Japan Sir -- 1945

Japan Since 1945

From Postwar to Post-bubble

Edited by

Christopher Gerteis
and Timothy S. George

B L O O M S B U R Y
LONDON • NEW DELHI • NEW YORK • SYDNEY

Bloomsbury Academic

An imprint of Bloomsbury Publishing Plc

50 Bedford Square	175 Fifth Avenue
London	New York
WC1B 3DP	NY 10010
UK	USA

www.bloomsbury.com

First published 2013

British Library Cataloguing-in-Publication Data
A catalogue record for this book is available from the British Library.

ISBN: HB: 978-1-4411-7524-3
PB: 978-1-4411-0118-1

Typeset by Deanta Global Publishing Services, Chennai, India
Printed and bound in India

Contents

List of Illustrations

Figures

Tables

Acknowledgments

This book grew from the papers presented at a conference hosted by the Institute of Comparative Culture at Sophia University in the spring of 2009. We are particularly grateful to Tak Watanabe who organized the Sophia conference as well as everyone who joined us in Tokyo to help plant the seeds for what eventually became this book. We had to make some hard choices from the more than 45 presentations given in Tokyo, and to commission several others later, and our only regret is that we were unable to select more of the many wonderful papers from the Tokyo conference. Financial support from a number of organizations enabled us to reconvene in 2010 as a workshop held at the School of Oriental & African Studies, University of London (SOAS). The chapters that comprise the core of this book are all the stronger for the critical insights offered by our many friends and colleagues in attendance in both London and Tokyo, and we are greatly indebted to all those who participated in the process, from first draft to final publication.

None of this would have been possible without the generous support of a number of organizations and individuals. We would like to thank the Japan Foundation Endowment Committee, the Daiwa Anglo-Japanese Foundation, Meiji Jingu, the Great Britain Sasakawa Foundation, and the Japan Research Centre at SOAS for their very generous financial support. We are particularly grateful for the administrative support we received from Jane Savory and Rahima Begum, who manage the Centres & Programmes Office at SOAS, without whom our London workshop would never have gotten off the ground. We are also thankful for the administrative support of Miwa Higashiura at the Institute for Comparative Culture at Sophia University who cheerfully accommodated our first conference, even though we had no idea what we were getting ourselves into. This book is all the stronger for their hard work.

We are also much in the debt of many colleagues and friends, and wish to take this opportunity to thank a few, though certainly not all. While all errors and omissions remain our own responsibility, we are nevertheless very thankful for intellectual critique and moral support from Penelope Francks, Harald Fuess, Sheldon Garon, Carol Gluck, Andrew Gordon, Janet Hunter, Toru Imajo, Griseldis Kirsch, Barak Kushner, Fujiko Kobayashi, Angus Lockyer, Helen Macnaughtan, Rajyashree Pande, Jordan Sand, Naoko Shimazu, Martyn Smith, Sarah Teasley, Subodhana Wijeyeratne, and Mai Yamashita. Our particular thanks also go to Jennifer Anderson for picking the book cover, and Claire Lipscomb, our editor at Bloomsbury, for helping transform this project from thoughtware to book.

About the Contributors

Bruce Aronson is Professor of Law at Creighton University School of Law. Prior to joining the academy, Aronson practiced law as a corporate partner at Hughes Hubbard & Reed LLP (1989–2000), where he served as co-chair of the Financial Services Group. He has also been a Senior Fulbright Research Scholar at the University of Tokyo (2000–02) and Waseda University (2011–12), an Associate Research Scholar at Columbia Law School (2002–04), and Visiting Professor of Law at the University of Michigan (2004) and the University of Washington, Seattle (2011). Aronson researches in the area of comparative corporate governance with a focus on Japan. He was the first holder of the Chair on International Markets Law at the University of Tokyo, endowed by Tokyo Stock Exchange, Inc. (2004), and a Visiting Scholar at the Bank of Japan (2010).

Lonny E. Carlile is Associate Professor in the Center for Japanese Studies and the Asian Studies Program at the University of Hawai'i – Manoa. His research focuses on the processes that mediate polity, economy, and society in the Japanese context and he has written extensively on such topics as business-state relations, the labor movement, and the travel industry. Recent publications include *Divisions of Labor: Globality, Ideology, and War in the Shaping of the Japanese Labor Movement* (University of Hawai'i Press, 2005); "The Japanese Labor Movement and Institutional Reform" in *Institutional Change in Japan*, edited by Magnus Blomstrom and Sumner LaCroix, (London: Routledge, 2006); "From Outbound to Inbound: Japan's International Travel and Tourism Promotion Policy Rationales" in *The Impact of Globalization on Japan's Public Policy*, edited by Hiroshi Itoh, (Lewiston, NY: Edwin Mellen Press, 2008); "The Evolution of 'Area Studies' in Japan: The Impact of Global Context and Institutional Setting" in *Remaking Area Studies: Teaching and Learning Across Asia and the Pacific*, edited by Terence Wesley-Smith and Jon Goss, (Honolulu: University of Hawai'i Press, 2010).

Katarzyna J. Cwiertka is Professor of Modern Japan Studies at Leiden University, the Netherlands. Her research to date has utilized food as a window into the modern history of Japan and Korea. Cwiertka is the author of *Modern Japanese Cuisine: Food, Power and National Identity*

(London: Reaktion Books, 2006) and *Cuisine, Colonialism and Cold War: Food in Twentieth Century Korea* (London: Reaktion Books, 2012). She has also edited several volumes with a larger geographical focus, including *Asian Food: The Global and the Local* (Honolulu: University of Hawai'i Press 2002), *Critical Readings on Food in East Asia* (Brill, forthcoming), and *Food and War in East Asia* (Farnham: Ashgate, forthcoming).

Martin Dusinberre is Lecturer in Modern Japanese History at Newcastle University. He served as Visiting Professor at Heidelberg University in the academic year 2011–12. Dusinberre's research interests focus on the social and cultural history of Japan from the mid-nineteenth to the late-twentieth centuries. His first book, *Hard Times in the Hometown: A History of Community Survival in Modern Japan* (Honolulu: University of Hawai'i Press, 2012), is a microhistory that reconstructs the lives of "ordinary people" in the Inland Sea town of Kaminsoseki as they tried to make sense of modern transformations. Dusinberre's current research investigates nineteenth- and early twentieth-century maritime history and the connected histories between rural Japan and the wider Asia-Pacific region.

Tetsuya Fujiwara is Professor of the English Division at the University of Fukui, School of Medical Sciences. He is a contributor to *Rekishi no Naka no Shōgaisha* [The Disabled in History] (Tokyo: Hōsei University Press, 2012). His PhD dissertation, entitled "Japanese Pacific War Disabled War Veterans from 1945 to 1963," (University of Iowa, 2011) explores the lives of Japanese disabled war veterans during the difficult years of reintegration that followed in the wake of World War II. Fujiwara's current research interests include comparative histories of disabled veterans' experiences in the United States and Japan.

Timothy S. George is Professor of History at the University of Rhode Island. His interests include environmental history, postwar history, local history, and citizen-corporation-state relations from Meiji to the present. He is the author of *Minamata: Pollution and the Struggle for Democracy in Postwar Japan* (Cambridge, MA: Harvard University Asia Center, 2001) and of "Tanaka Shōzō's Vision of an Alternative Constitutional Modernity for Japan" in *Public Spheres, Private Lives in Modern Japan, 1600-1950: Essays in Honor of Albert M. Craig*, edited by Gail Lee Bernstein, Andrew Gordon, and Kate Wildman Nakai, (Cambridge, MA: Harvard University Asia Center, 2005); co-author with John W. Dower of *Japanese History and Culture from Ancient to Modern Times: Seven Basic Bibliographies*, second edition, (Princeton, NJ: Markus Wiener, 1995); and co-translator and co-editor of Saitō Hisashi, *Niigata Minamata Disease* (Niigata: Niigata Nippō, 2009) and of Harada Masazumi, *Minamata Disease* (Kumamoto: Kumamoto Nichinichi Shinbun, 2004).

Christopher Gerteis is Lecturer in the History of Contemporary Japan at the School of Oriental & African Studies, University of London. His first book, *Gender Struggles: Wage-earning Women and Male Dominant Unions in Postwar Japan* (Cambridge, MA: Harvard University Asia Center, 2009) examines the extent to which customary notions of work, gender, and ethnicity influenced the formation of the socialist labor movement in postwar Japan. He is a contributor to *Recreating Japanese Men*, edited by Sabine Frühstück and Anne Walthall, (Berkeley and Los Angeles: University of California Press, 2011) and *Labor's Cold War: Local Politics in a Global Context*, edited by Shelton Stromquist, (Urbana, IL: University of Illinois Press, 2008). Gerteis' current work explores the intersection of consumer capitalism, history, and the politics of culture and identity in contemporary Japan.

Sally A. Hastings is Associate Professor of Japanese History at Purdue University. She is editor of the *U.S.-Japan Women's Journal* and author of *Neighborhood and Nation in Tokyo, 1905–1937* (University of Pittsburgh Press, 1995). She has published several essays on the history of Japanese women, most recently "Assassins, Madonnas, and Career Women: Reflections on Six Decades of Women's Suffrage in Japan" (*Asian Cultural Studies* No. 35, 2009), "Empress Nagako and the Family State" in *Handbook of the Emperors of Modern Japan*, edited by Ben-Ami Shillony, (Leiden: Brill, 2008), "Gender and Sexuality in Modern Japan" in *A Companion to Japanese History*, edited by William Tsutsui, (Oxford: Blackwell, 2007), and "Hatoyama Haruko: Ambitious Woman" in *The Human Tradition in Modern Japan*, edited by Anne Walthall, (Wilmington, DE: Scholarly Resources, 2002). Hastings is currently working on a book manuscript entitled "Gender and Japanese Politics: Women Legislators, 1946–74."

Laura Hein is Professor of Japanese History at Northwestern University. She has published two books on economic policy and economic ideologies, most recently *Reasonable Men, Powerful Words: Political Culture and Expertise in Twentieth-Century Japan* (Berkeley and Los Angeles: University of California Press, 2004; Japanese ed. Tokyo: Iwanami, 2007). A related essay, "Growth versus Success: Japan's Economic Policy in Historical Perspective," appeared in *Postwar Japan as History*, edited by Andrew Gordon, (Berkeley and Los Angeles: University of California Press, 1993). She has also co-edited five books on war remembrance, including *Imagination Without Borders: Feminist Artist Tomiyama Taeko and Social Responsibility* (Ann Arbor, MI: University Michigan, 2010), which is accompanied by a website http://imaginationwithoutborders.northwestern.edu/. She is one of the coordinators of the online peer-reviewed journal *Asia Pacific Journal: Japan Focus* at http://www.japanfocus.org/. Hein's current research focuses on a variety of institutions that the Japanese created after 1945 to prevent another disastrous war.

David Tobaru Obermiller is Associate Professor of East Asian History at Gustavus Adolphus College in St. Peter, Minnesota, where he teaches an array of courses, including East Asia-US foreign relations, Asian-American history, and trans-national environmental history. Obermiller's scholarship centers on Okinawa's modern history. His PhD dissertation, "The US Military Occupation of Okinawa: Politicizing and Contesting Okinawan Identity 1945–55" (University of Iowa, 2006) examined the formation of Okinawan national identity as a central aspect of local opposition movements against the American military and the Japanese government. He is currently researching the role of Senaga Kamejirō in the Okinawan resistance movement.

Hiraku Shimoda is Associate Professor in the Faculty of Law at Waseda University. He is the author of *Lost and Found: Recovering Regional Identity in Imperial Japan* (Cambridge, MA: Harvard University Asia Center, forthcoming), which examines the historical tension between locality and nation in Aizu from the late Tokugawa period to the early twentieth century. His articles have appeared in *Modern Asian Studies* (July 2001) and the *American Historical Review* (June 2010). His current research examines how Japan's popular media has mythologized postwar history, especially the economic contributions of baby boomers.

Satsuki Takahashi is Assistant Professor in the Department of Sociology and Anthropology at George Mason University. She completed her PhD in the Department of Anthropology at Rutgers, the State University of New Jersey in 2010, and is currently working on a book manuscript entitled *The Current of Modernity*. Her research interests include the politics of nature and modernity, fisheries science and technology, rumor, and discourses of survival.

Stephen Vlastos is Professor of Modern Japanese History at the University of Iowa. He has written on agrarian political economy in the Tokugawa and Meiji periods, agrarianism as an ideology in prewar Japan, protest upheaval in the nineteenth and twentieth centuries, "tradition" and modernity in Japanese culture, and Vietnam War historiography. He is the author of *Peasant Protests and Uprisings in Tokugawa Japan* (Berkeley and Los Angeles: University of California Press, 1986) and editor of *Mirror of Modernity: Invented Traditions of Modern Japan* (Berkeley and Los Angeles: University of California Press, 1998). Vlastos' current interests center on Japanese foreign relations in the prewar period, including representations of Japan in Hollywood cinema, and postwar Japanese national myth-making.

Christine Yano is Professor of Anthropology at the University of Hawai'i – Manoa. Her books include *Tears of Longing: Nostalgia and the Nation in Japanese Popular Song* (Cambridge, MA: Harvard University Asia Center,

2002); *Crowning the Nice Girl* (Honolulu: University of Hawai'i Press, 2006); and *Airborne Dreams: Pan American World Airways and Japanese American Stewardesses* (Durham, NC: Duke University Press, 2011). Presently, Yano is working on a book about "pink globalization," or the spread of cute goods from Japan to other parts of the industrial world.

1

Revisiting the History of Postwar Japan

Christopher Gerteis and Timothy S. George

Of course Japan matters. It was the first non-Western nation to have a constitution and to industrialize. It avoided being colonized and became a colonial power itself. It plunged into a devastating war that killed tens of millions in East and Southeast Asia and the Pacific and ended with Japan as the first and only nation to suffer the horrors of nuclear warfare. In defeat, Japan arose from the ashes of war to become an even greater industrial power while simultaneously establishing itself as a vibrant, pacifist, and contentious democracy. Japan's spectacular economic growth made it a model for its neighbors and even, at the height of its economic dominance and hubris in the 1980s, a model for business leaders in the Americas, Europe, and Pacific Asia. By the early 1990s, the collapse of mammoth real estate and stock market bubbles launched the nation on two decades of stagnation or fitful growth, deflation, and soul searching. And then, on 11 March 2011, the state's anemic response to the earthquake, tsunami, and nuclear disaster in northeastern Japan heightened popular debate over whether the nation was doomed to a slow decline or might yet be able to recover its vigor and discover a new path and new purposes.

The flurry of media coverage that erupted after the Tōhoku Earthquake in March 2011, known in Japan as the Great East Japan Earthquake, focused an intense global interest on Japan, interest that then faded just as it had during the long recession of the 1990s. International media interest in Japan during the affluent decade of the 1980s arose from what appeared to be the start of an era that would be defined by Japan and East Asia's Tiger Economies. And then the bubble burst. While financial reports seem to regularly declare Japan "out of recession," media discussions in and outside Japan after

March of 2011 remained haunted by the devastation inflicted by one of the strongest earthquakes in recorded human history. Yet the earthquake, tsunami, and nuclear disaster that swept across eastern Japan seem to have merely intensified the preceding two decades of political paralysis at the top, and a sense of frustration and hopelessness at the bottom.

Politicians, intellectuals, and philanthropists have all publicly wondered whether Japan really matters anymore. Of course Japan matters—but not in the way most journalists, commentators, business leaders, and politicians have been talking about it these last few decades. The problem lies in how media attention more than scholarly debate has driven the discussion of what lessons Japan has and has not yet learned from its successes and failures. Actual scholarship on Japan generally receives less attention than it ought. While many members of the international media are often eager to report on the successes and failures of Japan, a disturbing majority prefer to explain the so-called secrets of Japan's success, and many public failings, as resulting from a quaint culture defined by its relationship with the traditional and not at all by social, political, or even economic forces that shape the contemporary world.

These sorts of media reports have deflected attention from some very real problems, such as how the Japanese state will finance the reconstruction of the quake-devastated Northeast—much less ensure the welfare of a population that is anticipated by 2020 to be comprised of more septuagenarians than teenagers. This is a shame not only because of the missed opportunity to discuss Japan in a meaningful way, but also because Japan's achievements since the end of the nineteenth century remain a highly relevant yardstick for policy makers, business leaders, and citizenry across the globe. Having been the first Asian nation to achieve modern economic power, by blazing paths that have had substantial influence on the developing world, Japan in the twenty-first century has become the first nation in Pacific Asia to struggle with the consequences of declining industrial significance. While this is an unwanted and perhaps dubious honor, it is no less the fact that Japan shares its current trajectory with many highly industrialized societies even while remaining a model of achievement for much of the developing world.

Japan is not the only nation to face the sorts of problems we have generally thought characteristic of a postindustrial society. There is yet much to be learned from the mistakes and successes of a society that, despite everything, still features the highest standard of living in East Asia. Indeed, most of the highly industrialized nations of Europe and the Americas have faced the social, economic, and political problems that arise in the wake of high youth unemployment, aging populations, industrial decline, financial crises, and even natural disasters. Why so many of us worry about whether or not Japan matters is in itself a worrying question, motivated by a fear that the standard of living enjoyed by most Japanese since the 1960s was only sustainable by ever-expanding production built on the premise that

Japan was the world's industrial base. With decreasing birth rates and a general shift of industrial production overseas, many Japanese have come to believe that the inevitable result is the end of affluence and the start of a long decline into irrelevance.

While one aim of this book is to offer comparative contexts for Japan's recent history in a way that may prove useful in understanding the world's emerging industrial and postindustrial societies, there are, however, problematic antecedents to this endeavor. Making Japan matter has long been the purpose of the field of Japanese Studies. At the height of the Cold War, the United States government sponsored a series of scholarly workshops presenting modern Japan and Turkey as alternatives to the Marxist models under consideration in much of the developing world. Both Japan and Turkey took paths that significantly diverged from those predicted by the "modernization theorists" who decided the course of much of our field with a series of workshops held in Kyoto and Tokyo, and the rapid, unexpected growth of the Japanese economy significantly shifted the global balance of economic power. By the 1980s, intellectual fashions had shifted to decrying Japan's unprecedented economic success. The so-called "Japan-bashers" of the 1980s made the contradictory claims that a unique culture, ethnocentric outlook, and collusive relationships said to characterize Japanese society gave "Japan, Inc." an unfair advantage in the global marketplace.

The "Cold War" and "Trade War" frameworks failed to provide nuanced consideration of what it meant for Japan to experience the first 40 years of the postwar era. It often takes dramatic turning points or conceptual breakthroughs to make us see the past more clearly, and to see it as truly past. For much longer than necessary, Japan's experiences after 1945, or after the Allied Occupation ended in 1952, were not seen as appropriate subjects for study by historians. Despite professional disdain, even animosity, toward those who wrote the history of Japan since 1945, two things emerged to lend credibility to the study of postwar Japan as history. The first was the sense that an era had ended for Japan in the late 1980s and early 1990s with the death of Hirohito, the bursting of the financial bubble, the end of the Cold War, and the economic development of China.

The second was the publication in 1993, as that awareness of historic change was setting in, of *Postwar Japan as History*, a pioneering collection of essays that inspired a new generation of historians to look at Japan since the war through a wide variety of lenses.[1] The feeling that times had changed, which had set in over the several years since the book was first conceived, made it all the more timely and added to its impact on the field. The "Japan-bashing" by pundits and leaders of business and government in the 1980s may have been replaced since the 1990s by "Japan-passing" as they flocked to China, but at the same time, thanks partly to *Postwar Japan as History*, there has been an explosion of innovative scholarship on postwar Japan. The book moved the discussion of Japan beyond the then-dominant narratives by introducing a nuanced historical consideration of what it meant for Japan to experience rapid economic growth during the first 40 years of the postwar era.

As the field took shape in the mid-1990s, a renaissance of scholarship began to suggest new frameworks for thinking about the society, politics, economy, and culture of postwar Japan. Some scholars even found room for the modernization narrative of the 1960s, despite its Cold War origins, since by the 1980s it had become a defining myth for the postwar national consciousness. The naturalization of the ideas constructed by the modernization theorists of the 1960s made Japan matter in a way that it had not mattered before. That even the Japanese came to see Japan's "economic miracle" as part and parcel of what it meant to be Japanese was a construct made real by the power of belief as much as by the wealth created during the rapid economic growth of the postwar era. Indeed, the past two decades of lament over the decline of Japan might be seen as an expression of the power and persistence of the modernization mythology.

At several points in Japan's modern trajectory—particularly 1868, when its centralized feudal system was replaced by a centralizing and modernizing imperial government, and 1945, when its land, people, and governing ideology were devastated—it has been fashionable for some to argue that it was starting anew with a clean slate; that it had "no history." The triple disasters of March 2011 have similarly been described as a break with the past. This collection of essays cannot attempt to predict how or whether those disasters will change Japan or the ways its history is told. But it is the consensus of the contributors to this volume that, whatever directions Japan takes now, it will be building on its past, particularly its experiences, accomplishments, and failures in the period since 1945. Our purpose here is to sample some parts of that experience—and of the extensive and thought-provoking study of Japan since the mid-twentieth century that has flowered in the past two decades—in the hope of better understanding where Japan is and what trajectories it may follow from here.

This book is divided into four sections, in which the authors individually explore issues of civic life, the legacies of war and military occupation, the emergence of a postindustrial economy, and the interaction of public memory with the social, political, and economic trajectories from the postwar to the post-bubble eras. The intellectual boundaries where history leaves off and other disciplines begin can be complex to navigate, and therefore these essays are necessarily interdisciplinary in their consideration of the simultaneous transformations that defined the emergence of contemporary Japan. They examine the historical context to the social, cultural, and political underpinnings of Japan's postwar and postindustrial trajectories.

By reengaging earlier discourses and introducing new veins of research, they raise questions about the extent to which the history of Japan since 1945 might yet serve as an indicator for the economic and social trajectories partly shared with the late-capitalist, heavily industrialized societies of

Europe, North America, and Pacific Asia. Often integrating gender, class, and race within thematic narrative frames, the multidisciplinary essays explore topics that range from the postwar histories of the plight of Japan's disabled veterans of World War II and the rise of women's professional organizations within the political machinations of electoral politics, to the recent histories of the state's efforts to formulate industrial policy and foster financial reform, to the contemporary context of resource management strategies within Japan's rural communities.

These essays encourage us to take fresh looks at the ways the Japanese and those outside Japan have defined and understood its postwar paths. They also insist that there are no simple answers to the question of when or whether the postwar period has ended, or what the decisive turning points since 1945 have been. In complicating these questions by approaching them from a multiplicity of angles, the authors may even offer some hints as to what to look for as debates develop about whether the disasters of 11 March 2011 constituted a decisive turning point in postwar Japanese history.

Part One

Civic Imaginations

Japan's war in Pacific Asia from 1931 to 1945 wrought the greatest bloodshed the region had ever known, with a total cost in lives that may have reached as many as 20 million people dead.[1] Yet, the domestic experience of war, culminating with the incendiary bombings of Tokyo and Osaka and nuclear bombings of Hiroshima and Nagasaki, also brought death and hardship to many ordinary Japanese. In the wake of Japan's surrender in August 1945, war crimes tribunals tried, convicted, and hanged only a handful of the political and military leaders who were most responsible for the war. While issues of war responsibility remained unresolved, the people and government of postwar Japan were remarkable for their ability to convert the experiences of the wartime era into productive, long-lived alliances with many of Japan's former enemies.

Positioning themselves in the dual role of proconsul and tutor, the mostly American officials of the Allied Occupation of Japan (1945–52) translated their social and political vision of democracy into a constitutional monarchy for Japan that embraced the rights of free speech, gender equality, and a minimum guaranteed level of cultured living. While the Allied Occupation is often characterized as a "New Deal" for Japan, reactionary strains within American political discourse, in particular the rise of anti-Communism and the onset of the Cold War, also had tremendous repercussions for Japan. As consequence, there are numerous historical problems from this era with which scholars must grapple, some of which we have discussed in the introduction to this book.

One persistent myth about Japan is that it has suffered for its lack of a historical tradition of an engaged citizenry. Yet, the Meiji, Taishō, and even the early Shōwa eras (1868–1912, 1912–26, and 1926–31) witnessed considerable political activity, some of it quite radical. And the postwar years saw an even greater level of civic engagement. Indeed, the postwar era was a model of democratic capitalism even though the citizen movements of the era are rarely remembered. As a result, the postwar era is largely remembered within the narrow, sometimes stultifying context of the "economic miracle" narrative.

While the 1950s are customarily thought of as the era that saw the emergence of one-party rule by the Liberal Democratic Party (LDP), the same period also saw an upsurge in civic organizations and mass movements at odds with the state. From the efforts by the citizens of Hiroshima and Nagasaki to see the end of the nuclear arms race to the unionization struggles led by coal miners who sought to force their employers to provide basic safety equipment and pay fair wages, the 1950s were indeed witness to social and economic turmoil at odds with the middle-class family lives most often portrayed by television and motion picture melodramas.

By 1960, the political dissatisfactions of millions of Japanese had grown into a national movement calling for the rescinding of military treaties with the United States that most Japanese believed to have been agreed to without popular consent. These dissatisfactions grew by the end of the decade into national movements calling for the end of Japanese support for the Vietnam War and the reversion of Okinawa from American to Japanese sovereignty, while local civic movements focused on industrial pollution in Minamata and resistance to state encroachment upon the rights of farmers in Narita. The national social movements of the 1960s were squelched by extraparliamentary and occasionally extrajudicial action, as well as by co-optation; yet, many of the politically active refocused their civic engagement onto more local concerns.

The social movements from the late 1950s to the early 1970s defined the outer boundaries of democracy in Japan. Citizen involvement in national political movements, enthusiastic for the first 15 years of the postwar era, hit several road blocks between 1960 and 1970 that demarcated what has customarily been characterized as a decline in participatory democracy and the consolidation of one-party rule. Although leftist political movements exerted considerable influence on postwar politics, the center-right emerged as the more powerful force. The formation of the Liberal Democratic Party (LDP) in 1955 marked the beginning of an era of conservative politics that remained the norm until 2009.

Part One features chapters exploring how Japan's postwar democracy translated into—or was defined by—local practice by examining the shape of civic engagement that developed in local communities nonetheless influenced by the national politics that flowed to and from the capital city. By reconstructing narratives of civic life in a historically significant satellite of Tokyo and two towns deep in Japan's rural periphery, each examines from a different angle the structures of civil society that emerged within the postwar constitutional order. Running against a tide of literature that depicts postwar Japan as a nation driven by an interventionist state in league with vertically integrated marketing and banking systems, the chapters in this section reconstruct a more accurate portrait of civic life in postwar Japan than those focused on the national center.

"Civic Imaginations" explores what Japan's postwar democracy meant at the local level. Laura Hein, Timothy S. George, and Martin Dusinberre each examine the shape of civic engagement that developed in communities outside Tokyo that were nonetheless influenced by the national politics of the capital city. Chapters by George and Dusinberre also explore the boundaries of the nostalgic longing for "traditional" village Japan that accompanied the rise of the *"furusato"* (native place) movement in the 1990s. By reconstructing narratives of civic life and regional identity, these chapters examine from a different angle the structures of civil society that emerged within the postwar constitutional order.

2

The Art of Bourgeois Culture in Kamakura

Laura Hein

When *Postwar Japan As History* appeared in 1993, it represented some important new trends. One was greater attention to the complex manner in which the wartime experience affected postwar history. The scholars who participated in that project developed a "transwar" analysis that recognized both the ways that postwar Japanese built on planned wartime developments and how they responded to effects of unplanned wartime changes.[1] For example, Japan entered the Asia-Pacific War as a highly stratified society, but by 1945, wartime policies had laid the groundwork for a broad social safety net, while American bombing raids, because they targeted cities, had disproportionately destroyed urban accumulations of wealth. This research stream has expanded enormously in recent years, and has been augmented by much excellent work on the Japanese empire, a topic essentially missing from *Postwar Japan As History*, and one that revises our understanding of Japanese national history in crucial ways. We now know that the Japanese wartime state was highly modern, as were its strategies for mobilizing the population. Most scientists, social scientists, humanists, and other professionals used their expertise to support the empire and the war, in part because they felt a responsibility to make Japan more modern. Other private actors disseminated their ideas through such activities as popular science magazines and heritage tourism. Meanwhile, the general public took pride in the same aspects of their nation's military might and enthusiastically participated in many celebrations of Japan's domination of East Asia.[2]

Second, *Postwar Japan As History* consolidated a trend already well underway, to abandon the sterile debate between proponents of modernization theory and its corollary idea that Japanese historical development was "converging" on the Euro-American model on one hand, and the assertion that Japan was uniquely unique on the other. Embedded in this debate was the desire of both groups to refute Marxist analyses, a philosophy of history that shaped the views of many twentieth-century Japanese. Jettisoning all three frameworks, which were both too generic and too rigid, has allowed us to treat historical change as a far more fluid and multidirectional process than in the past. Leaving them behind also meant moving away from normative assessments that all too often treated Euro-American history as a template and the histories of all other people as deviant.

Finally, the contributors to *Postwar Japan As History* rethought Japan's place in the Cold War system, particularly how the American hegemon structured its relationships to other Asians, both US clients, such as the Republic of Korea, and its foes, notably China.[3] And, in a subtheme here, not only did postwar Japanese differ among themselves about the nature and best direction of their own society, so did Americans about Japan. The Occupation years formed a fundamentally transnational moment—and while the big story is of American domination of Japan, many of the little stories are of cooperation and alliances that cut across those national lines.[4]

When combined with the new work on the Japanese empire, this research stream has led to a reassessment of the East Asian region throughout the twentieth century as the site of competing imperialist powers, with much greater attention to their borderlands and colonies, and to the important ways in which such places affected the hegemons/metropoles.[5] Framing the recent past this way also reminds us that attention to local places in Japan's home islands often challenges nation-level generalizations about what it means to be Japanese, as argued here by myself, Timothy George, Satsuki Takahashi, and David Obermiller, and only addressed in the earlier book by William Kelly.

Another major trend since 1993, for the discipline of history as a whole, not just Japan, is greater attention to cultural formations, cultural processes, and the "cultural work" being done by representation, both words and images. This trend was inspired by frustration at older analyses that treated culture as mere "superstructure" for "real" economic and military power. Such studies not only failed to explain why people acted in ways that seemed to undercut their own best interests, but they resorted to unsatisfying and condescending conclusions, such as that their historical subjects suffered from "false consciousness." Scholars pursuing this cultural turn hoped to understand how hierarchies of power—particularly of race, class, and gender—were created and maintained through mechanisms other than formal politics and economics. Often this meant identifying the processes by which new "social imaginaries" are created, to use Sarah Maza's term from her essay on the French bourgeoisie.[6] The "social imaginary" is composed of "the cultural elements from which we construct our understanding of the social world." As she explains, "the crucial historical question is whether a middle class is seen: whether the existence of a unified and pivotal middling or upper-middling group is, first, acknowledged, and second, invested with historical,

moral, and/or political importance." The processes of reimagining are, of
course, particularly active in times of radical change, as in societies riven by a
disastrous war of choice, a failed empire, and a discredited political ideology.

A new postwar "social imaginary," that modern Japan was fundamentally
a peaceful, homogeneous, and middle-class society, developed very quickly.
Fifteen years after the war ended, the proudly belligerent, multiracial, and
intensely hierarchical empire had been relegated to the historical broom-
closet, along with samurai topknots and pagodas. The social forgetting
involved in distancing postwar from imperial wartime Japan was more a
performative stance that accomplished specific kinds of cultural work than
a compelling theory of history, even for those who espoused it.[7] Most of that
cultural work centered on moving past fascism. The main mechanism for
doing so was to equate fascism with feudalism and treat the postwar reforms
as bringing Japan into the modern age; this "feudal = fascist" framework
was adopted by American Occupation reformers, the Soviet Union and the
Japan Communist Party, the civilian bureaucracy, and millions of Japanese
who were suddenly required to reimagine their social identities. Yet, depicting
Japan as emerging from feudalism, while highly useful, elided the fact that
most people had been attracted to fascism for its modern core rather than
just its mystical trappings.

Problematically, a central aspect of fascism's appeal had been its promise
that submitting to the state (and Emperor) would eliminate class conflict at
home. Treating wartime Japan as if it had been feudal offered no new ways
to address that issue, even though many Japanese, including the individuals
discussed here, thought that anxiety about working-class identity had caused
elite Japanese to embrace fascism. And expressions of working-class identity
were everywhere in postwar Japan. Labor union membership went from
zero in August 1945 to 4.8 million workers (40 percent of the workforce) by
the end of 1946 and continued to grow after that, while the Japan Socialist
and Communist Parties regularly attracted well over a third of votes cast.

Then, around 1970, nearly all Japanese began to think of themselves—
and of one another—as middle class. That shift was in part the result of a
concerted effort by some of Japan's most prominent elite intellectuals to
make bourgeois society more welcoming to "the masses" without reviving
the core element of cultural fascism, which Doug Slaymaker and Bert
Winther-Tamaki have recently defined as "discourses that tie national
to personal identities."[8] Their narrative of Japanese and global history
proposed a strategy built around cosmopolitan rather than national identity
and urban rather than ethnic community. As J. Victor Koschmann argued
in *Postwar Japan as History*, this group of "postwar cultural and political
critics," "enjoyed a very large and well-informed readership," and played "a
very important role in molding, and to some degree constraining, the range
and terms of discourse." In the same volume, Carol Gluck wondered why
their domination of national media did not result more directly in political
power. Part of the answer surely lies in the strategy outlined here, which

shrewdly challenged the central anxiety that had generated fascism but later seemed vague to younger Japanese who had not experienced the war.[9]

Today, this antifascist perspective no longer dominates Japan's public sphere, but it is still embedded in many of the institutions these intellectuals created, such as the Kanagawa Prefectural Modern Art Museum, which opened its doors on 18 November 1951, as Japan's first museum dedicated to modern art.[10] Fundamentally transnational in origin and in their stance toward art, the museum's founders, curators, and trustees wanted to establish a local institution that could assuage the anxieties that had, in their view, explained the appeal of fascism to so many Japanese, including their friends, their families, and their own younger selves. They proposed an alternative that celebrated the modernity of diverse urban societies, defined culture as both local and transnational, and sought to resolve conflict between social classes by encouraging direct interaction across class lines. They invented an antifascist, cosmopolitan back-story for Japan's future, and the Kamakura museum was only one of many structures—literal and figurative—that institutionalized this narrative.

Founding the museum

The museum got its start through the efforts of both Kanagawa's first postwar prefectural governor, Uchiyama Iwatarō (1890–1968) and the American Occupation forces. While Uchiyama was a conservative in the mold of fellow-diplomat-turned Prime Minister Yoshida Shigeru, he consistently sought support for his administration among the group of left-liberal intellectuals described by Koschmann, as shown by the choice of both Hasegawa Nyōzekan and Osaragi Jirō to introduce his authorized biography. Uchiyama's diplomatic postings had included Paris, Madrid, and several Latin American nations before he became Governor of Kanagawa Prefecture in January 1946, a post he held for 21 years. Osaragi praised the governor for "without prejudice, immersing himself in the customs and society of each place he was assigned, for sharing the feelings of the people of that country, doing as they do, and fully experiencing their lives ... something that is impossible for [those who] stay within the walls of the embassy." He was particularly impressed that Uchiyama did not limit himself to the elegant parts of town, but also "lightheartedly walked the back streets among the local crowds, entering into their moods."[11] In other words, Osaragi valued Uchiyama for his ability to connect with both elites and working-class individuals in a transnational context.

Drawing on his experience in Paris in particular, Uchiyama thought contemporary art should be supported by the government. In August 1949, he convened local artists and asked them to name their biggest problem. Not surprisingly, given that both Yokohama and Kawasaki had been bombed multiple times during the war, the response was "exhibition space."[12] Uchiyama then allocated 28.5 million yen (almost $80,000 US) in 1950 to establish a new museum, a highly unusual move at a moment when most local governments were focused on building housing, schools, and commercial infrastructure. The museum was only one of a string of new spaces Uchiyama erected to enhance public life in the prefecture. Nicknamed the "assembly hall governor" (kaikan chiji), Uchiyama built a center for educators in 1948, a Workers' Building in 1949 at the request of the Sōdōmei and Sanbetsu labor unions, and then a Farmers' Hall in 1952. As his biographer explained, he built them because "his philosophy was that in a democracy people needed places where they could meet and talk with each other."[13]

Uchiyama acted at an opportune moment, just when Occupation officials dismantled the powerful Home Ministry, giving prefectures considerable independence from the national government, although Tokyo later reconsolidated some of that power.[14] Uchiyama also had excellent connections with both SCAP in Tokyo and US Eighth Army headquarters in Yokohama, where he regularly met General Robert L. Eichelberger and once took General Walton H. Walker boar hunting. The museum would soon benefit from these connections, from Uchiyama's "lack of an inferiority complex" toward all these authorities, and from his "amateur's bravery and passion," as Osaragi put it.[15]

SCAP's philosophy of decentralization and democratization explicitly included encouraging local museums at the expense of national ones. As Satō Kaori notes, the Americans issued a directive on 10 August, 1946 to democratize art in Japan in this manner.[16] The Fine Arts Advisors to SCAP, first Sherman E. Lee and then J. M. Plumer, wanted to block the efforts of the National Museum to establish ten regional branches. Plumer argued that establishing independent prefectural and municipal museums was preferable, explaining that "proposed branches of National Museum, (e.g. as at Fukuoka and Nagasaki) should be frowned upon as coming into conflict with basic SCAP policy of decentralization." In a later memo, Plumer argued even more forcefully that "no other branches should be permitted" of the National Museum. He went on to argue that the policy of sending to the Tokyo museum "broken-off heads and other fragments from the gradually crumbling Buddhist stone caves in Oita-ken . . ." was problematic because it promoted the "unfortunate possibility of draining Kyushu of cultural objects that should remain in Kyushu."[17]

Plumer had very little success in his drive to promote local art centers. Despite stated policy, in practice, most of SCAP's museum-related efforts aided the National Museum in Tokyo. In mid-1949, for example, Plumer traveled to Kyushu to inspect art-related activities in the region. He "noted with regret" that projects to establish prefectural museums in Kagoshima and Miyazaki were on hold, because the relevant buildings were temporarily occupied by a police training academy and a girls' school, respectively. Few of Plumer's superiors shared his view that SCAP resources—such as the cost of sending him to Kyushu—were usefully spent on local arts development, and his other requests were brusquely refused. [18]

Yet, in the case of the Kamakura museum alone, the Occupation seems to have played a significant role in establishing a local museum by securing an affordable location. Governor Uchiyama at first planned to use a building erected for the 1948 Yokohama Trade Fair, but it proved inappropriate. Another Yokohama building was too expensive. Uchiyama then somehow persuaded the Tsurugaoka Hachiman Shrine to rent 71,080 square feet (2000 tsubo) of its land near Kamakura station at essentially no cost to the prefecture. While many people would have preferred to build the museum closer to the main population centers, the ideal price, together with proximity to a station on the national train line, eventually carried the day.[19]

The agreement with the shrine was highly unusual, and almost certainly involved Occupation officials. SCAP's structure shows the likely internal channel of communication. The Arts and Monuments Branch was housed within the Religions and Cultural Resources Division of the Civil Information and Education Section (CI&E) of SCAP, meaning that the officials monitoring art-related activity interacted with those who oversaw religious reform every day. Shintō shrines were just then under orders to privatize, and donating this land would have tempered SCAP criticism of a shrine dedicated specifically to the god of war. Although no records seem to exist today, this effort surely stands as one of many examples of the ways in which mid-level Japanese and Americans at times worked together to create an outcome that was a low priority for top officials in both Tokyo governments. Uchiyama, Plumer, and others were all interpreting the Occupation goals of demilitarization and democratization to mean decentralization of cultural institutions away from Tokyo, establishing public support for artists at the local level, and creating new structures that would aid Kanagawa citizens in creating a fresh collaborative public culture. And this arrangement has endured despite the fact that shrine officials have openly regretted the lost opportunity to build a money-making enterprise on the museum site.[20]

Creating an antifascist back-story

Other individuals were more influential in shaping the message of the museum after it was built. They included Wakimura Yoshitarō (1900–97), Osaragi Jirō (1897–1973), and Hijikata Teiichi (1904–80), all involved with the museum for decades. Nearly exact contemporaries, these three men were friends for 30 years and saw themselves as jointly strengthening Japanese democracy through their writing, although Wakimura was an economist, Osaragi a writer of both novels and nonfiction, and Hijikata a poet, art critic, and museum curator. Sarah Maza locates the three main mechanisms by which people bring new social imaginaries into being as political discourse, academic commentary, and fictional representation.[21] As a group, Wakimura, Hijikata, and Osaragi purposefully intervened in all three areas as well as the additional space of the museum. They also clearly were among Koschmann's influential public intellectuals, as shown by their many widely read books and the fact that each has been memorialized with an annual prize. Wakimura was also simultaneously creating national structures for collective bargaining between managers and workers, as I have discussed elsewhere.[22]

Anticipating Hobsbawm and Ranger's explication of the ways that tradition is reinvented all the time for modern—and nationalist—purposes, Wakimura, Hijikata, and Osaragi strove to show other Japanese the extent to which such manipulation was ubiquitous, and not just in Japan.[23] They wanted to make visible the cultural work that had been performed by fascism and replace it with a different narrative of the past that valorized urban culture in ways that promoted class cooperation without nationalism. They reframed the relationship between tradition and modernity as interactive rather than a simple one-way and one-time transition, and eliminated the distinction between "the West and the rest." They also treated national culture as something that was cobbled together out of a variety of disparate activities by people acting both locally and transnationally. They did so by celebrating Japan's cities and urban institutions as cosmopolitan and sophisticated, by creating a modern past that stretched back far enough to claim simultaneity with European modernity, and by rejecting the idea of "the Japanese aesthetic tradition" in favor of a range of diverse, eclectic, and fundamentally interactive pasts. Given that only seven years before the museum opened, it was both illegal and dangerous to suggest that Japan's nineteenth-century leaders had invented the modern emperor system, rather than venerating "an unbroken line" of divine emperors, this stance was widely recognized as a political statement. These individuals also looked to local culture in order to rebuild international connections that had been lost during the war. They wanted to integrate Japan back into the community of nations in a way that cut across Cold War lines and located Japan in an international field that spanned Europe and Asia. Perhaps most crucially, the men at the Kamakura museum simply rejected the concepts of an injured or thwarted nationalism or the alignment of individual identity to national identity, assumptions that had formed the heart of fascist political culture.

Wakimura and Osaragi had known each other before the war but only met Hijikata in 1951, when he was hired as the Assistant Director of the new Kamakura Modern Art Museum. Hijikata quickly became the museum's dominant intellectual presence, long before succeeding Murata Ryōsaku (1895–1970) as Director in 1965. His consistent vision until his death in 1980 gave the museum considerable thematic continuity at a time when many in the Japanese art world characterized their era as one of disruption and discontinuity.[24] Wakimura was a member of the founding board of directors, later moving to the managing board, which he chaired from 1969

FIGURE 2.1 *Wakimura Yoshitarō and Hijikata Teiichi at the museum in the late 1970s. Photograph provided courtesy of the Museum of Modern Art, Kamakura and Hayama, and used with permission.*

to 1997.[25] Osaragi supported the museum in a variety of ways, including lending objects for exhibits and celebrating it in *The Journey* of 1953. The novel's heroine, Okamoto Taeko, the daughter of a rich man and his maid servant, reveled in the new opportunities of the postwar years when the circumstances of her birth no longer limited her so greatly. In one of the first scenes in the book, Taeko accepted an invitation for tea at the museum cafe after visiting her cousin's grave and meeting one of his friends, Tsugawa, for the first time. The tea room was "a light, cheerful place, and Tsugawa introduced it to Taeko as being the most pleasant spot in all Kamakura." Later, he called the museum "a little bit of the modern world at last." Osaragi welcomed the new museum in his nonfiction writing too, praising its boldness. He told his readers that he had worried that the "white block of the Corbusier-style building would not harmonize with the natural setting of the Tsurugaoka Hachiman shrine grounds but the completed building worked beautifully, and every corner within it happily surprised me with an unexpected new vista of the landscape."[26] Clearly, the museum symbolized for him a new way of combining past and present, one that represented a thoroughly modern and cosmopolitan local culture.

Although they championed regional identities and decentralization of power from Tokyo, these individuals shared a bias in favor of cities. Their urban preference was rooted in political-economic theory. Cities were the sites for the development of capitalism and therefore of the engine of social transformation globally. All three men argued that cities were the primary

FIGURE 2.2 *Osaragi Jirō in his study in the 1950s. Photograph by Yasuda Saburō. Used with permission of Nojiri Masako and Ebina Satomi.*

location where democracy and individualism, that is, bourgeois culture, had first flourished in Europe. Based on his own prewar research, Wakimura's university lectures on economic history highlighted the importance of urban venues for Britain's early development as a capitalist powerhouse. As he explained, the creative forms of disaster insurance provided by Lloyd's of London developed in the quintessentially urban space of the coffee house. The merchants who met there every day developed a trust in one another that transcended old-fashioned kinship or hierarchical ties, and this trust led both to capitalist expansion and democratic politics. Auction houses performed similar social functions in his view: they had gradually developed because people desired a mechanism for defining a public price for art and rare books. Wakimura was fully aware of the ways that aesthetic discernment worked to entrench class differences while hoping to change that dynamic. In a 1967 book, he explained that elegant manners and clothing were one of the requirements for succeeding as an art appraiser in eighteenth-century Great Britain, deconstructing for his readers precisely the conundrum that French sociologist Pierre Bourdieu presents as opaque.[27]

Hijikata made a similar case for urbane modernity in sixteenth-century Netherlands in his prize-winning study of Pieter Bruegel, while Osaragi was well known for his nonfiction books on late nineteenth-century France, beginning with *The Dreyfus Affair (Dorefyusu jiken)*, which was serialized in *Kaizō* in 1930. Osaragi emphasized the way that French military officers had been blinded by their prejudice against Jews. Rather than focusing on race or religion, he argued that anxiety about class tensions had led to militaristic nationalism, stigmatization, and oppression of vulnerable individuals. According to Kuroda Reiji, an activist in the leftwing student organization Shinjinkai, many young Japanese read this story as an analysis of Japan as much as France, describing it as a contest for "the soul of the military."[28] All three men were known for the depth of their historical research and their commitment to presenting a complex story of the past to a general audience.

They also approvingly charted the rise of urban bourgeois culture in Japan, particularly in Kanagawa Prefecture. They were particularly interested in the last years of the Tokugawa regime, because attention to that moment buttressed the argument that Japanese modernity had diverse origins before the Meiji state formed. Osaragi's best-selling, multivolume transwar series, *Kurama Tengu* (1924–59), was set in these years, as was his transposition of Mark Twain's *The Prince and the Pauper* of 1939. *Kurama Tengu* featured a nineteenth-century swordsman who used his weapon—only when attacked—for equality and human liberty. Although Kurama Tengu supported restoration of the Emperor, he did not do so out of ideology, and samurai on both sides were presented as groups of individuals, some worthy and some cowardly. His closest relationship was with a plucky young street acrobat, who was adept at evading the authorities, and whose courage, loyalty, and especially ingenuity, far exceeded those of Kurama's samurai allies.[29] The boy's urban street-smarts saved the swordsman again and again.

Many of Hijikata's exhibits and publications, such as *Bakumatsu Meiji Shoki* of 1970, surveyed various artistic genres to present a synthetic analysis of nineteenth-century Kanagawa's contribution to modern Japanese art history, in order to "prevent [this modern art] from being forgotten."[30] He mounted a large November 1957–January 1958 show that focused on 100 years of Japanese crafts, such as metal flower vases, glass from early-Meiji glassworks, sketches by Japanese of exhibits at nineteenth-century European trade fairs, woodcarving, and Western-style dining sets. Many of the objects originated in Kanagawa, and most included attribution to individual artists, erasing the class distinction between artists and artisans often used to assign low status to these genres, and to denigrate the modernity of their creators. His shows argued that Japanese modernity reached back into the Tokugawa past, was not led by the state, and had more localized and multiple origins

than national celebrations would suggest.[31] Emphasizing Yokohama's role
as one of the first official treaty ports, or "Japan's front door" (*nihon no
genkan*), Hijikata framed Kanagawa prefecture as more international than
Tokyo. He suggested that Kanagawa enjoyed more cultural resources to
overcome feudalism (= fascism), because its practical and realistic values
were rooted in mercantile rather than samurai society, giving Kanagawa
culture greater flexibility on issues of honor and identity than that of Tokyo.
Sawatari Kiyoko made this argument recently in essays and exhibits at
the Yokohama Museum of Art and was praised by Ellen Conant in 2006
because "Her research ... challenges previous scholarship stressing the role
of Edo/Tokyo and government institutions there," but Hijikata consistently
preceded her from 1951 to 1980.[32]

More unusually, Hijikata also pushed this argument several centuries
deeper into the past, dating the origins of bourgeois culture in Japan to
roughly the same time as in Europe. He organized an enormous two-part
exhibit in 1956 on the cultural history of the prefecture in the twelfth
through seventeenth centuries, and another in April–May 1959 on *The
Japanese City*, of maps and genre paintings of urban scenes from the
fourteenth through late nineteenth centuries, particularly of Yokohama. In
these exhibits, Hijikata argued that ancient and medieval Japan was less
a centralized national culture than a highly diffuse and varied society. He
located the origins of Japanese modernity in the century of early contact
with Europe, noting that in 1550–1650, Europeans were just beginning
to think in terms of a world history that involved Asia and the Americas.
(He also pointed out that European expansion was built on the plunder
of older American civilizations.) Hijikata argued that Kanagawa was an
important meeting place for cosmopolitan people interested in foreign
cultures in that "era of the eastward advance of Christianity" (*Kurisutokyō
tōzen jidai*).

In these exhibits and publications, Hijikata argued that comprehension
of the scientific spirit was widespread enough in Yokohama that it affected
both artists and artisans, making the city a center for modern aesthetics
and protocapitalist manufacturing a century before it became a treaty port
in 1858.[33] By the eighteenth century, Kanagawa was home to a large group of
Rangaku scholars, who developed rational and empirical approaches to the
world by studying both European and Asian texts. By the early nineteenth
century, many skilled artisans proficient in techniques such as copper-plate
etching made their homes there. Moreover, these two groups interacted with
each other, despite official separation of the social classes, just as in European
coffee houses. Joel Mokyr has recently argued that high levels of sustained
interaction between scientists and artisans explain why industrialization
first developed in Great Britain, suggesting that Hijikata was on to
something important.[34] Hijikata was also integrating Kanagawa prefecture
spatially with this argument, by linking its twentieth-century urban centers
of manufacturing, such as working-class Kawasaki, to the artisanal and

artistic communities in elite Kamakura, and treating both as cosmopolitan. Nagasu Kazuji, Uchiyama's successor as Governor of Kanagawa Prefecture, said about Hijikata in a 1980 eulogy: "You encouraged us to see local and regional culture as brimming over with individuality and originality,"[35] making it clear that he engaged others with this narrative.

While the museum founders had a formal responsibility to present art related to Kanagawa prefecture, they extended the same philosophy to other Japanese regions as well, showing that their approach was based on a social vision rather than mere local boosterism. A 1973 show featured Wakayama prefecture as an incubator for creative modern innovation, in part because of its long tradition of elite patronage of the arts. It foreshadowed the argument recently made by Eiko Ikegami that Tokugawa artistic communities (many in Wakayama) provided indigenous models of egalitarian community that later became resources for democratic modern society.[36] Wakimura, who had grown up in Tanabe, Wakayama's second city, helped organize this show by contacting collectors and encouraging them to lend their art.[37]

In his publications, his behind-the-scenes activities on behalf of the Kamakura museum, and his activities in Wakayama, Wakimura argued that local rather than national elites typically first provided modern cultural opportunities to their communities, because provincial leaders were responding to the condescension of the national capital. In his 1967 book, he gave the example of Detroit, where the municipal art museum opened its doors in 1896, eight years before the first automobile plant began producing cars. In Japan, businessmen in Kansai were similarly the first modern art patrons precisely because they felt patronized by Tokyo. Wakimura highlighted Sumitomo Shunsui, the 15th head of the Sumitomo family, who bankrolled artist Kanokogi Takeshirō to study in Paris and then establish a major art school, the Kansai Bijutsuin. The Sumitomo family later donated both land and art to establish the Osaka Municipal Museum of Art. Elsewhere, Wakimura profiled Ōhara Magosaburō who founded Japan's first museum of European art in Kurashiki in 1930, and Ōsaka businessman Yamamoto Hatsujirō, who bought over 120 paintings by Saeki Yūzo (1898–1928) in the 1930s for a planned museum, although his project was disrupted by the war. Some of these works are now housed in the Osaka Municipal Museum of Art in an arrangement brokered by Wakimura.[38] In all of these cases, Wakimura, like Hijikata, was proposing that Kamakura and Kurashiki—the home of Japan's industrial revolution—offered more civic-minded engagement across social class lines than did Tokyo.

Their version of both European and Japanese history presented urban bourgeois culture as an important counterweight to national mobilization. By contrast, none of them expressed interest in the mutual aid mechanisms created by Tokugawa-era peasants, as recently celebrated by Tetsuo Najita.[39] Their disdain for the rural past also underscores the fact that, while some Japanese elided the difference between ethnic and local, as Kevin Doak has cogently argued, these men did not, because their understanding of historical change equated urbanity with modernity. In this regard, their thinking resembled only one strand of the historical vision evoked by Irokawa Daikichi, one of the key practitioners of the popular "folk" *minshūshi* history being developed at the same time, which celebrated the rise of *both* bourgeois and village society over the samurai state. Rather than romanticizing the communitarian nature of rural life, they sought to valorize and expand bourgeois culture.[40]

Deconstructing the canon and the nation

The museum offered other strategies for decentering nationalism. Hijikata frequently expressed scorn for the annual art competitions begun by the national government in 1907 and continuing into the 1950s, because they mobilized art for nationalist unity. He criticized this structure of "feudalistic art nurturance" and thought Japanese needed spaces such as his museum where the status conveyed by the imprimatur of the state could be challenged and reevaluated.[41] He shared this disdain with many others, including SCAP officials, who saw the juried shows (known by the acronyms *Bunten*, *Teiten*, and, after the war, *Nitten*) as antidemocratic state control of artistic expression. Plumer lambasted the main national art organization, particularly its art competition: "Greatest evil is its annual 'Nitten' exhibit which perpetuates and advertises ugliness on a large scale," explaining his enthusiasm for decentralizing art institutions.[42]

Hijikata rejected the idea of establishing a Japanese national canon for several reasons. As he pointed out, the Tokyo government had established these shows in order to articulate a unified national culture to the world. Therefore in the prewar decades it had not displayed more experimental Western-style painting, such as the techniques associated with the *Nikakai* artists, meaning that it could not convey the central debates among artists of the era. Hijikata complained in 1951 that the planned Tokyo modern art museum, like the Louvre and the British Museum, would try to determine what a classic was. As the old joke put it, he quipped, "the museum is the mausoleum for masterpieces."[43] Elsewhere he explained that, "my plan as a modern art museum professional was to follow the system of modern art history that my research had indicated since the prewar years [that emphasized heterogeneity]. By making the art museum an institution of social education, we had an opportunity to radically revise modern Japanese art history. I want to correct the distorted art history created by the government's nineteenth-century-style arts policy and its administrative control through the official exhibition system." In contrast to national museums, Hijikata thought, "we must explore the artists whose work was made invisible, compile lists of their work, and organize materials on them," in short, bring them into history. Hijikata also displayed media neglected by the national museum, such as prints.[44]

Another reason, in his opinion, that art critics and museum curators should avoid canon making was that they simply did not know which contemporary artists would become most influential. Indeed, he noted, more than half of the art purchases by modern art museums took place after the artist in question had died.[45] Finally, like Plumer, Hijikata thought that establishing a narrative of an unbroken national art tradition required the Tokyo museum to display some lower-quality art, specifically identifying its collection of Edo-era paintings as mediocre.[46]

More fundamentally, however, Hijikata not only rejected a Japanese national canon, he rejected the idea of a canon itself. If all kinds of art are in the process of being revalued retrospectively all the time by many different people, a stable core tradition cannot exist. As he put it, "rather than placing importance on the existence of objective worth from the past, we focus on what contemporary people see and value, and what people in future might get out of it" in Kamakura.[47] His shows often emphasized the ways that new art historical categories gave older images modern meanings (keimō no imi), a line of thought that the national museum, by the way it framed its mission, neglected.[48]

This was an unusual stance at the time, and contrasted starkly with that of Imaizumi Atsuo, who had already accepted the job of assistant director for the planned national museum of modern art when the Kamakura museum opened its doors.[49] As art historian Mitsuda Yuri explains, rather than focusing on the ways that historical contexts change an image's meaning, Imaizumi treated "the nation" as a unified entity that yearned for cohesion, a concept that Hijikata had found attractive before 1945 but later rejected. Imaizumi championed a single abstract notion of "the modern"—which Japanese painting had not yet achieved—while Hijikata sought out many different moderns and found them everywhere[50] Masaaki Morishita has recently argued that, because both Hijikata and Imaizumi structured their exhibits around individuals rather than around art groups, they shared a philosophy of art history. He is surely right that both sought to diminish the power of the art groups in order to entrench the authority of curators, but this formulation misses the major differences in their intellectual concerns.[51]

In the early postwar years, Imaizumi was only one of many art critics to express the anxiety that Japan was not yet modern or still feudal. For example, in 1953, the distinguished architect Tange Kenzō (1913–2005) called the first exhibit at the new national modern art museum "a chance to someday achieve modernity," although he dismissed Maekawa Kunio's renovations to the building as having rendered the paintings "nothing more than brightly colored artificial flowers. Beautiful living blossoms may have existed there once but mysteriously they all seem to have died." After a lengthy celebration of French culture, Tange commented that "the meaning and the role of the Japanese modern art museum cannot be the same as of the Parisian one. Why? In a place where there is no domestic lineage [for modernity] one cannot start with historicism, nor be able to proceed in a straight line from the past . . . . Japan is still in the stage of pre-Impressionism."[52] This was precisely the attitude that Hijikata, Osaragi, and Wakimura thought had led Japanese to embrace fascism.

Hijikata, like Wakimura and Osaragi, treated the past as a resource that is constantly reinterpreted by modern people everywhere, in a global and interactive process. By the 1950s, Hijikata thought modernity had occurred everywhere at roughly the same time rather than in nation-specific chunks, explaining why he used the terms "modern (*kindai*)" as a straightforward chronological marker for the nineteenth plus early twentieth centuries and "contemporary (*gendai*)" for the postwar years. His exhibition strategy highlighted the ways in which aesthetic categories and artistic conventions were historical human creations, rather than timeless truths, and then explored the implications of this insight for the way contemporary people see the world.[53]

Hijikata's dialectical concept of historical change began with individual artists, not as representatives of their nation's culture, but as people in various parts of the globe who grew excited about specific ideas and artistic styles such as Impressionism, Symbolism, Fauvism, and Surrealism. These individuals discovered new (to them) cultural concepts in one place and then "transplanted" (*ishoku bunka*) them elsewhere, both transforming the original idea and (often) becoming an inspiration for another individual, creating a new synthesis somewhere else.

Precisely in order to undermine a nationalist reading of the process by which culture became both global and modern, Hijikata frequently combined American, Asian, European, and sometimes African artifacts, such as in two very large shows, Global Glass of 1955 and Jars of the World in 1957. These exhibits demonstrated his signature point: that modern artists borrow from a range of traditions, not just those of their own biological ancestors. Similarly, as Wakimura and Hijikata agreed in a 1979 discussion, rather than articulating timeless "western" versus "eastern" theories of painting, it made far more sense to trace historical trends, such as a return to realism in the 1920s and 1930s by individuals such as George Grosz and Otto Dix in Germany and Kishida Ryūsei and Matsumoto Sannosuke in Japan.[54] Hijikata also challenged the fiction that the Japanese enjoyed an empire in the prehistoric period, working closely with scholars such as Egami Namio, best known for his provocative argument that prehistoric horse riders from Korea had won political power in ancient Japan rather than the reverse. In fact, Egami lent Hijikata money for a trip to Europe in 1952.[55]

The first modern Japanese artist "whose work was made invisible" that Hijikata chose to highlight in this manner was Saeki Yūzō in 1952, followed by two more shows in 1966 and 1968. Hijikata focused on Saeki's desire to portray as beautiful the back streets, cafes, and other urban places of working-class Paris.[56] Wakimura Yoshitarō commented that Saeki was a bold and unusual choice for the museum's first one-man exhibit on a Japanese artist, particularly since Yasui Sotarō and Umehara Ryūzaburō were far more famous, followed more logically from the museum's inaugural exhibit on Cezanne and Renoir, and had local connections to Kamakura.[57] Another early two-man exhibit featured the work of Matsumoto Sannosuke and Shimazaki Keiji, neither of whom had won national prizes in their lifetimes. As Mark Sandler has shown, in 1941, Matsumoto was one of very few artists to openly criticize government control of the arts; so this show was perceived by many as a critique of fascism as well.[58] Matsumoto interested Hijikata as someone whose distinctively cosmopolitan and modern sensibility had given his paintings great individuality and humanism, despite the fact that he enjoyed neither the benefit of an elite education nor of overseas travel.

The same arguments are discernible in Hijikata's exhibit of African prints in 1959 and of modern Mexican prints in 1960. In both he depicted them as participants in a world-wide modern dialogue on art. Hijikata had developed this idea in 1952, after talking at length with two artists who "transplanted" Mexican art. One was sculptor Henry Moore, whom he visited in London in the spring to arrange an exhibit and the other was Isamu Noguchi, whose first big Japanese show was at the Kamakura museum in the fall. These experiences sparked his interest in Mexican art, and Hijikata published a brief book on that subject in 1955, shortly before Japan's first big Mexican art show opened at the Tokyo National Museum. Once again, Hijikata's view of this art as an example of universal, globally simultaneous modernity starkly contrasted with the opinions of other experts. In Winther-Tamaki's analysis of the 1955 Tokyo exhibit, most Japanese critics lingered on the power of the images in ways that telegraphed nationalist anxiety: "Indeed, perhaps the repetition and intensity of the rhetoric of expressive strength was driven by a desire to suppress an alternate reading of Mexican culture as impure hybridity, an impression that was demoralizing because it resonated with insecurities about the hybridity of Japan's own modernity."[59] Hijikata simply did not think that hybridity was either deviant from a stable norm or a problem.

Wakimura's 1967 book on the rise of the international art market similarly argued that there was only one modern—and transnational— experience. Even objects generally presumed to be traditional expressions of national identity had long ago become fundamentally modern items that required coordination and supplies from far-flung places. In one chapter-length example, Wakimura explained that the quality of Persian carpets had declined over several centuries until the late nineteenth century when modern local entrepreneurs, hoping for profits, revived the rug trade by combining a variety of new inputs, such as imported wool from Australia, cotton from Manchester, and new synthetic German dyes, all made possible by injections of capital from New York firms.[60] The "Persian rug" was a global artifact.

Hijikata and Wakimura both got attention for these views. Other museum professionals described the Kamakura museum as completely free of "the stink of bureaucracy" (*kanryōshū*), and many prefectures and municipalities modeled their institutions on it in later decades.[61] The young assistant curators at Kamakura, such as Yagyū Fujio, Asahi Akira, and Sakai Tadayasu, who reveled in the opportunity to "slip away from the reach of meddlesome conservative bureaucrats," also went on to head up other museums. (Yagyū's commitment must have been high because he accepted a substantial salary cut of 2000 yen from the 7000 yen he made as an editor at Heibonsha.)[62] Wakimura's book, *The Value of Taste*, was also celebrated as boundary-crossing and innovative, explaining its enduring "long-seller" status at Iwanami publishing house.[63]

These men were reclaiming Japanese modernity, emphasizing its ordinariness and connecting it to cosmopolitan local cultures. Their main antifascist strategy was to offer middle-class status and bourgeois culture to as many Japanese as possible, and was widely understood as such at the time. Yet, while their stance made intuitive sense to Japanese who remembered the decade of fascist mobilization, their valorization of bourgeois culture as a way to divorce individual from national identity was too abstract a concept for younger people. This, far more than either "forgetting" or "false consciousness," helps explain why Japanese pivoted so rapidly into thinking of themselves as peaceful, homogenous, and middle class.

3

Furusato-zukuri: Saving Home Towns by Reinventing Them

Timothy S. George

Japan had achieved its modern goal of building a wealthy nation by 1968, when its GNP became the third largest in the world, or certainly by the 1973 oil shock. But as farming, fishing, mining, and smokestack industries were marginalized in an increasingly high-tech, service-oriented economy, and as the population aged, rural areas, towns, and small cities struggled to redefine themselves, keep their young people, protect from redevelopment the buildings and places to which they attached special meaning, and reorient their economies. They did these things partly through processes often described as *furusato-zukuri* ("home town-building"), or *machi-zukuri* ("town-building"). This chapter traces the process in Minamata and briefly surveys three other cases of *furusato-zukuri*.[1]

In recent decades, the city of Minamata has attempted to recover from its poisonous past, the tragic mercury poisoning that made it the ultimate symbol of the dark side of Japan's high growth and also the symbol of the rise of the citizens' movement.[2] The people of Minamata have worked to rebuild their community, economy, and reputation, striving to reinvent their city as a symbol of community revival and environmental responsibility. Minamata, in addition to dealing with the persistent legacies of a long-term industrial pollution disaster, was responding to many of the sorts of problems common to many other areas throughout Japan.

In Minamata and elsewhere, the *furusato-zukuri* processes have involved the following questions:

Identity and Vision: What tangible and intangible things should be preserved, restored, or recovered, and what must be created anew? What should the town or city look and feel like?

Economy: How can and should the town or city survive and prosper economically?

Society and Community: How should citizens organize, relate to, and work with one another?

Power and Politics: Who makes these decisions, and how?

A sampling of *furusato-zukuri* processes in several other areas can illustrate a range of both distinctive and common patterns. Here, Minamata's experiences are compared with those of three other places: the old post town of Tsumago on the Nakasendō inland route from Edo to Kyoto, the port city of Otaru on Hokkaidō, and the Shikoku farming town of Uwa.

The background in Minamata: Success and tragedy

Growth under Chisso, and then decline

Minamata's current project is not its first attempt to recover from problems by redefining itself. At the start of the last century, it faced economic disaster, with jobs lost when its salt-making industry was nationalized and then eliminated, and when a new dam brought electricity to the gold mines inland of the city that had employed men from Minamata to haul coal for power. The creative solution was to turn the agent of this latter problem into the village's savior: Noguchi Shitagau was planning to build a chemical factory to be powered by the excess electricity from his dam, so they persuaded him to change plans and build it in Minamata. The factory opened in 1908 and the Nihon Chisso company moved to the cutting edge of technology in prewar Japan.

This solution was a model for local industrial policy in twentieth-century Japan and was quite literally *machi-zukuri* (town building): the growth it brought built Minamata from a village into a town by 1912, and a city by 1949. The population grew to 20,000 in 1921, 30,000 in 1941, 40,000 in 1948, and peaked at 50,000 in 1956. In the mid-1950s, Chisso provided a quarter of the city's jobs and half of its tax income.[3]

By then, however, the risks of being a factory town, an *unmei kyōdōtai*— a "community sharing a single fate" with the company—were becoming painfully clear. In Japan's third industrial transformation—the move to petrochemicals, automobiles, and electronics—Chisso fell behind. The factory employed nearly 5,000 workers in 1950, fewer than 4,000 in 1960, fewer than 2,000 in 1970, and a mere 680 in 1994. Population declined to just over 30,000 by 1990. The population declined only slightly after that but continued to age due to the low birth rate, longer life spans, and the exodus of young people, so that the percentage of Minamata's population over the age of 65, which was under 5 percent in 1955 and under 10 percent in 1970, was approximately 30 percent by 2010.[4]

Tragedy of a pollution disease

In 1956, Minamata discovered that the factory had brought it a disease the world had never before seen: the large-scale poisoning of human beings from mercury dumped into the sea, concentrated in the food chain, and consumed in fish and shellfish. Minamata disease destroys brain and nerve cells, causing symptoms ranging from ringing in the ears and narrowing of the field of vision to difficulty walking and speaking, and even death. Before the end of 1956, there were 52 officially designated patients, 17 of whom had died.

There have been four rounds of responses and so-called solutions to this disaster. The first "solution," at the end of 1959, involved "sympathy payments" by Chisso to victims, compensation to fishing cooperatives for loss of income, and pollution control equipment that did not remove mercury. The settlement was brokered by local elites, who kept the issue out of the national spotlight and enabled Chisso to evade responsibility. Most people believed that the issue had been resolved.

By 1968, however, the issue resurfaced. Chisso's moral and economic authority had declined, economic growth had made Japan more willing and able to pay some of the costs of growth, citizens' movements created the possibility of a nationwide network of support, and victims of pollution diseases in other areas filed lawsuits. The second Minamata "solution" ended this round of responses in July 1973, after a court victory climaxing a period in which the issue was brought to the attention of the nation by victims and supporters. Chisso accepted legal responsibility for the disease and began substantial regular payments to certified victims, who as of 31 August 2010 numbered 2,271, of whom 1,712 were deceased.[5]

For most people, this is where the story ends. And it was the end for the mediagenic national networks bringing victims and supporters and their creative forms of protest and pressure into the nation's homes. In fact, however, there was a third, lesser known, and again apparently last "solution" put in place in 1996. Under this, over 10,000 patients who were uncertified and therefore ineligible for compensation under the 1973 settlement received one-time payments, if they promised never to request full certification or to sue the government.

But this was not the end either. About 50 patients refused to accept this 1996 settlement and drop their suits alleging government responsibility. In 2004, the Supreme Court upheld lower court rulings in their favor. For the first time the highest court found the national and prefectural governments, not just the company, responsible for Minamata disease, though these authorities were only found negligent for not acting to stop the pollution

FIGURE 3.1 *The Minamata Memorial. The suspended box contains the names of victims of the disease.*

in 1959 when a research group deduced the cause. After thousands of
people newly applied for certification and filed lawsuits in the years after
2004, the government and patients' groups agreed in spring 2010 on a plan
to give one-time payments and monthly medical allowances to as many as
50,000 uncertified patients. This may truly be the last attempt at a "full
and final solution," but there has been no decision regarding governmental
responsibility for preventing the pollution and disease in the first place, and
some patients will remain uncompensated. Neither of these issues is likely
to be fully resolved before the last patient dies. So, like the legacies of the
Asia-Pacific War, Minamata remains, to adapt a phrase Carol Gluck uses
for the emperor system, a "ghost at the historical feast" that simply will not
go away.[6]

Approaches to *furusato-zukuri*

Before looking briefly at *furusato-zukuri* in Tsumago, Otaru, and Uwa,
and then returning to Minamata to survey its experiments in recovery
and rebuilding from the devastation caused by the disease, a discussion
of the approaches to and terms for such efforts is in order. There are not
only innumerable versions of the process, but also many different terms:
furusato-zukuri ("building" or "creating" "the old home town"), *machi-
zukuri* ("town-building"), *machi-sodate* ("raising the town" or "bringing
up the town," or "urban husbandry"), *chiiki-zukuri* ("region-building"),
mura-okoshi ("rousing the village" or perhaps "village revival"), *kasseika*
("activating"), and various combinations of these terms. *Furusato-zukuri*,
as Jennifer Robinson notes, is a logical impossibility: the past is not built or
created today.[7]

   The "traditional" village created in the process of *furusato-zukuri* is of
course an invented tradition, and in some cases what is built is rather like a
theme park. But precisely because the term *furusato-zukuri* is a reminder of
the invented nature of the "traditions" created in the process, and because
it implies the importance of the community and the past more than the
other terms do, I usually use this term, even if it is not always used by
participants.

   Furusato-zukuri or *machi-zukuri* efforts may be categorized in various
ways. One division is between those in major metropolitan areas, which
are usually called *machi-zukuri* and have been the focus of most studies
of the phenomenon, and those in towns and smaller cities, including all
those discussed in this chapter. Another dichotomization would separate
them into those that involve historic preservation of buildings and other
physical assets, and those that do not. Minamata's case is mostly in the latter
category, while the others discussed here do involve preservation.

   Much work on *machi-zukuri* beyond Minamata has been done by
sociologists and by scholars of urban planning, for whom the classic

examples of *machi-zukuri* are the movements in Sakae-Higashi in Nagoya in the 1950s and 1960s and in Maruyama and Mano in Kōbe in the 1960s and 1970s.[8] More recently there has been a great deal of interest in efforts in Kōbe since the 1995 Hanshin earthquake.[9] The focus of most of the literature on *machi-zukuri* is on major urban areas, and the overriding theme is the attempts by organized citizens to have a voice in the city planning decisions that the authorities wish to impose from above. This chapter complements such work by looking at rural towns and smaller cities, and looking at a range of issues beyond the formal city planning process.

Tsumago: Historic townscape preservation

Tsumago, familiar to readers of Shimazaki Tōson's *Yoakemae* (*Before the Dawn*), is one of the first and best-known cases of *furusato-zukuri*.[10] The intent was to make Tsumago, or at least the areas visible to tourists strolling through the town along the old Nakasendō, look and feel as much as possible as it had a century or more earlier in the late Tokugawa period, when it was one of the post stations on the Nakasendō and its inns hosted travelers of all kinds, including daimyō and their retinues. Discussions began in 1966, and in 1968 a campaign to redevelop the town by preserving it was launched as part of the centennial celebrations of the Meiji Restoration. The goals were to preserve, restore, and redevelop in order to attract tourists to revitalize the community, and to do this without relying on investment or control from outside. That it was largely successful is attested to by the 800,000 tourists who visited every year in the early twenty-first century.

By the late 1950s, Tsumago was in economic trouble. The railroad and modern roads had left much of the Nakasendō unused and overgrown, and the village was in danger of being abolished. When in the mid-1960s the prefecture began a campaign to attract tourists, and Nagano prefecture began planning for the Meiji centennial, tourist visits to Tsumago increased, and a few people looking for ways to keep the town alive stepped up their activities. The "Love Tsumago Association" (Tsumago o Aisuru Kai) was established in a meeting on 22 August 1968 and the movement took off.[11]

Their principles were spelled out in a remarkable "Residents' Constitution to Protect Tsumago" adopted in 1971. The section on "The Principle of Giving Priority to Preservation" includes what became their motto for preserving the town and keeping control and profits in the hands of the residents: "Do not sell, do not rent, do not tear down" (*uranai, kasanai, kowasanai*). Residents were enjoined to consult with the organization before transferring, remodeling, or restoring properties in the historic area along the Nakasendō, not to display advertisements, signs, or posters, and not to cause noise pollution with advertisements or cars or by keeping inns and shops open past 10 p.m.[12]

FIGURE 3.2 *A quiet evening on the Nakasendō in the center of Tsumago.*

FIGURE 3.3 *A souvenir and snack shop in Magome, the next post station on the Nakasendō. Such a display would not be allowed in Tsumago.*

One question that arose in Tsumago and elsewhere was how true to the past they should be. Shops were at first prohibited from serving coffee to tourists, but after great debate this was allowed. Horikawa Saburō describes in another context a transition from "preservation by freezing" the town in its past (*tōketsu hozon*) to "town-building" (*machi-zukuri*) involving some changes to accommodate present-day realities.[13] Despite such small concessions, Tsumago has done a remarkably successful job of providing visitors with what is widely regarded as the most authentic version of a Tokugawa-period post station. Shimazaki Tōson's boyhood home of Magome, the next post station along the Nakasendō toward Kyōto, was mostly burned down in a fire in 1895, and now appears much more touristy, with its modern signs and ice-cream stands. Tsumago, by contrast, became a model of *machinami hozon,* or "townscape preservation."

Otaru: Preserving a twentieth-century cityscape

The preservation movement in Otaru on Hokkaidō began some years after Tsumago's pioneering township preservation movement, but as the first significant example of a movement to preserve a twentieth-century township, it too was a pioneer.[14] Like Minamata in Kyūshū, Otaru had grown rapidly from late Meiji to early Shōwa, and until the 1920s, its population was greater than that of Sapporo.[15] Otaru's good harbor led Meiji planners of

FIGURE 3.4 *The canal and warehouses in Otaru.*

Hokkaidō's development to make it a major trading port, boasting handsome branch offices of so many banks that it was nicknamed the "Wall Street of the north." Small barges loaded the ships, and a canal was built in the center of the city between 1914 and 1923 to enable barges to dock at downtown warehouses. After the Asia-Pacific War, with little trade with the Soviet Union and less coal shipped from Otaru, and with ports such as Tomakomai building modern loading facilities and linked to Sapporo with better roads, Otaru declined. To keep the city alive, its planners decided in the 1960s to modernize the port and pave over the canal to improve the road system.

A citizens' movement began in 1973 when part of the canal had already been paved over for a road, more of it was scheduled to be lost, and the historic stone warehouses that had lined the canal were being destroyed. A group called the "Association to Protect the Otaru Canal (Otaru Unga o Mamoru Kai)" argued that the canal and warehouses should be preserved because they were central to Otaru's identity.

Horikawa Saburō identifies a shift in the nature of the movement, which in its first four years was unsuccessful, from 1977. New groups such as the Association to Realize the Building of the Town of Our Dreams (Yume no Machi-zukuri Jikkō Iinkai) symbolized a change that had also happened in Tsumago. Now activists argued for preservation of the canal and warehouses not for their own sake, but to revitalize the city, and they were willing to compromise. They promoted economic revitalization as the main goal, explained the educational value of a protected urban historical

FIGURE 3.5 *The Otaru branch of the Bank of Japan, built in 1912 and designed by Tatsuno Kingo, who also designed Tokyo Station and the headquarters of the Bank of Japan in Tokyo.*

environment, and sponsored an annual port festival that brought citizens together, reminded them of the city's past, and attracted large numbers of tourists. By 1980, the city and the Ministry of Construction agreed to cut in half the length of the canal to be paved over.

Despite this success, or perhaps partly due to it, the movement split and withered after 1984. Volunteers held the port festival until 1994, but then canceled it over concerns that it and the preservation project as a whole had led to what they called a "rootless," "souvenir-oriented" tourism.[16] There are concerns among residents that Otaru's townscape belongs less to them than it does to the tourists who come (though more now come only on day trips and fewer are staying overnight) to see the canal, warehouses, and old bank buildings and to buy souvenirs at the gift shops popping up everywhere. The city government even began a campaign to collect donations ("*furusato* tax payments") from "Otaru fans" around the country to support Otaru's "*furusato machi-zukuri*;" donors can choose to support any of five projects to preserve historic buildings or fund museums.[17] Civic activists want to reclaim the process and the historic areas for the community, but where the process will go next remains unclear.

The accomplishments in Tsumago and Otaru were significant, however. In addition to preserving historic buildings in both places and part of the canal in Otaru, the movements changed government policies and planning processes by insisting that their communities were "places" (*basho*) made what they were by the life of the community, and essential to its survival.[18] In other words, they were not just interchangeable "spaces" (*kūkan*) of

FIGURE 3.6 *Tourists visiting the canal and warehouses in Otaru.*

certain dimensions that could serve any function at any particular time. And the movements persuasively argued that preservation of the past could serve the needs of the present, as in the slogan used by the movement in Bologna, Italy: "an old town for a new society."[19]

Uwa: A more typical version of *furusato-zukuri?*

Gail Bernstein, in *Haruko's World*, her participant-observer account of the Shikoku town of Uwa in the 1970s, describes a case of *furusato-zukuri* that is probably more similar to most of those in Japan's rural areas than are the others described in this chapter.[20] In the 1970s, Utsunomiya Shōichi, whose family Bernstein lived with for her research, led a campaign to reorganize the rice fields in his Besshō district of Uwa to make farming more mechanized and efficient. The model for this project, far from being something in the local past, was the large-scale, mechanized farming he had seen in the United States in 1955 as a member of one of the early groups of Japanese sent to study American farming. This project helped cement Utsunomiya's leading role in the community. As mayor from 1982 to 2004 (Bernstein was called back to help with his first campaign), he presided over a town with fewer residents farming, and with more of the income of those who still farmed coming from other jobs. Education and economic changes

FIGURE 3.7 *Utsunomiya Shōichi near his home and the rice fields he reorganized, bisected by the new "Hydrangea Road."*

FIGURE 3.8 *Part of the preserved area of Unomachi.*

led the older generation to fear that the town's young people would reject farming and even the town itself for other ways of making a living and other places in which to live.

In fact, unlike many other rural areas, the population of Uwa had stopped declining, but it was rapidly aging at the time of Bernstein's 1993 return to Uwa, described in her epilogue. Uwa's population peaked at just under 25,000 in 1950. From 1970 to 1990, it stayed between 17,500 and 18,500, but the number of households rose from 5,018 to 6,659.[21] By 1993, Mayor Utsunomiya had secured prefectural and national government funding (the "construction state" was alive and well) for a nursing home and day care center for the elderly, a health center, a group home for mentally handicapped residents, a culture center, and two museums, including one explaining how rice was grown. The latter is in the old elementary school building from 1928, so Uwa too has found historic buildings to preserve and promote. It has also protected part of the Edo-era townscape of its old main street in the Nakanomachi area of the Unomachi district, the "downtown" area of Uwa.[22] Uwa also sold itself as a tourist destination, and the campaign included internationalization (*kokusaika*) by promoting the town as the one-time home of Japan's first female doctor of Western medicine, Philip Franz von Siebold's daughter Kusumoto Ine (1827–1903), who was educated in Uwa by one of Siebold's students.

Uwa's *furusato-zukuri* projects are more typical than those of Tsumago and Otaru. Its transformation was made possible by huge amounts of money from the prefectural and national governments, and was designed to provide jobs, build facilities, attract tourists and retirees from cities, and entice some who had moved away to make a "U-turn" (as the Utsunomiyas' grown daughter did). Some programs to rebuild community, such as a rather artificial-feeling new festival, seemed to be afterthoughts, but others, such as the "Ajisai (hydrangea) Road," a walking path built along the irrigation canal that flows through the rice fields Shōichi rationalized in the 1970s, continue to bring community members together. So does the Donburikan, a market complex built under Utsunomiya Shōichi's stewardship that functions as a farmers' market and a market for other local products, and includes a popular restaurant that uses local ingredients. Thanks to all of these efforts, Uwa seems to have survived the second half of the twentieth century better than many other rural farming areas.

Furusato-zukuri in Minamata

In Minamata, unlike most other rural towns and cities, it can be difficult to argue that what needs to be created is something that existed in a better past. The old "Chisso *jōkamachi*" (Chisso's castle town) is obviously a less than attractive model. And Minamata before Chisso was just a village, not something today's small city, built around an old factory, can even pretend to be or to recreate. There is the Tokutomi family home, where Sohō and Roka were born, but few other premodern buildings.

Keeping memories alive

Prior to the 1990s, activism in Minamata was almost exclusively by and for Minamata disease patients. One urgent task was to prevent the victims from being forgotten. This was a central purpose of a new organization established in 1974, the Minamata Disease Center Sōshisha. In addition to providing a place for patients to meet, the Sōshisha began collecting, organizing, and preserving documents, publishing a newsletter, and operating a museum. Thanks to the progressive teachers' union, Nikkyōsō, the museum attracted students on school trips. The Sōshisha was staffed mostly by young activists who had moved to Minamata and decided to stay and make Minamata their lifework.

Getting by: Fishing and farming

Of course, the patients themselves, on top of their concerns involving certification, government responsibility, and maintaining memories, had to find ways to live from day to day. Even if they were physically able to work, opportunities were limited. The job market was shrinking, even more so than elsewhere in rural Japan. Although the government never actually banned fishing in the bay, fish from the bay could not be caught and marketed because of a "self-restraint" policy the fishing cooperative had followed since the late 1950s. Chisso made a deal under which coop members would catch fish in the bay and sell them to Chisso, which sealed them in oil drums and buried them in land reclaimed from the bay.

Other patients concentrated on farming. Many turned to citrus fruit, which grows well in the warm climate and steep hills of southern Kyūshū. But clambering around the hills was difficult even for patients with relatively mild symptoms. Some decided they would never poison the consumers of their produce in the way Chisso had poisoned them, so they reduced or eliminated their use of pesticides and chemical fertilizers. The Sōshisha helped them market their products, first by mail order to its newsletter subscribers, and now online as well.

The Sōshisha was partly responsible for two other new business endeavors designed both to provide jobs and model environmentally friendly activities. One was a soap factory that made soap from used cooking oil collected from the city's restaurants. Another was a Japanese paper-making operation that employed Minamata disease patients and other physically and mentally disabled people.

Through the 1980s, though, Minamata remained a city divided and declining. Patients struggled to get by, to keep memories of their tragedy from being forgotten, to get certified, and to have local and national governments found responsible for their plight. Most of the rest of the city's residents did their best to ignore them.

The 1990s and beyond

That began to change in the 1990s, as the end of the world's Cold War was reflected in a thaw in Minamata as well. A few brave opinion leaders came to believe that Minamata's problems—the city's own sickness—could not be separated from the problems caused by Minamata disease, which had sickened not only citizens but also Minamata's economy, society, and politics. By 1994, this movement had been given a name: *moyainaoshi*, which means to re-moor a boat, or lash two boats together, as is often done by Minamata fishers. In this context, it means to come together to start things over or make things right.

This *moyainaoshi* movement was sparked in part by the mayor elected in 1994, Yoshii Masazumi. A member of the LDP, he was from a mountain village that had been incorporated into the city. His family was in the lumber business and grew rice; they were not tied to the Chisso factory in any way. He had donated much of the lumber used to construct the Sōshisha out of sympathy for the patients, some of whom had bought lumber from his family for their fishing boats over the years. As mayor, he insisted that the Minamata disease issue be confronted head-on, and sponsored a series of public lectures and forums on Minamata disease. Most importantly, on 1 May 1994, at a city-sponsored memorial service for disease victims held on land reclaimed from the most polluted parts of the bay, Yoshii became the first mayor to formally apologize on behalf of the city. Victims, he said, had suffered from "defamation, prejudice, and discrimination," and the city had failed "to take proper measures for those who were victims." He called for all citizens of Minamata to begin *moyainaoshi*.[23]

Mayors, of course, do not plan or carry out such projects on their own, and Yoshii's breakthrough was made possible in part by a group that had begun informal meetings the previous December, the Minamata Kenkyūkai (Minamata Study Group). This group, which met one or two evenings a month, included people from the city hall, the chamber of commerce, the agricultural association, the prefectural government, and others. Through their organizations, the results of the group's wide-ranging discussions were disseminated. The members of this diverse group, who had sometimes considered one another enemies, discovered over beer and *sake*, and sometimes while soaking in hot springs, that many of them had something in common: they had been university students during the late 1960s and early 1970s, and most, even those who were conservative members of the establishment by the 1990s, claimed to have been radical activists.

This group was partly responsible for Minamata's adoption of the most extensive recycling program in Japan, in which citizens voluntarily sort their

recyclable trash into 23 separate categories every week. The Kenkyūkai also
helped press the mayor to apologize on behalf of the city and to accommodate
a group of patients who petitioned him to allow them to place Buddhist stone
statues on the reclaimed land. They helped start an annual environmental
festival and memorial service on that land as well. This group also helped
make it possible for the city's Minamata Disease Museum and the Sōshisha
to cooperate in staging a joint exhibit at the museum and in jointly writing
and publishing a pamphlet entitled *Ten Things to Know about Minamata
Disease*. The pamphlet, which was published in Japanese, English, German,
Korean, Chinese, and French, pushed the city much further than it had
previously gone by clearly and repeatedly naming Chisso as the cause of the
disease.

One patient, a woman named Hirakida Rimiko, exemplified the breaking
of taboos on discussion of the disease. In 1994, at the age of 43, she first
admitted in public that her family suffered from Minamata disease. Her
father had gotten sick in 1954 and died in 1956. The disease also killed her
mother, grandmother, and grandfather. "But for many years I did not want
to talk about Minamata disease," she says. "Minamata owed its prosperity
to Chisso. Minamata existed for Chisso. That's how nearly everyone in
Minamata felt. But . . . I don't want the deaths of my father and grandfather
and the many people who have died from the disease to be in vain. If we

FIGURE 3.9 *Stone statues placed by Ogata Masato and others on the reclaimed
land that was once part of Minamata Bay.*

don't rethink this, the same tragedy will be repeated somewhere else in the world."[24]

So, Hirakida finally decided to speak out, to join and help channel the *moyainaoshi* movement. She began speaking regularly as a *kataribe*, or storyteller, at the city's Minamata Disease Municipal Museum. In 2002, she and Sasaki Kiyoto, head of a patients' group, traveled with supporters from the Sōshisha to Johannesburg for the United Nations Global Summit on the Environment. There she told her story, both in lectures and to visitors to a large booth set up in the conference exhibition hall. She and Sasaki also met and exchanged stories of suffering and struggle with members of black South African citizens' groups. Hirakida invited the head of one of these groups from Soweto to visit Minamata, and this led her to establish the Association for Minamata-South Africa Exchange.

One of the most fascinating activists is Ogata Masato. Born in 1953, he left home at 16 and took up with pimps and gangsters before returning home, applying for certification, and becoming a leader of the applicants' movement. Eventually he realized that "we could not fight the system unless we were in it." He left the movement, and in 1985 withdrew his application for certification, still pending after 11 years. He enjoyed the officials' confusion: "I was no longer a member of the movement but Ogata Masato; they were no longer officials but human beings."[25]

Since then Ogata has demonstrated how a pollution victim can define himself and his community by rejecting what he calls the "System" in favor of alternative forms of interconnectedness. He built a wooden boat named *Tokoyo*, the Buddhist "Other World," and took it to Minamata almost daily, sitting in front of the factory displaying "open letters" with a simple, direct message: "The Minamata Incident began when people stopped seeing their fellow humans as human beings," and it was time for them to reconnect. Ogata also visited Auschwitz and Okinawa to put Minamata in the context of other tragedies of the twentieth century.

A symbolic focus of his activity is the new land created by dredging the mercury-laden sludge and confining it in the innermost part of Minamata Bay. Ogata has worked to make this "a place of atonement." It was he, among others, who placed the small Buddhist stone statues there "to serve as our guides, leading us on a path of healing and restoration."

But Ogata does not simply trust in the gods, or withdraw from society. On that reclaimed land in 1995 he hosted a concert by Kina Shōkichi, the Okinawan folk-rock singer (and a National Diet member from the Democratic Party since 2004) on his way to perform in Nagasaki and Hiroshima. That linkage, and the way this furthered the patients' claim on this land, was powerful. Earlier, Ogata had lobbied against a concert there sponsored by the governor, arguing that it was in poor taste. Now Ogata said, "I heard someone complain that the man who had fought against the governor's concert was . . . staging his own on the same ground. . . . It's OK if it's me."[26] In 2002, when Sasaki and Hirakida went to Johannesburg for the United Nations World Summit on Sustainable Development, Ogata suggested that they perform a ceremony there for the souls of Minamata victims, while he did so under the same moon at home. They did this on a hilltop in Soweto with a local citizens' group whose distrust of the system mirrors Ogata's.

Hirakida's mentor in this spiritual performance was Sugimoto Eiko. In 1996, Sugimoto stood in a white robe on an open lot outside Tokyo's Shinagawa station, welcoming the spirits of the people and all living things that had died of Minamata disease to the first Minamata Exhibition. Sugimoto, long thought to have inherited her father's magical ability to know where and when to find fish, had also come to be considered to have a special ability to speak with or for the souls of the dead. Sociologist Kurihara Akira has compared her to a *goze*, the blind female singers and *shamisen* players who wandered Japan performing folk songs as well as recitations and chants with Shintō or Buddhist themes, and were often considered to have supernatural powers.[27] It almost seemed as though she were coming close to creating another of modern Japan's so-called new religions, but in fact she generally stayed within the bounds of the Pure Land Buddhism that dominates Minamata and the surrounding areas of Kyūshū. Her first such performance was at the 1994 Hi no Matsuri, or "fire festival" in Minamata, the first of those annual environmental festivals sponsored by the city.

In recent years, people such as Hirakida (now Ōya), Ogata, and Sugimoto (who died in February 2008) have become respected community leaders rather than pariahs, and citizens and the city government have learned from them. One of the people who has done the most to move the city government in this direction is Yoshimoto Tetsurō, a city hall official who was a leader of the Minamata Kenkyūkai founded in 1993, and who published a remarkable book in 1995, *Watashi no jimotogaku: Minamata kara no hasshin* (My *Jimotogaku*: A Message from Minamata).[28] *Jimotogaku*, which literally means "study of a local area," or "study of one's native place," is what he sees as the key to healing Minamata society, and the cornerstone of *furusato-zukuri* or *machi-zukuri*, for Minamata and elsewhere. He encourages people to get organized and get interested in their *jimoto*; to get out and study its nature, its history, its traditions, and its people. Most symbolic for him, as it was for Tanaka Shōzō, the patron saint of environmental activists who fought for the victims of the Ashio copper mine poisoning a century earlier, is the studying and cherishing of the watercourses. Water and its flow is what ties the area together.

The city has taken up his call in a big way, as some of the maps and posters it produces clearly show. It has declared itself "a city in which people value the environment, health, and welfare." It gives environmental prizes every year. It bought a number of kayaks that citizens can use without charge to explore the rivers. It is building on its position as the most recycling-aware city in Japan with a plan to become a "zero garbage city." The last of seven projects listed in its third general plan, covering the years 1996–2005, was the "Project to Support *Chiiki-zukuri* carried out by the citizens themselves" (*"shimin mizukara okonau chiiki zukuri shien" purojekuto*). The fourth plan, covering 2005–09, aimed to create "Ecopolis Minamata," and ended by describing five principles for Minamata's *machi-zukuri*, the last of which was "*machi-zukuri* through *moyai*." The fifth plan, for 2010–17, describes Minamata as "understanding better than anywhere else in the world the importance of the environment" and "placing the environment at the center of [our] *machi-zukuri*."[29]

Clearly, what has happened in Minamata since the early 1990s goes beyond the usual *furusato-zukuri* or *machi-zukuri*. The key roles of individuals throughout the story suggest that historians should pay more attention to the sorts of people that leading *minshūshi* (people's history) scholar Irokawa Daikichi calls "small leaders."[30] I strongly believe—taking gentle issue with Irokawa here—that had Yoshii Masazumi, Hirakida Rimiko, Ogata Masato, Sugimoto Eiko, or Yoshimoto Tetsurō not thought and acted as they did, the forces of history might *not* have created others to do the same things.

And just as Minamata's *machi-zukuri* initiative of a century ago was envied and copied by other towns, the people of Minamata today once again believe that their rebuilding project can provide a model for recovery for other rural towns and cities in Japan. This may turn out to be the case. But the history of Minamata over the past half-century has taught its people skepticism. Some question whether the *moyainaoshi* movement is aimed at the political "denaturing," to borrow another phrase Carol Gluck used in a different context, of issues that should not be removed from political discussion.[31] Still, if this reinventing of Minamata fails to have the long-term positive effects residents hope for, they know at least that it cannot bring the sort of tragedy of their first attempt.

Conclusion: Bringing rural towns and cities back in

Before the disasters of 11 March 2011, rural areas and regional cities had drawn relatively little attention in English-language scholarship on postwar Japan. Little wonder: one of the greatest transformations in the postwar resulted from mass migration to the major urban centers, so that the Tokyo, Osaka, and Nagoya areas alone held 43.4 percent of Japan's population by 1993.[32] Only 4.9 percent of Japan's workers in 1996 were farmers.[33] For most Japanese, in the first two and a half postwar decades, farming, fishing, and rural areas represented the dirtier and more difficult lives they had recently escaped. That changed when Japanese realized that they had achieved their goal of a wealthy society, and were able to feel nostalgia for a simpler, less crowded, and less polluted past.

Yet, despite the newfound appreciation of city dwellers for the pleasures of the (partly imagined) rural past, symbolized by the "Discover Japan" travel boom, rural areas struggled with economic and population realities. In many ways, they were struggling with problems that Japan as a whole would begin to confront later: declining, aging populations, and hollowed-out economies. There is a case to be made for looking more closely at the *furusato-zukuri/machi-zukuri* phenomenon and broadening our gaze beyond the major urban areas to bring them back into postwar history. This case is even stronger given the fact that most of the areas severely affected by the earthquake, tsunami, and radiation leaks of 2011 were rural, and had long struggled with the same sorts of difficulties as other rural areas.

4

Searching for *Furusato* in Kaminoseki

Martin Dusinberre

FIGURE 4.1 *Sakai Yoshinori lighting the Olympic Cauldron at the Opening Ceremonies of the 1964 Tokyo Olympics. Used with permission from the International Olympic Committee.*

As iconic images go, the photograph of Sakai Yoshinori holding aloft the Olympic torch at the opening ceremony of the 1964 Tokyo Summer Games is one of the most defining of postwar Japan. Born in Hiroshima on 6 August 1945, Sakai embodied the recovery of the nation from the deepest traumas of World War II. His igniting the Olympic flame invited the world to celebrate not just a two-week festival of sport, but a country once again on the rise, with the speedy new bullet trains symbolic of Japan's then record-breaking economic growth.

If the opening of the Tokyo Olympics spoke to the optimism of the high economic growth years that characterized the postwar era, then perhaps the closing ceremony of the 1998 Winter Olympics, hosted by the mountain city of Nagano, might represent the more pessimistic mood of Japan's post-bubble era. Here, the memorable image is of Japanese vocalist Anri, who took to the stage as the Olympic flame withered in the chilly night air. Bathed in icy blue light and against a backdrop of thousands of handheld paper lanterns, she began to sing a well-known folksong:

Usagi oishi kano yama	That hill where I chased rabbits
kobuna tsurishi kano kawa	that river where I fished for carp
yume wa ima mo megurite	even now they appear like a dream
Wasuregataki furusato.	the *furusato* I can't forget.

The song laments the loss of an old (*furu*) village (*sato*) left behind by the rapid modernization that swept Japan in the late nineteenth century. Almost from the moment of its composition in 1914, "Furusato" became an instant hit, and to this day is familiar to consecutive generations of Japanese. That the "Furusato" lyrics were written by a native of Nagano prefecture, Takano Tatsuyuki, made it doubly perfect for an Olympic closing ceremony: the song symbolized both the local culture of the region in which the games had been held, and more generally the national culture of Japan televised to the international Olympic audience.

In domestic terms, however, the evocation of *furusato* at the end of the Nagano Olympics inadvertently spoke to a sense of loss—of local communities, of an unspoiled landscape, of a preindustrial innocence—that had become particularly acute by the late 1990s. Yet, this late-twentieth-century sense of loss was different in a number of important ways to that articulated in Takano's 1914 song, even if the word itself—*furusato*—remained the same. The first part of this chapter thus briefly traces the ways in which popular discourses of *furusato* modulated from the first decades of the twentieth century to the last, drawing on the work of numerous scholars, both Japanese and non-Japanese, who have studied this most ubiquitous of terms. As will be shown, these discourses tend to reveal more about the sentiments of the people who left their old village behind—people such as the narrator of Takano's song—than they do about the lives of those who remained in their ancestral hometowns. Focusing instead on the latter, I then turn to the ways in which ordinary villagers attempted to reconcile the "dream"-like quality of the idealized *furusato* with the exigencies of rural life in late-twentieth-century Japan. This reconciliation led to the construction of a grassroots interpretation of the *furusato* and its history that both drew on and differed from national discourses. By examining these representations of *furusato* history in one particular town, this chapter offers an important and hitherto understudied local perspective on the bright "history narrative" (*rekishi monogatari*) also identified at a national level in Hiraku Shimoda's chapter later in this book—a narrative that creates a lacuna out of the twentieth century as a whole, and which therefore glosses over the very *furusato* memories that Takano's song claims we cannot forget.

As with a closing ceremony, the discourse of *furusato* usually takes as its starting point a physical departure. In the late nineteenth and early twentieth centuries, this departure was from the old village to the city, with tens of thousands of young men and women migrating every year from the countryside to urban factories. As they settled into new rhythms of everyday life, they consumed popular expressions of nostalgia for the communities they had left behind. Thus, the ballad "Ryoshū" (1907) recalled "the *furusato* I miss, the parents for whom I yearn," while *furusato* folk songs in the New Folk Song Movement (c.1915–25) enabled city dwellers to "send their hearts" back home, creating a comforting, fictional image of village harmony for countryside immigrants still finding their feet in the big cities.[2] In the emerging *furusato* literature, moreover, nostalgia for the hometown became "a means to articulate the perceived shortcomings of city life" (even if, as in Kunikida Doppo's 1901 story, "Let me return," the hometown could also be a site of unrequited love and grief).[3] One of the Japanese words for "nostalgia," *kyōshū*, shares its first character with the second character in the word *kokyō*, which is the alternative phonetic reading for *furusato*. Thus, just as the English word "nostalgia" grows out of the Greek term *nostos*, "return to a native place," so, in Japanese, "the village" (*kyō*, *sato*) was at the etymological root of prewar longing for a rural life left behind.

The so-called *furusato*-boom of the 1970s, by contrast, was premised on a different type of departure—from city to countryside. One of its most famous expressions was Japan National Railways' "Discover Japan" campaign, launched by the advertising giant Dentsu in the fall of 1970.[4] As Account Executive Fujioka Wakao later recalled, the young, urban women who were the target consumer group for the campaign made it clear to Dentsu researchers that they were less interested in traveling to specific locations than in "seeking a stage on which they might play out their *own* journey." Reflecting this, the working slogan for the campaign was "Discover Myself"—or, as Fujioka interpreted it, "my Japanese self." Even when this later changed to "Discover Japan," the campaign title still stood for the anticipated discovery that young women would make of not only a physical landscape but also of their own sense of Japanese identity.[5] The campaign thus featured iconic images of modern, Western-dressed young women strolling pensively through beautiful but unidentified Japanese landscapes: a woman crossing paths with a Buddhist monk on an ancient forest path bathed in sunlight, for example, or meeting a wrinkled old farmer on her descent from a quiet mountain shrine. Running eventually for eight years,

Discover Japan was typical of domestic travel advertisements throughout the 1970s that spoke to a popular desire to "travel home."[6]

But whereas Kunikida Doppo's "Let me return" had as its object an actual community, the *furusato* "home" of the 1970s was far more abstract, thus highlighting some of the crucial differences between the early and late-twentieth-century discourses. The narrators of early-twentieth-century songs and stories were almost always first-generation city immigrants: their *furusato/kokyō* comprised specific "memories of the land where each individual was born and raised."[7] Moreover, as they "yearned" for their parents, the old village became synonymous with the mother figure in particular, in implicit comparison to the modern, masculine city. The mother took on the role of "biological *furusato*," becoming deeply associated with the hearty, healthy food of the hometown.[8] Once the older generation passed on, the ancestral grave also became a centrifugal force in *furusato* memories.

By the 1970s, however, the wandering minstrels of the *furusato*-boom were second- or third-generation city dwellers. As such, many of them had few or no personal memories of rural village life, and no connection to an ancestral grave; robbed of direct, personal nostalgia for a preurban past, they instead had to create that emotion in different ways. One way was domestic travel, through which they could choose potentially anywhere in Japan to become their *furusato*. For city dwellers with less time or money, television programs broadcasting Japanese-style popular songs (*enka*) in the 1980s and 1990s were another way of sating the desire for nostalgia. The producer of one such program explained, "Everyone probably has a *furusato*, a place to which he or she wants to return. Probably people who have left their rural hometown, as well as those who have no such rural hometown, have a nostalgic desire to return."[9] As with Discover Japan, the *site* of return was less important than the emotional act of returning.

The nostalgia of the postwar *furusato*-boom was thus once-removed. As Jennifer Robertson has argued, the boom was characterized by a longing for the emotion of nostalgia, by the desire to experience first-hand the yearning for a "home" landscape that early twentieth-century songs and literature expressed. This shift, from first-generation nostalgia to second- and third-generation "nostalgia for nostalgia," was also accompanied by a new development in the way the word *furusato* was written: instead of the "old village" Chinese characters (also read as *kokyō*), the word was increasingly spelled out using the Japanese phonetic script hiragana, thus connoting the *emotion* of hometown as much as its physical location. As "my *furusato*" became synonymous with "my Japan"—both stages for emotional self-discovery—so local hometowns became "nationalized as Homeland."[10] In travel advertising copy, even graves lost their individual meaning and instead became markers of a generic, Japanese "spiritual homeland" (*kokoro no furusato*). Elsewhere, local historical traditions, such as Noh performances in Kurokawa, Yamagata prefecture, were repackaged as paragons of middle-class "Japanese" culture: in William Kelly's words, the *furusato*-boom thus "appropriated the individual's homeplace as the nation's heartland."[11]

The notion that *furusato* could be a matter of individual choice, as opposed to the ancestral land of one's birth, was perhaps best articulated by Takahata Isao's 1991 anime, *Omoide poroporo* (*Only Yesterday*). In the film, the protagonist is a 27-year-old woman named Taeko, who takes a vacation to the northern Tōhoku region in order to experience farm life. During her short stay, she has multiple, life-changing flashbacks to her childhood and upbringing in an entirely different area of Japan. The film ends with her adopting the Tōhoku village as her "second *furusato*" and moving there to marry a local farmer's son. The individual choices made by Taeko in *Only Yesterday* reinforce the generational divide apparent in the results of a survey carried out by Yagi Tōru in 1995. Yagi's survey revealed that whereas half of the women aged over 60 in his sample still took the association of *furusato* with ancestral and household ritual to be given, three-quarters of women under 60—the generation first depicted in Discover Japan—saw "no relation" between *furusato* and the ancestral grave.[12]

Starting with the Discover Japan campaign, therefore, late-twentieth-century *furusato* became a discourse of searching rather than returning, of "Japan" rather than a specific site of childhood memories, and of young, female travelers rather than the mother left behind. As such, it could be argued that the *furusato*-boom tells us more about a generation of disaffected postwar urbanites than it does about the "old village" itself: *furusato* as a discourse of the center, not the periphery. But by the late 1980s, even within that centrally constructed discourse, there was a shift back toward focusing on individual communities rather than on abstract, generic ones. In this regard, the establishment of the Furusato Rejuvenation Fund (*Furusato sōsei kikin*) by the government of Takeshita Noboru, in 1988, was an important new development. Through the fund, Tokyo offered every municipality in Japan a one-off grant of 100 million yen. The money was to be used to promote the local community to the wider world, leading to the development of what Yasui Manami has called "consumer *furusato*." For people living in those municipalities, the *furusato* could now be exploited as a resource, as a way of selling each community's unique qualities to all and sundry: our unique beauty, unique history, unique cuisine, unique friendliness (even if, in some cases, that uniqueness was very much in the eye of the beholder). From the Discover Japan notion of "*furusato* as anywhere," this was a shift back to "*furusato* as only here."[13]

Yet, to assume that municipalities simply took their lead from the center would be to fall into the trap of denying local communities any agency in the construction of *furusato* discourse. In the small port town of Kaminoseki, for example—a town located in southeast Yamaguchi prefecture, 25 kilometers from the nearest train station and thus beyond the railroad frame of Discover Japan—officials articulated a shift toward "A Rich and Lively *Furusato*-making" in their discussion of the 1985–86 municipal budget, several years before Takeshita's Rejuvenation Fund. This focus on the policy implications of *furusato*-making (*furusato-zukuri*, see also Timothy George in this volume) dated from at least the late 1970s, when the phrase was used by the town mayor in the context of counter-measures to Kaminoseki's ongoing depopulation crisis.[14]

Meanwhile, in a different example of local *furusato* discourse, town appeals in the early 1980s for a "clean *furusato*" referred both to efficient trash collection and to protection of Kaminoseki's beautiful "blue sea." In this way, such appeals drew on the very first postwar use of the word *furusato* in official publications, in November 1971: "Cultural assets," announced an article in the *Kaminoseki Town News*, "are said to be the spiritual homeland (*kokoro no furusato*). These kinds of cultural assets in the natural world— the various assets that over time have been nurtured in our midst—are now gradually being lost owing to pollution and the transformation of the social environment."[15] *Furusato* as municipal policy, *furusato* as environmental protection, *furusato* as cultural assets, and thus, as the "spiritual homeland": even a cursory examination of official publications in one small town reveals that at the local level, no less than at the national, the malleability of *furusato* discourse facilitated the construction of multiple layers of meaning. In that sense, Kaminoseki was surely no different to thousands of other municipalities in the 1970s and 1980s as it began to articulate its own version of the *furusato*-boom. But Kaminoseki *was* very different in one respect. By the early 1990s, visitors to the town were assailed by a number of large billboards erected in each district of the municipality, many of which echoed the mid-1980s' rhetoric of a "rich" or "lively" town. Read one: "[Through nuclear power], a *furusato* where young people gather, and where we have heart-to-heart communication!" Or another: "Bright and rich *furusato*-making through a nuclear power station—[bringing] vitality to young people and comfort to the elderly." A third billboard included artwork depicting delighted elderly townspeople welcoming young workers back to the hometown: "Charming town-making, together with nuclear power."

A planned nuclear power station, therefore, was Kaminoseki's claim to uniqueness, to the *furusato* as only here. Exactly how nuclear power came to Kaminoseki is a story too long to be recounted in these pages; briefly, however, in 1981–82, town officials were so desperate to halt Kaminoseki's depopulation crisis that they invited Chugoku Electric Power Company to build a new nuclear power station in the town.[16] Thus, discourses of *furusato* and *furusato*-making in late-twentieth-century Kaminoseki were inextricably tied to a policy debate about nuclear power in the town. In this way, discourses of *furusato*, far from being "dream"-like, were politicized to the extent that they became sites of conflict. In one district of Kaminoseki where the majority of residents did not support the power station plan, for example, and from which activists launched an antinuclear campaign that delayed power station construction until early 2011, a billboard announced: "Preserve our rich fishing and important *furusato*: complete opposition to the Kaminoseki nuclear power station!" Within the town, the emotional connotations of *furusato*, and even of adjectives such as "rich" (*yutakana*), differed by district and by political stance.

Political divisions in Kaminoseki also exposed an aspect of *furusato* discourse that has been largely overlooked by scholars of postwar Japan.[17] The *furusato*-boom, as we have seen, was a discourse primarily of space: travelers embarked on a journey in which they sought a place that they might call "home," and that might serve as their "second *furusato*." This was a physical place for Japan National Railway customers and an imaginary place for consumers of *enka* and other popular songs: in both cases, a physical or imaginary distance needed to be covered. Residents of Kaminoseki, by contrast, did not have that problem: in spatial terms, their *furusato* was what they experienced as they got on with their everyday lives in the hometown. And yet, no less than their urban counterparts, Kaminoseki residents also articulated a longing for the *furusato* in the slogans of the roadside billboards. Thus, instead of spatial distance, *furusato* discourse in Kaminoseki appears to have been characterized by temporal distance. The promises of a "bright" and "rich" community were promises for the future, but they were predicated on communal memories of a bright and rich past—brighter and richer, implicitly, than the crisis times of the 1980s and 1990s. The antinuclear appeal to "preserve" the *furusato* was similarly founded on an assumption that townspeople shared memories of an "important" and "rich" past. To understand *furusato* discourse of the 1980s and 1990s in Kaminoseki, we need to ask not, "Where was the *furusato*?" but rather, "*When* was the *furusato*?"

A number of sites and texts in Kaminoseki help us answer that question. Together, they enable us to identify the emergence of a *furusato* historical memory in the late twentieth century—a body of memories that simultaneously conformed to the contours of national memory construction in the troubled 1990s, and yet which also displayed important local variations.

Following the success of Discover Japan between 1970 and 1978, Japan National Railways launched a new advertising campaign in 1984 entitled, *Ekizochikku Japan (Exotic Japan)*. This was a campaign that both reflected and fueled a popular Japanese fascination with the non-Japanese Orient. As Marilyn Ivy has argued, Exotic Japan drew particularly on the imagery of the Silk Road, which, following NHK's extraordinarily popular television series in 1980, became a late twentieth-century "metaphor for Japan's ancient, tenuous, and winding connections with a greater world of cultural and material splendor."[18]

Such exoticism was apparent in a large billboard that stood on the main road into Kaminoseki, until it was blown down by a typhoon in September 2004. Erected by one of the town's civil society associations in September 1990, it illustrated a number of important historical encounters between Kaminoseki and the outside world under the banner, "Kaminoseki: the Silk

FIGURE 4.2 *"Kaminoseki: The Silk Road of the Sea," Kaminoseki Town, Yamaguchi Prefecture, 2004. Author's photo.*

Road of the Sea." Focusing in particular on the narrow straits that offered natural shelter to passing travelers in times past, hand-drawn icons on the sign depicted the Dutch ships of the 1820s, which brought the German physician Philipp Franz von Siebold to Japan and thence through Kaminoseki on his way to meet the Tokugawa shogun in Edo; the Dutch-built ship, *Hei'in-maru*, bought and commandeered by the revolutionary Takasugi Shinsaku in the buildup to the overthrow of the shogunate in 1868; the embassy ships sent by the Ashikaga shogunate to Ming China in the fifteenth and early sixteenth centuries; the *shuinsen* trade ships that sailed between Japan and southeast Asia in the late sixteenth century; the Korean Embassies of the Tokugawa period, which first came to Japan in 1607; and, closer to home, the *kitamae* ships of the eighteenth and nineteenth centuries, which facilitated interdomain commerce along the important Western trade circuit of the Inland Sea (*Nishi mawari kōrō*). As if through the eye of a needle, multicolored threads from each icon passed through the Kaminoseki straits, in the center of the map, thus weaving the town into a rich tapestry of historical engagement between the local community and the outside world.

That each icon referred to an important chapter in the histories of both Kaminoseki and Japan is indisputable. The Korean Embassies, for example, were a key part of the Tokugawa state's diplomatic strategy in the seventeenth and eighteenth centuries, as Ronald Toby has shown: they enabled the shogunate to maintain cultural and diplomatic ties with the Asian mainland even as it cut off all direct contact with the European world (with the exception of the Netherlands).[19] On 11 of the 12 occasions that the Embassies came to

Japan, they stayed overnight in Kaminoseki on their way to and from Edo: not just ambassadors, but also doctors, musicians, craftsmen, and scholars, numbering (in 1711) some 569 people. In addition, scores of accompanying officials from the Tsushima domain and that of Chōshū, to which Kaminoseki belonged, also stayed overnight, in a town whose own early eighteenth-century population was less than one thousand people. Quite apart from the sheer numbers of visitors, the pomp and circumstance of the Embassies clearly made a profound impression on Kaminoseki residents. A retrospective painting from 1821, which survives in one of the town's temples, depicts the arrival of one Embassy in panoramic detail, from the scores of tiny row boats that welcomed the Ambassadors' junks, to the ceremonial curtains hanging from the doorways of Kaminoseki's freshly cleaned houses.[20] This was the East Asian world of material and cultural splendor entering the everyday lives of individual townspeople—households such as the Awaya, which survives to this day on the main street of Kaminoseki, and which first appears in historical records as hosting several minor officials of the Chōshū domain on the occasion of the 1764 Korean Embassy.[21]

The Silk Road sign was designed by the late Nishiyama Hiroshi, a local history enthusiast who had returned to his *furusato* in 1977 after two decades of working for Mazda in Hiroshima.[22] In 1990, Nishiyama was working for the Kaminoseki Chamber of Commerce, a pronuclear lobby group whose chair would be a prime mover behind the establishment of the Kaminoseki Town-Making Liaison Committee, in October 1991; it was the latter organization that erected the aforementioned *furusato* and town-making (*machi-zukuri*) billboards found all over the town. The Liaison Committee brought together a coalition of 18 pronuclear organizations in the town, one of which, the Kaminoseki Youth and Young Men's Liaison Committee, had commissioned the Silk Road sign. In other words, Nishiyama was at the hub of a network of pronuclear individuals and organizations in Kaminoseki, and to a certain extent, the Silk Road sign echoed the contemporary rhetoric of pronuclear campaigners. A slogan at the bottom of the sign, for example, proclaimed: "With this history as our backdrop, we are tackling a new town-making." The implication was clear: a basic overview of Kaminoseki's history would help townspeople understand the specific (and controversial) town-making policies of the 1980s and 1990s.

This implicitly pronuclear framing of the past could also be found in the explanatory text, "Kaminoseki's History," in the bottom left-hand corner of the sign. After summarizing the historical development of the town in five paragraphs, the text concluded: "Since the Meiji period, the role of Kaminoseki as an entrepôt has weakened due to the development of land routes and the appearance of machine-powered boats; but even now, more than one thousand boats pass through the Kaminoseki straits every day, and everywhere in the town one can see the heights of prosperity in the image of the past." On its own, there was nothing controversial about this summary: located in one of the most prosperous regions of mid-nineteenth-century

Japan, Kaminoseki did indeed display "advanced" patterns of employment, as Thomas C. Smith has shown, and the town did indeed suffer a severe economic decline in the decades following the Meiji Restoration.[23] But when set alongside the explicitly pronuclear signs erected by the Town-Making Liaison Committee in 1991–92, Nishiyama's summary was susceptible to a more overtly political interpretation. Through the Silk Road sign, townspeople were reminded of a more prosperous past; through the nuclear power station, townspeople were offered a "rich" and prosperous future. (The site of the planned two-reactor power plant, incidentally, was marked on an inset of the sign by two white flowers.)

In fact, Nishiyama's text was a good deal more restrained than other expressions of *furusato* history at the time. In a two-volume collection of essays on Kaminoseki's history, *Seeking the furusato of Kaminoseki* (1984–86), nonresident Kawamura Toshiyuki concludes:

> With the turning point of the Meiji Restoration, Kaminoseki was transformed from port-of-call (*kikōchi*) to fishing town; and, in 1969, another turning point occurred. In that year, Kaminoseki Great Bridge was opened. As a result, Nagashima island was joined to the mainland, and the flow of goods and culture into the town dramatically improved.
>
> But the Kaminoseki of today is facing the great problem of the outflow of young people from the town. There are few local industries, and although in terms of tourist resources the town has good basic materials, these have not been developed. The number of places at which young people can work is certainly not large.
>
> However, a beautiful natural environment, a rich and abundant sea, and warm-hearted townspeople: for the young people of Kaminoseki, the rebirth of a charming town is surely close at hand.[24]

Kawamura's volumes were published by the pronuclear lobby group, The Association for Considering the Development of Kaminoseki, a predecessor of the Kaminoseki Town-Making Liaison Committee. At the time of its foundation, in 1982, the Association characterized Kaminoseki as a town with a "bright history" (*akarui rekishi*), but one that had now lost its old identity.[25] Kawamura's optimism for the "rebirth of a charming town" thus spoke directly to this characterization: the nuclear power station promised to be a metaphorical bridge that connected a brighter past to a brighter future, thus lifting townspeople out of their present crisis. Nishiyama's sign, juxtaposing the Silk Road past and the new town-making future, echoed this vision of *furusato* history.

If we were to assume that the Silk Road sign only reflected the nuclear context of the 1980s and 1990s, then it would be possible to explain its time frame, which focused exclusively on Kaminoseki's pre-1868 history, as if nothing of importance in the town occurred after the Meiji Restoration.

By this logic, a story of modern economic decline was not as relevant to pronuclear campaigners as one of premodern prosperity—a golden age, as it were, to which Kaminoseki's town-making policymakers might aspire to return. In fact, however, there *was* a history of prosperity after 1868, at least for some townspeople. Moreover, that history was one of interaction with the outside world—one deserving, we might assume, of a commemorative icon on the Silk Road sign.

To follow this equally colorful thread in town history, let us return to the Awaya household, on the main street of Kaminoseki. In the mid-eighteenth century, the Awaya was in a position to host officials connected to the Korean Embassies because it was a successful merchant household, engaging in trade with the passing *kitamae* ships depicted on the Silk Road sign. By the mid-1820s, when Siebold stayed in Kaminoseki, business was so good that the Awaya built a new, two-storied house which survives to this day, and which is an important focus of tourist interest in Kaminoseki (that is, when tourists come to the town, which is not very often). But Meiji period economic transformations had a profoundly negative impact on the *kitamae* ships, and thus a knock-on effect on merchants such as the Awaya; this, as much as the reasons noted by the Silk Road sign, explains the declining role of Kaminoseki as a port-of-call and trade entrepôt by the turn of the twentieth century. Thus, just a few months before the death of the Emperor Meiji in 1912, Awaya Torazuchi, the then head of the household, took the radical step of emigrating with his family to Korea.

In fact, neither Awaya's decision, nor his destination, were as radical as they might seem. From the 1870s onward, shippers formerly involved in the Western trade circuit had begun to emigrate to Korea from the southeast of Yamaguchi prefecture. By the mid-1890s, more than a quarter of the 12,000 Japanese residents in Korea came from the prefecture, including not only shippers but also merchants.[26] In 1895, for example, a 28-year-old merchant called Kōno Takenosuke emigrated first to Busan and then to Incheon from Murotsu village, on the mainland side of the straits from Kaminoseki. Kōno's business activities in Korea made him so rich that 15 years later, in 1910, he became the principal donor in a fundraising campaign to build a new assembly hall for his hometown elementary school: his contribution of 300 yen earned him a personal commendation from the Governor of Yamaguchi prefecture, while 93 other Murotsu villagers living in Korea in 1910 also made donations to the campaign, totaling 3,200 yen. Perhaps it was the extraordinary success of men such as Kōno, neighbors across the water, that prompted Awaya Torazuchi to seek new fortunes overseas. Although such fortunes did not accrue overnight, nor for everyone who ventured to Korea at the turn of the twentieth century, they did eventually come his way: by 1936, Awaya could afford to build himself a new farmhouse in Gyeonggi, using the best building material shipped over from Japan. At the end of the 1930s, he was the owner of 45 hectares of pear orchards and rice fields—45 times more land than the average landowning household back in Kaminoseki. In 1937, he celebrated his newfound wealth by donating 100 yen toward the installation of electric lights on the steps leading up to his hometown's Kamado Hachimangū shrine. For men such as Kōno and Awaya, as much as for the schoolchildren of Murotsu or for the worshippers of Kaminoseki, the silk road connecting the Japanese port town to the Korean peninsula brought material splendor indeed.

But the silk roads led not only to Korea. In the mid-1880s, at the same time as Kaminoseki villagers started moving to Korea, the Meiji government's sponsored emigration program offered hundreds of Awaya's and Kōno's fellow villagers the opportunity to go and work in Hawai'i. After 1894, when the emigration system was liberalized, hundreds more villagers crossed to the mainland United States, Canada, Brazil, and Peru, even as they also continued to move to territories which would ultimately become part of the formal Japanese empire—Taiwan, the South Seas Islands, Karafuto (Sakhalin), Manchuria, and China. The demographic impact of such overseas migration on the hometown was significant. For example, the number of pupils attending Murotsu Elementary School fell by a fifth in the 1910s as migrants educated their children overseas. But Kaminoseki's diaspora community also had a profound impact on the material culture of the hometown: remittances sent back from successful overseas relatives enabled individual households to pay off their debts and thus escape abject poverty; successful returnees in Yamaguchi and Hiroshima prefectures built fancy two-story homes, or extra-large Buddhist altars to their ancestors, or new agricultural warehouses.[27] Murotsu Elementary School, at which the so-called Korean Assembly Hall was constructed after the 1910 campaign, also received donations toward the construction of an America-Hawai'i Hall in 1916. Other elementary schools in Kaminoseki were rebuilt in the late 1920s and early 1930s as a result of donations from villagers living in the mainland United States, Hawai'i, Korea, Taiwan, Manchuria, and Karafuto. Overseas donations paid for shrine and temple repairs, a new school radio, and the construction of a Russo-Japanese war memorial.

Thus, the financial and material impact of the diaspora community's donations on everyday life in the hometown was considerable. Successful returnees to the hometown were said to return "wearing brocade" (nishiki o kazaru), such was their prosperity.[28] But the metaphor could equally apply to the town itself: by the early 1930s, it would have been impossible to walk down a street in Kaminoseki, or to attend elementary school, or to worship at the local shrines and temples without becoming aware of Kaminoseki's connections to, and reliance on, the beneficence of villagers living overseas. Brocaded streets, silk roads: the material evidence alone suggests that these overseas connections were one of the most important historical characteristics of everyday life in the town from the mid-1880s to the late 1930s.

All these connections, however, are absent from the Silk Road sign—a sign that celebrates such intersections of local and world history as the Ming Embassies, the southeast Asian trade ships, the Korean Embassies, and the Dutch ships, and yet which ignores the very transnational interactions that provided the greatest material splendor to the everyday lives of post-1868 townspeople. "Kaminoseki: the Silk Road of the Sea" is a memory map that forgets an important aspect of local history.[29] But it is not the only example of such amnesia. Not one of Kawamura's 61 essays on *furusato* history discusses overseas emigration. Similarly, *A Walking History Guide to the Port Town of Kaminoseki*, a pamphlet published in 1996 by the Ninja-tai, a town history association, includes no emigration-related relics in its list of must-see sites—relics such as surviving memorial stones that mark a prewar overseas contribution, and which can be found throughout the town. Ninja-tai volunteers take tourists to look at the material culture of the Tokugawa period in the form of the Awaya residence (no mention is made of the Awaya's twentieth-century Korean connection), but not to the two-story houses built by Hawaiian returnees in the 1930s, on an adjacent street. Meanwhile, in the town history museum, the only reference to overseas emigration is a one-line entry on the main date-line panel. A video on display in the museum in the early 2000s, "The Silk Road of the Sea: A Tale of the Kaminoseki Straits" (1995), made no mention of the prewar diaspora, but in an echo of Kawamura's dream of municipal "rebirth," it concluded with an image of a freight ship passing beneath the Kaminoseki Great Bridge. "Even in the present day," the narrator intoned, "ships pass through the Kaminoseki straits, and in those straits—the Silk Road of the Sea—a new tale is being born."[30]

Just as the nuclear context of the 1980s and 1990s explains the particular emphasis on prosperity in the Silk Road sign, so we might assume that the sign's amnesia is also explained by nuclear politics. One would be hard pressed, however, to explain why a story of townspeople's dependence on outside largesse in the early twentieth century would be inimical to a lobby group actively encouraging major external investment in the late twentieth century. Indeed, *Fūdoki: Exploring the History of the Furusato*, a short book on regional history published by Chugoku Electric itself, *does* include a chapter on overseas emigration (mainly on Hawaiian emigration, but with a brief reference to benefactions from Korea).[31] Moreover, the language of amnesia, or forgetting, is actually misleading. When the Ninja-tai was established, in 1989, one of its founder members was the late Ueda Kichisuke, who had been born on Hawai'i Island in 1918, and who grew up there until his father decided to return to Kaminoseki in 1932. If Ueda did not sport brocade on his first day at Kaminoseki Elementary School, he did at least dress up in a suit, necktie, and hunting cap, for which he remembered being roundly mocked.[32] Another founder member was Nishiyama Hiroshi himself, who once showed me photographs of the huge colonial residence at which his older stepsister had worked as a domestic maid, in Karafuto in the 1930s.[33] Local history enthusiasts had not "forgotten" about prewar overseas emigration and its impact on the hometown; they just chose not to study it as part of their Ninja-tai activities or to mention it in publications on *furusato* history.

As far as I could work out, the decision not to study a particular aspect of Kaminoseki's history was an unconscious one (a pesky British researcher asking questions interrupts that unconscious process, of course). Members of the Ninja-tai did, however, make a conscious decision to focus on the history of the Korean Embassies in Kaminoseki. In 1997, for example, they published a manga, *Crossing Time and Sea*, which tells of Minoru, a sixth-grade elementary school student who, by an extraordinary feat of time travel, witnesses one of the Embassies. Once again, the Korean Embassies are framed within the discourse of "the silk road of the sea."[34] Members of the Ninja-tai also established a historical document reading group in which they translated newly discovered local accounts of the Korean Embassies into modern Japanese and then published them through the Municipal Board of Education.[35] In designing explanatory panels for the town history museum (opened 2002), they focused particularly on the history of the Korean Embassies; and on the 400th anniversary of the first Embassy, in 2007, they dressed up in Korean costumes and went to Hiroshima, to take part in a celebratory parade.

One impetus for all this activity was a simple desire to preserve and record municipal history. Indeed, the Ninja-tai was formed in response to one of the most striking Tokugawa-period structures in Kaminoseki, the Yoshida household in Murotsu district, being sold and removed to the town of Shimo-Kamakari in Hiroshima prefecture, for want of money to restore the building in Kaminoseki itself.[36] In the early 1990s, there was similarly talk of the town selling the *go-bansho* office, the administrative center for the Chōshū domain in Kaminoseki, and a building that actually appears in the 1821 painting of the Korean Embassy. In response, the Ninja-tai lobbied "day and night" for its retention, classification as a town cultural asset (in 1992), and ultimate restoration (in 1996). Given that the town's oldest cultural assets seemed to be under threat, the Ninja-tai's focus on the history of the Tokugawa period, and of the Korean Embassies in particular, made good sense.[37]

A second impetus for the association's Embassy-focused activities was revealed by another founder member of the Ninja-tai, Inoue Midori, in a newspaper interview she gave in 2006. Speaking as debates raged over whether Prime Minister Koizumi would again visit the Yasukuni Shrine in August, thereby once again inflaming relations with Korea and China, Inoue said: "Given things such as the Yasukuni Shrine problem, it's necessary to have solid private citizens' exchange (*minkan kōryū*). I want to be of some small help in binding the hearts of [Japanese and Koreans] together."[38] In other words, by focusing on the Korean Embassies, members of the Ninja-tai were studying what we might characterize as "safe" international relations—ones far removed from the contentious relations of the twentieth century, and ones that reminded local people of a happier history of "exchange" between Japanese and Koreans.

Inoue's comment reveals not only why the history of the Korean Embassies was the focus of the Ninja-tai in the 1990s and early 2000s, but also, we might speculate, why the history of the prewar Kaminoseki diaspora was not. That is, the colonial history of the Awaya and Kōno households, and of hundreds of others in Korea, Taiwan, Manchuria, and Karafuto, was too embarrassing to be commemorated at a local level, especially as—in the case of the Awaya and many others—the story ended with an ignoble and impecunious return to Kaminoseki in the final months of 1945. These were histories which survived at the individual level of "living memories," freely shared with outside researchers, but which had never been translated into the kinds of group-based "cultural"—or even transcultural—memories that might find expression in a museum or on a public billboard. To this extent, the curious silence surrounding the transnational material splendor of the prewar decades conformed to a wider pattern of Japanese war memories identified by Sven Saaler, in which individual memories rarely made the "translation" process into group memories.[39]

All this goes some way to explaining why Japan's prewar colonies were not part of the Silk Road discourse of *furusato* history, but it does not explain why that silence extended to those town residents who emigrated in their hundreds to Hawai'i and America, and who were not colonists. (The thousands of Hawaiian and North American emigrants from neighboring Ōshima County, to the east of Kaminoseki, have been honored with an excellent museum and resource center.) One reason for this silence may be that the distinctions between "emigrants" and "colonists" were becoming blurred by the 1930s, as the Japanese state attempted to subordinate Japanese-American emigrant history into a wider discourse of imperial overseas expansion.[40] Disaggregating "emigrants" and "colonists" in a town that sent hundreds of people to both the Americas and to Asia, sometimes from the same household, was perhaps beyond the energies of Ninja-tai members (it certainly felt beyond my energies, at times). But more importantly, the material splendor of prewar overseas benefactions made, and continues to make, such disaggregation impossible. This is because the schools, Russo-Japanese war memorials, donations to shrine electrification, and so on, came from emigrants who were residing in both Hawai'i *and* in Korea, in California *and* in Karafuto. As a townsperson gazing at these sites in the postwar period (or at the memorial stones, where the original buildings have been demolished), one's pride and appreciation of the prewar American diaspora would inevitably lead to pride and appreciation of the Asian diaspora: the two were inseparable to the beneficiaries of overseas donations who had stayed in the hometown. Thus, rather than engaging in a false exercise of distinguishing the local impact of the Asian diaspora from that of the American one, perhaps it was easier simply to remain silent about all emigrants and their impact on hometown history.

The construction of the Silk Road discourse in 1990s' Kaminoseki was framed not only by local nuclear politics, but also by the more general challenge of how to commemorate twentieth-century Japanese history—a challenge that the town's historians were not alone in facing. But there is a third and final framework of *furusato* history that we need to consider, namely, the site of the local history museum.

The Shikairō is a uniquely shaped building in the heart of Murotsu port, on the mainland side of the Kaminoseki straits. Standing at four stories (*shi-kai*) and 11.4 meters, it was twice the height of any other building in Murotsu or Kaminoseki at the time of its construction, in 1879. Its owner was a merchant called Ogata Kenkurō (born 1835), who had fought with the Chōshū forces in the mid-1860s against the Tokugawa shogunate and been rewarded generously for his efforts. With three-fingered arabesque dragons ornamenting the four main pillars of its structure, with fretwork peonies carved over the second floor, and with stained glass windows on the top floor, the Shikairō was a bold statement of its owner's cosmopolitan aspirations. Indeed, the stained glass—vivid blues, reds, oranges, and greens—was directly imported from the Saint Gobain company, best known for its Hall of Mirrors at Versailles: Ogata ordered the glass in Yokohama, and it seems likely that he was influenced by imitative Western architecture that he would have seen in the treaty port.[41] In May 1993, doubtless due to campaigning by the Ninja-tai, the Shikairō was the first building in Kaminoseki to be designated a Tangible Cultural Asset by Yamaguchi prefecture. Between 1999 and 2001, it was then meticulously restored, at the cost of 140 million yen (partly financed by Japanese government subsidies paid to municipalities that offer to host nuclear power stations). Following its opening as the Kaminoseki Municipal Hometown History Museum (Kyōdoshi gakushūkan) in 2002, it was designated as a national Important Cultural Asset in December 2005.

The Shikairō's contemporary status suggests that we may view its history through a cultural lens, as an embodiment of early-Meiji Japanese-Western eclecticism (*wayō setchū*). It is the kind of building that would interest scholars of 1960s and 1970s "people's history" (*minshūshi*) in Japan, built as it was by an educated member of the village elites and displaying what Irokawa Daikichi would call the creative potential of early Meiji culture.[42] Moreover, as a statement of architectural engagement between Kaminoseki and the outside world, it complements—and may be taken as an example of—the Silk Road discourse of hometown history (even if its construction occurred after 1868).

However, such a cultural lens distorts an alternative reading of the Shikairō, as a statement of social status. The building cost 3,000 yen to construct in 1879—just under 10 times the combined village income raised through local levies, education fees, and festival levies in the following year. Such extravagance underlined Ogata's status as one of the four richest landowners in a village of more than 500 households. Thus, just as the Shikairō towered over Murotsu in a physical sense, so Ogata towered over his neighbors figuratively, both in terms of his financial assets and his political career as a village elder and then village councillor from the 1870s to the 1890s.[43] For all the architectural uniqueness of the Shikairō, the fact that this building in particular became the municipal history museum suggests that the only material culture worth preserving in the twenty-first century is that of elite households: the Awaya in the Tokugawa period (and the Yoshida household, had it not been sold) and the Ogata in the Meiji period. By contrast, the material culture of nonelite households—the Hawaiian returnees, the commemorations of donations much smaller than 3,000 yen yet no less important in their contribution to Meiji period village culture—is quietly ignored.

In other words, a third frame for understanding the Silk Road discourse of *furusato* history is that of social hierarchy, in which the richly documented lives of local elites were preserved at the expense of everyday history. The hundreds of destitute farmers applying to the village office—just down the road from the Shikairō—for permission to emigrate to Hawai'i in the mid-1880s are present in the historical records, and their names can be retrieved from the shadows for posterity, with a little work; but that kind of history is a lot less "bright" than the Saint Gobain glass.[44] By focusing on the histories of men such as Ogata Kenkurō, Philipp Franz von Siebold, and the Korean ambassadors, members of the Ninja-tai in the 1990s chose to weave a smooth narrative of Great Men in Kaminoseki, rather than patching together a rougher story of everyday Kaminoseki people's contributions to the history of the wider world. Perhaps, we may argue, this choice had less to do with nuclear discourses of the *furusato*, or with the troublesome problem of how to remember pre-1945 imperialism, than with a basic, rather elitist assumption of what good history is and who should be its protagonists.

I first met Nishiyama Hiroshi in September 1998. It was my first day as an Assistant Language Teacher at Kaminoseki Junior High School, and afternoon classes were canceled so that the whole school could walk over to Jōyama (Castle Hill). There, an excavation team was meticulously piecing together the foundations of a castle built in the mid-fifteenth century by the Murakami Suigun, an important medieval sea militia. Nishiyama spoke enthusiastically to the students (who listened somewhat less enthusiastically), and a colleague translated for my benefit. "It's good that the students study their own town history," she added. The excavation appeared to be part of a wider interest that town administrators were beginning to show in the history of the Murakami. In 1991, for example, Chamber of Commerce officials rebranded the town's annual summer festival the Kaminoseki Suigun Matsuri, now sponsored by Chugoku Electric and funded with central government nuclear subsidies. As one official later explained, this was an attempt to "image up" the town after the bitter nuclear arguments of the 1980s.[45]

On my return to Kaminoseki in 2003, after a three-year absence, I noticed some significant changes in the town. Murotsu Bay, over which Ogata Kenkurō could gaze from his four-storied Shikairō, had been filled in by a major land reclamation project. A roadside sign facing the Shikairō announced, "With the beautiful sea, a great future," but plans to fill the site with a new Municipal Culture Center would not be approved until the 2011–12 budget. In the intervening years, the land reclamation area became a less than beautiful wasteland, fit only for the Suigun Matsuri festival. Thus, when I attended in 2007, drink stalls and food tents were erected around a temporary stage on which local children performed in *taiko* ensembles and B-list celebrities enjoyed muted adulation. An enthusiastic Master-of-Ceremonies waxed lyrical about Kaminoseki's "*furusato* history," while festival-goers cooled themselves with plastic fans provided by Chugoku Electric: "Toward a Bright Future: Kaminoseki Nuclear Power Plant, hand-in-hand with the local community." Meanwhile, in the distance behind the stage, it was possible to make out the original Murakami base rising above the waters of the Kaminoseki straits. Except that Jōyama is now several meters lower than it was in the fifteenth century: it has been relandscaped as the Kaminoseki-town Castle Hill History Park, while the rocks and stones so carefully excavated in 1998 now lie at the bottom of the sea, having been used to fill in Murotsu Bay. In attending the Suigun Matsuri, or visiting the History Park, townspeople thus trample on the very *furusato* history that their leaders purport to celebrate.

Given these ambiguous foundations, searching for the past in Kaminoseki requires two acts of retrieval. We need to acknowledge that local representations of the *furusato* and of municipal history did not just mirror the uncertain age of 1990s' Japan, nor do they do so today. Instead, multiple local agendas, conscious and unconscious, went into the construction of *furusato* history in Kaminoseki. Although many scholars of Japan's "memory problems" in the 1990s focus their studies at the level of national or international history, the complex interplay of nuclear politics, diaspora memories, and social history in Kaminoseki demonstrates that memory construction was no less contentious—and is no less worthy of study—at a local level too. In this sense, the excavation of everyday voices from the *furusato* past requires the rescuing of history from the overarching historiographical frame of the nation, to paraphrase Prasenjit Duara.[46] But at the same time, the development of Kaminoseki's Suigun Matsuri in the 1990s, and of the History Park in the 2000s, suggests that we equally need to slow down the reclamation of the past by myopic bureaucrats and their corporate partners. Despite the best efforts of the Ninja-tai, we need also to rescue history from the local.

Such a conclusion is more than just a plea for abstract academic rigor. The post-tsunami nuclear crisis at Fukushima in 2011 forced a question previously debated in the scholarly community once again to public consciousness: why did the only country to suffer the horrors of nuclear weapons come to embrace nuclear power? There are many answers to that question, but one concerns the way the nuclear debate has been framed at a local level in postwar Japan, in the very communities that host nuclear power plants. As this chapter demonstrates, the discourses of *furusato* history in 1990s' Kaminoseki helped project an image of prosperity in the past—an image that aided pronuclear campaigners predicting prosperity in the future. One cost of such framing was the lacuna created of post-1868 history—the darker stories of decline, deprivation, and latterly depopulation that together undermine the "bright history" of pronuclear campaigners. But perhaps more importantly, especially in light of the Fukushima crisis, *furusato* history also contributed to a campaign in which the hosting of a nuclear power plant became a debate primarily over prosperity, rather than one over safety. In this way, questions much more important than historical veracity were bypassed by bureaucrats and company officials intent on selling a nuclear future to the town. If George Orwell was right in observing that those who control the past control the future, then the debate over *furusato* history in Kaminoseki is one that should concern us all.

Part Two

Legacies of War and Occupation

If anything has been proven by the endless debates about when or whether the "postwar" has ended, it is that Japan has never escaped the long shadow of its Asia-Pacific War. The "postwar" was declared over many times, including when the Allied Occupation ended in 1952, again when the nation's GNP regained its prewar peak in 1955, when Japan's economy passed that of West Germany in 1968 to become the third largest in the world after those of the two superpowers, once again in the 1980s when Japan was the world's largest creditor and foreign aid donor and home to the world's ten largest banks, and in 1989 when the Shōwa emperor died after 63 years on the throne.

Yet, there remained ever-present reminders that the war was not buried in the past. Okinawa was occupied and administered by the United States until 1972. Former victims of Japan's invasion of the Asian continent reacted in anger in the 1980s and after, when textbooks in Japan called that invasion an "advance" and Japanese politicians denied that there had been a Rape of Nanjing. Such discontent again appeared when Asia's former "comfort women," forced into sexual slavery by Japan during the war, spoke out for the first time to demand compensation and apology. Throughout the postwar and into the twenty-first century, many Koreans and Chinese repeatedly insisted that Japan had never fully apologized for its actions.

Even the scenes of devastation left by the earthquake and tsunami in 2011 revived for many Japanese strong public memories of the hard times that followed in the wake of surrender in 1945, as did the Heisei emperor's decision to address the Japanese people in the immediate aftermath of the March 2011 disasters as his father had done 66 years earlier.

The decision by the International Military Tribunal for the Far East of 1946–48—the "Tokyo War Crimes Trial"—to blame a small number of top leaders (not including the emperor) for the war further discouraged most Japanese from considering their individual responsibility for the nation's actions. Many came to think of the war as a tragedy that had happened *to* them, brought on by those above. Even more so for later generations, the shadow of the war was something bequeathed to them by others and with which they simply had to live.

Japan's two constitutions—the Meiji constitution of 1890, and the current constitution in effect since 3 May 1947—were both literally handed to the Japanese people from above, the former from the Meiji emperor and the latter from their postwar occupiers. The Allied Occupation, the legacies of the war, and the new constitution were an infrastructure that the Japanese could do little to change. What they could control, however, was how they responded to them, and what meanings their responses gave to them. In doing so, they were writing new chapters in the story of Japan's continuing redefinition of its modern identity and its place in the world, a process that had been ongoing since the 1850s.

Conventional periodizations of history, which tend to focus on decisive breaks in 1868, 1945, and 1952, can obscure as much as they illuminate. David Obermiller shows how Okinawa experienced a much longer and very different sort of occupation, and how it complicated questions of national and regional identity. The ethnographic emphasis in American views of and policies toward Okinawa had a decidedly colonial flavor. So, too, did American attempts to shape the ways Okinawans defined themselves and remembered their past. Katarczyna Cwiertka describes the continuity in food shortages and distribution systems across the assumed great divide of defeat in August 1945. By focusing on patterns of distribution and consumption, she shows that actual practices did not always change immediately in the wake of changes in rulers, laws, and policies. Wartime mobilization strategies were found useful by citizens and occupiers alike in the early years after the war.

In the postwar period, marginalized groups with grievances, like all Japanese, were no longer subjects but citizens, with a much greater space for political activism. They could, in theory, choose between attempting to win seats at the tables of power to enable them to participate in making policies that affected them, or simply attempting to win recognition and compensation from "those above" (*okami*). The nurses described by Sally A. Hastings chose the former path, organizing and electing representatives to the National Diet. She shows us the complicated nature of such gender and occupational politics, which involved not simply female nurses rebalancing their power vis-à-vis male doctors and politicians, but also contestations between nurses and midwives. Tetsuya Fujiwara's disabled veterans chose to demand recognition, but in doing so they also had to contend with some of their own, the "white gown" beggars who threatened to undermine their attempts to avoid social and economic marginalization.

5

Dreaming Ryūkyū: Shifting and Contesting Identities in Okinawa

David Tobaru Obermiller

Arakawa Akira, a noted Okinawan intellectual and polemicist for Okinawan independence, once told me that what it meant to be Okinawan (Uchinanchu) was simple, "it meant you were not Japanese." Likewise, Chibana Shōichi, who gained notoriety when he burned the Japanese flag (*Hinomaru*) during a national sporting event in the early 1980s, saw himself as being Okinawan, but understood that identity formation depended on context. When asked whether he considers himself Japanese, Chibana Shōichi, replied "I want to say, 'I'm Ryūkyūan;' there's something that keeps me from saying I'm Japanese outright." Yet, Chibana acknowledged that from the perspective of Asia, he would be perceived as being Japanese, "just like the ones who went to war against Asia." At the same time, within Japan's polity, "I want to say, I'm different, at least I'm not the same as the Yamato race."[1] A recent popular car sticker in Okinawa reflects their pride: *Uchinā to Ryūkyū kokoro nankurunaisa,* "What will be, will be—the spirit of Uchinā (Okinawa) and the Ryūkyūs," a slogan that aptly captures Okinawa's contemporary ethos of a timeless *Uchinā* spirit.[2] While most Okinawans do not support Arakawa's call for independence, most feel that the spirit of *Uchinā to Ryūkyū kokoro* (the spirit of Uchinā) has *always* made them different from Japan.

While these examples show that contemporary Okinawa possesses a vibrant and confident ethnic identity, for the vast majority of modern Okinawan history, most island inhabitants desired to be Japanese and thus sought to suppress or minimize their Okinawan heritage. In the 70 years of prewar Japanese rule, the majority of Okinawans strove to be loyal Japanese subjects. Despite the Japanese military atrocities committed

against the Okinawan populace during the Battle of Okinawa, the majority
of Okinawans supported reversion to Japan during the postwar American
occupation. In the summer of 1951, an Okinawan group called the *Ryūkyū
Nippon Fukki Sokushi Kiseikai* (Reversion to Japan Association) obtained
200,000 signatures on a petition drive, representing 76.2 percent of the
eligible Okinawan voters.[3] A major force behind the petition drive, the
Okinawa People's Party (Jinmintō), issued a "Declaration Concerning
Reversion of the Ryūkyū Islands to Japan" that echoed the popular sentiment
among Okinawans:

> There can be no doubt that the *Ryūkyūans are Japanese*, and it is very
> natural that *the same race be under the same political organization* . . . .
> separation of one from the other would mean a total nullification of the
> hard efforts of one century made by us Ryūkyūan people, and that is too
> unbearable . . . The return of the islands is most naturally desirable.[4]

How do we reconcile the contemporary Uchinā spirit with the historic
inertia of Okinawans advocating for full integration with Japan? It is
widely understood by scholars that national and ethnic identities do
not occur in a vacuum but have to be produced in order for a critical
mass of an "imagined community" to exist. This chapter examines how
US occupation officials, during the occupation of the Ryūkyū Islands,
manipulated Ryūkyūan-Okinawan culture to construct a national
consciousness that, in theory, would elicit an identity estrangement from
Japan and simultaneously strengthen identification with Okinawa's cultural
benefactor, the United States. (Ironically, Japan had used a similar approach
in its 70-year occupation of the Ryūkyūs prior to World War II, except
that Tokyo used Japanese culture to break identification with the Ryūkyūan
past.)[5] The United States viewed Okinawa as its most important military
base to fight the Cold War in East Asia. In order to build a massive military
complex on Okinawa, the United States had to convince Okinawans that
they were not Japanese, which meant encouraging an Okinawan national
identity. Officials embarked on an ambitious nation-building program to
instill among the people a "natural" affinity that Okinawa should exist
as an independent nation. In essence, the United States had to invent and
nurture a new national consciousness, which meant not only overturning
70 years of Japanese assimilation programs, but also to find indigenous/
traditional Ryūkyūan (Okinawan) symbols that could be used to create a
modern national consciousness. This chapter specifically examines how
occupation officials attempted to invent modern Okinawan national
symbols based upon Ryūkyūan traditions. The result was a complex and
often contradictory legacy of political, social, and cultural currents that
together explain the acute ambivalence toward "Japan" that Okinawans
continue to experience to this day. Finally, this chapter will address the law
of unintended consequences as the US occupation efforts to establish an

acute Okinawan consciousness bore fruit, but 30 years too late and much to the detriment of the current national interests of both Japan and the United States.

The genesis of a Ryūkyūan imagined nation

In September 1944, the Joint Chiefs of Staff (JCS) unexpectedly canceled the long-anticipated invasion of Taiwan and ordered Admiral Nimitz to prepare for an invasion of the Ryūkyūs in March of 1945. The Navy's Civil Affairs team (NCAT), who were responsible for occupation planning for Taiwan and other Japanese possessions in the Pacific, had published Civil Affairs handbooks for every major island group in the Pacific, including the Kuriles. Yet, when NCAT received word in September to begin planning for operations in the Ryūkyūs, they had no data nor had conducted any research on the Ryūkyūs. J. D. Morris, who served as a Navy Civil Affairs officer in Okinawa, wrote that an invasion of Okinawa "might just as well have been assaulting the planet Mars."[6] Adding to NCAT's information vacuum was the fact that they only had a few months to produce civil affairs manuals for the Ryūkyūs. What information they did have on the Ryūkyūs came from two recent sources. The first, a book published in early 1944, entitled *The Pacific World*, was compiled and edited by "thirty men from eminent institutions of higher education and was doubtless the best information at hand." Yet, the authors failed to fill even one page on the Ryūkyū archipelago—and not all of this information was correct.[7] The second, and more substantial source, was the ethnographical research conducted by the Office of Strategic Services (OSS) on the Okinawan immigrant community in Hawai'i. The OSS published a series of reports, the most significant being *The Okinawas of the Loo Choo Islands: A Japanese Minority Group*, which by default, became the starting point of NCAT's learning curve regarding the Ryūkyūs.

The conclusion of the OSS's ethnographical research indicated that, at best, mainland Japanese viewed Okinwans as rustic cousins, and at worst as no better than Japan's other colonial subjects. "It is claimed that, at one time," the OSS report stated, "the Japanese authorities would not allow the natives of the islands [Okinawa] to visit Korea as they did not wish the Koreans to know that there was *any question of disunity between the Japanese and the Okinawa[n]s*."[8] The OSS report led NCAT to view "Okinawa as being not only a physical minority but a linguistic and ethnic one."[9] Building upon the OSS findings, NCAT assembled all available information from Japanese language sources. Synthesizing these sources, NCAT compiled a 334-page *Civil Affairs Handbook: Ryūkyū (Loochoo) Islands OPNAV 13-31*, which was published in mid-November of 1944. The *Handbook* largely reflected the conclusions reached in the earlier OSS report, *The Okinawas of the Loo Choo Islands: A Japanese Minority Group*, namely, that the Ryūkyū Islands and their people were not an organic part of Japan. Consequently, NCAT saw the invasion as an opportunity to liberate the Ryūkyūs and restore a sense of Ryūkyūan/Okinawan nationalism.

From imagining to inventing the Ryūkyū nation, 1945–47

When US military forces began the invasion of Okinawa on 1 April 1945, American civil affairs personnel immediately began a process of creating identity dissonance among Okinawans. During the battle, American propaganda reminded Okinawans of their unique heritage and the 70-year history of Japanese oppression and discrimination. The US Army's secret "Psychological Warfare Plan" stated that Okinawans "will be continuously reminded of the repeated discrimination against them by the Japanese."[10] The purpose of one propaganda leaflet was to "turn local inhabitants against Japanese soldiers." It asked Okinawan civilians a series of questions such as "What obligations do you have to the Japanese?" and "Is this your war? Or is it really the war of Japanese leaders who have dominated you for many decades?"[11] Another leaflet, which drew directly on the OSS report, tried to undermine civilian participation in the defense of the island by reminding Okinawans of discriminatory treatment by the Japanese, who were often referred to on Okinawa as *Naichi*:

> What have you received from the *Naichijin* to warrant these sacrifices? Are not you of equal ability with Japanese, yet given employment at menial tasks? *Do not the Naichijin consider themselves superior to you?* As proof of that, do not the *Naichijin* scorn intermarriage with your women? Do not *Naichijin* teachers in schools show preference to *Naichijin* children? Are not the chief political administrative posts held by the *Naichijin*? . . . . . Is not clear, then, that the Japanese are needlessly killing your men and *destroying your homeland*? This is not your war, but you are being used as a cat's paw by the Naichijin. You are sacrificing for them and getting nothing in return![12]

Whether in response to the brutality of Japanese soldiers or US propaganda, the Battle of Okinawa provided cause for Okinawans to question their identity as Japanese and rethink what it meant to be Okinawan. One such Okinawan was Hayashi Iko, who during the prewar period was part of the small yet influential prewar Okinawan intellectual class that had long advocated assimilation with Japan. Hayashi, shocked by Japanese propaganda lies, said that "after the war, Okinawa should sever all connections with Japan . . . . Okinawa should be independent although militarily and politically under the control of the United States."[13] Hayashi's reawakened consciousness undoubtedly reflected a larger identity crisis among Okinawans, who were willing to explore a new identity. NCAT quickly exploited this identity vacuum and began the process of Ryūkyūan nation building.

NCAT immediately began to collect and preserve Ryūkyūan cultural assets because they believed that the people needed more than the basic necessities to survive, and with their connection to Japan shattered by war, they intuitively understood that a reconstructed Ryūkyūs could fill the vacuum caused by the war.[14] Even before Japan had surrendered, NCAT authorized the construction of a new museum and cultural center and hired Okinawans to house the artifacts rescued from the rubble of Shuri Castle, the former capital of the Ryūkyū Kingdom.[15] Omine Kaoru was hired to be the museum's first director, as it was recognized that the entire enterprise needed to be run by Okinawans, not Americans. Omine and his employees wasted little time in scouring the island for surviving artifacts. "Before the shells had stopped going off, we had got busy collecting prize specimens of Okinawan pottery, lacquer, textiles and of the other arts and crafts" and even managed to recover "rare items from the prewar Shuri Castle museum" amidst the "rubble and corpse-littered caves of Shuri Castle hill."

NCAT saw an opportunity to demonstrate the richness of Ryūkyūan civilization by holding an exhibit of the recently salvaged artifacts. Omine and NCAT produced a pamphlet entitled "Okinawan Exhibit" to commemorate the opening of the museum. NCAT wanted to use the exhibit to demonstrate American appreciation of the "tastes of the Okinawan people in home architecture, home furnishings, landscape gardening, clothing and textiles, pottery, and other matters concerned with daily living and artistic expression." Moreover, American officials hoped that the "exhibit may help to indicate why both emigrant and resident *Okinawans looked with pride and affection upon the isle of their birth*, and also why the rehabilitation of the by no means unsophisticated people of Okinawa under Military Government auspices is no mean undertaking."[16] This patronage of the museum and the Ryūkyūan heritage also sent a clear message to the people that unlike the contempt prewar Japanese rule had for Okinawa, the Americans respected the unique Ryūkyūan heritage.

NCAT also promoted the Ryūkyūan traditional performing arts.[17] At an outdoor, NCAT-built cultural performing center next to the museum, a small a troupe of "leading Okinawan actors and actresses" performed traditional music and plays for the displaced Okinawans living in Ishikawa. The troupe's success led to performances throughout the island.[18] Eventually, orders were given to build an outdoor "stage in every city, town, and village." After extensive rehearsals at the military government's headquarters in Ishikawa, the "troupe had taken to the road for as rugged a schedule of appearances as could be encompassed in open six-by-six trucks, roaring over rough coral highway through wind, rain and dust."[19] Lacking formal instruments, the resourceful troupe made their own *sanshin* (three-stringed instrument) "from cans and then sewed costumes from parachutes and traveled around from neighborhood to neighborhood performing."[20] Throughout Okinawa, "each village, town and city had a *rotengekijō* (open-air theater) where the actors performed" and crowds numbering tens of thousands were usual.[21] After the shock of the war and especially the treatment Okinawans suffered at the hands of the Japanese military, the performances were not only a welcome break from the arduous task of rebuilding, but also served to resurrect a Ryūkyūan past that had nearly been effaced by 70 years of Japanese assimilation.

These performances, complete with traditional costumes, textiles, music, and songs, served as a powerful reminder that before they were Japanese, Ryūkyūans had their own unique culture. For example, a play entitled "Old Man's Dance" was a "poetic eulogy to the ancient Kingdom of Ryūkyū while the gold-robed, white-bearded dancer performed the stately steps which had been admired by Chinese and Japanese emissaries to the royal court at Shuri."[22] *Ryūbu*, a traditional Ryūkyūan dance, was also popular with the masses. It originated as a special performance for visiting dignitaries from Ming China in the fifteenth century, but over time had evolved "into an art form popular among commoners."[23] These performances were extremely popular as the audiences were "large and patient" as the "programs last[ed] up to six hours."[24] Ruth Ann Keyso's assessment of *Ryūbu* holds that in the "immediate postwar years," the Ryūkyūan performing arts helped Ryūkyūans to "regain their lost sense of self." Overall, the "preservation of this performing art, many islanders claim, was the key to conserving Okinawa's heritage."[25]

Navy Lt. James Watkins, one of the ardent advocates of Ryūkyūanization in NCAT, urged the restoration of a Ryūkyūan political identity. With the military government and the Okinawan Advisory Council based in Ishikawa, far from the traditional centers of political power, Watkins was attentive to a "consideration for dignity—and a befitting setting—so important in oriental eyes."[26] Watkins, after meeting with the Okinawan Advisory Council, wrote in his diary that "I am convinced that if possible we should secure Shuri, the ancient (pre-Naha) capital, for the Okinawans" because in reference to the existing location in Ishikawa, "without either Naha or Shuri, one can as easily find a center for national life as one might for America in Arkansas."[27] Watkins eventually raised the issue of establishing a new capital. Nakasone Genwa, a member of the Okinawan Advisory Council (OCA), agreed with Watkins that the OCA had to "consider the subject from the perspective of Okinawa's future benefit, though not all on the Council agreed with the idea" because of the reality that Shuri had been leveled in the fighting.[28] Nevertheless, Watkins told the Okinawan Advisory Council that "military government officers would continue to bend their efforts *towards the rebirth of Okinawa*."[29] Since establishing a new capital in Shuri was premature,

Watkins informed the Okinawan Advisory Council of his intention to "use the museum .... as a means of propaganda to show them that Okinawa had once been something more than an island of broken-down farm houses and pig-sties." Watkins, continuing his lecture, noted the importance of using other significant historical and cultural sites, such as Nakagusuku Castle, for the same purpose.[30]

NCAT initial efforts of nation building created an identity space where Okinawans, for the first time, could at least entertain the possibility of Okinawa and the entire Ryūkyū archipelago being independent. The Okinawan elite responded favorably to the American efforts. On 24 April 1946, Shikiya Kōshin became the first native Okinawan to head an Okinawan governing authority, a highly auspicious moment in Okinawan modern history because in Japan's prewar administration of the islands, mainlanders dominated all of the top administrative posts.[31] Shikiya, understanding the historical significance of the day, stated in his inaugural speech that "with thankfulness for the kind intentions of Military Government, we Okinawans are filled with hope that, in striving *to build a better Okinawa than before, we will achieve the golden age for Okinawa with our hands*."[32] Shortly thereafter, Military Government (MG) allowed the formation of political parties and they collectively shared Shikiya's optimism for a Ryūkyūan "golden age," as none advocated for reversion. In its inaugural party platform of 1946, the Okinawa People's Party (OPP) argued for the continuation of democracy "in political, economic, social, and cultural fields" in order to create an "autonomous Okinawa," and thanked the Americans for "liberating the Ryūkyū race."[33] Ogimi Chotoku, founder of the Okinawa Socialist Party, called for US annexation, arguing that this "would save Okinawa from repeating the past tragic experience of Japanese exploitation and poverty."[34] Echoing this sentiment, the OPP platform noted the marked distinction between their former "protectors" and their former "enemy," in that "we Okinawans, who were extremely mistreated under the aggressive war waged by the Japanese militarists," exist now because of the American "humanistic good will and material assistance."[35]

On the defensive: Ryūkyūan culture and the reversion movement

The first two years of the occupation of the Ryūkyūs, however, represented the apex of US-Ryūkyūan relations and Okinawan desires for independence. In mid-1946, the US Army took over the administration of the Ryūkyūs, and the era of Army rule until 1950 has been referred to as the era of "apathy and neglect." During this time, NCAT's effort to promote a Ryūkyūan identity was displaced by an ethos of incompetence, cultural insensitivity, and contemptuous actions toward the idea of Ryūkyūan sovereignty. Not only did cultural rehabilitation of the Ryūkyūs flounder, but economic recovery came to a halt and any notion of fundamental human rights became nonexistent as military justice was an oxymoron. This cultural reversal in occupation policies destroyed any hopes among Okinawans for independence, but more importantly, disillusioned and embittered Okinawans came to feel that their only political option was reunification with Japan. At the same time, a series of geopolitical events in 1949 and 1950, such as the Communist victory in China, the Soviets' successful detonation of an atomic bomb, and the outbreak of hostilities in Korea, made US Cold War planners belatedly aware of the strategic importance of the Ryūkyūs. The onset of the Cold War in Asia forced Washington to reignite an enlightened administration of the islands, but in the face of Okinawan demands for reversion to Japan, the US-Ryūkyūan relationship was seriously compromised. In 1950, Pentagon officials appointed General Josef Sheetz to troubleshoot the Army's maladministration of the Ryūkyūs.

Cognizant of the level of damage incurred during the four year era of "apathy and neglect," Sheetz embarked on an ambitious cultural and political program to "win the hearts and minds" of the Okinawan people. Sheetz was well aware of NCAT's earlier accomplishments and understood that greater political autonomy and the nurturing of a nascent Ryūkyūan identity might stem Okinawan demands for reversion.[36] US Army Colonel James Tull, who was Sheetz's right-hand man in promoting Ryūkyūan nation building, was also influenced by the 1944 reports and NCAT's efforts.[37] Tull later commented that the OSS report "emphasized the enduring nature of the cultural attachments to China" and that under Japanese rule, "Satsuma labored sedulously to eliminate the Chinese cultural influence . . . . and the people were urged to imitate things Japanese."[38] Hence, both Sheetz and Tull considered it imperative to revive NCAT's cultural project to encourage a Ryūkyūan identity.

Sheetz pushed Military Government (MG) to respect Ryūkyūan history and culture, thereby respecting a people long accustomed to disrespect by outsiders. George Kerr, an occupation consultant, candidly pointed out to US officials that "the biggest and most consistent failure has been the neglect of the rich Ryūkyūan cultural heritage." Exploiting the history and culture undoubtedly would have provided a "feeling of national consciousness," but the failure to do so had led many to "dislike being addressed as Ryūkyūans."[39] Beginning in 1950, Sheetz initiated a systematic approach to the rehabilitation of Okinawan cultural and historical sites with emphasis on reconstruction projects in Shuri because the former kingdom's capital was the key to resurrecting Okinawans' links to their past. MG built Shuri Museum and Shuri High School, and reconstructed both *Sonohyan Utaki*, which was a shrine to the fire god that the battle had destroyed, and stood symbolically "near the entrance of the University in Shuri," and the crown jewel, Shureimon. Each project touched "on the religious life, the cultural life, and the education life of the past." In the end, Sheetz believed that the "psychological value of a demonstration of American interest in them would far outweigh the necessary cost in dollars or yen."[40]

Sheetz, understanding that "Okinawa" reflected the prewar relationship between Okinawans and mainland Japan, consciously attempted to break this political identification by emphasizing the term "Ryūkyū." Because the Meiji government consciously invented "Okinawa" in order to erase historical memory of the Ryūkyū Kingdom, Sheetz understood that continued use of "Okinawa" would reinforce Japan's claims to sovereignty and popular support for reversion. Sheetz, therefore, ordered that "Ryūkyū" would become the exclusive authorized nomenclature and renamed the military government as the "Ryūkyū Command (RYCOM)." Sheetz even renamed the annual report on the occupation's state of affairs the *Ryūkyū Statistical Bulletin*. The first *Ryūkyū Statistical Bulletin* noted in its preface that the "Ryūkyūans were a proud people, with their own history and culture, they were treated as social inferiors by the Japanese." Moreover, the *Bulletin* noted that Japan had sacrificed and discarded the Ryūkyūs during the war, yet the Ryūkyūan people were "preparing now, with the help and guidance of United States Military Government, to reach full stature with individual identity, culture and prestige which is truly their own."[41] Sheetz renamed the Okinawa Advisory Council as the Interim Ryūkyūs Advisory Council. Other reforms also reflected the change, as seen in the new newspaper *Ryūkyū Kōhō*, Ryūkyū-American Education Week, and *Voice of the Ryūkyūs (Ryūkyū no Koe)*. Even the political leaflets and posters distributed throughout 1950 conspicuously avoided the term "Okinawan people" (*Okinawajin*) and instead used "*Ryūkyūjin*." In December 1950, General Douglas MacArthur renamed the US Army's administrative authority on Okinawa the United States Civil Administration of the Ryūkyū Islands (USCAR) to emphasize America's "civil" commitment to the "Ryūkyūs."[42]

Sheetz understood that the change in the official name would not by itself create a Ryūkyūan identity, as a "Ryūkyūan central government can be measured in direct proportion to the degree to which the people develop national consciousness and national pride."[43] Sheetz attempted to complement the semantic emphasis on "Ryūkyū" and the development of a national consciousness by creating a new national symbol, and asked Governor Shikiya Kōshin to find local artists to design a flag. Shikiya, probably in conjunction with the most ardent supporter of independence, Nakasone Genwa, commissioned the Shuri Fine Artist Association (*Shuri Bijutsuka Kyōkai*) to design a Ryūkyūan flag. Whether or not Shikiya instructed the artists to use a design that reflected the American flag, the lineage of the Ryūkyūan-designed flag was quite apparent. The flag had three equal-sized horizontal stripes of blue, white, and red (from top to bottom). In the upper left hand corner of the flag (on the blue stripe) was one white star. The blue, white, and red stripes represented peace (*heiwa*), liberty (*jiyū*), and passion (*nessei*), respectively. The white star represented the morning star (*myōjō*) and it symbolized hope (*kibō*) for the dawn of a new era of independence built upon peace and liberty.

With the support of Nakasone Genwa, an ardent advocate of Ryūkyūan independence, Governor Shikiya presented the flag to a surprised audience of political elite on 25 January 1950. Supporters of independence applauded the flag, but the majority of the audience stood in disbelief, apparently at the audacity of creating a Ryūkyūan flag, especially one reminiscent of the American flag. Fearing a backlash during a sensitive time of political reform, military government officials quietly pulled the flag on 1 March 1950. For many, the entire incident seemed surreal and hence, came to be referred to as the *maboroshi no Ryūkyū kokki* (the phantom illusion of the Ryūkyūan national flag).[44]

USCAR reinforced these symbolic efforts with more tangible actions, most notably in establishing the first university in Okinawa, the University of the Ryūkyūs. To great fanfare, on 22 May 1950, University of the Ryūkyūs opened its doors to 28 faculty and nearly 600 students.[45] American authorities stressed that "the first and only institution of its kind in the islands" resulted from American patronage.[46] The university, it was hoped, would remind Okinawans that Japan had failed to build an institution of higher learning during its 70 years of rule and that this failure largely stemmed from Japan's discriminatory neglect of the prefecture. The establishment of the first university in Okinawa allowed US authorities to claim that "Ryūkyūans were a proud people, with their own history and culture, they were treated as social inferiors by the Japanese" and moreover, that Ryūkyūans were "preparing now, with the help and guidance of United States Military Government, to reach full stature with individual identity, culture and prestige which is truly their own."[47] While the new university allowed the United States to favorably contrast their occupation with Japan's prewar rule, it also played a pivotal role in the promotion of Ryūkyūanization.

In addition, USCAR consciously built the university on the site of the former capital of the Ryūkyū Kingdom, Shuri. When Japan forcibly annexed the Ryūkyūs in the 1870s, it moved the political capital to Naha and renamed the islands Okinawa Prefecture. Tokyo sent down a military company to force King Shō Tai's abdication, and on 30 March 1879, "Shō Tai and his household passed from the castle grounds through the *Kokugaku-mon* (Gate of National Learning) into forced exile."[48] George Kerr, who was commissioned by the USCAR to write a history of the islands, argued that this exile represented a "symbolic break with the past" because "for the first time in five hundred years the palace [Shuri Castle] ceased to be the seat of authority and the symbol of nationhood." Tokyo's two decisions effectively rendered Shuri and the Ryūkyūs as anachronisms, as Shuri became a garrison for Japanese soldiers and during the Battle of Okinawa it was reduced to rubble.[49] The decision to locate the university at Shuri was made with great deliberation. Some officials worried that the university's location would be perceived by the people as sacrilege, both in terms of what it represented historically and what had transpired during the battle. But Yamashiro Atsuo, a leading Okinawan educator, reassured American officials that Shuri was indeed the perfect location for the Ryūkyūs' first university.[50] Yamashiro understood that the university's location linked the present Ryūkyūs to the Ryūkyūan past, and simultaneously conveyed American respect and support for the Ryūkyūan heritage.[51] General MacArthur's congratulatory message captured the essence of what US planners hoped to convey to the assembled Ryūkyūan audience:

> Establishment of the University of the Ryūkyūs is an event of outstanding importance in the cultural and intellectual history of these Islands. It is, moreover, particularly appropriate that the University, founded upon the ancient site of the throne of Ryūkyūan kings . . . . so too the eventual greatness of this institution will depend not on the multiplicity but the quality of its resources and its wisdom in using them.[52]

US officials, anxious to extract full propaganda value, commemorated the opening by issuing special postal stamps. These stamps, drawn by Okinawan artists, captured the historical link between the University of the Ryūkyūs and the Ryūkyū Kingdom. In the stamp's design, the building in the foreground represented the university, but was shadowed by a larger, looming outline of Shuri Castle.[53] The dragon pillar, on the left part of the stamp, was a stone marker that designated the approach to the king's throne. American officials managed to salvage one of the dragon pillars from the castle's ruins; it represented the only tangible artifact to survive the battle and was highlighted by the Americans as an example of their efforts to preserve the Ryūkyū heritage.

The post office also issued a special "first day issue" envelope that reinforced the stamp's connection to the Ryūkyūan past. The envelope's specially commissioned art work, on the left, conveyed the auspicious moment of the opening day and linked the university to what American officials hoped would come to represent Ryūkyūan national symbols. Once again, the artist represented the signature dragon pillar and Shuri Castle in a silhouette. A new "national" symbol, however, was conspicuously added. This symbol, Shureimon, was one of Shuri Castle's main gates, and more importantly, due to its unique architecture style, symbolized a golden age in Ryūkyū history. Built in the early sixteenth century, Shureimon remained intact until the Battle of Okinawa, when it was destroyed. While Okinawans revered the gate, US officials believed that the gate, even more than Shuri Castle, had even greater utility in their goal of Ryūkyūanization.

In fact, US officials believed that Shureimon was such a potent symbol for representing the Ryūkyū-American relationship that they commissioned Okinawan artisans to reconstruct a scale model of Shureimon. Upon completion, the model was strategically displayed in the University of the Ryūkyūs "to show students what [had] once stood outside their classroom doors," and to show that thanks to US support, students could be proud of their Ryūkyūan heritage.[54] Later, in 1958, with US support, Okinawan officials rebuilt Shureimon in its original location, which allowed students to pass under this historic gate on their way to the university. US authorities also sponsored school field trips to the newly reconstructed Shureimon and provided teachers handouts on the symbolic value of Shureimon.

It is also worth pointing out that on the eve of Okinawa's reversion to Japan, US authorities published the last edition of *Shurei no Hikari*, a long-standing US occupation magazine used to show Okinawans the American efforts to promote Ryūkyūan heritage. For the magazine's final cover, American officials decided to place Shureimon on the cover, as an "enduring symbol" of American-Ryūkyū relations and perhaps a subtle reminder of Japan's prewar rule of forced assimilation. Japanese officials, well aware of American patronage of Ryūkyūan history, responded with their own acknowledgment of Okinawa's special place by issuing a special Shureimon stamp in 1972.

In 1954, USCAR once again resurrected the idea of creating a new Ryukyan national standard, drawing upon the lessons of the failed attempt of 1950. In a memo to General Ogden, Colonel Walter Murray, USCAR's Deputy Civil Administrator, reported on long-term discussions with key "members of the GRI (Government of the Ryūkyū Islands) and the University" and recommended that "some paper flags containing the device of the old Shō kings to be used in decorating the various Ryūkyūan-American cultural centers." Murray believed that the people would accept this design because it derived from Ryūkyūan history, implying that the effort to introduce a Ryūkyūan national flag in 1950 had failed because it was too "American" in design. Cautiously optimistic, Murray concluded that the new design might create more "Ryūkyūan nationalistic feeling," and more importantly, "wean them away somewhat from the Japanese."[55]

USCAR designated Edward Freimuth, USCAR's primary liaison with the GRI, to assess the flag's feasibility because his liaison department understood the GRI and the Okinawan "pulse" better than anyone else within USCAR. A week after Murray's initial proposal, Freimuth responded with an in-depth and thoughtful analysis. Freimuth immediately acknowledged that USCAR faced a problem in implementing Ryūkyūanization because the Japanese flag "continues to be the emblem the people are inclined to respect," and of course rally around. Fundamentally, as long as the Ryūkyūs remained a part of Japan, Freimuth believed that by default the people would view the Japanese flag as the "most desired emblem." To counter this situation, Freimuth believed that a Ryūkyūan national flag would "create a nationalistic spirit around which the people will automatically rally, and furthermore . . . give the Government [GRI] an emblem which it can display from its buildings, ships and installations thereby designating them as Ryūkyūan."[56]

Freimuth, however, urged that the matter be handled with great care and sensitivity. Since the United States acknowledged that Japan had "residual sovereignty" over the islands, Friemuth believed that designating the

Ryūkyūan flag as a "national" flag would be "inappropriate" and bound to cause a diplomatic row with Japan. If USCAR decided to introduce a new flag, he urged that it not be done via a "USCAR directive or ordinance," as a top-down approach would elicit "enmity against the proposal rather than developing a nationalistic feeling." Freimuth, perhaps addressing the "military mind," pointed out the obvious, namely that popular support for a "Ryūkyū Banner must stem from the people." Finally, Freimuth urged patience, as Ryūkyūan acceptance for the new flag would take time. In fact, he warned USCAR that acceptance might never occur, because he "doubted that under the present conditions the desire for display of a Ryūkyū banner will supplant the desire to display a national emblem as the Japanese flag." At the same time, acceptance could "possibly be developed with the initial steps already having been taken by CI&E (Department of Civil Information and Education) in its Information Centers [Ryūkyūan-American Friendship Centers]."[57]

Given the green light from Freimuth's department, USCAR's CI&E department attempted to use the national flag, the *Tomoebata*, to promote a sense of Okinawan identity. First, they decided to keep the Shō family crest and colors as the new national standard, and thus, "Americans in Okinawa became advocates for a separate Okinawan identity."[58] CI&E displayed the banners at the Ryūkyū-American Friendship Centers with the Stars and Stripes and the *Tomoebata* placed side by side. Freimuth, who witnessed this effort, wrote that "unofficial and informal this may have been, the military's printing resources reproduced the crest on paper flags and used them extensively for decorative purposes on strings along with the paper flags of other allied nations."[59] By placing the Ryūkyūan flag along with the Stars and Stripes and other national flags, officials hoped to confer legitimacy on the nascent Ryūkyūan national symbol.

USCAR, undaunted by its failure to raise Ryūkyūan national consciousness through the *Tomoebata*, next attempted to create a national anthem based on traditional music. One USCAR official, Adjunct William Brewer, believed that Okinawan music offered a means to develop a Ryūkyūan consciousness. USCAR wanted to create a distinctively Okinawan "musical composition that can be forever identified with the Golden Age of Okinawa and its resurgence." Officials met with a distinguished group of Okinawans and discussed which traditional songs to use and urged the group to consider a traditional song that would be acceptable to both Okinawans and Americans. Working together, the committee developed 14 questions designed to help compose an appropriate national anthem. For example, one question asked "which music has the same appeal to Okinawans that *Kimigayo* [Japan's National Anthem] has to the Japanese?" Another asked, "Are there any outstanding things in Okinawa's past that will always be remembered?" In the end, they concluded that a "march medley consisting of several of the more popular Okinawan songs" provided the best path to create a Ryūkyūan national anthem.[60] In the end, the power of the reversion movement overwhelmed American efforts to produce an identity gap between the Ryūkyūs and Japan. Nevertheless, this entire flag and anthem saga unequivocally demonstrated USCAR's intent to promote Ryūkyūan national identity whenever the opportunity presented itself.[61] These efforts, however, only fueled Okinawan desires for reversion.

In the 1960s, Okinawan demands for reversion to Japan entered into a new and more dynamic stage and became a much broader social movement which incorporated Okinawan labor and youth participation, and was energized by massive support and sympathy from demonstrations in Japan. At the same time, Okinawan intellectuals, especially those who came of age during the process of Ryūkyū nation building, began to critique Okinawa's relationship with the "fatherland," Japan. The most prominent manifestation of this turn in sentiment was Ōta Masahide's best seller *Minikui Nihonjin* (*The Ugly Japanese*), which sold tens of thousands of copies in Okinawa. A less known work, *Nihon wa sokuku ja nai*, (*Japan is Not our Fatherland*), was written by Yamazato Eikichi in 1969. Yamazato, vice president of the "Okinawa for the Okinawans Association," believed that Okinawans had failed to ask a vital question: what is the fatherland? If this question had been asked in 1879, Yamazato stated, nine out of ten would not have hesitated to say that their fatherland was the Ryūkyūs. Yamazato explained how Japan's forcible colonization of the Ryūkyūs had turned the people into "artificial" Japanese. He decried the Japanese assimilation programs that robbed the people of their mother tongue and made speaking in their native tongue a crime punishable by death. Yamazato concluded:

> Our fatherland can never be Japan. Our fatherland is the Ryūkyūs. All Ryūkyūans will only be saved when the Ryūkyū government flies the flag of independence that will restore our self-respect and teach all Ryūkyūans to be proud of our identity before ever becoming Japanese.[62]

Another Okinawan intellectual, Sakihara Mitsugu, in the preface to his book *A Brief History of Early Okinawa Based on the Omoro Sōshi* (1987), noted his confusion and ambiguity about his identity, stating that while studying in Oregon on an American scholarship, he assumed he was Japanese; after all, "I fought and was wounded in the defense of Japan in the Battle of Okinawa."[63] Yet, his time away from Okinawa led him to doubt his "Japanese" identity.

> The uncertainty of whether I was an Okinawan or a Japanese led to the question "What is an Okinawan, and how is he or she different from a Japanese?" An Okinawan may legally be a Japanese, but is he or she a Japanese in the same sense that a person from Tokyo is Japanese? Okinawa is said to have been annexed by Japan in 1879. Does that mean Okinawa was not a part of Japan before 1879? *Is an Okinawan therefore a colonial?*[64]

Although the views of Ōta, Yamazato, and Sakihara were clearly in the minority in late 1960s Okinawa, they nonetheless represent the genesis of an acute Okinawan ethnic nationalism. In addition, the confidence gained in the two-decade struggle for reversion, plus the social and temporal space provided by occupation nation-building policies, allowed Okinawans to take their experiences into the postreversion era. In 1972, however, few could have predicted that Okinawa's postreversion era would be as contentious as the occupation period, and that once again the politicization of Okinawa's identity and culture would spark controversy.

Asserting identity and resisting the state

For the first time in history, at the famed 71st Annual Kōshien High School Baseball Spring Tournament on 4 April 1999, an Okinawan high school team (Okinawa Shōgaku) won Japan's most prestigious baseball tournament. This victory was more than a long coveted baseball championship; it represented a poignant event in Okinawan history and identity. The outpouring of euphoria was stunning, especially among the elderly, who with tears in their eyes shouted: "we finally beat them [the Japanese]!" One elderly woman, with tears running down her cheeks, told me that now she could die in peace knowing that Okinawa had finally beaten those mainlanders. Others shouted "never forget where you were on 4 April 1999." For weeks after the victory, the letters-to-the-editor page of the two local newspapers (*Okinawa Times* and the *Ryūkyū Shinpō*) contained numerous emotional letters about the game. "Remember the date 4 April 1999!" was a frequent refrain in these letters, and surprisingly, many of the authors were elderly women. More recently, another Okinawan high school (Kōnan) won for the first time both the spring and the summer Kōshien tournament (2010). Kōnan's double victory gave it a place in Kōshien history as it was only one of eight schools in Japan to win both championships in the same year. Not surprisingly, on 21 August 2010, celebrations erupted throughout the island and seemed akin to the national thrall exhibited by Spain after its team won the World Cup. When both high school teams returned to Okinawa, massive victory parades were conducted throughout the island, producing a de facto "national holiday" as many took the day off to celebrate Okinawa's victory.

Okinawa's recent political culture also mirrored the combative spirit exhibited by the Kōshien baseball championships. On 4 September 1995, three US military personnel abducted, beat, and gang-raped a 12-year-old Okinawan girl, a crime that galvanized latent Okinawan anger into a potent social movement that was both antibase and anti-Japanese. Okinawa's governor, Ōta Masahide, who had written *The Ugly Japanese* 27 years earlier, used the criminal act and the subsequent demonstrations to challenge both the bases and Tokyo's tacit support for the US presence, resulting in significant concessions in the Status of Forces (SOFA) agreement and forcing pledges to remove the Futenma airbase. Not content with these concessions, Ōta continued to press the issue and stunned Tokyo when he refused to sign off on the land leases as required in the Land Acquisition Law (LAL). Without his signature, American bases would technically be occupying Okinawan land illegally. Prime Minister Murayama Tomiichi sued Ōta to force him to comply with LAL, but to the surprise of many, Ōta appealed to the Japanese Supreme Court, which agreed to hear his case in 1996.

Ōta's appearance represented the first time in Japanese history that a governor had challenged the state in the Supreme Court. Moreover, he asserted that culturally and historically, Okinawa was distinct from Japan, implying that Okinawa should be seen as an independent entity. In the face of Japanese claims to being a peaceful nation, he argued that Japan had forcibly conquered the Ryūkyū Kingdom and for the next 70 years imposed cultural assimilation policies on a reluctant people. Given this context, he claimed that "Okinawa, formerly a peaceful nation-state (*heiwa kokka*), had no choice but to go along with a military state (*gunkoku*), Japan. This, one might say, was the beginning of Okinawa's fortification (*Okinawa no kichika*)." With this statement, Ōta challenged the prevailing notion that Okinawa was an integral part of Japan, and more importantly, asserted that Japan, rather than the United States, should bear responsibility for Okinawa's base problem (*kichi mondai*). He reminded the court that Japanese militarism bore primary responsibility for the killing of one-third of the island's population during the Battle of Okinawa, and that the destruction of Shurijō had destroyed irreplaceable national treasures and subsequently cut off Okinawans from the "cultural heritage of their ancestors." Finally, he warned that Japan's continuing refusal to recognize the base problem would have "implications for Japan's sovereignty and democracy."[65] Ōta's warning was not an idle threat, as Okinawans took to the streets and voted in plebiscites to show their opposition to Tokyo's tacit support for the massive US military presence on the island.

Governor Ōta and the antibase movement pressed their cause by organizing a prefecture-wide referendum in 1996 that asked Okinawans if they wanted to review the SOFA treaty and to reduce the US base presence. This prefectural referendum, one of the first in the nation, sent a clear message as 89 percent of the voters expressed support for revisiting SOFA and reducing the bases, although the voter turnout was lower than expected at 40 percent.[66] Nevertheless, Okinawa's nonbinding referendum challenged the state's authority, as the status of the US bases fell under the purview of national security and maintaining treaty obligations. The demonstrations, Ōta's refusal to sign off on the Land Acquisition Law, Ōta's Supreme Court appeal, and the prefecture-wide plebiscite did force significant concessions to SOFA, most notably giving Okinawa legal and judicial jurisdiction over crimes committed by US military personnel. Efforts to move the airbase from Futenma to Henoko in northern Okinawa also encountered substantial opposition. Despite substantial pledges of economic aid for the long-depressed region and overt arm-twisting by conservative forces, Nago residents rejected the new base in a 1997 local referendum, with nearly 54 percent voting in opposition to the new base.[67] Not surprisingly, Okinawa's continued intransigence elicited reactions from policy makers in both countries.

The empire strikes back: Politicization of Okinawa culture

Both Tokyo and Washington pursued a "carrot and stick" approach to deal with the "Okinawa problem." Tokyo, and specifically, the governing Liberal Democratic Party (LDP), took an active role in preventing the reelection of Ōta in 1998. Ōta's opponent, LDP-endorsed Inamine Keiichi, reminded Okinawans that Ōta's contentious stance with Tokyo and Washington was destroying the local economy as Tokyo had frozen millions of dollars in development funds for Okinawa, causing 10 percent unemployment, nearly double the national rate. Inamine, who made it clear that his election would open Tokyo's purse strings and that he supported the new base in Nago, prevailed with 52 percent of the vote.[68] Despite Ōta's appeal that "Okinawans should not sell their soul to Japan," it was hard for economically depressed Okinawans to ignore the ¥100 million secretly disbursed by Prime Minister Obuchi's office through a front organization to various constituents in Okinawa.[69] The day after Inamine's inauguration, Obuchi announced that ¥100 million in special development funds would be earmarked for Okinawa, nearly double what the government had provided Ōta. Obuchi made it clear the increase in funds was directly tied to Inamine's victory by stating "I sincerely hope various problems on Okinawa, including the issue of US bases, will move toward resolution through deeper cooperation between the central government and (Okinawa) prefecture."[70] In addition, Obuchi further legitimized newly elected Governor Inamine by meeting with the Ministerial Committee on Okinawan Affairs, which he had refused to do during Ōta's term.

Hoping to further solidify Inamine's political position and to ingratiate the LDP with Okinawa, Obuchi shocked the nation, Okinawa, and the United States by announcing in April 1999 that Okinawa would be the primary host for the annual meeting of the G8 Summit for the year 2000.[71] Obuchi, however, had one additional surprise when he announced in the fall that a new ¥2000 note would be introduced to both commemorate the new century and acknowledge Okinawa's importance by placing its iconic Shureimon on the front of the new note. Rather than just a commemorative note, treasury officials stressed that the Shureimon Bill was permanent currency and that it would be released the following spring, "in time for the G8 summit next July," to be held in Okinawa.[72]

FIGURE 5.1 *Two thousand yen bank note depicting "Shureimon" issued on 19 July 2000. Author's photo.*

Owing to Obuchi's patronage of Okinawan culture, the year 2000 turned out to be an auspicious year for Okinawa. On 19 July 2000, the Shureimon ¥2,000 note was issued. Two days later, as Okinawa hosted the G8 summit, the Japanese government, now led by Mori Yoshirō, lavished ¥81 *billion* on Okinawa and the summit (In comparison, the German government spent ¥700 million for the 1999 G8 summit in Cologne).[73] Clearly, cooperation was rewarded.

For the next three days, Okinawa showcased the island's distinctive culture and history for the G8 heads of state. President Bill Clinton, the first US president to visit Okinawa since President Eisenhower's disastrous visit in 1960, gave a speech at Okinawa's Cornerstone of Peace, the memorial site for the Battle of Okinawa where roughly one-third of the island's population had perished in the battle.[74] Clinton's administration, displeased by Obuchi's decision to have Okinawa host the G8 summit, decided that the President would take a cue from Obuchi's playbook and acknowledge Okinawa's unique heritage. In his speech, Clinton acknowledged Okinawa's suffering from the war, and moreover, astutely noted the uniqueness of Okinawa's war memorial. Clinton also paid homage to Okinawa's claim of being a country of courtesy and peace, as he observed that the memorial "is more than a war memorial—it is a monument to the tragedy of all war, reminding us of our common responsibility to prevent such destruction from ever happening again."[75]

Clinton's acknowledgment of Okinawa's wartime suffering and the burden of hosting the US military bases for the previous 50 years was no surprise. Yet, his speech was more remarkable for its emphasis on Okinawa's non-Japanese historical and cultural pedigree and the previous American efforts to nurture this unique heritage. First, he made reference to the Bankoku Shinryō, a famous bronze bell that once hung in Shurijō (Shuri Castle), the capital of the Ryūkyū Kingdom. When it was cast in 1458, the Ryūkyū King had the phrase "*bankoku shinryō no kane*" inscribed on the bell, meaning "the bell that bridges the world." Clinton stressed how the forging of the *bankoku shinryō* bell coincided with the "Golden Era" of the Shō Dynasty when "this land served as the crossroads for all trade that flowed through Asia." The American president also highlighted the 50th anniversary of Ryūkyū University, reminding the Okinawans that "the United States played a leading role in its creation; equally proud that so many young Okinawans studied in the United States through the Garioa and Fulbright programs."

Clinton concluded by quoting the last king of the Ryūkyū Kingdom, Shō Tai, who wrote a poem in 1879 urging his Ryūkyūan subjects to maintain hope. Quoting the King's poem in Uchināguchi, Clinton said "*Ikusa-yun sumachi, miruku-un yagate*. The time for wars is ending, the time for peace is not far away. Do not despair. Life itself is a treasure. May Shō Tai's words guide our friendship and our work in the months and years to come." While quoting King Shō Tai's poem seemed an innocuous act, the subtext was quite profound. In 1872, Meiji Japan conquered the Ryūkyū Kingdom and renamed it Ryūkyū *han*, unsure whether to make it a full-fledged prefecture of Japan. In 1877, Japan renamed the main island Okinawa and designated the Ryūkyūs Okinawa Prefecture to give the illusion that the islands were an integral part of Japan. King Shō Tai and his court, however, resisted by refusing Tokyo's orders to appear in front of the Meiji emperor. Feigning illness, he staved off Japanese demands for abdication until 1879 when the Meiji military forced their way into Shurijō and "persuaded" the king and his family to live in Tokyo as the emperor's guest. Prior to his departure, King Shō Tai wrote "*Ikusa-yun sumachi, miruku-un yagate*" under distress as the Ryūkyūs became the first victim of Japanese imperialism. By mentioning both the poem and the phrase *bankoku shinryō*, Clinton had simultaneously reified Okinawa's contemporary claim of being the true peaceful nation while offering a subtle reminder that much of Okinawa's suffering had resulted from its relationship with Japan.

The capstone of the summit, highlighting Okinawa's rich heritage, occurred at the G8 signature dinner at Shurijō, a plan that was made in Tokyo. Following the dinner, the assembled G8 leaders had their picture taken with Shurijō as the backdrop. The nighttime photo only served to emphasize the distinctive architecture of Shurijō and clearly conveyed Okinawa's distinct identity, culture, and history across the front pages of newspapers all over the world.[76]

While the prominent display of Shureimon on the ¥2000 note, President Clinton's historic speech at the Cornerstone of Peace, and the overall attention received from the G8 Summit provided positive coverage for Okinawa, UNESCO's November announcement capped the year in a dramatic way. UNESCO announced that nine historical sites of the former Ryūkyū Kingdom would be designated as UNESCO World Heritage Historical Sites. All located on the main island of Okinawa, five were former castle sites and the other four were in the Shuri/Naha region where the Ryūkyū Kingdom's royalty had resided.[77] Celebrations erupted throughout the island, in part because most had expected that only Shurijō would be selected, and no one had expected that UNESCO would designate nine locations as World Heritage sites.[78] The role of Obuchi's cabinet in lobbying for these designations was not widely known, and yet the timing of this announcement certainly capped a notable decade in which Okinawan culture and identity were paramount.

Conclusion

During the 27 years of the occupation, US efforts to create a Ryūkyū national identity failed, and in fact only served to increase Okinawan desires for reversion. Yet, Okinawan aspirations to be an integral part of Japan unraveled as the US military footprint on Okinawa remained unchanged, and their frustrations were increased by Tokyo's tacit collusion in maintaining the status quo. The 1995 rape incident turned latent discontent into a full-fledged, vocal antibase movement, which was also strikingly anti-Japanese. Embracing the politics of ethnic nationalism, Okinawans used their identity, heritage, and culture to create solidarity and also to point out how Japan's policies continued to discriminate against Okinawa. While many in Okinawa believed that *Uchinā to Ryūkyū kokoro* (the spirit of Uchinā) was a timeless and innate identity of the Ryūkyūs, this chapter shows the critical role US nation building efforts played in nurturing ethnic nationalism in Okinawa. While this effort failed during the occupation period, it can be argued that Ryūkyūanization provided the genesis of a contemporary Okinawan ethnic nationalism, with the unintended consequence of undermining the American military presence on Okinawa, challenging Japanese state authority, and fundamentally threatening the long-term stability of US-Japanese security arrangements. Historicizing Okinawa's postwar experience not only challenges the homogenizing narrative of postwar Japan but also serves as a powerful reminder that identity formation does not occur in a vacuum but rather is subject to the forces of historical contingencies.

6

Beyond the Black Market: Neighborhood Associations and Food Rationing in Postwar Japan

Katarzyna Cwiertka

Centralized control of local affairs has been one of the principal features of totalitarianism in Japan. The neighborhood association system was one of the devices by which such control was achieved and maintained during the war years. Today it continues as an important feature of Japanese life, retaining its principal wartime functions in respect to the distribution of commodities and the operation of the official rationing system.—John W. Masland, *Far Eastern Survey*, 1946[1]

Food shortage is a key factor in the history of the immediate postwar period.[2] It features as a backdrop in practically every monograph that deals with the second half of the 1940s, regardless of research focus. Few studies fail to mention this fundamental condition that affected political and economic strategies of the time, as well as left a lasting imprint on the social and cultural development of Japan. The quest for food was central to postwar life: from orderly lines at rationing points and meal coupon restaurants to rowdy food stalls at the black market (*yamiichi*) and crowded trains carrying city dwellers to the countryside to barter their belongings for food (*kaidashi*). In a variety of different forms, the 1940s' food shortage not only assumed a prominent place in the everyday practices of the time, but has also become engraved in the public memory of the decade.[3]

When describing the food-supply situation in urban Japan between 1945 and 1947, expressions such as "near-starvation," "on a verge of crisis," and "narrowly averting famine" are frequently used.[4] According to Chris Aldous, it is the clamor associated with the prospect of famine—rather than reliable statistics to sustain such predictions—that is responsible for leaving a historical impression of large-scale starvation among urban Japanese during the early years of the occupation.[5] Following the surrender, the Japanese authorities repeatedly issued warnings of mass starvation. One of the first, announced on 15 October 1945, predicted that 10 million Japanese might starve to death if food imports were not immediately forthcoming. Such announcements, along with understating crop yields and underestimating stocks of staple crops, were the strategies employed by the Japanese government to ensure sufficient flows of food aid. Warnings about impending famine, as Aldous explains, "shaded into declarations of actual starvation, with the imminence and scale of the problem perhaps escalating the rhetoric."[6] Although the actual food relief fell far short of the minimum amounts requested, the predicted disasters did not occur.

While mass starvation did not take place, hunger and malnutrition did prevail in the immediate postwar years, especially in the cities. Symptoms such as weight loss, anemia, chronic diarrhea, delayed menstruation, and stunting of children were recorded in nutritional surveys conducted by the Welfare Ministry between 1946 and 1948. Indications of nutritional deficiencies were already apparent in similar surveys that had been conducted by the ministry in the final years of the Asia-Pacific War (1937–45).[7] Between 1940 and 1946, the food supply in Japan deteriorated rapidly, with the most severe shortages experienced by the urban population. At the same time that food was becoming increasingly scarce, over six million Japanese were repatriated from the colonies and occupied territories during the first two years following the surrender—additional mouths to feed which had thus far relied on food resources produced outside of the four main islands.

A fair body of literature covers the 1940s' food crisis, largely from the macropolitical and economic perspective.[8] An exception is Owen Griffith's groundbreaking study of the black market, in which he depicts *yamiichi* and *kaidashi* as social practices that defined the times. At the beginning of his paper, he quotes a statement by Mishima Yukio, made 20 years after the war, that the black market was "one of the unmistakable points of origin for postwar peoples' history."[9] In this work, Griffith corrects a widely accepted misconception of the black market as the historical marker of "postwar." "It did not arise," he explains, "phoenix-like, from the ashes of defeat, but grew steadily into a compelling structure of daily life from the late 1930s to the late 1940s; . . . the black market was, in fact, a structure of continuity linking war and defeat as a single historical era."[10]

In a fashion similar to the black market assuming an iconic place in public memory as the foundation of postwar life, the food rationing system is customarily associated with the wartime era of state control, despite the fact that it continued to function practically undisturbed after 1945. This also happens, unconsciously or not, in the historical literature, which tends to discuss rationing in relation to the first half of the decade and the black market when dealing with the post-1945 development.[11] Delineation of the black market as the beginning of "postwar" and the state rationing system as a "wartime" phenomenon helps to sustain the myth of 1945 as a symbolic turning point in Japanese history, a moment "when the past ended and the present began," to borrow the words of Carol Gluck in her contribution to a volume the current collection aspires to complement.[12] In reality, as Gluck argues in the essay, the postwar could never be truly separated from the wartime, and the body of evidence that reveals intricate connections between the first and the second half of the 1940s has only become more convincing during the two decades since the publication of *Postwar Japan as History*. These continuities are particularly pronounced when one looks into trivial practices of the everyday, with food shortages in the forefront as a persistent indicator of the 1940s' continuities. With the exception of soldiers and civilians repatriated from the colonies and occupied territories, there was more continuity than change in the daily life of ordinary Japanese before and after 1945.

This chapter will illuminate the 1940s continuities by focusing on food rationing. From November 1940, when nationwide rationing of foodstuffs was introduced, to June 1952, when all but rice disappeared from the list of controlled commodities, the food rationing system played a critical role in the daily lives of urban dwellers. To be sure, the reliance on the rationing system diminished during the first years of the occupation. Estimates reveal that the per capita daily amount of calories provided by rationed food decreased from 1400–1600 kcal during 1943 and 1944, to 1000–1100 kcal in 1945 and 1946, reaching the lowest point of 577 kcal in 1947.[13] Nonetheless, rationing remained an important source of nutrition, fluctuating depending on the season. For example, approximately 10 kg of food (in brown rice equivalent) was rationed per month per person in Tokyo between December and March 1946, but the ration dropped below eight kg during May, June, and September. In April 1947, over 15 kg of rationed food was available, but the level dropped below eight kg again in June.[14]

Along with food rationing remaining the lifeline of survival in the midst of the mid-1940s' food shortage, there is another reason why it deserves our attention. Unlike black-market transactions and direct purchases of foodstuffs from farmers, which were illegal and usually conducted individually and in secrecy, delivery of rationed foodstuffs and the collection of staple food at rationing points were collective activities that engaged entire neighborhoods. Procedures to acquire rationed foodstuffs constituted the core of community life in the urban areas during the 1940s, a powerful force that shaped daily interaction between relatives, neighbors, acquaintances, and strangers.

The rationing system and *tonarigumi*

The promulgation of the Foodstuffs Control Law (Shokuryō Kanrihō) on 21 February 1942 was one of the key measures employed by the wartime government to deal with food shortages that worsened rapidly after the outbreak of the Pacific War. Sugar was the first item to enter the nationwide rationing system, effective on 1 November 1940.[15] It was soon followed by a wide range of other foodstuffs, from luxuries such as *sake*, confectioneries, and fruit to daily necessities like *miso* (soybean paste), fish, and vegetables. Before 1942, rationing was conducted on an individual basis, consumers collecting their rations at shops of their choice. There was a great degree of local variation in the range of foods that were being rationed, their allotted quantities, and procedures to acquire them. Rationing of perishable items such as seafood and vegetables remained uneven throughout the 1940s, depending on available local resources, dietary customs, and the organizational capacities of the authorities.[16]

A fairly uniform system of rationing under the direct control of the central government was created for staple food only. It was introduced in the six largest cities in April 1941 and extended nationwide the following year. The Foodstuffs Control Law established a comprehensive control over collection and distribution of staple food in Japan. Rice was designated as the main staple, but other cereals and foods processed from them, such as flour and noodles, as well as sweet and white potatoes, assumed an increasing prominence in the category of "staple food." In order to simplify the structure of trade by eliminating middlemen, the government facilitated a merger of the Japan Rice Company, the National Flour Distribution Company, the National Federation of Rice Merchants, the Japan Vermicelli Manufacturers' Federation, and the Japan Wheat Federation into a semipublic corporation that was named the Central Foodstuffs Management Corporation (Chūō Shokuryō Eidan). It functioned under the direct control of the Ministry of Agriculture and Forestry and its chief responsibilities were imports, exports, storage, and reserves. The distribution and sale of the staple rations was handled by the Regional Foodstuffs Management Corporations (Chihō Shokuryō Eidan), which were established in each prefecture through a merger of guilds of wholesalers of grain, flour, and noodles.[17]

From October 1942, the task of coordinating rationing of foodstuffs on the consumers' side was entrusted to *tonarigumi*, or "neighborhood associations." Composed of approximately ten households from each urban neighborhood, the associations functioned de facto as the lowest level of municipal administration.[18] Although set up with the original purpose of spiritual indoctrination within the framework of the Imperial Rule Assistance Association (Taisei Yokusankai), *tonarigumi* soon assumed a wide range of practical functions, such as certification of changes of address, collection of taxes, sale of war bonds, and dissemination of government propaganda. None of them, however, acquired such an important role as food distribution.

The wartime system of neighborhood associations (*tonarigumi*), block associations (*chōnaikai*), and hamlet councils (*burakukai*) emerged in September 1940, when Home Ministry Ordinance No. 17 called for the establishment of these organizations, making membership compulsory for each household. Only seven months after the ordinance was issued over a million neighborhood associations had been created.[19] By December

1942 the six largest cities—Tokyo, Yokohama, Nagoya, Osaka, Kobe, and Kyoto—counted together 282,677 neighborhood associations, each comprising approximately ten households. Tokyo counted 2,286 block associations (on the average comprised of 51 *tonarigumi*), Osaka 3,583 (on the average comprised of 18 *tonarigumi*), Nagoya 2,656 (on the average comprised of 10 *tonarigumi*), Kyoto 3,651 (on the average comprised of 7 *tonarigumi*), Kobe 1,418 (on the average comprised of 19 *tonarigumi*), and Yokohama 805 (on the average comprised of 26 *tonarigumi*).[20]

In theory, the three organizations derived from the *goningumi* ("five man bands"), a forced system of five families that was created in the seventeenth century by the Tokugawa administration for the purpose of nurturing corporate responsibility among its taxpaying (overwhelmingly rural) population.[21] The origin of the system itself went back to the ancient Chinese structure of *baojia* conceived with a similar goal in mind.[22] Despite the claim of common roots, only a few of the wartime neighborhood associations could be traced back further than the early twentieth century. Most of them sprang up after calamities such as the Russo-Japanese War (1904–05) or the Kantō Earthquake (1923) with the goal of self-help for the community. After 1936, municipal administrations supported the establishment of such associations, and the mobilization campaign of 1938 provided an additional boost.

There was a degree of rivalry between the Imperial Rule Assistance Association and the Home Ministry over the function of the neighborhood associations. The former saw them primarily as cells for political integration, while the latter envisaged them as small-scale local agencies that served administrative purposes.[23] The official involvement of *tonarigumi* and *chōnaikai* in food rationing from April 1942 not only marked the growing influence of the Home Ministry over the associations, but also set the stage for embedding them into local communities.[24]

Scholars have argued that involvement of *tonarigumi* in rationing was motivated chiefly by efficiency and convenience, and was part of a larger strategy of readjusting channels of distribution and consolidating units of consumption for the purpose of wartime mobilization.[25] As an increasing number of foodstuffs had to be collected from shops and distribution centers located at long distances from one another, and long hours of waiting in line were required to obtain them, delegating one or two members of a *tonarigumi* as full-time "food procurers," or issuing joint purchase permits for entire *tonarigumi*, seemed a logical solution to a logistical problem of wartime shortages.

Rationing as daily practice

The implementation of nationwide measures concerning food rationing remained diverse, depending on administrative capacities and available resources, as well as consumption practices of each locality. Generally speaking, staple food rations were collected at the distribution stations by individual families or jointly by a representative of the neighborhood association, usually its head (*kumichō*). Supplementary foods were distributed through private retail establishments, individually or collectively to the neighborhood associations, whose leaders were entrusted with the task of distributing them further.[26] For example, in the entry for 16 February 1942 in the wartime diary of Sakamoto Tane (1900–82), wife of a judge in the District Court of Kōchi in Shikoku, we find the following note: "Got up at six. Before seven Yamamoto *kaichō*[27] announced through the megaphone that celebratory *sake* would be rationed to rejoice in the fall of Singapore. I immediately got my share, together with other members of the neighborhood association."[28] In contrast, a detailed analysis of food rationing in Amagasaki, a middle-size town in Hyōgo prefecture, conducted on the basis of data in the local newspapers *Amagasakishi Kōhō* and *Shimin Jihō* reveals that supplementary foodstuffs were often rationed directly to individual households rather than through neighborhood associations (see Table 6.1 and Table 6.2).[29]

Accounts of rationing procedures in different locations suggest that they were by no means uniform, but rather differed from case to case. Regardless

TABLE 6.1 *Instances of supplementary food items rationed through neighborhood associations, Amagasaki, January 1943–May 1945*

Food Item	1943	1944	1945
Yakifu		once	
Kiriboshi daikon	once	once	
Tsukemono		once	
Matsutake	once		
Nori, konbu, kanten	3 times	3 times	
Chirimenjako, iriko, kezuribushi	6 times	1 times	
Salted fish	twice	4 times	
Surume (for New Year)	once		
Tsukudani, shiokara	twice		
Fruit wine			once
Canned food		once	

TABLE 6.2 *Instances of supplementary food items rationed to individuals/households, Amagasaki, January 1943–May 1945*

Food Item	1943	1944	1945
Eiyō mushipan flour	once		
Kanpan	once		
Tokubetsu senji pan	twice	4 times	
Noodles	once	once	
Sugar	6 times	6 times	
Beans	5 times	twice	
Soybeans	once		
Aburaage, tōfu	10 times	19 times	
Yuba (for pregnant women)	3 times	once	
Kiriboshi daikon (for pregnant women)	once		
Apple jam	twice		
Kazunoko (for New Year)	once		
Meat	once	once	
Eggs/dried eggs	9 times	3 times	
Vegetable oil	twice	twice	once
Namagashi	5 times	once	
Higashi (for infants)	6 times	4 times	once
Kashi		once	
Sake	4 times	4 times	twice

(*Continued*)

TABLE 6.2 (Continued)

Food Item	1943	1944	1945
Beer	3 times	3 times	once
Salt	once	once	
Vinegar		3 times	
Miso	once		
Sakekasu		once	
Ajinomoto	once		

of whether the rations were delivered to an individual household or not, however, the chances were small that the occasion would ever pass unnoticed by the neighbors. Over the years, the distribution of rations came to form the core of community life, regulating the pace of life of each neighborhood. We may presume that it also determined the menus cooked in the households belonging to the same neighborhood. This was contrary to black-market transactions and direct purchases of foodstuffs from farmers, which were illegal and not only had to be conducted in secrecy, but were also prepared and consumed away from the prodding gaze of the neighbors. Illegally acquired food tended to be boiled rather than broiled to keep the appetizing smell in the house.[30]

An excellent source for studying the central role that neighborhood associations assumed in the life of the community is *kairanban* ("circulating bulletin boards"). Usually made of a piece of wood or cardboard measuring approximately 40 × 25 cm, they served as a base to which posters, printed notices, or handwritten announcements were attached and then passed from one household to another. Each family would stamp the attached notice with their family seal (*hankō*) after reading the notice, and after circulating to all member households, the *kairanban* would be returned to the *kumichō*.[31]

Kairanban notices issued by the block association of Den'enchōfu district in Tokyo between December 1943 and November 1946 are an outstanding source for the study of the role of food-procuring activities—which included both distributing rations and managing vegetable gardens—in the life of a wartime *tonarigumi*. Out of 170 circulars issued by the Denenchōfu block association throughout 1944, more than half (91) contained information related to distribution of supplementary food, either in the form of regular food rationing (*haikyū*) or extra rations (*tokuhai*).[32] For example, a circular dated 28 February prohibited cooking of rice on the mornings of 29 February and 1 March, announced the issue of new rationing books for household goods and the rationing of *narazuke* to the whole neighborhood association; the circular of 8 March announced the rationing of *tōfu* and dried eggs, and the issuing of bread coupons; the circular of 11 May announced rationing of starch for infants and fruit for pregnant and nursing mothers, and the issuing of bread coupons; the circular dated 6 June announced the rationing of beer and informed members of the possibility of unexpected air defense training; the circular dated 4 July announced the rationing of dried *nori* and soy sauce, and included a notice related to air defense; the circular of 4 August announced the rationing of dried *shiitake*, *nori* and guard strips (*kanpyō*); the circular of 17 August announced rationing of *nattō* and included a notice on rice bag repairs; the circular issued on 11 September announced the arrival of special bread coupons, warned that the consumption of seafood was only allowed once in four days, and informed residents about shoe repairs; the circular of 11 October announced the rationing of *sake* and beef, and issued information on the annual festival at Hachiman shrine; and the circular dated 30 November announced the rationing of *konbu* for *tsukudani*, and a concert in which recorded music would be played (*onban ensō*).[33]

As food resources became increasingly scarce, food-related announcements became less pronounced in the circulars: only 29 out of 99 circulars issued by one block association in 1945 included food-related announcements, and 28 out of 133 circulars issued by the same block association in 1946 included food-related announcements. A striking feature of the food-rationing notices on the circulars issued after the surrender is a dominant presence of canned food, beer, and Western-style foods, most probably carryover stock from the Japanese military and donations by the occupying forces (see Table 6.3).

Along with the *kairanban* ritual, most urban families followed the following procedure for the procurement of rations, with possible local variations: the chief of each association (*kumichō*) gathered ration books, the money needed to pay for the items, and the *hankō* of his ten or so families and departed to the rationing points to collect the rations of the entire *tonarigumi*. Upon his return, he divided the rations and returned ration books and *hankō* to the families, though it was customary at some associations for *kumichō* to retain the ration books of all members. The procedure was repeated several times a week.[35]

Scholars such as Braibanti and Masland, who observed the rationing practices first hand as members of the administrative apparatus of SCAP, stress that the system opened the way to widespread maldistribution of civilian supplies.[36] It was not uncommon for the rations to be somehow "lost" during this complex process of collection and redistribution, and diverted to black market channels or otherwise removed from the official lines of distribution. Though most irregularities were difficult to prove, prosecution of mismanagement was not uncommon, before and after 1945. For example, records of the public prosecutor's office between 1941 and 1944 include a case of a *kumichō* in Osaka who "adjusted" ages in ration books

TABLE 6.3 *Rationed supplementary food items recorded on kairanban notices of Denenchōfu block association in Tokyo, 18 January–28 October 1946*[34]

Date	Food item
18 January	*Asakusa-nori*
25 January	New Year's *sake*
26 January	"nourishing vinegar" (*eiyōsu*) for repatriates
19 February	beer
9 March	canned food
14 March	margarine
22 March	fresh whale meat, flour for infants
28 March	beer
14 May	beer
21 May	starch for the sick
25 May	*konbu tsukudani*
31 May	butter for pregnant women
21 June	margarine
3 July	beer
2 August	"nourishing sauce" (*eiyō sōsu*) for repatriates
28 August	chocolate candy
5 September	imported canned food and dairy products, sake
12 September	*konbu tsukudani*
8 October	imported canned food for school children
28 October	*sake* for celebrating new constitution

to get higher rations, and a case of a wife of a *tonarigumi* head who kept 18 kg of rice obtained through ration books of a neighbor for herself. Other instances testify to such malpractices by heads of neighborhood associations as adding nonexisting persons to the ration books, favoring relatives and friends, and blackmail. Bribery and black market trade dominated in the latter half of the decade.[37]

A close look into informative materials for *tonarigumi* heads reveals plentiful opportunities for fraud that stemmed from the central position that the heads of block and neighborhood associations were assigned within the food rationing system. For example, in the case of Tokyo, rice ration books (*haikyū tsūchō*) were issued by the municipal office to household heads, but if the family decided to move out of the city, their ration book was to be handed over to the head of the block or neighborhood association. In theory, the ration book was supposed to be returned to the municipality which had issued it, but in practice, the *kumichō* could keep it for his own use. Similarly, the daily allotment for the entire household was entered in the ration book by the municipal office, but any corrections, such as deaths or births of household members, or changes in occupational classification (which had implications for the size of rations) were to be entered by the head of the block association. He was then required to forward the record of the specific changes to the local distributing station where the family was registered, so that the consumption card kept there for each household could be accordingly corrected. In the case of visitors staying with a family for longer than a month, the additional mouths to feed also had to be recorded in the ration book.[38] All these procedures could potentially be used by household heads to draw additional rations.

An interesting detail in the bureaucratic structure of the Japanese rationing system is a rather broad application of the concept of "household." For example, lodgers within the same building were treated as members of a single household, as were occupants of boarding houses and dormitories. The managers of these institutions acted as de facto household heads of rather large families, leaving plenty of room for "doctoring" rationing books.[39]

Mission impossible?

In the eyes of SCAP, *tonarigumi* were a "feudalistic. . .institution, by means of which the personal lives, activities and even the thoughts of the people of Japan were brought under the effective overall control of a mere handful of central government officials."[40] Still, they remained closely involved in food rationing for the remaining part of the decade. Even after 1 April 1947, when the occupying forces undertook persistent efforts to weaken the role of *tonarigumi* in the process of food distribution, altering the daily routines perpetuated for years proved close to impossible, and the established practices were carried on.

After the surrender, the Home Ministry continued to consider *tonarigumi* an essential part of local government; this status was not altered even by the amendments of local government laws in September 1946. Steiner reports that between August 1945 and May 1946 a single *chōnaikai* in Tokyo

FIGURE 6.1 *"US authorities inspect a food rationing facility, 1945." Reprinted with permission from the Mainichi Newspapers.*

received 512 instructions from the metropolitan and national government, and that the subsidies for all *chōnaikai* in Tokyo in 1946 amounted to more than six million yen.[41] SCAP tolerated neighborhood associations chiefly due to the essential role they fulfilled in the system of food distribution. The report "Food Situation during the First Year of Occupation" made it quite clear that "although the Japanese rationing machinery had certain undesirable and undemocratic characteristics, particularly in its reliance on monopolistic, quasi-governmental control companies, it was decided that the existing machinery should be retained intact in order to cope with the critical food shortage which was anticipated."[42] Extreme caution was exercised with regard to any organizational changes that might result in a deterioration of the food situation.[43]

The first steps toward altering the existing system, in the autumn of 1946, were taken at the initiative of the Government Section of SCAP, which was charged with the task of reforming local government, rather than by the Economic and Scientific Section that was entrusted, among other things, with keeping the food situation under control. These steps coincided with other reforms within the system of local government, such as the passage of the Local Autonomy Law (which prohibited the delegation of municipal duties to quasigovernmental bodies) and the first nationwide elections for prefectural governors, mayors, village heads, and local assembly representatives in April 1947.[44]

"The distribution of staple food rations will after 1 April be based on the convenience of the consumer instead of the government. No pressure or intimidation of any sort on any individual consumer to draw rations for neighbors will be tolerated."[45] These are the two final sentences of the press release issued on 21 March 1947 by the President of the Food Management Board on the subject of abolition of *tonarigumi* and staple food ration distribution. The first public statement had already been made a few days after the Cabinet Decree on the dissolution of neighborhood associations was issued two months earlier. On 22 January 1947, Home Ministry Instruction No. 4 rescinded Home Ministry Instruction No. 17 of 1940, relinquishing the ministry's control over them and turning all their functions over to the municipalities.[46] The decree would take effect on 1 April to provide enough time for implementation, stressing that the functioning of *tonarigumi* as organs of food distribution would thereafter end.[47]

At the beginning of the 21 March press release, the president of the Food Management Board offered an explanation for *tonarigumi* assuming a central position in the rationing system in the first place:

> During the war years there were many places where due to the acute shortage of labor the ration distribution had to be made on the basis of *Tonarigumi*, but the fact that *Tonarigumi* were used for the purpose of ration distribution was merely based on convenience. It never meant that the right of the consumer to receive rations was contingent on their membership in *Tonarigumi*.[48]

A few months earlier, in November 1946, prefectural governors received the first instructions from the Food Management Board of the Ministry of Agriculture and Forestry concerning the necessary steps to be taken in order to ensure that in the future the staple food rations would be distributed directly to individual households. The Board emphasized that consumers were to receive their rations without the necessity of belonging to any sort of compulsory membership organization. Additional instructions were issued to prefectural governors and to Directors in Chief of Food Distribution Corporation (Shokuryō Eidan) in each prefecture, on 4 January, 24 March and 9 April of 1947, suggesting measures such as expanding transportation facilities, increasing the number of staff and the number of rationing points, and the employment of "liaison men" who would be responsible for the delivery of information concerning ration distributions to individual households.[49]

In the letter of 4 January it was stressed that anyone, "regardless of whether member or not of *Tonarigumi*, is entitled to direct ration distribution. Officials of the Shokuryō-Eidan should be duly informed that they have no right to refuse rations to anyone on the ground that he or she is not a member of a *Tonarigumi*."[50] In a letter dated 24 March 1947—a week before the abolition of *tonarigumi* took effect—the President of the Food Management Board alerted prefectural governors and heads of Shokuryō Eidan that distribution of staple food rations should be made directly to individual households, and that an individual is legitimately entitled "to direct ration distribution at the rationing point during office hours. A consumer may go to a rationing point on *any* day after the ration is available to get the ration and it is *not* necessary for him to go on the expected date of distribution."[51]

One more press release was issued to the public on 28 March, with the following six points specified:

1   Each individual is entitled to the direct and individual distribution of staple food rations.

2   To ensure the afore-mentioned right of the consumer, Eidan should do everything possible to effect direct ration distribution to the individual households.

3   In case the meager stock does not make it possible to do so, an advance notice must be given promptly and without fail to the individual consumers regarding the expected date when the ration is ready for distribution. The advance notice shall be posted in front of rationing points, or delivered orally, or both. In order to ensure the effectiveness of the advance notice, the rationing points should employ special messengers charged with the delivery of the notice to individual households.

4   Individual consumers are entitled to direct ration distribution at any time during the office hours at the rationing points after the date when the ration is announced to be ready for distribution.

5   It is not forbidden for consumers to pool in a voluntary and friendly way their ration cards for the purpose of receiving ration distribution. If the inhabitants in an appropriate area form a group by their own wishes in order to receive their rations, it is not forbidden, provided that it is strictly informed and voluntary. The right of the consumers to receive rations should never be made contingent on membership in such a group. It should be entirely free for the individuals whether to or not to join it.

6   For the convenience of consumers, rationing points are taking positive steps to increase the number of rationing points as well as their personnel.[52]

In addition to this correspondence, the Food Management Board organized three conferences on the topic. On 31 March and 10 May, over a hundred Directors of Food Distribution Corporations of each prefecture were invited to Tokyo, and on 8 May, they were joined by chiefs of Prefectural Food Sections. At the last meeting, the President of the Food Management Board stressed that despite repeated instructions to enforce the direct distribution of staple food rations to individual households—thus with no involvement of *tonarigumi*—"the progress so far made in this regard is still unsatisfactory."[53]

He set up 1 June as the absolute deadline for implementing the new policy, which should have gone into effect already on 1 April.

A standard reaction to the legal dissolution of *tonarigumi* was changing the name into allegedly voluntary organizations, such as "rationing associations" (*haikyūgumi*) or "cooperative living guilds" (*seikatsu kyōdō kumiai*), while continuing as usual under the same leadership.[54] The Government Section of SCAP saw a danger of *tonarigumi* continuing their existence in disguise, and believed that the participation of any organization, voluntary or not, was an undesirable interference in the rationing process. A deadline of 1 June was set for the dissolution of *haikyūgumi* and the establishment of additional distribution points.[55]

The views of SCAP were translated into a Cabinet Order issued on 3 May, which specified that a variety of new organizations, into which *tonarigumi* had evolved after 1 April, were to be dissolved by 31 May. The decree stressed that all functions thus far performed by *burakukai*, *chōnaikai*, and *tonarigumi* would, as of 1 June, be entirely taken over by offices of government administration. Moreover, the heads of the block associations who held office continuously from before 1 September 1945 to 1 September 1946 were to be prohibited for the period of four years to hold municipal offices that had similar functions in the same city, ward, town, or village. The decree further specified that the former heads of block and neighborhood associations were prohibited from issuing orders to their former subordinates, on penalty of jail sentences of up to a year or a fine of up to ¥15,000. The same penalties were reserved for individuals involved in rationing who demanded from consumers proof of membership in any organization as a condition for issuing rations. On top of that, they would be fired and prohibited from public employment for a period of 10 years.[56]

The content of the new decree reflects very well the impediments encountered in the process of dissolution of *tonarigumi*, but it proved rather ineffective. Two months later, little progress seems to have been achieved, as the old patterns persisted.[57] For example, increasing the number of rationing points was considered to be a prerequisite for the success of the operation, but by 1 June, their number had increased by less than 10 percent (from 16,880 to 18,520), which was far below the set goals.[58] From yet another letter, dated 26 January 1949 and written by the Director-General of the Food Management Bureau, it is quite evident that two years later, dissolution of *tonarigumi* was still far from completed.

> In accordance with the purport of the provisions of Cabinet Order No. 13 of 5 May 1947, subject: "Cabinet order concerning the dissolution, exclusion, or exhibition against organizations, offices, and other matters relating to *Chonaikai*, *Burakukai* or Federations thereof and others," instructions have been given repeatedly from the time of Food Distribution Eidan onward so as not to distribute the staple food through *Tonarigumi* or other organizations corresponding thereto. Notwithstanding these

instructions, food distribution through *Tonarigumi* is still prevailing. In this respect, a warning has recently been given to us by the General Headquarters. In connection with this, you are requested to supervise fully the work done by the agencies at the lowest level so as to strictly prevent food distribution through *Tonarigumi* from now on.[59]

The Central Foodstuffs Management Corporation was dissolved in February 1946, but its local branches, commonly known under the name Shokuryō Eidan, remained responsible for food rationing in each prefecture for two more years.[60] As of 1 January 1948, a public corporation with the name Staple Food Kōdan (Shokuryō Haikyū Kōdan) took responsibility for storage, transport, processing, and distribution of staple food to consumers. For SCAP, the major advantage of the shift from Shokuryō Eidan to Shokuryō Haikyū Kōdan was the fact that as wholly government-owned and uniform organizations, the latter were easier to control than the semigovernmental fragmented Shokuryō Eidan, which had grown from the amalgamation of organizations involved in trade and processing of rice and wheat (see section 2). Moreover, this administrative transformation was closely related to the efforts toward dissolution of *tonarigumi* undertaken at the beginning of 1947.

Discussions in favor of the Staple Food Kōdan replacing the existing Shokuryō Eidan began among the SCAP staff in June 1947. However, actions in this direction were postponed to November when the 1947 rice crop would be available, since it seemed "inadvisable to attempt to make changes in the staple food distribution machinery in the middle of the period of acute ration curtailment."[61] The situation in the summer of 1947 was particularly difficult because the rice supplies were practically exhausted, so that imported grain and highly perishable white and sweet potatoes constituted a large proportion of staple food rations. In the deficit areas, distribution was made at frequent and irregular intervals as supplies were received, which made the situation far from ideal for any institutional or procedural changes. For example, in June 1947, Eidan stock in Tokyo was equal to only a three-day supply, only 1/3 of the minimum requirement.[62]

According to the Food Management Board, the personnel of Shokuryō Eidan strongly opposed the idea of transformation into a government corporation. "The Eidan was formed by merging former rice merchants into a single organization, so a majority of the members are former small food dealers who are interested in going back into business on a free basis as soon as the food situation permits. They look upon the establishment of a Government Kōdan and their becoming government employees as jeopardizing their opportunity to return to food distribution on a private basis in the future."[63] SCAP pursued the original plans for a governmental body for staple food rationing, primarily with the ultimate goal of dissolution of *tonarigumi* in mind. The life span of the Shokuryō Haikyū Kōdan indeed proved rather short. It was dissolved as of 1 April 1951 and rice merchants were gradually able to reemerge as part of the urban landscape.[64]

Conclusion

Operational provisioning of the troops and supply of food for the home front are absolutely essential for the functioning of a war machine. Food assumes strategic significance not only due to its basic purpose of strengthening the troops and enabling the productivity of workers, but also due to its potential effect on the morale of the population. Hunger can undermine people's trust in their government and may cause a serious threat to public order.

The implementation of measures to deal with the deteriorating food situation remained a central concern in 1940s' Japan, and in particular after 1945 when the crisis had reached the most severe magnitude. The pivotal position of food policies was stressed by Steven Fuchs in his analysis of the occupation: "from 1945 to 1947, SCAP's economic policy *was* its food policy" (emphasis added).[65] Whether by reducing consumption by occupation personnel, sponsoring land reclamation and land reform, establishing incentive programs, strengthening the collection and distribution systems, or enhancing enforcement measures, SCAP's number one priority was feeding the Japanese. Food had an importance beyond its nutritional value: satiating the peoples' hunger was critical for ensuring democratization, stabilizing the economy, and overcoming the distorted images created by wartime propaganda.[66]

The decision to allow the wartime rationing system to continue operation practically undisturbed for over a year, including the central role that *tonarigumi* played in it, attests to the pragmatism of the men in charge of the occupation. Insistence on dissolution of *tonarigumi* is an interesting example of how this pragmatic orientation of the early days gave way to the ideological agenda of the Government Section.

A series of measures implemented after 1947 aimed at dissolution of *tonarigumi* did not seem to bring about the desired results. Neighborhood associations continued to function, "often with the aid of municipal subsidies of doubtful legality."[67] Their enduring quality derived from the intricate connection with the channels of food rationing, which remained critical for survival. Until the end of the decade, when the food supply situation stabilized, getting enough food on the table remained the chief worry of most urbanites. While in principle the abolition of *tonarigumi* was welcomed by many and the impetus for opposition against the ban came from a comparatively small number of people,[68] divorcing neighborhood associations from the food rationing system was a mission doomed to fail. By then, the practices related to food rationing had become engraved in the community life of urban Japan, a stable element in rather unstable times.

Brought together by the genius of conscription society with the aim of tackling the problem of economic mobilization and popular resistance to mass war,[69] by the mid-1940s, the relationship between *tonarigumi* and the food rationing system became mutually constitutive. With tasks such as air raid defense and disseminating wartime propaganda removed from their responsibilities after the surrender, and the food supply situation steadily deteriorating, procuring food became *tonarigumi's* chief mission. Food shortages were the most important argument for its post-1945 continuation and only when most foodstuffs entered the free market could this legacy of the wartime system begin to fade away.

The ordinance prohibiting the neighborhood associations became void on 24 October 1952, when Law No. 18 of April 1952, which kept ordinances of the occupation in force for 180 days, expired. While reversing policies instituted during the occupation once an autonomous government was again in power was by no means unusual, no steps have ever been taken toward the reestablishment of the *tonarigumi* system.[70]

7

Political Representation for Nurses in Postwar Japan

Sally A. Hastings

In the 2009 election for the lower house of the Japanese legislature, Abe Toshiko, vice president of the Japanese Nursing Association (JNA), won a second term. Abe's electoral victory occurred under adverse circumstances. Her political party, the Liberal Democratic Party (LDP), lost badly; its share of the seats fell from 300 to 119.[1] As one of the "Koizumi Children," Abe was particularly vulnerable. The fledgling politicians whom Prime Minister Koizumi recruited into the LDP in 2005 as "assassins" to punish party members who opposed his privatization of the postal system were not well integrated into the party.[2] Abe's success in 2009 was the result of the strong support she enjoyed from her party, which placed her so high on the proportional list that she won a seat and remained in politics, despite having lost the race in her district.

Abe is the latest of several women who have held seats in the national legislature with the formal support of the JNA. The political activities of nurses complicate our understanding of Japanese women and their place in politics. Japanese politics has remained a predominantly male space and women's activities have been presumed to emanate from the home rather than from the workplace. With few exceptions, scholarly attention to women in politics has focused on the feminist movement, with the presumption that women's political activities are part of broader movements to reform or even topple the status quo. The JNA presents the spectacle of never-married career women inserting themselves into the political scene and allying themselves with the conservative LDP. Although the nursing profession in Japan as elsewhere has constituted relatively low paid work performed almost exclusively by women subordinate to male physicians, the leadership of the nurses' association has conceptualized themselves as worthy of political representation.

This chapter shows how professionally organized Japanese nurses
secured political representation in the national legislature and used it
to defend both their economic well-being and their professional status.
Their political involvement was facilitated by the national constituency
of the upper house: one hundred seats elected from the nation at large,
a structure that allowed organizations with large memberships to propel
candidates into office. Further, the working conditions of nurses in Japan
made political representation useful. Finally, this chapter will show
that the alliance between the JNA and the LDP has persisted precisely
because, despite major changes in the electoral system and the educational
attainments of women, women remain disadvantaged in the Japanese
workforce and under-represented in Japanese politics. Nurses continue
to need political representation and the LDP continues to need women
representatives.

Historiography of invisibility

Although nurses have participated in the Japanese work force in significant
numbers—over a million in 2006—throughout the postwar era, they have
been largely absent from English-language histories of postwar Japanese
women, labor, and society.[3] Nurses are a poor fit with the dominant
paradigms of women as housewives, women workers as short-term or part-
time, and women's politics as feminist or maternal. The centrality of the
urban middle-class housewife to scholarly research on Japanese women
was foreshadowed by Ezra Vogel's study on Japan's new middle class, but
the emergence of the housewife in the 1980s as the stereotypical Japanese
woman was the product of new scholars and new scholarship.[4] When in
the 1980s women became an appropriate subject of academic scholarship,
American women from a number of disciplines investigated Japanese women
and their homes. These studies rescued Japanese women from their status
as feudal remnants and showed that the sexual division of labor in Japanese
middle-class families empowered women by giving them autonomy within
the home.[5]

The workforce participation of Japanese women is widely acknowledged,
but scholars stress the structural factors that encourage a woman to work
full-time until marriage or childbirth and then return to the work force part-
time until she is required to care for elderly parents-in-laws. Government
emphasis on women's obligations in the home, tax laws that allowed wives to
earn a certain amount tax free and heavily penalized any additional income,
and company policies that mandated retirement at marriage discouraged
women from full-time employment.[6] Although court decisions outlawed
forced early retirement and the Equal Employment Opportunity Law of
1985 opened up career-track positions to women, the majority of women
remained in low-wage jobs with little security.[7]

Career nurses do not conform to this pattern of discontinuous employment. The specific training for the nursing profession implies a commitment to long-term work. The prewar Red Cross required nurses to work 15 years to repay their education.[8] Thus, nurse's training was associated with long-term employment, economic need, and lower class status. Moreover, care work in East Asia has generally been devalued and lowly paid.[9] Nursing was not, like office work, employment that women from middle-class families might undertake as preparation for marriage. One informant of anthropologist Takie Lebra welcomed the economic autonomy nursing afforded her in 1945, the family home reduced to ashes. Another informant faced resistance from her high-ranking samurai family when she chose to train as a nurse.[10]

In contrast to office workers in large companies, nurses have had the option of staying on the job, but the rigidity of job requirements has forced them to choose between career and marriage. Dorothy Robins-Mowry mentions a cohort of Japanese women trained at American universities through the Fulbright program who left the nursing profession because their employers inflexibly insisted on a full work load even after women were wives and mothers.[11] One of Takie Lebra's informants was a single woman who enjoyed a fulfilling career as a nurse, well aware that marriage would have prevented her accepting the transfers that had advanced her career.[12] As wage earners supporting themselves and their families, nurses had every reason to organize to protect their employment conditions.

Nurses have remained as obscure in medical, political, and institutional histories of postwar Japan as in women's history. Studies of healthcare focus on physicians rather than the women who care for patients on a daily basis. Ruth Campbell points out that information on hospitals, where most nurses work, has been hard to come by; many hospitals are small facilities, owned by a founding physician.[13] Nursing homes, which employ nurses, have been better studied, but often with a focus on care workers rather than on nurses. Nurse legislators have been irrelevant to discussions of women's exclusion from politics. Issues of class have distanced foreign ethnographers from nurses and contributed to the low profile of nurses in the women's movement.

Finally, nursing has sparked no interest as a peculiarly Japanese practice. American nurses working in Japan during the occupation deplored the low wages of Japanese nurses, the time they spent on cleaning and janitorial duties, their self-conceptualization as attendants of doctors rather than of patients, and their subordination to men. The appointment of a woman, Hayashi Shio, as chief of nursing education for the Japanese Red Cross was hailed as a milestone.[14] Although in the mid-1950s rural patients were sufficiently poor as to merit comment, an American nurse noted that Japanese urban medical centers "are not so vastly different from any modern public health agency in any country."[15] The struggles of nurses in the workplace attracted attention only when they were focused on peculiarly Japanese issues such as pay for menstrual leave.[16]

Women's suffrage and the nursing profession

The JNA dates its representation in the national legislature to 1959 and the founding of the Japan Nursing Federation as a political lobbying organization, and Hayashi Shio, who won a seat in the upper house in 1962, was the first woman the association elected to the Diet.[17] In fact, nurses and midwives entered politics as soon as Japanese women were able to vote and hold office in 1946. This section examines postwar elections with emphasis on two cases of election to the upper house, Inoue Natsue, president of the JNA, in 1947, and Yokoyama Fuku, president of the Midwives' Association, in 1953.

Women in the health professions were integral to Japan's twentieth-century imperial project. Japanese efforts to enhance the physical and intellectual qualities of the population incidentally created institutionalized ways in which women could earn an independent living while exercising feminine functions in the public realm. Often counties and villages paid the cost of midwife training programs, making the education free to the recipients.[18] Teaching and nursing were two other possible routes to financial independence. In 1890, the Japan Red Cross, an organization patronized by the imperial family and thus closely tied to state aims, initiated a three-year training program for nurses.[19] A number of accounts suggest that midwifery offered an optimal combination of independence, flexibility, and financial stability.[20] Midwives took pride in their contribution to the modern Japanese state and organized as a profession. Prefectural associations of midwives, the first of which was founded in Kyoto in 1875, had close ties with the bureaucracy. In 1927, the Japan Midwives Association (Nihon sanbakai) linked the widespread prefectural organizations into a national federation.

In the lower house election of 10 April 1946, the first in which Japanese women could vote and run for office, work experience outside the home was a common characteristic of the 39 women who took office. Their ranks included a midwife, physicians, a dentist, teachers, professors, and school principals.[21] Tanaka Tatsu, head of the Tottori Midwives Association, won a seat, although Shibahara Urako, an activist midwife, failed in Osaka.[22] Midwives claimed special expertise on women's bodies and, in contrast to physicians, dentists, and teachers who were in professions dominated by men, had the advantage of performing indisputably gender appropriate work.

Because the state regulated their professions, nurses and midwives were strongly motivated to secure a voice in government, especially right after the war when the American military occupiers were intent on reorganizing the medical professions in Japan and raising the level of training. The Americans found that nursing as they understood it was not a recognized profession in Japan. Although formal nurses' training was available through the Japanese Red Cross, St. Luke's Hospital in Tokyo, and a few institutions related to Christian missions, many of the women designated as nurses were merely attendants to the doctors or even cleaning women.[23] As one American complained, "[T]housands have had no formal training but have merely read a manual or two and attended a few hygiene classes."[24]

In November 1946, the American occupiers disbanded the existing government-controlled associations of women medical workers and established a new professional organization with officers elected by the membership. Initially known as the "Japan Midwives, Clinical Nurses and Public Health Nurses Association," the new organization incorporated three types of medical workers all encompassed by the American concept of "nurse" but expressed in Japanese by three separate words representing separate histories. "Clinical Nurse" referred to a wide range of hospital nurses (*kangofu*), from graduates of British and American institutions to cleaning women. The public health nurses (*hokenfu*) were graduates of a government training program. The midwives had the longest history of formal training and licensure.

Formally trained Japanese nurses welcomed the official recognition of their credentials and became the first officers of the new association. The first president was Inoue Natsue (1898–1980), a graduate of Tsuda College and the Bedford Women's Public Health School of London University.[25] Inoue's experience living in London stood her in good stead as she forged close ties with Major Grace Alt, head of the Nursing Affairs Division, and Virginia M. Ohlsen, who succeeded Alt in April 1949.[26]

A firm link between the JNA and the political world was established in April 1947 when the president, Inoue Natsue, won a seat in the national constituency of the newly created upper house of the national legislature. In the election of 1947, 100 of the 250 seats in the upper house were elected from the nation at large; those who finished in the top 50 won a six-year term; those who finished in the second 50 won three-year terms. Candidates who already had national reputations enjoyed an electoral advantage. As president of the JNA, Inoue had a status that commanded respect and a recognizably female name, an advantage when voters were eager for change. Moreover, her candidacy resonated with hopes that the upper house might represent professional or functional groups.[27] She won a six-year term and the opportunity to articulate the professional interests of nurses and midwives. Inoue contributed to the 1948 national legislation that provided for the education, examination, and qualification of public health nurses, midwives, nurses, and practical nurses.[28] In May 1949, when revisions to the Eugenic Protection Law increased access to abortion and thus reduced the projected number of live births, she asked for government funds to retrain midwives whose employment opportunities would thus be reduced.[29]

The election of Yokoyama Fuku to the upper house in 1953 reflected the strong sense of community among midwives and their concern about the status of their profession. The American reforms threatened the midwives, challenging their preeminence as experts on childbirth. In 1947, midwives attended 92.1 percent of births, in contrast to physicians who attended only 3.5 percent. The 1948 legislation, however, brought all clinics, including birthing clinics, under the supervision of physicians.[30] Further, the Americans regarded midwifery as a postgraduate specialty of nursing. Consequently, the educational standard mandated by the 1948 law required that midwives complete a three-year nursing degree before commencing midwife training, greatly increasing the time and expense required to qualify as a practitioner.[31]

Yokoyama Fuku ran for the Diet as a champion of midwives, well aware of the many changes military occupation had brought to their work. She said, "I was brought up as a midwife and I have lived as a midwife."[32] Born in 1907 in Tokyo, she referred to herself as an Edokko (child of Tokyo), a person with origins in the old commoner section of the capital.[33] As a young woman in professional training, her mentors were the leading midwives of Tokyo, for instance, Ichikawa Ishi, president of the Midwives Association when it was founded in 1927.[34] Following in the footsteps of her mentors, Yokoyama took office in the postwar JNA by 1949, becoming a vice president in 1950. At the same time, she was executive secretary for the Midwives' Section, becoming its head in 1951.[35] Leadership in the JNA made Yokoyama nationally known. As vice president of the JNA, she had high visibility at the annual meeting and she occasionally attended regional meetings, for instance, the Tokai and Hokuriku branch meetings in November 1950 and the Yamaguchi City one in January 1951.[36] Once she became head of the Midwives Section, she ventured into the prefectures yet more often.

Leadership in the JNA also allowed Yokoyama to reach into the homes of midwives and nurses through two official publications. Yokoyama wrote occasionally for *Kango*, the monthly magazine of the JNA. She was a major contributor, however, to *Hoken to josan*, the publication for public health nurses and midwives. Her comments on the weather or season gave a personal touch to the columns. Noting the deaths of prominent members of the association and celebrating the pioneers of the profession, Yokoyama cultivated a sense of community among midwives. For instance, she reported on the eightieth birthday celebration held 18 November 1951, for Tsuge Ai, a founder of both the Tokyo and the national midwives' associations.[37] The sense of community among midwives extended to the entire nation when Yokoyama reported in great detail on districts hit by natural disasters.

For all her chattiness and personal compassion, however, Yokoyama's writings never strayed far from the political. For her, the rupture in modern Japanese history was the American Occupation rather than the outbreak of war and she was openly critical of the Allied occupation. In April 1952, as Japan was about to recover its independence, she wrote, "After the war various changes were inflicted on our national ways and some of these were not appropriate to our national conditions. I think that it goes without saying that many of the changes inflicted on our system of midwifery do not suit the conditions of the Japanese people."[38] Professionally educated in an era of reverence for the imperial institution, she welcomed the installation of the Crown Prince in November 1952. She was glad to see national flags flying in doorways, lantern parades, and crowds pushing in the square in front of the imperial palace. Despite her strong attachment to Japan as it once was, Yokoyama took note of international women's activities within Japan. She denied learning anything new from Margaret Sanger's 1952 appearances at the Japan Medical Association (JMA) on 4 November and at Mainichi Hall on 7 November. She took the occasion, however, to reflect on how both Japan and midwifery had changed since Sanger's 1922 visit. However much she might grumble about the American presence in Japan, Yokoyama still noted the 23 October welcome party for Virginia Ohlsen, formerly of GHQ, back in Japan as an employee of the Rockefeller Foundation.[39]

Yokoyama had no patience with those who merely grumbled about postwar changes in midwifery. "The distress of midwives has become a commonplace. When midwives meet each other, the first words out of their mouths are on this subject. But complaints are the words of the defeated. They are the words of people who will stop progress."[40] She issued a call to action, urging Japanese midwives to work together at their annual meeting, scheduled for 20 April 1952, to discuss policies to address the root causes of their problems and to cooperate in carrying those policies out.

By the time she ran for office in 1953, Yokoyama had already acquired political experience. In the special election of 20 September 1947, necessitated when part of Tokyo's Itabashi Ward broke off to establish Nerima Ward, she won a seat in the Itabashi Ward Assembly.[41] She ran unsuccessfully for the upper house in 1950, finishing 65th (the top 50 candidates won seats) with a respectable 104,752 votes.[42] In that event, she had at least some support from her fellow midwives, for Yokoyama recalled receiving flowers from her mentor Ichikawa Ishi.[43] During the election campaign in the fall of 1952, Yokoyama and the other employees of the section headquarters worked on the loudspeaker trucks of candidates who supported the interests of midwives so that, should they be elected, the midwives could call upon them for further assistance. The issues Yokoyama was particularly concerned about were birth control and income taxes.[44]

Yokoyama won her first electoral victory on 24 April 1953 in the third election for seats in the upper house of Japan's parliament. The prominent *Asahi* newspaper described her as a mother of four who had first opened her midwifery practice in 1932. Her campaign slogans, "Protect Motherhood" and "Prevent War," addressed the concerns of many women in postwar Japan.[45] Yokoyama ran, however, not simply as a mother but explicitly as a midwife with special expertise on motherhood. In her official listing as a candidate, she identified herself as the head of the midwives section of the JNA. The May issue of *Hoken to josan*, the official publication of the midwives section, announced her candidacy and an editorial in June celebrated her electoral victory.[46] She ran without party affiliation in 1953, but she soon aligned herself with the Liberal Party.[47] When the Liberal Party participated in the formation of the LDP in 1955, she automatically became a member of the party which, with a minor break in 1993, dominated Japanese politics until 2009. In 1957, she was head of the Tokyo Women's Section of the party.[48]

As a legislator, Yokoyama evoked for the public health nurses and midwives who read *Hoken to josan* the sights and sounds of a legislator's life: car horns in the streets and the footsteps and voices of petitioners in the corridors of the Diet building. Her activities for 13 to 30 November 1953 provide us with a glimpse of her life as a legislator.[49] On 13 November, she skipped the social hour that followed a meeting of midwives in the Matsudo area in Chiba in order to be back at the Diet building for the opening of a social work conference. Two days later she was in Toyokawa for a training course for the Aiichi prefecture midwives. On the sixteenth she went to Odawara, where a childbirth center was under construction, thanks to cooperation between a united midwives' association and the local authorities. On 18 November, she left the Tokyo area as a member of the Diet Welfare Committee to go to the Northeast, which had suffered cold weather damage. In Akita, she accepted a petition opposing any change in the nursing law. On the 22nd, she went to a women's meeting and a midwives meeting, on the 23rd to the Iwate midwives meeting in Morioka, and on the 25th to the Miyagi midwives meeting in Sendai. Back in Tokyo on the 25th, she attended the opening ceremonies for the Tokyo Midwives National Health Insurance Union. The next day she set out in the opposite direction, to view flood damage in Kyushu. Because, however, the Diet was to convene on 30 November, she cut short her visit to Kumamoto to return to Tokyo. Leaving Sasebo at 2:20 a.m., she arrived in Tokyo in time for the 2:00 opening of the Diet. These 12 strenuous days of travel demonstrate how Yokoyama's life as a leader of midwives was thoroughly entwined with her activities as a Diet member.

During Yokoyama's first few months as an elected legislator, changes in the JNA prompted her departure from the organization. In the same election in which Yokoyama won office, Inoue Natsue, the president of the JNA, lost her seat, leaving Yokoyama as the only high-ranking member of the JNA in the legislature. At the JNA annual meeting, Hayashi Shio became president in Inoue's stead. When Inoue returned from the International Nursing Conference, her report that the Japanese midwives, because they were not trained as nurses, were not eligible for full membership in the International Nursing Association prompted Yokoyama and the majority of the midwives to leave the JNA and set up their own independent organization.

The stories of Inoue and Yokoyama show how the suitability of nursing as women's work, the prominence of the nursing profession, and the structure of the nursing organization could project a nurse or a midwife into the national legislature. Their political fortunes, however, did not leave the JNA with effective representation. By the end of 1953, Inoue was no longer a Diet member. Yokoyama had a Diet seat, but she was no longer a member of the JNA.

Galvanized into political action

The members of the JNA were galvanized into political action in 1956, when the JMA sought to revise the 1948 nursing law so as to reduce the qualifications and thus the prestige of nurses. Sentiment had been growing among physicians that the qualifications for nurses were too high. Acting through a Diet member whose election it had supported, the JMA drew up legislation without any consultation with the nurses. In response, the JNA held an emergency meeting of the board of directors in October. When the JMA failed to respond to its strong request for the withdrawal of the proposal, the JNA issued a formal statement from President Hayashi Shio.[50] Hayashi complained that the physicians had acted without consultation and asserted that lowering the educational standards for nurses would have an adverse effect on society. She ended by proclaiming that 300,000 public health workers, midwives, and nurses opposed the JMA proposal.[51] Although Hayashi did not say so, the JMA represented a far smaller number of professionals, roughly 70,000.[52] Soon, cries of "Absolutely oppose weakening the nursing system!" and "Do not submit to the Japan Medical Association's feudal system!" were raised across the country.[53] In their quest for support, the nurses even called on the prime minister's wife. In the end, the proposed legislation did not pass. One other governmental matter that irked the leadership of the JNA in the mid-1950s was the decision to abolish the Nursing Section of the Welfare Ministry effective April 1956.[54]

The proposed revision of the nursing law and other legal battles prompted the JNA to secure its own representation in the Diet. In October 1958, the board of directors (rijikai) of the JNA formally resolved to support its current president Hayashi Shio as a candidate for the upper house in the next election.[55] Hayashi's educational qualifications and professional experience made her an attractive candidate to represent the nursing profession. Her education at the Osaka Red Cross Hospital Nurses' Training School was among the best available in Japan at the time. Born in 1904, Hayashi entered Red Cross training before women's higher school became a requirement for admission. After three years of work as a nurse, however, she was among a small number of Red Cross nurses selected in 1928 to enroll at Tsuda College in order to acquire foreign language skills that would make them better representatives of Japan in the international community. Upon graduation in 1932, she continued working for the Red Cross, with a brief interruption

to serve on a hospital ship in the late 1930s. In June 1949, she went to
the United States for a year of study at Emory University.[56] As president of
the JNA from 1953 to 1959, she faced formidable challenges such as the
departure of the majority of the midwives from the nursing association and
the construction of a new headquarters building after a disastrous fire.

When she announced her candidacy for the 2 June 1959 upper house
elections, Hayashi presented herself as a single woman with over 30 years
of service to the sick and the weak. She proudly claimed the backing of
300,000 public health workers, midwives, and nurses who cared for the
sick, pregnant women, the handicapped, and the mentally weak and she
promised to make Japan a welfare (*fukushi*) state.[57] In 1959, Hayashi was
not without rivals as a care-giver candidate. Yokoyama Fuku, the head of the
midwives' association, won reelection. Inoue Natsue, the former president
of the JNA and former Diet member also stood for election, although with
even less success than Hayashi, who, in spite of strong support from the
association, failed to win a seat.

The JNA responded to Hayashi's electoral defeat by establishing a
political federation (*seiji renmei*). At the annual meeting in Nagoya on 16
June, a mere two weeks after the election, Yumaki Masa, the newly elected
president of the JNA, said, "Let's stop thinking emotionally about the
cause of our past defeat and with this feeling resolve to set up a supporting
political organization." The six-member ad hoc committee set up to establish
a political league included one representative from each of the three sections
of the association (public health workers, midwives, and nurses).[58] On 14
October, the board of directors ratified the work of the ad hoc committee
and named Hayashi Shio as chair of the federation. The JNA provided start-
up funds of a hundred thousand yen and an office on the fifth floor of its
building.[59] The founding meeting of the federation took place in April 1960
immediately following the JNA annual general meeting.[60]

The JMA, which spurred the nurses of Japan to enter the political
arena, also provided models for political organization. The Japan Doctors'
Federation was formally established in 1952 "to engage in political
activities necessary for the achievement of the goals of the Japan Medical
Association." For both the physicians and the nurses, the formation of a
political federation skirted the potential legal problem of having a "public
interest juristic person," the category into which the JMA and the JNA fit,
engage in political activities.[61]

Securing political representation

Despite some internal dissension, the JNA proceeded with its plans for the
1962 upper house election. At the annual meeting in Shizuoka on 12–14
May 1961, the members restored Hayashi Shio to the presidency. Outgoing
President Yumaki reported the recommendation of the Board of Directors

that the association nominate Hayashi Shio as its only candidate for the upper house. The measure passed with few dissenting votes.[62] The choice of the JNA to endorse only one candidate stands in contrast to the policy of the JMA, which in 1959 endorsed 47 candidates.[63]

In the 1962 election, Hayashi continued to position herself as a representative of 300,000 public health workers, midwives, and nurses and she promised to improve their treatment and raise their status. Widening her appeal, she vowed to protect the rights of all working women to marriage, childbirth, and access to a greater number of day-care facilities. These pledges, combined with her promise to foster the health of housewives and protect mothers' bodies, made her a candidate for all women. She asserted that as a nurse who protected the bodies of all citizens (*kokumin*), she was absolutely opposed to war. She promised to protect the spirit of the constitution and to construct a welfare state.[64]

During the campaign period, when Hayashi, wearing a two-piece dress, a hat, and gloves, was out making speeches from the requisite loudspeaker car, the headquarters of the JNA was transformed into a billboard on Hayashi's behalf. Beneath the permanent sign identifying the building were two horizontal white banners. One read "Nurses' Voices to the Diet" and the other "Politics on Behalf of Women and Children." At the entrance to the building, a small vertical sign bore Hayashi's name.[65] A paid advertisement for Hayashi appeared in the *Asahi shinbun* for 7 June 1962. As election day approached, Hayashi's candidacy drew press attention. The *Asahi shinbun* paired her with Yamataka Shigeri of the National Association of Regional Women's Clubs as an independent candidate appealing to women voters and thus likely to win a seat.[66] In fact, Hayashi finished with a considerably higher vote total than Yamataka. *Kango*, the official journal of the JNA, celebrated Hayashi's victory. Photographs showed Hayashi, goal achieved, painting the eye of a daruma and the members of the association and the office staff, arms raised as they cried "*banzai.*"[67] Having run as an independent, Hayashi maintained her autonomy from political parties as a Diet member, affiliating with the "Independents Club." In her first year as a legislator, she served on the Social Labor Committee and the Preliminary Budget Committee.[68]

Institutionalizing representation

Encouraged by Hayashi's electoral success, the JNA resolved at its annual meeting in Tokyo in April 1964 to support a candidate in the upper house election in 1965.[69] Because members of the upper house serve staggered six-year terms, the members of the JNA could reasonably expect that a successful candidate in the 1965 election would run for re-election in 1971 and would thus not compete with Hayashi, whose term would end in 1968. It was not until an emergency general meeting on 5 December 1964 that the association chose Ishimoto Shigeru as the candidate for 1965.

Like Hayashi, Ishimoto was a never-married Red Cross Nurse. Born in 1913, she graduated from women's higher school in Ishikawa Prefecture and then from the Japan Red Cross Social Nursing program in 1934. Three years later, she was drafted into military service, serving a full nine years before her discharge in late 1946. As a civilian, she worked in a number of national hospitals. From 1958, she was the chair of the nursing section of the JNA.[70]

The JNA's 1965 electoral efforts were successful—Ishimoto won a seat, but as the last candidate on the national list to qualify for election, she won only a three-year term. The JNA held appropriate celebrations, but the celebrants no doubt recognized the looming problem, that both Hayashi and Ishimoto would come up for reelection in 1968. At the Board of Directors' meeting of 1 May 1967, decisions about nominations for the upper house election were deferred to the general meeting of the political federation.[71] In August 1967, Hayashi joined the ruling LDP.[72] Ishimoto remained an independent. On 9 September the nurses' political federation endorsed Ishimoto as its only candidate.[73]

The 1968 election revealed the difficulties a professional organization faced in navigating parliamentary politics. Hayashi and Ishimoto ran against each other, the former with support from the LDP and the latter with the backing of the JNA. Neither won. The community of nurses proved more influential than the political party, for Ishimoto did better than Hayashi. Building on that symbolic victory, the nurses began their preparations for the 1971 election early. At the annual meeting in April 1969, the JNA and the political league resolved to support Ishimoto as their only candidate in the next upper house election.[74]

In 1971, Ishimoto won a solid victory with JNA support and LDP endorsement; she placed 37th to win a full six-year term. Ishimoto's success was at the expense of at least two women candidates with medical expertise, Yamamoto Sugi (a physician) and Yokoyama Fuku, both of whom won seats in 1959 when Hayashi Shio lost. To be sure, when Yokoyama came up for reelection, she was running as a midwife with a shrinking constituency against a nurse in a growing profession. The midwives had turned their professional organization into a political instrument in 1953; the nurses lagged considerably behind. By 1971, however, a glance at the election statements shows that the nurses had surpassed the midwives not only in numbers of members and numbers of votes but also in the effectiveness of their campaign materials. Whereas Yokoyama's statement was a solid block of fine print, Ishimoto's statement displayed her name prominently and highlighted the central points of her argument in easy-to-read headlines. Hayashi Shio's political career was short, but her quest for the JNA to become an effective political force was fulfilled.

Ishimoto's electoral success stabilized the political representation of the JNA. In the 1977 and 1983 elections, she ran with the advantage of incumbency. She won further prominence when she was appointed as

Minister of the Environment in the second Nakasone cabinet in 1984.[75] By 1989, when Ishimoto retired from the Diet at the age of 76, the political system had changed. From the 1983 election, the national constituency was transformed into a system of proportional representation. No longer could a large national organization use the strength of numbers to elect its own representative. Nurses continued to enjoy political representation under this new system, in part because of the seniority Ishimoto had earned. To be sure, political parties were well aware that large national organizations could contribute to political party strength.

In establishing direct political representation for their profession, the nurses were engaged in activities parallel to those of doctors and dentists, whose political connections have been documented by Gerald Curtis and William Steslicke, and to those of midwives, who elected their own representative in 1953. The interests of nurses did not always coincide with those of doctors and midwives, and the JNA had to maintain a delicate balance among fellow medical workers and national bureaucrats in order to advance their own interests. At the same time, as the *Asahi* noted in 1962, the JNA operated at first like Ichikawa Fusae's League of Women Voters or like the women's organizations that supported other prominent women such as Oku Mumeo and Yamataka Shigeri as candidates for the national constituency. When the JNA abandoned its independent status to throw in its lot with the LDP, it broke ranks with other women's organizations. As a member of the ruling party, Ishimoto was tapped for cabinet office, only the third woman ever to become a cabinet member. Her successors in the Diet, Shimizu Kayoko, and Nōno Chieko, have likewise held cabinet positions.

Nurses and politics in Heisei Japan

In the era of economic uncertainty that began in 1989, the first year of the Heisei emperor's reign, Japanese nurses have continued to enjoy political representation, as their profession has expanded steadily.[76] Despite an increase in numbers every year, there remains a nursing shortage as Japan anticipates increased medical care for its aging population. In the 1989 upper house elections, Shimizu Kayoko was the successful candidate of the JNA. Born in Tokyo in 1935, Shimizu studied nursing at Tokyo University before entering the Welfare Ministry.[77] As a legislator, she continued the close alliance between the JNA and the LDP. She took office in October 1999 as Director-General of the Environment Ministry in the cabinet of Prime Minister Obuchi Keizō. In 1992, Shimizu was joined in the upper house by a second nurse, Nōno Chieko. Born in Manchuria in 1935, Nōno was educated in midwifery in Osaka. She worked as a nurse for 30 years before entering politics. She won re-election in 1998 and 2004 and served as Justice Minister in the first Koizumi cabinet in 2001. As a legislator, she was instrumental in the passage of the Law for the Prevention of Spousal

Violence and Protection of Victims.[78] Shimizu retired in 2007 in keeping
with party age limitations. Nōno Chieko, who was born the same year as
Shimizu, did not serve past 2010.

The JNA has also established a foothold in the lower house. Nose
Kazuko won a seat in 1996 and 2003. Because she voted against Prime
Minister Koizumi's postal reform, Nose lost her affiliation with the Liberal
Democratic Party and opted not to run in 2005. Although Nose lost out,
the JNA did not, for this was the same election in which Abe Toshiko, a
vice-president of the JNA, first won a seat.

Conclusion

This examination of the nursing profession in Japan and its long-standing
political representation shows that nurses have exercised agency to secure
political representation, not to reform society but rather to secure their
professional privileges within the existing order. Nurses, who function as
the "housewives" of hospitals, have not attracted public notice, because
their work appears gender-appropriate and attracts no interest as a
peculiarly Japanese institution.[79] The political activities of the care workers
who fall within the Japanese category of "nurse" highlight a number of
fissures in the body politic that are obscured by the term "nurse" as well
as by the even more problematic category "woman." The insistence of the
American occupiers on "nurse" as the overarching category inclusive of
midwives and public health workers has still not erased the differences
among the three groups amalgamated into one national organization.
Further, the strong alliance between both the midwives and the nurses
with the LDP highlights the lack of congruence between the politics of
women and leftist politics. The midwife Yokoyama was willing to use the
enfranchisement of women to advance the interests of midwives, but she
strongly supported the Japan of her youth rather than the reform agenda
of the occupiers. The differences in work history between Hayashi Shio
and Ishimoto Shigeru draw attention to class divisions among nurses
and women more generally. Hayashi Shio, with her broader education,
positioned herself as a representative of all women, a feminine yet expert
voice in the male political space. Ishimoto, who never attended college
or spent extensive time in the United States, is emblematic of the alliance
of low-paid health workers with power in pursuit of their own economic
well-being.

The alliance of the JNA and the LDP has persisted despite major political,
legal, and social changes. The system of election to the one hundred at-
large seats in the upper house that allowed midwives and nurses to convert
numbers of members, official publications, and professional solidarity into
political power changed in the 1980s to one of proportional election in
which parties slate the list of representatives. The number of women in

political office has increased dramatically since 1989. Because of legal changes in the interests of gender equity, nursing is no longer an exclusively female profession. Other factors, however, have remained constant. Nurses continue to be crucial to the delivery of health care, an activity in which the Japanese government is deeply involved. Women are still a novelty in politics, particularly conservative politics. One component of the long-lasting alliance has been the usefulness of the JNA as a reliable source of respectable women to include as cabinet members in the LDP's public presentation of itself as a party friendly to women. Cabinet appointments become more likely when politicians have a certain degree of seniority. The JNA has facilitated not only the entry of women into politics but also their advancement and retention there.

8

Japan's other Forgotten Soldiers[1]

Tetsuya Fujiwara

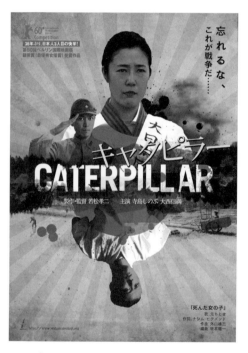

FIGURE 8.1 *Promotional poster from the motion picture film Caterpillar. Copyright Wakamatsu Production. Reproduced with permission.*

In a distant land, the Sino-Japanese front of the Asia-Pacific War draws to a shameful end. Kurokawa Kenzō hopelessly contemplates his son Kyuzō's living but war-ravaged body. Limbless, nearly voiceless, his face terribly burned, Kyuzō has been discharged as a highly decorated lieutenant from the army and sent home to his stunned Japanese family. With no idea of what to do with what is left of Kyuzō, his father and sister parade Kyuzō's decorations before Shigeko, Kyuzō's wife. "Look how highly our Emperor has honored Kyuzō! For the sake of our country, we beg you, please take care of him." The immobilizing sight of Kyuzō's disfigurement leaves Shigeko no alternative but to declare at a patriotic town meeting, "I am Kurokawa Kyuzō's wife. I solemnly swear to carry out my patriotic duty to him as a war god's wife."

Caterpillar (2010) vividly portrays the story of a Japanese couple on the home front in the Asia-Pacific War. Publicly, Kyuzō is manipulated as a "war god" in Japanese press propaganda and is almost forcefully revered by the villagers. Privately, however, the demands of his care, including his constant desire for sex, generate intense emotional undercurrents between Kyuzō and Shigeko.

Prior to his service, Kyuzō brutally mistreated Shigeko because of her infertility. However, after his discharge and return home, the balance of power between the two tips in quite the other direction. Shigeko takes full advantage of her new-found public respect as a dutiful war god's wife, and behind the closed rice paper doors of home, she exploits Kyuzō's loss of speech by verbally taunting him with her revelations of her mixed feelings about both her war god and his war.

This intensely private depiction of war enjoyed worldwide acclaim as evidenced by the receipt of the Silver Bear for Best Actress at the 60th Berlin International Film Festival by Terajima Shinobu, who plays the role of Shigeko. Terajima has explained the reason why Caterpillar achieved international fame by saying, "[Director] Wakamatsu, who experienced the war, portrays war not simply as the killing of others on the battlefield but as a tragedy actually occurring in family homes. I guess that appeals to people around the world."[2]

The popularity of *Caterpillar* rests principally on not only a meticulous portrayal of wartime Japanese people but also on a sense of crisis over the fading memory of war's brutality. Those who experienced the Asia-Pacific War are vanishing, and with them vanish any remnants of war's visible or invisible scars in the souls of younger generations. *Caterpillar's* successful capturing of those miseries of war that are difficult for young viewers to imagine is difficult to either ignore or forget. The movie's director, Wakamatsu Kōji, expresses his objective along these lines:

> In this movie, I was intent on depicting war as it is and what the human destruction of war truly means. Moreover, I wanted to achieve these goals by presenting the people of war not solely in action-packed battle scenes . . . [With this movie,] I hope to infuse young, war-innocent people with war's horrible immediacy. I want this presence to say to them, "Please don't forget such a horrifying war, and please don't destroy others' lives even for your country. In any way you can, please run from being a victimizer." In truth, all that I am has gone into this movie.[3]

Certainly, the visual imagery of *Caterpillar* is so intensely self-evident and compelling that the viewer hardly has room to question war's misery. However, once seen through historical eyes *Caterpillar* confronts its viewers with another important underlying theme: war's business of manufacturing disabilities. The very sight of war-ravaged Kyuzō provides us with a wrenchingly different perspective on disabled persons. Indeed, the social presence of disabled soldiers is easily, perhaps adaptively, forgotten. Although disabled persons tend to be marginalized or isolated from the rest of society, the movie communicates how one disabled soldier was honorably treated and paid considerable attention in the context of a wartime effort. This anonymity-heroism gap astutely illustrates that our mental images of disability are painted upon sociohistorical canvases.

This chapter represents a merging of two vital Japanese war veteran issues: their social welfare and their memories of war. Historiographies of the Allied occupation of Japan and war memories in the postwar period provide the conceptual cornerstones of the work. John W. Dower, in *Embracing Defeat* (1999), strives to understand the perspectives and emotions of the defeated Japanese in the aftermath of war as they sought to redefine their identity and values. *Inside GHQ* (2002) by Takemae Eiji provides a comprehensive picture of the Allied occupation of Japan. Takemae examines the welfare reform for disabled persons from the viewpoints of both the occupiers and the Japanese bureaucrats. He does not, however, specifically differentiate disabled or wounded soldiers from the general disabled population. Lori Watt, in her *When Empire Comes Home* (2009), delves into experiences of the repatriates who had returned to Japan from its former imperial colonies after the war. Watt pays specific scholarly attention to the readjustment of the repatriates into postwar Japanese society. Thus, a substantial number of disabled ex-soldiers, being merged with the more general category of war veterans, are left beyond the reach of analysis.

Recently, a broad growing concern has stirred scholarly efforts with regard to the Asia-Pacific War's impacts on the memories and social welfare of Japanese war veterans. Yoshikuni Igarashi, in his *Bodies of Memory* (2000), employs the imagery of human bodies as portrayed in Japanese popular culture in the 1950s and 1960s to examine how war memories lingered among the Japanese during the period of their country's recovery from the defeat of the war. In one instance in his work, panhandling disabled veterans become the target of police who crack down on them for the sanitation of public spaces.

James Orr, in his *The Victim as Hero* (2001), provides a historical analysis of how Japanese war memories were molded in the postwar decades into a victim consciousness which yet tends to neglect Japanese wartime aggressions in Asian countries. Orr focuses on various aspects of the Japanese sense of victimization, one of which is the Japanese government's compensation of groups of war victims such as the bereaved families of war dead and atomic bomb survivors. Yet, the exclusion of disabled war veterans as a group of war victims once again leaves them beyond the reach of historical analysis. Franziska Seraphim, in *War Memory and Social Politics in Japan, 1945–2005* (2006) traces the shaping of Japan's social political discourse by public memory of the Asia-Pacific War. Examining five prominent civic organizations, Seraphim argues that the organizations played leading roles in shaping the social political war memory of postwar Japan. Yet, in selecting organizations for study, Seraphim bypasses disabled war veterans as a collectively significantly influential social force. As observed above, then, in English sources, historical scholarship of the Allied occupation of Japan and Japanese war memories has largely been unable to reach beyond convention far enough to embrace within its analyses the welfare of disabled war veterans and their postwar lives.

Previous Japanese language researchers, too, have largely bypassed examining the lives of disabled war veterans in Japan during the postwar period. A few notable researchers, however, have accorded these forgotten warriors some well-deserved attention. Yamada Akira does distinguish between the general population's disabled citizens and disabled war veterans in describing how the movement initiated by veterans illustrates a significant postwar pioneering activity of Japanese disabled populations.[4] Murakami Kimiko analyzes the treatment of disabled veterans in the formulating process of the Law of Welfare for Handicapped Persons of 1949 (*Shintai Shōgaisha Fukushi-hō*).[5] Ueno Masumi added an examination of the conditions of "white gown beggars" in the context of postwar Japanese society.[6] Still, the activities of Japanese disabled war veterans during the postoccupation period have yet to be investigated to an extent that truly honors these broken patriots.

Specifically, this chapter addresses initial efforts of war veterans and activities of the Japan Disabled Veterans Association (JDVA: Nippon Shōi Gunjin-kai) during the postoccupation period. Formed on 16 November 1952, the JDVA played a pivotal role in organizing the disabled veterans' movement to attain their political goals. Among their primary targets was the right of those obligated to military service to be compensated for this service through the receipt of a military pension. In particular, they drew a distinction between pensions provided to disabled veterans and those providing general welfare. The Act on Relief for War Victims and Survivors (*Senső Byōsha Senbotsusha Izokutō Engo-hō*) of 1952 indicated an increasingly favorable climate for veteran initiatives, and the JDVA aimed to put pressure on the government to establish preferential provisions for disabled war veterans and their families. Taking this period into consideration within a broader historical context, I will argue that the achievement of numerous goals contributed to the restoration of honor to disabled war veterans immediately following the end of the Pacific War.

Japanese disabled war veterans during the occupation period

One sees examples on city streets and on trains of disabled veterans soliciting money. One also sees organizing activity in the formation of local patients associations and organizations that are nationwide in scope such as The National Hospital Patients League. The appearance of these organizations is open to various interpretations. But the case of the white gown beggars (who are not necessarily hospitalized patients) reveals a moment of individual despondency. While the organizational activity reveals the despair and resentments of patients over government policy.... Viewed together they are twin responses to the objective situation produced by [the failure of] social policy in the postwar period.[7]

In his essay titled, "*Shōisha wa sukuwareruka*? (Can Disabled Veterans Be Saved?)" Imamura Yuzuru, an official of the Ministry of Health and Welfare (MHW), called attention to two characteristics attributable to disabled war veterans during the Allied occupation period (1945–52). Imamura's remarks refer to policies initiated by both the Allied Forces and the Japanese government that drove them to begging on the streets and trains as well as the activism of patients' groups in the national hospitals. He concluded that it was virtually impossible for disabled veterans to provide for their most basic needs. And without protective policies, the disabled were left to rely on relatives who may or may not have been capable and willing to support them. Thus, disabled veterans were caught between the harsh economic realities of Japan following surrender and the Allied occupation which obstructed the development of policies specifically addressing the needs of disabled veterans.

Allied occupation policy doubtless imposed tough living conditions on veterans.[8] The restriction or prohibition of granting preferential treatment during the occupation years stripped disabled veterans of what privileges they had enjoyed prior to 1945 and forced many of them to fight for survival. Following surrender, two principal objectives of the Allied countries, democratization and demilitarization, decisively affected the status of Japanese disabled veterans. Under the Allied mission, the Public Health and Welfare Section (PHW) of General Headquarters (GHQ) formulated a new framework for disability policy in cooperation with officials of the MHW that forbade the privileged treatment of veterans, a policy that extended to disabled veterans but without consideration of their obvious special needs.

GHQ successively ordered the abolition of preferential treatment for all former Japanese military personnel as part of the demilitarization effort from late 1945 to early 1946. On 24 November 1945, "SCAPIN 338: the Memorandum on Pensions and Benefits" announced that all military pensions would be suspended.[9] Following the GHQ order, on 1 February 1946 military pensions were terminated except in the case of severely injured ex-servicemen.[10] The suspension of these benefits resulted in a critical loss of support that affected an estimated 5.7 million ex-military pension recipients.[11] Then, SCAPIN 775, titled "Public Assistance" and issued on 27 February 1946, marked one of the watershed moments in public welfare policy with major consequences for the treatment of disabled veterans and their families.[12] It declared three new principles of public assistance: (1) operational responsibility of the state, (2) no discrimination or preferential treatment in provisions of public assistance, and (3) no limitations on the amount of aid furnished. In fact, the nondiscriminatory clause was primarily intended to terminate the legal status and privileges of war veterans, their families, and the families of deceased soldiers.[13] Rather than a special population classified by their service to the country, disabled veterans henceforth were to be treated simply as disabled persons. Citing SCAPIN 775, GHQ and PHW subsequently intervened when they suspected that Japanese policy makers might violate the tenet of fairness by making special provisions for disabled war veterans.

As an alternative to preferential assistance to disabled veterans, the Japanese government adopted more inclusive welfare policies that provided relatively equal assistance to veterans and nonveterans. The essential concern of GHQ and PHW was whether the MHW's proposals violated the nondiscriminatory principle outlined in SCAPIN 775. In response to concerns over its implementation, on 9 September 1946, the Diet passed the Public Assistance Act (*Seikatsu Hogo-hō*). Nevertheless, the initiative did not adequately provide for the livelihood of disabled veterans and their families. The main beneficiaries of the law were the families of deceased soldiers, including widows and their children. Furthermore, the payments under the act failed to properly support families faced with soaring commodity prices. In addition, the enactment of the Law of Welfare for Handicapped Persons of 1949 did not necessarily meet the demands of disabled veterans. The MHW assumed that welfare laws would cover the majority of disabled persons including veterans. But due to the limited benefits offered and restrictive provisions, disabled veterans did not gain substantially from the new laws. Although veterans expected respect and adequate welfare measures, few benefited owing to the language of the legislation.

Such barriers to access to public assistance led some disabled veterans to resort to activities such as patients' associations at national hospitals to secure their livelihoods. In response to the dire situation in the spring of 1946, local patients' associations began to form in the national hospitals among disabled veterans who capitalized on GHQ's democratization policies to protest. Patients' associations at the hospitals initially aimed to expand and improve local self-help programs for the rehabilitation of patients. However, shortages were so pervasive that hospitals even lacked sufficient fuel to meet their energy needs. These shortages increasingly limited the medical services provided, which denied even the possibility of providing adequate treatment for patients. Thus, the movement became increasingly politicized and took positions strongly critical of both GHQ and the Japanese government.[14] In March 1947, patients at national hospitals organized the National Hospital Patients League (Zenkoku Kokuritsu Byōin Kanja Dōmei), prompting GHQ and Japanese authorities to keep a watchful eye on increasing communist sympathies among patients.[15]

Toward the end of the occupation, GHQ discreetly allowed the Japanese government to address the needs of veterans as well as civilian war victims. During this latter phase, the burgeoning cold war, including the outbreak of the Korean War, transformed the initially democratic reform agenda of GHQ into the so-called reverse course, which prioritized Japan's economic and political stability. In addition, the holding of the San Francisco Peace Conference in September 1951 gave the Japanese responsibility for postoccupation policy. Hence, measures for disabled war veterans and war victims were altered in tune with Japan's international relations and the restoration of Japan's sovereignty.

In 1951, frustrations with the failure of government policies led to protests in Tokyo. Even as the restoration of Japan's sovereignty approached, assistance to disabled veterans showed little sign of improvement. On 25 June 1951, more than 200 disabled veteran protesters marched from Sukiya Bridge to the office of the prime minister. Participants in the demonstrations, including veterans who had been blinded and/or lost limbs, were surrounded by a number of armed police officers, which further invited the attention of passing citizens.[16] On 13 October 1951, about 80 hospitalized patients, mostly from the Sagamihara National Hospital, presented a written petition to the prime minister and the MHW. The petition called for the abolition of prioritized military pensions for former high ranking soldiers and the forced discharge of veterans from national hospitals. When they did not receive a satisfactory response, six inpatients resolved to go on a hunger strike in Sukiya Bridge Park near the Imperial Palace.[17]

During the occupation years, GHQ monitored organizations associated with prewar and wartime militarism and oppressively restricted veterans' activities. While the Japan War-Bereaved Association (Nihon Izokukai) was permitted to organize under the government's guidance on 17 November 1947, the League of Revival of Military Pension (Gunjin Onkyū Fukkatsukisei Renmei) and the JDVA were eventually established in July and October, 1952, respectively.[18]

Birth of the Japan Disabled Veterans Association

The end of the Allied occupation allowed Japanese war veterans to associate freely for the first time since 1945. By mid-1952, local disabled veterans became increasingly organized. On 15 August 1952, a group of disabled veterans in Yamanashi prefecture formed the first prefecture-wide organization, which gave an impetus to nation-wide organizing efforts by disabled veterans. Tanaka Teruo, an executive officer of the Yamanashi Branch, issued the call to create a nationwide body for disabled veterans. The verterans' associations in Ishikawa, Kōchi, and Yamaguchi prefectures immediately responded to Tanaka's appeal. In response to requests from disabled veterans, on 10 September 1952, the MHW announced a preparatory meeting of the Japan Physically Disabled Persons' League (Nihon Shintai Shōgaisha Renmei), which presumably had intended to integrate their initiative to create a national organization of disabled veterans into the comprehensive organization for disabled people.

However, the first preliminary meeting of the Japan Physically Disabled Persons' League at the head office of the Japan Red Cross in Tokyo faced an unexpected event. To disabled veterans, the creation of the league was different from what they originally envisioned. When Fuji Tatsumi, a delegate from Chiba prefecture, delivered the opening speech, a representative from Yamanashi prefecture suddenly circulated a manifesto calling for the creation of an independent disabled veterans group. Confusion ensued, leading to a temporary halt in the proceedings. However, the participants eventually agreed to hold what would become a preliminary meeting of the JDVA. By taking direct action, disabled veterans asserted their will to establish an autonomous domain for securing their rights and honor.

On 11 September, representatives from 22 prefectural associations discussed their objectives at the first preliminary meeting of the JDVA. Their prime concern was how the newly created organization would treat the reintroduction of military pensions in their political agenda. As a consequence, they reached three resolutions: (1) revival of military pensions for veterans between the ranks of seven-degree *kōshō* and seven-degree *kanshō*, (2) pegging pensions to the price index, and (3) formation of a national organization for disabled veterans. They also resolved to petition for immediate implementation of military pensions at the meeting of the Council for Special Provision of the Pension Law on 19 September.[19]

With approximately 350 disabled veterans from 37 prefectures to celebrate its birth, the JDVA held its first national convention on 16 November in the auditorium of Nagata elementary school in Chiyoda ward, Tokyo. Nomura Kichisaburo,[20] the newly elected JDVA president, opened the first meeting with the following declaration:

> In beginning Japan's reconstruction after seven years of the Allied occupation, the government should immediately compensate war victims in the name of the state. Bearing numerous burdens and enduring financial difficulties, we disabled veterans and army civilian employees have been waiting for this day since the end of the war. The current

provision of assistance to all war victims including disabled veterans does
not provide compensation for what we have endured in the past seven
years. Now we hold the first convention with the hope of achieving this
original goal, and contributing to the reconstruction of an independent
Japan and world peace. Be it so resolved by the Japan Disabled Veterans
Association![21]

The JDVA leaders asked that the members serve as role models for their
fellow Japanese citizens. Kaba Atsushi, the first chairman of the JDVA,
emphasized that disabled veterans should demonstrate their will and capacity
to contribute to society.[22] The JDVA encouraged them to nurture the idea
of patriotism as well as to respect foreign countries. The members were
also required to work hard for the good of society. Cultivation of religious
faith was endorsed as a path toward self-reflection. They pointed out the
importance of absorbing knowledge from the world to understand Japan's
place.[23] Instead of appealing for sympathy, they presented their disabilities
as a source of strength in reconstructing postwar Japan.

The JDVA's political agendas revealed the gap between the harsh
realities of disabled veterans and the inadequate provision for their needs
in the postoccupation period. The resolutions introduced at the first JDVA
convention urged recovery of the prewar perquisites of disabled veterans:
revival of military pensions, preferential treatment in using the national
railways, preferential quotas in employment for disabled ex-servicemen,
free medical care in case of recurrence of sickness, and exemptions from
national and local taxes. The organization also requested the enactment of
independent legislation for disabled veterans. In addition, it demanded the
resolution of long-standing war issues such as the return of the confiscated
property of the Great Nippon Disabled Veterans Association, immediate
release of war criminals, repatriation of Japanese detainees abroad, and the
problem of white gown veterans.[24]

The momentum generated by the first convention inspired disabled
veterans to hold a rally at Hibiya Park on the following day. The spectacle
of the JDVA members, including men with crutches and single-armed men,
caught the attention of people walking around the park. Despite inclusion
of welfare support for white gown beggars in the resolution, white gown
beggars' sudden intrusion onto the stage while the committee members
were lining up called attention to conflicts between JDVA members and the
beggars.[25]

After the convention concluded, the members organized groups
of petitioners to hand over the adopted resolutions to five concerned
government ministries including the MHW and the Pension Bureau, as well
as the prime minister's official residence. Then, they returned to the Upper
House hall to give reports on their contacts with the ministries. The meeting
concluded with a chorus of three loud cheers.[26] In response to the JDVA's

communiqué, the MHW recognized the JDVA as the official association for Japanese disabled veterans. At the same time, the MHW urged the JDVA to work together with other disabled persons' organizations:

> It is expected that disabled veterans' organizations will be formed in every prefecture. We earnestly ask you to pay special attention so that formation of these organizations will not interfere with other organizations of disabled persons, but, rather, contribute to mutually promoting the welfare of all physically handicapped persons including disabled ex-servicemen.[27]

Thus, the MHW acknowledged that the JDVA would play the leading role in promoting the welfare of disabled veterans, while it also considered their relations with the larger community of disabled persons.

The Revival of the military pension

The passage of the Act on Relief of War Victims and Survivors in April 1952 gave impetus to the reintroduction of military pensions. In fact, the Japanese government deliberately waited for the opportunity to reintroduce the military pension. By the end of the Allied occupation, the government already recognized that ex-soldiers including disabled veterans were a group that required special protection and welfare, since the Public Assistance Act was too comprehensive to cover needy ex-soldiers and their families. Instead, the comprehensive compensatory law aimed to cover a wide range of war victims, from widows and their families to disabled veterans. Although the law was premised on the reintroduction of the military pension, it was put on hold pending legislation to receive payment of military pensions for budgetary reasons.[28]

With the creation of the Council for Special Provision of the Pension Law (Onkyū-hō Tokurei Shingikai) on 20 May 1952, the Japanese government sought to find a way to revive military pensions.[29] Meanwhile, on 20 June, the government decided to extend the suspension of military pensions while thorough deliberations occurred in the Council until 31 March 1953.[30] The Council for Special Provision of the Pension Law subsequently aimed to replace the old pension scheme by drafting new legislation to redress disparities among pension beneficiaries. In reality, the gap between civil servants and military personnel widened during the occupation period. While the military pension was suspended, civil servants continued to receive a pension. Moreover, commissioned officers received more benefits and favorable conditions than noncommissioned officers.[31] Considering the postwar financial constraints on governmental spending and favorable public opinion toward ex-soldiers, the Council focused on three points: prioritizing of recipients, method of payment (regular payment or one-time payment), and payment of a supplement for overseas service.[32]

On 22 November 1952, the Council finally submitted draft legislation on the reintroduction of military pensions to the Yoshida Shigeru Cabinet. While recognizing the necessity of military pensions, the proposal also stressed the need for numerous modifications of the pre-1945 military pension system. The Council explained the main rationale for the proposed legislation:

> After many years of public service, they become older, or suffer from sickness and wounds, or die, and in the end, lose the means of earning their own living. The payment and savings under military service will not cover such inability to work sufficiently. Therefore, the state as an employer should compensate for the serious loss of their inability to work.[33]

The draft prepared by the Council took into consideration both military rank and length of service in determining the amount of military pensions.[34] However, considering the difficult lives of noncommissioned disabled veterans, the revised pension plan gave greater weight to the severity of injuries than to military rank. In addition to the standard military pension, in the new plan, severely injured veterans received supplemental pensions, and less severely injured veterans received lump-sum payments. Not surprisingly, the final figures proposed struck a balance between the grim realities of disabled veterans' lives and financial constraints on governmental spending.

Yet, many Japanese remained suspicious of the revival of the military pension system.[35] Soon after the Council made its proposal, on 23 December, a report submitted by the Council of Social Security System (Shakai Hoshō Seido Shingi-kai) under the General Administrative Agency of the Cabinet raised possible objections to the reintroduction of military pensions:

> The renewal of military pensions gives preferential treatment to certain groups of military personnel. The argument that they deserved this, which is predicated on vested rights, has a weak foundation. Considering the balance of social security expenditures for the general population, and in consideration of the fact that the sacrifices of this war influenced the entire nation, we cannot find valid reasons for this.[36]

From its foundation, the JDVA engaged in lobbying the Diet for legislation to revive military pensions. The JDVA instantly created a Diet Affairs Committee (Kokkai Taisaku Iin) for effective mobilization of its constituents. The bill for the revision of the Pension Law was submitted to the Fifteenth Diet in early 1953. JDVA representatives actively lobbied key figures in both the Upper and Lower Houses. As a result of extensive interviews with national Diet members, eight regional groups lobbied in succession at the Diet from 12 January to 11 March. The JDVA utilized numerous strategies such as face-to-face meetings with Diet members; submission of petitions, appeals, and questionnaires; attendance at proceedings of the concerned committees and Diet sessions; and giving testimony at the hearings. On 1 March, presenting actual cases of disabled veterans, Kuroda Akira, representative of the JDVA, explained the reasons for the revival of military pensions for veterans of ranks below seven-degree *koshō* at the hearing of Lower House.[37] In spite of the all-out campaign by JDVA members, dissolution of the Lower House on 14 March resulted in failure to pass the bill. At the same time, the government decided to prolong the suspension of military pensions until the end of July.

In preparation for breaking the gridlock at the Diet, the JDVA focused their agenda on three goals for the Sixteenth Diet: (1) revival of increased military pensions for the seven-degree *koshō*, (2) revival of disability pensions from the first to the fourth-degree *kanshō*, and (3) payment of additional family pensions from the special degree to the seven-degree *koshō*.[38] At the hearings of the Lower House, Kuroda Akira agreed to the general plan for the revised pension law with two exceptions. The Council for Special Provision of the Pension Law agreed to suspend the seven-degree *koshō* military pensions and disability pensions from the first to the fourth-degree *kanshō*. The council gave three reasons: public sentiment, national budget, and degree of injuries. Nevertheless, Kuroda countered the Council's concerns:

> As for public sentiment, we regret that they consider the granting of military pensions issued to disabled persons only from a sentimental perspective or legal argument. . . . In the second issue of the national budget, we have never asked for a specific amount of compensation. . . . In the last hearing, the Council said that mildly injured persons such as those who lost one thumb would be excluded from the final report. The decision makes us furious because the chart of disability does not mention anything about it. I protest such irresponsible words.[39]

The Diet consequently passed the revised Pension Law on 31 July. The revised law aimed to fill in the gap within the national pension system between the treatment of public officials and former military personnel, particularly to aid lower-ranked ex-soldiers. Moreover, mildly injured veterans would receive increased military pensions.

Nonetheless, the primary goal proposed by the Council was not incorporated into the enacted bill. The final plan was based on the idea that military personnel and civil public officials should receive equal treatment, but the pensions of lower-ranking soldiers would be less than the pensions for officers. Also, the planned pension amount would be reduced due to budgetary restrictions.[40] Despite these changes, it was a significant step that the military pension was once again part of the national pension system as it had been before 1945.

The problem of the white gown beggars

Veterans who wore white gowns and solicited money on streets were recognized as a social problem, particularly after the war. White gown veterans begged to sustain their lives. Nevertheless, they stained the JDVA's reputation because Japanese citizens frequently identified them as members. Accordingly, the JDVA considered them an obstacle to promoting the welfare of its members. On 21 October 1953, a declaration concerning the white gown beggars proclaimed at the JDVA second national convention firmly condemned the practice:

> We have observed disabled veterans asking for donations on the streets or in the trains after the war. The suspension of military pensions and inadequate public assistance made us think they had no choice. However, with the reinstitution of new support services provided by the government, we now believe that 300,000 disabled veterans should practice self-restraint, stop asking for donations, work to improve the lives of members, and act as honorable role models in accordance with the JDVA charter.[41]

Alarmed by the seriousness of the problem, the MHW conducted a national survey of the white gown beggars on 22 and 23 October 1953. Three hundred and eighty-seven white gown beggars responded to the survey. According to the findings, their average age was 39 years old, they had 2.5 dependent family members on average, and they had solicited donations for an average of one year, 6 hours and 40 minutes per day, and 17 days per month. Nearly 80 percent of respondents engaged in begging to meet survival needs. About 90 percent of beggars answered that they would quit begging once a job or self-employment was secured. Surprisingly, more than half of the beggars were now receiving military pensions or disability payments. Thus, this demonstrates that legal pitfalls affected their living conditions even after the revival of the military pension system. The MHW recognized the need to adopt new cooperation with prefectures. On the other hand, the JDVA announced that they would continue efforts to support unfortunate injured ex-servicemen under the guidance of the MHW.[42]

The JDVA's statement ignited a host of criticisms of the white gown beggars from its members. As the result of a survey of its members, the Nagano Prefecture Disabled Veterans Association eventually advocated a complete ban on their activities. They found that most of the beggars were from outside of the prefecture, and mostly from Tokyo and Kanagawa. Some of them appeared to have become professional beggars, who controlled their "market" for collecting donations and appeared to fake or exaggerate their disabilities. The association eventually advocated a complete ban on their activities in Nagano prefecture. In addition, on 5 December, the *Yomiuri Shimbun* uncovered the fact that the Takinokawa police station in Tokyo, which had conducted an undercover investigation, ordered the Hakuyu-kai Foundation for Welfare of Disabled Veterans to present themselves for questioning regarding fraudulent charity activities. However, representatives of charity groups refuted such suspicions and criticisms. In an interview with the *Sangyō Shimbun*, Takahashi Kiyotake, secretary of the Committee of Rehabilitative Assistance for White Gown Donation, found fault with the JDVA's recommendation. "The military pension is not paid as was planned. . . . If the country were to provide adequate living support, we are always ready to quit. Who dares to wish to stand under this wintry sky?"[43]

Amid growing concerns about the disturbances caused by white gown beggars, several local disabled veterans organizations took full-scale measures for eliminating them. On 28 January 1954, about 100 members of the Katori District Disabled Veterans Association in Chiba prefecture engaged in an all-out campaign for eradicating white gown charity. White gown beggars primarily collected donations at shrines where large numbers of visitors came to pray. Members chartered three buses and hung white banners on the buses saying "Please help us put an end to white gown charity!" and headed for numerous destinations in Tokyo, including the National Diet, the Pension Bureau, and Yasukuni Shrine. One of the members recalled the scene when they walked under the big archway to Yasukuni Shrine:

> Under the archway, five white gown beggars were soliciting donations from visitors. They exposed their ugly features to visitors whose loved ones may have once been comrades of the drifters, even sharing cigarettes. . . . Since the restoration of Japan's sovereignty, the bereaved families who come up to Tokyo from afar and other people are surely pleased to meet the spirits of war dead. When they pass under the big shrine gate, they should hear the voices of the spirits of the heroic dead and embrace the spirits of war comrades. . . . Nevertheless, the band of ungracious white charity panhandlers disturb what should be a profoundly spiritual moment! We disabled veterans cannot tell you how sorry we are.[44]

Ordinary people at the shrine showed mixed reactions to the presence of a disabled veterans group in the precinct yard. A peddler said, "Why is the JDVA cracking down on the white gown beggars?" Another worker shoveling the snow pondered, "They gave us lots of troubles. . . . Well, the JDVA has nothing to do with them? If so, the donations would go into their pockets." An elderly lady resting at a restaurant sighed, "Oh, they have received pensions while soliciting donations." These observations demonstrated that the general public somehow equated the JDVA members with the beggars.

The Katori District Disabled Veterans Association officially stated, "White gown solicitors engaged in begging. As injured persons in the same war, we cannot ignore this fact anymore. Anyone who has a will should rehabilitate himself." They distributed a printed statement to white gown beggars and visitors at the shrine. In the statement to white gown beggars, they demanded that the beggars stop asking for charity:

> We profoundly sympathize with your handicaps as we do with all other injured veterans. However, you cannot be allowed to solicit donations publicly since it causes considerable discomfort to the general public. If you make the most of your abilities, you can survive one way or another. Our comrades already have demonstrated this in the whole country. . . . You should stop begging immediately. Why don't we join together and work for rehabilitation![45]

Simultaneously, the statement circulated to shrine visitors expressed appreciation and favor for disabled veterans' participation in society:

> We feel very grateful for the sympathy you have shown to white gown solicitors and the kindness in giving your charity. However, this does them more harm than good. . . . Even if you still feel sorry for them, what they need is tough love. At the same time, I would like you to encourage the government to provide adequate support to war victims. Moreover, we ask for your deep understanding and cooperation in addressing the problems of physically handicapped persons.[46]

In March 1954, the Shimane Prefecture Disabled Veterans Association also launched a campaign to eliminate white gown charity. White gown beggars at Izumo Shrine were an irksome problem to the Shimane Tourist Association. The Taisha town division of the prefectural association distributed fliers to the beggars in cooperation with local authorities and police. The fliers were titled "A Request to Gentlemen in White" and pleaded with them to stop begging:

> Dear gentlemen who are fund-raising! Have you heard of the statement on the elimination of white gown begging in the second national convention of the JDVA? We, disabled veterans in Shimane Prefecture, particularly disabled veterans living in Taisha town, cannot overlook such actions any more at all when we think how much visitors at the shrine are troubled and disturbed. . . . Now we, in the name of the Taisha town division, appeal to you gentlemen to stop white gown fundraising.[47]

One white gown beggar coldly received the fliers. Contrary to the members' expectation that he would act remorsefully, the beggar adamantly retorted: "I never thought that soliciting money was a good thing to do. However, who on earth would employ me even if I wish to find a job? I have neither a house to live in nor relatives. Actually, I am still a hospital inpatient."

Then, the beggar told the members about his difficulties and finally asked them to give him a couple of days' grace. Since the members did not have the authority to grant permission, they left the final decision up to him.[48] Contrary to the reports that beggars lived extravagantly, in reality many of them led hard lives. The JDVA members felt they were a menace to society. Meanwhile, their experience with charity panhandlers made them realize how important the charity they received really was to the beggars' lives.

The JDVA's relationship with disabled American veterans

Communications with foreign disabled veterans played a key early role in strengthening the JDVA's reputation and organization. The JDVA's relationship with Disabled American Veterans (DAV) was deemed crucial to participation in the World Veterans' Federation (WVF).[49] At the second annual meeting of the JDVA in Kyoto, Yasui Fukuzō, president of the Osaka Prefecture Disabled Veterans Association, explained the necessity of participation to JDVA members: "It would be very meaningful for the proper growth of the JDVA to join the WVF if we consider the current situation of fellow foreign disabled veterans and courtesy from DAV."[50] Consequently, the JDVA passed a unanimous resolution to participate in the WVF.

In June 1952, their first contact with the DAV accidentally took place. Representatives of the DAV traveled to Korea for the purpose of showing sympathy to wounded American soldiers. On their return trip to America, they paid a courtesy visit to Tokyo. The Japanese veterans were struck by their magnanimous attitude. Yasui remembered their solemn but warm demeanor.

> Americans in the delegation that greeted us expressed the warm friendship that is the bond of disabled veterans in their gracious deportment and speech. When we arrived, the party stood up and shook hands with us, and we kept shaking hands for a long time. Heartfelt feelings and silent eye-to-eye communication were enough to make us choke up.[51]

The JDVA members reiterated their wish to cooperate with the DAV as a partner organization dedicated to rehabilitation.

The DAV's second visit to Japan gave the JDVA an opportunity to develop a close relationship. On 12 December 1953, when the JDVA held a board meeting, three representatives of the DAV happened to visit the JDVA office in Tokyo. The Japanese members were impressed with the advanced technologies of the American's prosthetic hands. However, the American veterans were shocked by the meager military pension the Japanese veterans had received. When Mr. Jackson, a lieutenant commander who lost his eyesight, told them that he had been wounded in the battle of Bougainville Island, Tanba Keiji, a Japanese veteran who lost his arm immediately responded, "I was injured there too! So, we fought each other in the war?" The *Nisshō gekkan* reported this anecdote: "The mutual enemies from that time are friends in the present, which is evidence of the spirit that unites disabled veterans around the world."[52] In this way, Japanese veterans established a rapport with their American counterparts.

The DAV advanced several proposals to promote the friendship between them. To the JDVA's surprise, the DAV's offers included financial assistance to sustain JDVA activities. Although the JDVA expressed their appreciation, they demurred on the grounds that it would have an impact on their management as a whole.[53] The exchanges also led to an invitation to the JDVA President, Nomura Kichisaburō, to attend the national convention of the DAV in the summer of 1953. Nomura was pleased to accept their proposal.[54]

The JDVA decided to send Yasui Fukuzō to visit the United States for the national convention of the DAV from 11 August to 19 September 1954. His primary purpose was to introduce the JDVA to American disabled veterans to enhance communication and friendship, as well as to petition the United States to release Japanese war criminals who were still serving prison sentences.[55] At the annual convention of the DAV in Miami on 15 August 1954, Yasui delivered the JDVA chairman Kaba Atsushi's message to American colleagues: "It is an honor to speak at the National Convention of DAV. . . . Those who have directly experienced the horror of war are disabled veterans. Countries should establish world peace by respecting each other and cooperating together. In this regard, I long for the creation of an alliance between American and Japanese disabled veterans."[56] In his speech on behalf of President Nomura Kichisaburō, Yasui explained the rationale for the immediate release of war criminals:

> Considering the fact that the present international situation, and particularly the situation in the Far East, has drastically changed, and that in the Far East Japan is the only independent country that can serve as a defense against the threat of communism, it is against the national interest of the United States to prolong resolving this problem.[57]

DAV members gave thunderous applause to Yasui's remarks. Despite the fact that the release of Japanese war criminals was a politically charged issue, the JDVA aimed to take advantage of the fear of communism for mutual benefit. In addition, Yasui cited their families' predicaments in postwar Japan in order to elicit sympathy among American veterans.

Nevertheless, the problem of Japanese war criminals overshadowed relations between the two countries' veterans. A major stumbling block was the adamant opposition from hardliners in the American Legion. Yasui reasoned that political consideration toward the members of the American Legion who lost family members and friends in the Pacific War largely explained the DAV's negative posture. The wartime atrocities of the Japanese

Imperial Army such as the vivisection practiced on American soldiers at Kyushu University still remained a fresh issue in the minds of American veterans. Moreover, leaders of the American Legion insisted, "War criminals are criminals. Obviously, as long as justice against crime exists, they should be imprisoned." As a representative of the JDVA, Yasui was trapped in a vulnerable position, but received a positive response from his veteran constituency at home for expressing the call to Americans for the prompt release of Japanese war criminals.[58]

As a disabled veteran from a defeated country, Yasui was overwhelmed by American hospitality and the rehabilitation programs available to American disabled veterans. Yasui described his experiences with American disabled veterans:

> I'd say that's the American spirit. Although we fiercely fought each other, once the war was over, they treated me like an old friend as if they seem to have already forgotten the past, which made me surprised. I also want to tell you that they always warmly welcomed me as a representative from Japan, committed themselves not to hurt my pride, and adopted a respectful attitude toward me.[59]

Moreover, during his stay in Cincinnati, where DAV headquarters was located, Yasui inspected a factory managed by the DAV that was producing license plates. In the air-conditioned factory with well-equipped facilities, about 500 employees, the majority of whom were disabled veterans, appeared to work comfortably.[60] After he observed American rehabilitation and vocational reeducation programs, he admitted that the DAV could be highly influential to Japanese disabled veterans. "I cannot say whether this can be imitated as it is, though it would be helpful, but it is my honest belief that application of this system to Japanese disabled veterans is too difficult due to the differences of scale between the countries."[61]

On the way back to Japan, Yasui visited Japanese living in Hawai'i to gain support for the JDVA. Yasui reported on the activities of the JDVA and conditions of Japanese disabled veterans to Japanese and Nisei Japanese-Americans in Hawai'i. Many of the old Japanese cried over the predicaments Japanese disabled veterans faced. An old man lamented the contradictory situation between disabled veterans and Japan's reconstruction:

> Although the roads in Japan were fully rebuilt after the war and splendid buildings appeared in front of the station in Osaka, unless people who were injured for the country are truly consoled and the country provides generous assistance for them, we Japanese residents abroad can never feel that these are truly signs of either recovery or national prosperity.[62]

As a representative of the JDVA, Yasui's visit to the United States reminded him of the status of Japanese disabled war veterans at home in his own country. While the invitation from the DAV gave the JDVA a chance to express their opinions in accordance with mutual benefits, Yasui's encounter with his Japanese colleagues in Hawai'i reassured him that a significant gap existed between the status of disabled veterans and the recovering Japanese society.

Restoring honor to Japanese disabled war veterans was closely tied with the early postwar Japanese milieu. The presence of disabled veterans was reminiscent of bitter war experiences for the general Japanese population. Abolition of preferential treatment for disabled veterans not only increased the difficulty of their everyday life, but also gave average citizens a negative impression of them. Indeed, many Japanese citizens felt repulsion toward the revival of entitlements for military personnel including the military pension. Meanwhile, public opinion of disabled veterans showed sympathy for their sacrifice as war victims. This complex popular sentiment substantially impacted the movement in its early stages.

As a disabled veterans' group of a defeated nation in the Asia-Pacific War, the JDVA cautiously chose prioritized agendas: the revival of military pensions, a campaign to eliminate the white gown beggars, and friendship with the DAV. Members of the JDVA essentially regarded themselves not as welfare recipients but as those who served their country; they sought to make their country take responsibility for compensating them. By eradicating white gown beggars from the street, they aimed to dispel any identification of disabled veterans with the beggars. Furthermore, JDVA's strengthening of ties with the DAV served to obtain recognition from their counterparts in the United States and to elevate their status as comrades-in-arms.

The groundbreaking years of the JDVA clarified their raison d'etre and their mission as disabled veterans both at home and abroad. Although the Allied occupiers and the Japanese government originally intended to create a comprehensive national disability policy, the JDVA resisted as they devoted themselves to being identified not as disabled persons but specifically as disabled war veterans. Their endeavors subsequently led to a two-tier disability policy distinguishing between the general disabled population and disabled war veterans. Thus, the initial efforts of the JDVA played a decisive role in molding their distinct identity as war veterans and establishing their status in postwar Japanese society.

The plight of Japanese soldiers forgotten for decades on isolated Pacific islands was long a dark cloud over the postwar years of peace. The return home and honoring of the last of these forgotten warriors at long last granted Japan a sense of closure and honor following the blackness of war. This sigh of relief, however, may have been taken somewhat prematurely, for even now the other forgotten soldiers, those disabled by the brutality of their service to their country, may have yet to fully return to their rightful and honored places within their own home borders.

Part Three

State Policy for a Late-Capitalist Society

Journalist and oft-quoted "Japan expert" Karel van Wolferen, in his title for a controversial book, characterized the essence of Japan's rise to global prominence as *The Enigma of Japanese Power*. What he was referring to was not military but rather economic power. Written at the height of Japan's economic success, van Wolferen's book was an attempt to explain how Japan came to be the second largest economy in the world. Japan's postwar "economic miracle" is indeed an important subject for historical study, and the Japanese "success story" has been both envied and resented throughout the world. Japan's rapid rise to global economic prominence was by far the most famous of all its postwar accomplishments, yet many scholars and pundits have, since the bursting of the economic bubble in the early 1990s, sought to distance themselves from their earlier praise for Japan's accomplishments by aiming harsh criticism at the state's failure to effect economic recovery. There is, of course, an important back-story to this narrative.

Pundits and scholars often assert that economic policy was the secret of Japan's postwar economic success. Prime Minister Ikeda Hayato's 1960 income-doubling policy, in part precipitated by the strong showing by labor in the social protest movements of the 1950s, combined with the rapid economic growth of the middle and late 1960s to dramatically increase the standard of living of most Japanese households. By the end of the 1960s, the three Cs—car, "cooler" (air conditioner), and color television—were the longed-for icons of Japan's new material wealth. Unprecedented economic growth also enabled managers to refrain from mass layoffs while asserting that the company should be able to expect an ever greater commitment in return. Indeed, Japan's unemployment rate remained well below 3 percent until the late 1980s.

By the mid-1970s, most blue- and white-collar families had, or would soon have, the car, color TV, and air conditioner that served as three key indicators of their social and economic aspirations. By the 1970s, the majority of Japanese considered themselves to be middle-class, but middle-class affluence at the height of the economic boom of the 1980s took on a level of opulence unparalleled in modern history. But even at the height of the bubble years of the 1980s, it was becoming clear that Japanese affluence was built on unsustainable social, economic, and environmental models laid bare by the frenetic pace at which many Japanese sought to consume the trappings of extravagances theretofore unaffordable—from Gucci hand bags to gold-leaf sushi.

The economic bubble burst in 1991. Housing prices plummeted and suicide rates skyrocketed. Along with the increasingly bleak economic outlook came cultural and social issues that included the re-emergence of teenage prostitution (*enjo kōsai* or compensated dating) and increasing rates of unemployment and homelessness. Japan's long nineties, also known as the lost decade, stretched well into the twenty-first century. In 2002, the national unemployment rate exceeded 5 percent for the first time since the early 1950s. When disaggregated, the data revealed a more troubling concern: the average unemployment rate for persons aged 15–24 was double that for the overall population. All through the decade preceding the 2011 Tōhoku Earthquake, aggregate wages continued to decline, the ratio of part-time temporary to full-time regular workers rose, and the unemployment rate hovered around 5 percent. Meanwhile, critics blamed the state for having failed to develop viable social health and welfare strategies for the ageing population while simultaneously failing to provide adequate employment training for the nation's youth. Instead, pundits and politicians seemed keen on laying claim to their filial status while blaming young people for being too lazy to work.

The chapters of this section explore how state policy initiatives of the postwar era have shaped, to varying degrees of success, the economy and society of post-bubble Japan. "State Policy for a Late Capitalist Society" reconstructs state policy initiatives of the postwar and post-bubble eras as means of examining the ways in which the state has attempted to address some of Japan's most pressing policy problems. By examining the recent historical trajectory of industrial, fisheries, and financial policies, the chapters collectively examine how state policy initiatives, although not publicly praised and not always for the better, nevertheless effected considerable changes to the relationship between the postwar state and producer. Bruce Aronson and Lonny Carlile focus specifically on economic policies centered in Tokyo that, with varying degrees of success, attempted to address the interconnected milieu of pressing economic and social problems. Narrating geographical and topical territory akin to those of the chapters by Martin Dusinberre and Timothy S. George, Satsuki Takahashi paints a portrait of fisheries policies for rural Japan that illustrates quite plainly the persistence of Japan's historical rural/urban divide. All three chapters suggest ways in which the precedents of post-bubble policy may yet continue to shape the relationship between state and society in the wake of the 2011 Tōhoku Earthquake.

9

The Postindustrialization of the Developmental State

Lonny E. Carlile

There is considerable disagreement over what precisely the term "postindustrial society" refers to, and whether it is appropriate to use it to describe sociocultural and politicoeconomic conditions that have emerged since the 1970s in so-called advanced industrialized societies. In this chapter, the term postindustrial society will be used as a short-hand form to refer to four interrelated and much discussed transformations that have occurred in recent times, again most prominently in advanced industrialized countries.

The first transformation, a sociotechnical one, is that which is conventionally associated with the term, namely, the shift in the structure of employment from one dominated by manufacturing to one in which services account for the bulk of employment.[1] Behind this shift is a sustained rise in the amount of research and knowledge that goes into the production of goods and services (i.e. the arrival of the "information society" and "knowledge economy").[2] A key enabling innovation here is the incorporation of microelectronic components into a wide variety of producer and consumer machinery and the permeation of telecommunications networks (the so-called digital revolution) that have facilitated a dramatic rise in the role and significance of "information" in the economy and various aspects of social life.[3] The second transformation is primarily cultural in character, and is often referred to as "postmodernity." It is the simultaneous diversification and destabilization of tastes, interests, preferences, and identities, and the associated permeation and commodification of "signs," a trend that has been facilitated by the aforementioned sociotechnical changes.[4] The third is political-economic in nature. It is frequently identified with the term "globalization" and is rooted in the integration of economic activity across national boundaries that has eroded the relative discreteness and self-contained-ness of national economies. Driven by ever-expanding transnational flows of highly mobile capital, this process of "globalization" has given rise to an increased turbulence and instability of economic conditions, precipitating the collapse of the "long runs" and stable "productivity bargains" that characterized post-World War II industrialized societies, and their replacement by "flexible" institutional arrangements more conducive to rapid product innovation and rapid shifts in needs and taste (post-Fordism).[5] Finally, the fourth, sociological, transformation that has occurred in tandem with the preceding is what one group of researchers has evocatively labeled "the reconstruction of the intimate sphere."[6] That is, in combination with the other transformations listed, significant changes have occurred in interpersonal relationships, the institution of the family and society's overall demographic composition (notably, its aging) that have, in turn, precipitated changes in the way in which, among other things, intimacy and responsibility for care are understood and practiced.

Adapting to the arrival of postindustrial society as defined here has presented profound challenges to states everywhere, and there has been considerable debate as to what the best strategies for coping with them might be. One school of thought has it that the arrival of these new conditions has resulted in the erosion of the power, influence and effectiveness of the state as critical socioeconomic processes increasingly unfold in realms outside of a state's reach.[7] Others, however, argue that what is occurring is not an erosion of the state but rather a change in its methods.[8] The points at issue in this debate are clearly pertinent when it comes to understanding Japan's recent history. To begin with, Japan has met the basic benchmarks for identifying a postindustrial society since around 1970. Census figures indicate that the percentage of Japan's workforce in the tertiary or service sector came to account for the largest proportion of the workforce at some point between 1960 and 1965 and to account for the majority of employment between 1975 and 1980. Furthermore, by 1970, it was becoming readily apparent that many of the most technologically sophisticated sectors of Japanese industry had effectively caught up with the United States and Western Europe, and further industrial advancement would require the development of state-of-the-art "knowledge-intensive" industries of its own. Its electronics industry had already begun moving in this direction, and by the early 1970s, a wide range of industries were exploring ways to incorporate advanced electronic components into their production processes and products.[9] From the 1980s onward, Japan grew steadily in prominence as a mecca for postmodern culture, most notably in such areas as fashion and visual arts (*manga, anime*), and in the articulation of a distinctive style of cultural consumption (i.e. *otaku* culture).[10] Furthermore, even though the globalization of the Japanese economy in the area of trade and capital liberalization lagged behind the expectations of its partners, the internationalization of the Japanese economy had in fact advanced greatly over the course of the 1960s. A substantial jump in the outflow of Japanese investment would unfold during the 1970s, and this would pick up steam rapidly as time passed.[11] Economic turbulence in the form of accelerating inflation, along with labor unrest and other signs of political and economic instability permeated the Japanese economy as the decade of the 1970s opened. The Oil Crisis of 1973–74 in particular strained the country's industrial relations system, prompting corporate managements to scramble in search of means for attaining greater flexibility, a quest that led to fairly fundamental restructuring of the Japanese employment system during the latter half of the 1970s.[12] In addition, there was an additional somewhat distinctive feature in Japan's postindustrial profile that policymakers and the general population were beginning to take note of. This was the unprecedentedly rapid aging of Japan that was caused by the combined effect of a short postwar baby boom, substantially increased life expectancies, and a steadily declining fertility rate that have brought about major changes in the institution of the family and interpersonal relationships in Japan.[13]

What makes Japan a particularly interesting case for the study of state responses to the arrival of postindustrial society is the extensive and controversial role of the state in that country's economy historically. In the late 1980s and early 1990s, the study of Japan's political economy was overwhelmed by a debate over the contribution of the "capitalist developmental state" to the country's economic success and whether or not it was appropriate for other countries to adopt this ostensible model.[14] Japan's economic stagnation during the "lost decade" of the post-bubble 1990s, however, quickly dampened interest in these questions, and ironically, if the Japanese political economy is discussed at all today, it is more often than not in the context of a search for lessons on what *not* to do in responding to economic crises. To the extent that there is a prevailing view concerning the Japanese capitalist developmental state today, it is that it is a system that worked well in the postwar period prior to the arrival of what we have termed postindustrial society but became *dysfunctional* when confronted with these new conditions.[15] To the extent that there is a lesson to be learned, it is the neoliberalist one that the developmental state should be abandoned at the first signs of the arrival of postindustrial society, if not sooner.

This chapter represents an initial, tentative effort to address the question of what happened to the Japanese capitalist developmental state as Japan confronted the conditions of postindustrial society. Fully addressing the question would require a study of a size and scope that is well beyond what is possible in the context of this volume, along with analytical approaches and methods not utilized in this study. While referring to some extent—and in broad strokes and selectively—to the changes in administrative apparatuses, policy processes, and policy content and outcomes that would be the subject of a "full-fledged" addressing of the question, the central focus here is on the rhetorical dimension, and specifically how the role of the state in the economy was envisioned and justified in the discourse of prominent commissions in the 1980s and 1990s that were given the assignment of envisioning what the Japanese state should look like as it adapts to the changes associated with what we have just described as the arrival of postindustrial society. What the present study suggests is that in spite of calls for a radical rollback in the state's regulatory presence in the economy, we see a continued discursive embrace of a pilot role for the state that differs from the kind of laissez faire role associated with neoliberalist doctrine.

The capitalist developmental state

What is a capitalist developmental state and how and in what way is it applicable to the Japanese experience? While the bulk of the attention in the industrial policy debates of the 1985–95 period focused on issues of bureaucratic control over the economy and its contribution to economic growth, for Chalmers Johnson, the originator of the concept, the primary marker of a capitalist developmental state was not bureaucratic control or the fostering of economic growth *per se*, but rather the quality of *plan rationality* in a state's management of the national economy. Johnson contrasts plan rationality with the "market rationality" of a state whose primary role is to serve as a neutral referee enforcing the rules of play in an otherwise self-propelled and unconstrained market. By contrast, a "developmental, or plan-rational, state, has as its dominant feature precisely the setting of . . . substantive goals."[16] Put another way, it is a state that constructs broad blueprints of what it wants an economy or a part thereof to look like at some future time point and whose policies are intended to shepherd private sector industrial activity toward the realization of that blueprint. A capitalist developmental state is also to be distinguished from what Johnson calls a "plan ideological state" or a state exemplified by the former Soviet Union where an unmodulated state control over the economy is maintained for its own sake rather than merely as a means to an end.

Johnson went on to posit four key elements of what he sees as "the essential features of the capitalist developmental state," elements that he later succinctly summarized in a series of quotations from his original 1982 volume:

> The first element of the model is the existence of a small, inexpensive, but elite state bureaucracy staffed by the best managerial talent available in the system . . . . The duties of this bureaucracy would be first, to identify and choose the industries to be developed (industrial structure policy); second to identify and choose the best means of rapidly developing the chosen industries (industrial rationalization policy); and third, to supervise competition in the designated strategic sectors in order to guarantee their economic health and effectiveness . . . .
>
> The second element . . . is a political system in which the bureaucracy is given sufficient scope to take initiative and operate effectively. This means . . . that the legislative and judicial branches of government must be restricted to "safety valve" functions . . . .

The third element of the model is the perfection of market-conforming methods of state intervention in the economy [that is, interventions that harness or redirect rather than displace market forces] . . . .

The fourth and final element of the model is a pilot organization like MITI [i.e. the Ministry of International Trade and Industry, the forerunner of the current Ministry of Economy, Trade and Industry or METI] . . . . MITI's experience suggests that the agency that controls industrial policy needs to combine at least planning, energy, domestic production, international trade, and a share of finance (particularly capital supply and tax policy).[17]

Using Johnson's terminology where specified, the qualities associated with these four attributes can for the sake of convenience be labeled, respectively, plan rationality, autonomy, market conforming methods of state intervention, and a pilot agency.

As previously noted, the prevailing perspective on the Japanese capitalist developmental state today is that although state activity consistent with the model served a useful function during Japan's high growth era (or, alternatively, did not get in the way of economic growth), in the changed context of postindustrial society, this is now dysfunctional and a fundamental source of Japan's current economic, political, and social malaise. At first pass, the argument appears to make sense, since indeed, heavy handed controls, the concentrated channeling of capital to a small number of preidentified strategic industries, and restrictions on competition that are pointed to as constraints on the Japanese economy do not constitute a viable economic strategy under conditions where fast-paced innovation-driven change is demanded. However, deeper reflection suggests that there are at least two problems with this claim.

The first is the reification produced by equating the essential attributes of a capitalist developmental state with the industrial policy tools used in Japan during a particular era. The protectionist measures and the state's channeling of capital might rightly be identified as problematic in the context of postindustrial society, but historically they represent tools that were adopted for use in the context of a Fordist one. Carrying the argument forward, if deregulation and market opening—in essence an expansion of the scope of market forces at the expense of state control—are consciously embraced by a state with the intent of better attuning a national economy to the international and sociological context in which it operates (i.e. plan rationality), then such action should be considered consistent with the capitalist *developmental* state model. And to the extent that such market-enhancing "liberal" policies are associated with goal-oriented state policy initiatives claiming to address postindustrial conditions, then it is useful to distinguish them from "classic" industrial policy by using the term *postindustrial policy*. It is also useful to distinguish between a capitalist developmental state and a *post-developmental state* wherein the latter refers to a state that abandons the pursuit of developmental state goals in the economy altogether in favor of a passive referee-like role characteristic of a market rational state, as has been argued to have happened in France since the mid-1980s.[18]

A second point is that a dysfunctional mismatch between state economic intervention and the context in which it is exercised might not necessarily be the product of a developmental state at work. This leads to a second problem with the conventional interpretation—namely, the failure to recognize important divergences of the institutions of the Japanese state from the capitalist developmental state model. To make the argument that the Japanese developmental state failed under postindustrial conditions, one needs to start with the premise that what is being observed is a fully functional capitalist developmental state at work. Against this, one can make the case that the "dysfunctional" behavior is actually the consequence of critical departures of the Japanese political economic system from the developmental state model. This can be highlighted in a number of ways. One can, for instance, point to the contradiction between the capitalist developmental state's requirement of autonomy on the part of the state bureaucracy and a post-World War II governmental system based on principles of popular sovereignty and parliamentary supremacy. The reason why the Japanese state bureaucracy could act like a capitalist developmental state in spite of this was the consequence of certain extenuating circumstances. These include the continued hold of a political culture tied to the authoritarian prewar system of government, the extremely limited extent of the Occupation's reform of the state bureaucracy, the disarray and organizational weakness of the country's political parties that did not begin to be rectified until the mid-1950s, the resulting head start that the bureaucracy enjoyed in establishing a base of power in the postwar system, and the essential compatibility between the economic growth policies of the Japanese state and the needs and preferences of the ruling conservatives. These conditions combined to provide the Japanese state bureaucracy with an autonomy and power that allowed it to function as a developmental state for an extended period of time despite an institutional base that would not otherwise have been conducive to its operation. In time, however, party politicians developed mechanisms for flexing their institutionally grounded political muscle and began intervening extensively in state policy making and implementation.[19]

Another key departure from a "pure" capitalist developmental state was the extensive bureaucratic sectionalism that plagued the Japanese bureaucracy and hampered consolidated control. Although MITI was the designated "pilot agency" for steering the economy, it was just one of nearly two dozen cabinet-level ministries and agencies of roughly equal formal status. Implementation of national developmental plans and industrial policies required their cooperation. There was no centralized overarching development policy organ comparable to, for instance, the South Korean Economic Planning Board under Park Chunghee.[20] Given an institutional culture rooted in strong intraministry *esprit des corps*, coordination of policy across ministries was notoriously difficult. But as was the case in state-ruling party relations, extenuating circumstances allowed the Japanese state to nevertheless function reasonably well as a developmental state for an extended period. It was significant, for instance, that the heavy and chemical industrialization strategy that was at the core of developmental state's industrial policy program until the late 1960s was established prior to 1949.[21] When the state bureaucracy was reorganized in 1949 into a format that would remain in place with only incremental amendments until 2001 it was with this heavy industrial (re)industrialization strategy in mind. Having all of the relevant ministries on the same page, so to speak, clearly facilitated coordination across ministries. In time, however, interagency rivalry intensified, particularly when new initiatives that potentially crossed jurisdictional boundaries were involved, robbing the Japanese state of the consolidated oversight associated with a capitalist developmental state.

By the 1970s, just as postindustrial society was taking root in Japan, it became patently obvious that parliamentary supremacy and bureaucratic sectionalist tendencies were beginning to fuse in a way that could even be called *anti*developmental. The phenomenon that we are referring to here has been widely documented and goes by a variety of names, among the most familiar of which are patterned pluralism, *zoku* politics, and canalized democracy.[22] Diet members and politicians associated with the ruling LDP discovered the electoral benefit of mediating relations between politically strategic interest groups and the bureaucrats who oversaw the policy domains that affected the interests of that group, leading to the formation of "iron triangles" that tightly linked so-called *zoku* politicians, bureaucrats, and vested interests in a given policy domain. Although present earlier, the ubiquity and scale of this patterned pluralism grew dramatically over the course of the late 1960s and 1970s as rapid growth expanded the amount of government largesse that could be channeled through the system and an expanding productivity gap between Japan's internationally competitive industrial sectors and uncompetitive domestically based sectors created rationales for doing just that. Ruling party politicians began to use their constitutionally derived leverage to direct state subsidies and protectionist regulatory measures to farmers, small retailers, and other politically strategic interest groups that were falling behind.[23] Another sector that benefited immensely was the construction industry as LDP politicians exerted their influence to locate public works projects in electorally strategic districts with scant concern for their developmental significance.[24] The economic turmoil and problems of competitiveness created by the Oil Crisis magnified these trends. The rationale of stimulating economic recovery through deficit spending provided a convenient cover for patterned pluralist processes and was reflected in the rapid growth of government budgetary deficits over the course of the 1970s.[25] In any event, what happened during this period when described in the terminology of the developmental state model delineated earlier was that in addition to a loss of autonomy and consolidated control, patterned pluralism was severely undermining overall plan rationality and leading to a proliferation of policy interventions in industry that were not market-conforming mechanisms of state intervention in that they lacked a clear developmental rationale.

Although increasingly eclipsed by these patterned pluralist patterns, developmental state policies did not disappear entirely and were in fact placed on a new footing as MITI unveiled an industrial policy vision built around the concept of an "information society." The concept had received widespread attention in industrial policy circles between around 1968 and 1973 and, in a development that is of central significance for our purposes, was adopted as the central theme of the Spring 1971 report of the MITI-attached Industrial Structure Council. The premise of the proposals presented in that report, which paralleled what was being posited in "postindustrial society" theorizing in Europe and the United States around the same time, was that the emerging "information society" would be characterized by a form of production in which information and technical knowledge formed an ever-increasing source of value in the "goods" being produced. What the Industrial Structural Council was proposing in its report was that MITI focus on facilitating the transition of the Japanese economy to "a 'knowledge-intensive industrial structure' (*chishiki shūyakugata sangyō kōzō*), the main components of which would be machines controlled by integrated circuits, computers, robot development of ocean resources, office and communications machinery, high fashion (including furniture), and management services such as systems engineering, software, and industrial consulting."[26] This new vision would be in fact be pursued from the late 1970s onward, with varying degrees of success, most notably in the form of a variety of MITI-organized research consortiums identified by their various acronyms: ASPLA (Advanced System-on-a-Chip Platform Group), NEDO (New Energy and Industrial Technology Development Organization), PERI (Protein Engineering Research Institute), Selete (Semiconductor Leading Edge Technologies) Sigma (Software Industrialized Generator and Maintenance Aids), TRON (Real-Time Operating System Software), VLSI (Very Large-Scale Integrated Circuits).[27] It is noteworthy, too, that the line ministries of the Japanese state began to embrace visions of transforming themselves into developmentally oriented "policy ministries" like MITI. MPT (Ministry of Posts and Telecommunications) and MOC (Ministry of Construction) are examples. But as critics of Japanese industrial policy rightly point out, the effectiveness and payoff from these policies from the standpoint of strategic industry development declined over time.[28] The key problem was that in the turbulent, globalized, and rapidly changing competitive environment associated with the postindustrial condition, it was extremely difficult to predict which industries and technologies were in fact strategic, and even when the state guessed correctly, state-led guidance frequently proved to be too slow and cumbersome for the task. Also, strategic "industries" often straddled the jurisdictions of multiple ministries and here, the sectionalist instincts of the Japanese bureaucracy made coherent implementation extremely difficult.

During the 1970s and 1980s, the rise of patterned pluralism meant that much of the energy and resources of the state were now consumed by activities that were, from the standpoint of the developmental state, neither strategic nor developmental. Even the "pilot agency" MITI found itself mired in the pattern as it propped up the declining basic industries sector[29] and enforced voluntary export restraints in the automobile sector, the latter being a product of threats by foreign countries to lock out Japanese exports in retaliation for various Japanese restrictions that protected noncompetitive sectors from foreign competition. In the past, the terms dual economy and dual society have been used to describe the economic differentiation between internationally competitive exporters and internationally uncompetitive domestic sectors that was behind this diffusion of patterned pluralism.[30] A similar tack can be taken with respect to our effort to analytically interpret the consequences of this diffusion. We can speak of a dualistic state structure in which elements of a capitalist developmental state (notably in the high-tech sectors) coexisted with a clientelistic state whose tendencies were *anti*developmental in nature.

Framing Japan's response to postindustrial society: Rinchō

Rinchō, the abbreviated name given to what was formally known as the Second Provisional Commission on Administrative Reform (*Dai niji rinji gyōsei chōsakai*), was created in March 1981. Its establishment represented an initial culmination of a post-Oil Crisis reaction centered in the business community against Japan's ballooning budgetary deficit that, as we have noted, was driven by the rapid expansion of patterned pluralism. Although originating in the national business community, Rinchō and the administrative reform movement as a whole picked up the backing of a broader coalition that included portions of the state bureaucracy, certain neoconservative politicians in the LDP, and the enterprise-oriented right wing of the labor movement.[31] Over the course of its two-year life, Rinchō issued five reports, each of which was given widespread coverage in the media. Rinchō's significance for our purposes rests on the fact that it constituted the point of embarkation for, and set the ideological and policy framework of, the administrative reform movement of the 1980s and 1990s that culminated in the 2001 reorganization of the Japanese state bureaucracy. This movement, as I hope to demonstrate, can be understood as a kind of rectification effort aimed at reviving the Japanese capitalist developmental state under terms that were more attuned to the realities of postindustrial society. Here, we will focus on Rinchō's third or "basic" report[32] since it is there that the commission outlined the fundamental premises and rationales behind its various recommendations and fleshed out a reform agenda that would continue to drive the administrative reform movement for the next two decades.

That the arrival of postindustrial society Japanese-style was the context that framed the the commission's recommendations is allusively expressed in the following passage:

> In this way, amidst material affluence, the significance of knowledge and services in our national society has increased [postindustrial sociotechnical change]. The people's consciousness is maturing and diversifying ["postmodern" cultural change]. We anticipate even further advances in academia, culture and the arts. But there is also the danger that, in conjunction with imminent arrival of an aging society, society's robustness could dissipate as a result of a decline in the aspiration for technological progress and economic development, and that there will also be a decline in the self-sufficiency of individuals, households and groups [the reconstruction of the intimate sphere].
>
> At the same time, active contributions to international society commensurate with the rise in our nation's international status [globalization] will be expected from now on.[33]

The commission went on to offer "the construction of a robust welfare society" (*katsuryoku aru fukushi shakai*) as the encompassing theme for its suggested response to the arrival of these conditions: "The robust welfare society that our nation should be aiming for from now on refers to a society grounded in . . . self-reliance [on the part of individuals] and mutual assistance [within households, neighborhoods, and workplaces] and which can insure each person an appropriate place of employment under an appropriate rate of economic growth while assuring basic security in employment, health and old age." As numerous commentators have pointed out, the idea here was to minimize the growth of welfare *state* programs and spending, and to do so by relying to the greatest extent possible on *society* to provide for societal welfare, thereby avoiding the administrative "sclerosis" that was perceived to be incapacitating Western European states that had well-developed welfare state systems.

As befits a commission assigned to come up with proposals for administrative reform, the bulk of Rinchō's basic report is devoted to discussion of ways in which the state bureaucracy should be reformed. Here, it offered six rubrics:

1 With regard to that which is appropriately left to the independent and self-reliant activities of the private sector, reduce excessive administrative intervention;

2 Privatize where there is excessive competition and overlap between government and the private sector;

3 Eliminate and reduce selective assistance in market activities, as well as subsidies and licensing requirements that involve excessive intervention;

4 Remedy institutions that are problematic from the standpoint of income distribution;

5 Rectify areas where there is an imbalance between returns and costs; and

6 Elsewhere, reconsider areas where the significance [of policies] has dissipated due to changes over time.[34]

A superficial reading of these rubrics could easily give the impression that what we see here is an archetypal neoliberal pitch for free enterprise and *laissez faire* government *in principle*. Such a reading, however, misses the essential point of the exercise as it was understood by the commission, which it explained was "the securing of the flexibility that is required in order to address *new demands* on the state bureaucracy" (p. 174, italics added):

> At any time and under any circumstances state organizations should be rich in the ability to adapt to change, should be operated in a comprehensive, efficient and fair manner, and should be capable of attracting the confidence of the people.
>
> Given that our nation's economic society is highly developed, there is demand for complex and wide-ranging administrative services. Against this, there is an excessive division of administrative functions across ministries and agencies (so-called vertical administration). This results in barriers stemming from vertical functional divisions and a tendency for administration to lack comprehensiveness. And, there is a strong built-in tendency for administrative organizations to become bloated as they respond to new administrative demands while maintaining existing institutions and organizations.
>
> For this reason, it is important to focus on strengthening the function of comprehensive coordination and . . . on streamlining and rationalization when considering the desirable forms of administrative organization . . . .[35]

From there, the report spends a considerable number of pages presenting in detail concrete proposals for reforming the state bureaucracy in line with this under the theme of "strengthening the comprehensive planning function" of the state. These cover a wide range of areas that would remain items championed over the life of the administrative reform movement: (1) the strengthening of the powers and oversight authority of the cabinet and its staff; (2) a comprehensive reorganization of ministries and agencies with a focus on expanding the breadth of their jurisdictions; (3) giving bureaucratic agencies capacities for self-correction and greater adaptability and flexibility; (4) revisions of government personnel administration policies aimed at assuring that state bureaucrats maintain political neutrality and perform their duties with an eye toward national rather than particular interests; and (5) that functions and authority be devolved to local governments in order to more finely attune administrative activities to grassroots needs.[36]

In sum, what is clear here is that Rinchō's call for a slimming down of government and an expanded role for the private sector did not constitute a call for an abandonment of plan rationality. In fact, it was precisely the reverse—that is, these proposals were put forward as part of an effort to revive the centralized plan rationality that had been forced to recede in the face of trends that had steadily bled the Japanese state of its capacity to function developmentally.

During the 13 years that followed Rinchō's disbandment in 1983, the essential themes of the report were refined and elaborated by a series of follow-up administrative reform commissions. To the frustration of the administrative reform movement's proponents, however, following a brief period of success in slowing down the growth of the national debt and reversing to some extent certain of the more egregious and costly manifestations of patterned pluralist protectionism (e.g. rice), the Japanese political system seemed to rapidly backslide as the LDP found its hold on power threatened by public disillusionment fueled by recurrent and seemingly ever more spectacular corruption scandals. The collapse of Japan's bubble economy in 1991 only worsened these tendencies as the government enacted a series of massive stimulus packages that channeled huge amounts of government funding into construction projects and support programs without much impact in reviving the economy. The crisis in the financial system proved to be a source of even more dismay as state bailouts gave rise to further scandals that seemed to increasingly implicate state bureaucrats.[37] In the meantime, Japanese industrial policy appeared incapable of delivering decisive "winners." This was apparent, for instance, in the computer industry where a fixation on hardware caused the industrial policymakers and Japanese computer makers to be slow in recognizing the significance of standardized operating systems and off-the-shelf application software. Japanese policymakers and firms also lagged in telecommunications where among other things interministerial jurisdictional rivalries complicated and slowed the opening up of value-added networks and the infrastructure for digitized electronic communication.[38]

The postindustrialization of the developmental state

The economic and financial crisis of the mid-1990s served as a stimulus that reversed the neglect of administrative reform that had characterized the post-Rinchō years and precipitated a major restructuring of the Japanese state bureaucracy more or less in line with Rinchō's original recommendations. The culmination of this process, a review of which can be found elsewhere, was the so-called Hashimoto Administrative Reform program that was officially enunciated in the final report of the Administrative Reform Council (Gyōsei Kaikaku Kaigi) issued in December 1997 and implemented over the course of the next three years.[39] The translation of the Administrative Reform Council's program into enabling legislation proceeded quickly and smoothly. A Basic Law on Central Ministry and Agency Reform (Chūō Shōchō Tō Kihon Kaikaku Hō) was passed in June 1998 along with a related law on information disclosure. Subsequent preparations yielded a massively revamped state administrative bureaucracy that began operating right after the New Year holiday ended on 6 January 2001. Foremost among the changes wrought by the legislation was a fortification of the staff and oversight powers of the cabinet and a reduction in the number of cabinet-level ministries and agencies from 23 to 13.

It was in the midst of the scramble in Kasumigaseki to implement the provisions of the Hashimoto Administrative Reform's reorganization of the state bureaucracy by the 2001 deadline that MITI's Industrial Structure Council completed a report entitled "Challenges and Prospects for Economic and Industrial Policy in the 21st Century."[40] The report is a highly significant document for our purposes because it presents a systematic articulation on the part of the industrial policy bureaucracy of what in its view a postindustrialized developmental state should look like and the rationales behind it. As such, it represents the industrial policy bureaucracy's answer to the Rinchō-initiated administrative reform movement in that it re-envisions the industrial development process and the role of the state in that process in a manner that is consistent with the propositions championed by the administrative reform movement.

On the surface, the March 2000 report looks like a standard Industrial Structure Council vision. It frames its discussion as a presentation of a long-term strategy for adjusting Japan's industrial structure to global economic trends and changes in technology—specifically, the post-Cold War trend of rapid economic globalization and the equally rapid adoption of digital information and communications technology in a huge range of fields. But what distinguishes the report from previous industrial structure visions is that it spends as much time talking about the relationship between state and society and broader and deeper sociocultural trends as it does about industrial structure per se. Put another way, where earlier Industrial Structure Council visions offered up ideas on how the developmental state ought to restructure the economy and industry, the 2000 report in key ways turns things around and focuses on how the developmental state itself should be restructured. This can be illustrated quite succinctly through references to passages in the provisional English translation of the report's abstract.[41]

The document asserts that "the socio-economic system which supported Japan's economic development throughout the postwar period comprised a succession of self-sufficient circles, with each organization securing its own resources—technology, information and human resources, for example—handling evaluations in-house, and absorbing risk independently. Growing competitiveness based on technological advances and greater production efficiency, as well as the confidence in future development created by a company-based society and swift growth, formed a virtuous circle of supply and demand elements and produced an equitable and stable society." This was expressed graphically in the diagram reproduced in Figure 9.1. This postwar system, the report asserted, was no longer functional and it needed to be abandoned and replaced with one better suited to the times, the essence of which was depicted in the diagram reproduced in Figure 9.2. In contrast to the closed units characteristic of the old system, the system it advocated for the twenty-first century "must be more open and more interconnected—in other words, opportunities, information, evaluation and other elements must be opened out, while elements such as costs and risks are shared and minimized across society as a whole." The report addresses social concerns, something that was typically not directly incorporated into prior industrial policy visions, while proposing an altered structure of state-society relations: "The new Japanese system will emphasize sustainable growth, participation by senior citizens, and harmony with the environment, while the former two-dimensional public-private social structure will gain the extra dimension of NPOs." In other words, what we see here is not a vision whose purview is limited to objectives linked to industrial upgrading, but one that instead (1) reverses the vector connecting industrial restructuring to economic growth (i.e. instead of, how much economic growth do we need to sustain required restructuring, it is how much industrial restructuring do we need to attain "sustainable" growth?) and (2) embraces quintessentially "postindustrial" goals (participation by seniors and harmony with the environment). And with regard to the last point relating to the alteration of state-society relations, it goes on to suggest a system in which functions are devolved to individuals and the size of the state is whittled down to a bare minimum:

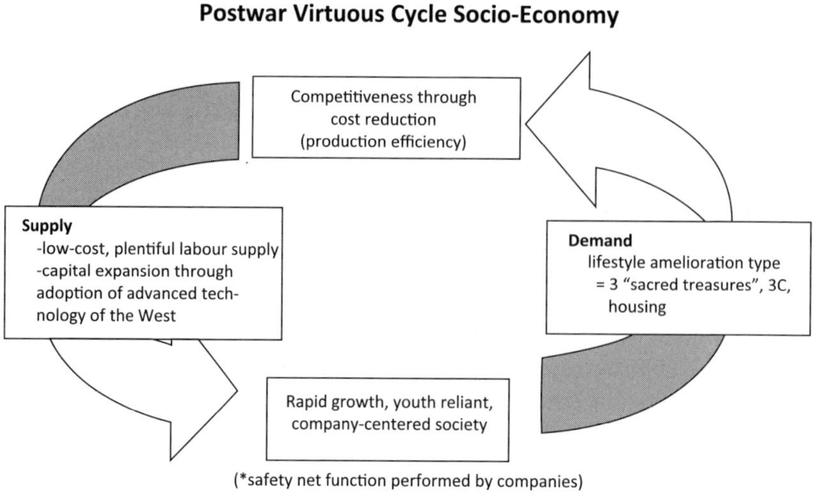

Postwar Virtuous Cycle Socio-Economy

Competitiveness through
cost reduction
(production efficiency)

Supply
-low-cost, plentiful labour supply
-capital expansion through
adoption of advanced technology of the West

Demand
lifestyle amelioration type
= 3 "sacred treasures", 3C,
housing

Rapid growth, youth reliant,
company-centered society

(*safety net function performed by companies)

FIGURE 9.1 *Nijūisseiki keizai sangyō seisaku no kadai to tenbō: Kyōsōryoku aru tasanka shakai no keisei ni mukete. Available at www.meti.go.jp/kohosys/ press/0000450/0/fintousin.pdf, p. 26. Accessed 1 May 2011.*

Source: Industrial Structure Council 2000b.

21st Century Virtuous Cycle Socio-Economy

Competitiveness through
creation of rent
(scarcity value of innovation)

Supply (qualitative improvement)
-systems reform
-technological innovation
-high quality human resources

Demand
Self-fulfillment type, individuality
enhancement type = diversivty of
value systems and demand (old
age, environmental, aesthetic)

Multi-participatory society
(diverse opportunities for and
self-realization by individuals)

Solid safety net
(Social security, etc.)

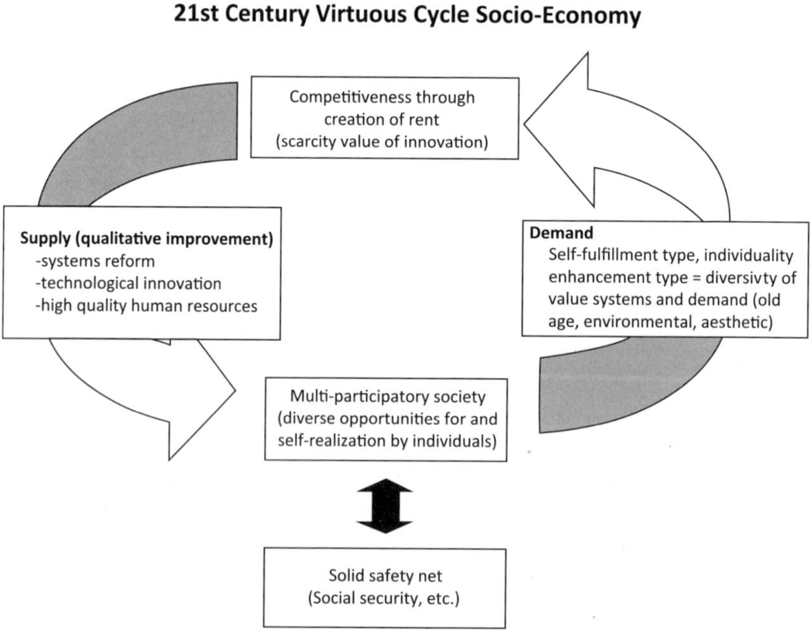

FIGURE 9.2 *Nijūisseiki keizai sangyō seisaku no kadai to tenbō: Kyōsōryoku aru tasanka shakai no keisei ni mukete. Available at www.meti.go.jp/kohosys/ press/0000450/0/fintousin.pdf, p. 34. Accessed 1 May 2011.*

Source: Industrial Structure Council 2000b.

The socio-economy produced by this new system will comprise, on the one hand, independent individuals with a strong sense of self who are also sympathetic toward others and understand public values, and on the other, a lean, effective state which provides the basic conditions for self-realization, and in which individuals and companies work actively toward value creation, engaging on their own initiative, for example, in the development of economic security, safety-nets, and an international economic order.[42]

NPOs are considered critically important as a medium for translating this individual-level public-spiritedness into socially beneficial outcomes.

It should be emphasized that, as with Rinchō, this is not quite the same thing as a classic libertarian position, and the state, the lightness of its presence notwithstanding, remains conceived as both the ultimate point of reference and guiding force:

> It is though the realization of conditions in which autonomous individuals can attain self-realization by harnessing their individuality and abilities, and in which the organizations that are their amalgamation can become the vehicles for value creation, that the state is put on a solid footing. And, at the same time, we believe that *the state* should put itself on a solid foundation in the sense of *establishing the robust environment required to attain this* and to perform its basic functions efficiently.[43]

Figure 9.3 provides a schematic that suggests how this would play out in the more concrete context of technology policy. What one sees is something akin to a technician gingerly fine-tuning the control knobs of a largely self-propelling machine—or, alternatively, a highly refined system of Foucaldian governmentality.

If (a) Rinchō introduced a new vision of the role of a developmental state attuned to postindustrial conditions, (b) the late-1990s' Hashimoto Administrative Reform reorganized Japan's state apparatus in line with this vision, and (c) the 2000 Industrial Structure Council report laid out a framework for translating this thrust into a new mode of state industrial management, then it is fair to ask if there are signs of a new approach to developmental policy in line with these during the first decade of the twenty-first century? In the remainder of this section, we shall look at two sectors that suggest that this was indeed happening.

The first is IT or information technology policy. As noted earlier, this was an industry where despite an early lead in the late 1980s, Japan fell substantially behind the United States and other nations over the course of the 1990s as a result of the difficulty that it was having in altering institutions and regulatory mechanisms in effective ways.[44] During the first half of the first decade of the new century, however, Japan made such rapid progress in the diffusion of broadband connections that by the end 2004, it was possible to legitimately claim that it "now ranked as one of the most

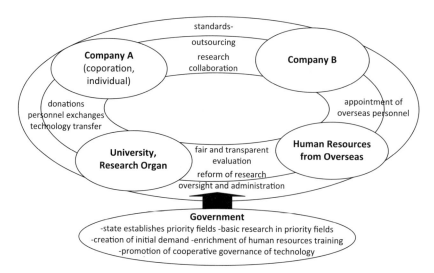

FIGURE 9.3 *Nijūisseiki keizai sangyō seisaku no kadai to tenbō: Kyōsōryoku aru tasanka shakai no keisei ni mukete. Available at www.meti.go.jp/kohosys/ press/0000450/0/fintousin.pdf, p. 41. Accessed 1 May 2011.*

Source: Industrial Structure Council 2000b.

advanced countries in the deployment of broadband services" and moved from having one of the highest to one of the lowest prices for broadband services in the world.[45] Behind this outcome was a major overhaul in the regulatory regime governing telecommunications services that included substantial changes in both the state's institutional apparatus for overseeing the sector and the state's role therein, the ultimate outcome of which was a "regime shift" from "a carrier-led, equipment manufacturer driven, hardware-oriented platform for producer-oriented investment and exports, to a carrier- and service provider-driven, service-oriented arena focused on domestic consumption."[46]

Behind the problems that Japan was having in the information technology sector was the dysfunctionality of the "controlled competition" regime that came into being following the Rinchō-inspired privatization of NTT (Nippon Telephone & Telegraph) in 1985.[47] For MPT, NTT's privatization had turned what had been a rather uninteresting supervision of a government monopoly into jurisdiction over a bona fide industry at the cutting edge of new technological developments. The ministry, which had long sought to become a true "policy ministry" a la MITI, proceeded to mobilize the classic tools of industrial policy to engage in the microeconomic management of the industry. However, it was also a regime in which a behemoth former public corporation and the companies in its "family" dominated the sector and maintained a chokehold over the critical infrastructure of landline telecommunications. Particularly problematic was the latter's ability to maintain extremely high prices for access to the national telecommunications network that it had a near monopoly over. It was these high interconnection costs and adherence to unique Japan-only standards that more than anything prevented the expansion of the market for new internet-based telecommunications services of the sort that were seen in countries at the forefront of the IT sector during the 1990s.

The organizational innovation that proved critical in the regime shift in the telecommunications sector was the 2001 government reorganization precipitated by the Hashimoto administrative reforms. Under the Basic Law on Central Ministry and Agency Reform, MPT's jurisdiction over the telecommunications sector was transferred to the newly created Ministry of Internal Affairs and Communications (MIC).[48] By this time, a major public debate was underway over just what could be done to rectify Japan's conspicuous lag in this strategically critical sector, and MIC's establishment was closely intertwined with a cabinet-led initiative to establish a national strategy for broadband deployment. This was concretized with the passage of the IT Basic Law in 2001 and the creation of an IT Strategy Headquarters in which the new minted ministry was assigned a central role. The Headquarters, in turn, promptly produced an e-Japan Priority Plan. The plan was premised on the proposition that broadband deployment was critical for Japan's adaptation to the postindustrial world ("Our country must undertake a rapid adaptation toward the realization of a knowledge creation-type society in which all of the nation's people can actively make use of IT and enjoy its benefits") and attempt to maximize the scope of the private sector's role ("Utilizing market principles, we aim to prepare an environment in which the private sector can manifest its robustness to the fullest and to become the world's leading IT nation within 5 years").[49] More concretely, the Japanese state altered regulations in order to open up the market to both foreign and domestic firms, let competing firms set prices for their products, and helped set the stage for an explosive rise in demand for broadband services. It did this by constructing a framework of rules that made both consumer- and producer-level electronic business transactions feasible and attractive while carrying through an "e-government" program of making government documents and services available over the internet. The initial strategy was followed in 2003 by an e-Japan Strategy II that involved similar policies, but this time directed at more specialized segments of broadband service. With its goal-oriented framing, plan-based coordination and a policy package in which the state maximized the role of the private sector, as well as in the very language that was used to describe the undertaking, the e-Japan Strategy's affinity with the Rinchō's vision of "postindustrial" development policy described in the preceding section should be readily apparent.

A similar argument can be made for the state's inbound tourism promotion policy, another new arena of government economic involvement in the early twenty-first century. The legal framework for Japanese tourism policy had been established back in 1964 via the Tourism Basic Law that was passed that year. Despite the existence of a basic law, however, tourism policy remained a rather low-key affair. Primary oversight over the industry was placed in the hands of the Ministry of Transportation, but the ministry was clearly too preoccupied with planning and overseeing the construction and maintenance of Japan's extensive and multimodal transportation infrastructure to devote serious energy and attention to tourism policy. Activity on the part of the ministry rarely extended beyond the compilation of an annual white paper as mandated in the law and sporadic initiatives that rarely involved any sort of systematic and sustained developmental initiative.[50] Dissatisfaction with this state of affairs had developed, and this dissatisfaction was targeted at what in the language of the Rinchō report was a lack of comprehensive coordination. Thus, it was observed with chagrin that the basic law was rarely referenced in related legislation, that there was no requirement for any sort of comprehensive planning in the tourism sector, and there did not exist institutional mechanisms for coordinating policies relevant to the development of tourism across the various ministries and agencies.[51]

Interest in boosting domestic and inbound tourism grew in the latter half of the 1990s as the hard times of the "lost decade" and high domestic travel costs relative to overseas travel sapped the industry of demand. The central pillar of the response was the passage—interestingly via Diet member sponsorship—of the Tourism Nation Promotion Act of 2006. The language used to outline the rationale for the policy reveals a concern for postindustrial conditions while echoing the language of the Rinchō basic report. Thus, the preamble of the law speaks of how changing values and affluence are creating an orientation toward leisure, more diversified travel behavior and demand for more sophisticated experiences. It also mentions "the arrival of a globally unprecedented low fertility/aging society" and in conjunction with this the pressing need to facilitate the "realization of local communities brimming with robustness" (*katsuryoku ni michita chiiki keizai shakai no jitsugen*). It notes that tourism is important in fostering an understanding of Japan and the Japanese and "plays a critical role in establishing a respectable status in international society" while lamenting that the number of inbound travellers "is not commensurate with our nation's status in international society" (*kokusai shakai ni okeru waga kuni no chii ni fusawashii mono towa natteinai*). The law mandates the compilation of a Tourism Nation Promotion Plan (Kankō Rikkoku Suishin Keikaku) and requires that the plan be used to coordinate a broad range of principles that includes various central ministries and agencies, local governments, tourism-related firms of various types, and local citizens.

Although not in the law itself, a resolution passed at the time of the Tourism Nation Promotion Act's passage called for the creation of an administrative agency to coordinate the nation's tourism promotion strategy. This was fulfilled in October 2008 with the establishment of Japan Tourism Agency (Kankōchō). The general spirit of the policies that are to be adopted in drafting and implementing tourism promotion policies are outlined in the agency's "5 Rules of the JTA":

- We will work with the private sector, regional government and other ministries and agencies to exercise a new kind of effectiveness.
- We will avoid sectionalism, cut waste, maintain speed and produce results swiftly.
- We will actively disseminate information, and disclose our work process and results.
- We will work to improve specialization, and to respond to a broad range of tourism-related calls for support.
- We will commit to free and flat communication, and create an employee-friendly workplace.[52]

Thus, the JTA's overall ethos is clearly developmental but in a way that is consciously attuned (at least rhetorically) to overcoming specific shortcomings in Japanese industrial policy administration discussed earlier.

Before concluding this section, it is useful to draw attention to the fact that politicians and developments in the arena of partisan politics were indispensable in bringing about the transition that we focused on. The reports of the administrative reform movement presented administrative reform as a set of ideas that should be put into practice but left no indication as to how its recommendations should be ferried from there to implementation in a political context that was not by any means fully welcoming of its ideas. In the event, it took the efforts of politicians championing both political *and* administrative reform, a change in government, and success in 1994 in getting legislation passed that drastically changed the logic of and the incentives produced by the electoral system to set the stage for the culmination of the administrative reform movement in the Hashimoto administrative reforms.[53]

Conclusion

As discussed in the introduction, this chapter constitutes an initial, exploratory attempt to address the question, what happened to the Japanese capitalist developmental state as Japan confronted the bundle of profound social changes that we labeled "postindustrial society?" It suggested the proviso that in critical ways Japan's was an imperfect capitalist developmental state, one in which the autonomy of the state posited in the model was limited by the institutions of a strong electoral democracy and by equally strong bureaucratic sectionalist tendencies. Working synergistically, the two tendencies together severely undercut the developmental effectiveness of the state's industrial interventions. These tendencies became undeniably

apparent from the latter half of the 1970s onward just as the changes
associated with the transition to postindustrial society were taking hold.
In this sense, for better or worse, the challenge from the standpoint of
realizing a developmental state in Japan was as much about finding a way
to bring a "plan rational" orientation to the country's vigorous democracy
as it was a search for policies and institutional reforms adapted to the
socioeconomic realities of postindustrial society. We then traced the effort
to formulate a response to this challenge at the rhetorical level as revealed in
a key report associated with the administrative reform movement. Looked
at in this light, the reforms of the Japanese governmental system that were
implemented at the turn of the century can be considered to have been an
exercise designed to revamp the Japanese system of government in a way
that harmonizes democracy and plan rationality in a way that is attuned
to the complex and fluid demands of postindustrial society. A brief look at
broadband and inbound tourism policies provides evidence that at least in
some sectors "postindustrial" policy initiatives of the sort that one would
anticipate in light of the preceding are indeed being pursued, although a full
assessment of the degree to which the postindustrial developmental state
model provides a meaningful framework for describing policy practice in
twenty-first century Japan requires research and analysis of a scope well
beyond what was presented here.

     In closing, one could also ask whether a postindustrial society represents
an inhospitable environment for the capitalist developmental state. The
Japanese experience suggests, perhaps not. Indeed, one of the most fascinating
elements of the Japanese trajectory has been the way in which a business-
centered movement, which conventional wisdom would suggest would be
adamantly opposed to any such revival, was at the forefront of the Japanese
efforts to reinstate it. At the same time, however, that country's experience
also suggests that survival over the long term will require adaptation of
its modus operandi; that is, a shift from industrial policy to postindustrial
policy as the tool set of choice.

10

Reassessing Japan's "Big Bang": Twenty Years of Financial Regulatory Reform

Bruce E. Aronson

The "lost decade" of the 1990s in Japan has now become two decades, with the latter decade being marked by persistent deflationary pressure. A number of factors contributed to this long period of low economic growth, including (1) significantly larger real estate and stock bubbles than experienced by the United States in 2007,[1] (2) monetary and fiscal policy mistakes (in 1989–90 and 1997, respectively) as, at least in hindsight, the government removed economic stimulus too early, (3) a banking crisis beginning in 1997 which exacerbated long-term growth and productivity issues and which preoccupied governmental policy making and actions, (4) an aging society with a declining number of productive workers that constrained economic growth, (5) pork barrel politics which supported ongoing subsidies for inefficient industries, particularly in rural areas, that exacerbated budget deficits and the national debt, and (6) bad luck, as the Asian financial crisis in 1997, the US-initiated financial crisis in 2008, and the Tōhoku earthquake in 2011 set back what might have otherwise been sustained economic recovery in Japan.

Beginning in the early 1990s, the Japanese responded with both short-term fiscal and monetary policies to stimulate the economy and long-term "structural reform." Two core elements of the wide-ranging reform efforts were substantive financial deregulation under the "Big Bang"[2] program initiated in 1996 and reform of Japan's regulatory style from one of administrative guidance to a transparent system based on legal rules and their interpretation. Such changes would transform a highly regulated bank-oriented financial system to a transparent, market-based financial system (i.e. the often-cited Big Bang slogan of a "fair, free and global" financial system). A newly efficient capital market would, in turn, lead to a sustained economic recovery and, ultimately, to a new postindustrial economic model. Thus, the long-standing effort to adjust Japan's economic model to conditions of a postindustrial society would center more on private market initiative rather than on government planning.[3]

Both popular opinion and academic literature view these reform efforts as a failure. Many cite Japan's continuing low economic growth, particularly in contrast to the perceived success of financial and technological innovation in the United States in the 1990s and strong economic growth in China in the 2000s. Economic stagnation is seen, especially by Western critics, as strong evidence that Japan did not, in fact, implement the promised reforms to change its system. However, this view is too broad and result-oriented to be used as a standard for evaluating Japanese reform efforts.

Judging the success of Japan's economic and other policies based on its economic growth rate is nothing new. In *Postwar Japan as History*, Laura Hein pointed out that through the 1980s, Japan's high economic growth rate was broadly equated with economic success. This led to a simplified view of the existence of a fully planned, carefully executed, and consistent economic policy in Japan. This view was accompanied by a number of myths such as bureaucratic omnipotence and cultural uniqueness as causes of Japan's success. It also ignored Japan's complexities, inconsistencies, and inconclusive, ongoing debates throughout the period of its perceived postwar success.[4]

Since the early 1990s, the opposite has occurred, as Japan's low economic growth rate has led to an equally simplistic view of Japan as a failure. This view is accompanied by corresponding myths of bureaucratic incompetence and rigid cultural traits that supposedly contribute to this ongoing failure. It similarly ignores complexities, debates, and policy shifts amid fast-changing and fluid circumstances in Japan. Apart from a seemingly poor substantive outcome, critics, including many within Japan, also cite concerns with administrative process. Skepticism remains about the ability and willingness of Japan to replace its often-cited bureaucratic-led model of postwar development with a new "hands-off" approach that will allow private businesses and markets to function efficiently, particularly in the critical and highly regulated financial services sector. Accustomed to a regulatory style of active administrative guidance, could Japan's bureaucracy really shift to one of a neutral umpire based on legal rules and their interpretation?

This negative view of Japan has been reinforced in academic circles by the increasing importance of globalization and the perceived success of the US postindustrial model in the 1990s. Scholars have focused on the possibility that international competition among economic and legal systems would lead to global convergence, presumably toward a US-based "global" or "standard" model that emphasized deregulation and the role of free markets.[5] Japan would, therefore, require a real transformation to compete in the future, but scholars in a number of fields noted the lack of such a clear, systemic transformation.[6] This generally led them to conclude that reform efforts in Japan were insufficient to effect "real change" and therefore not significant. If deregulation and the US model were successful, Japan merely had to "get serious" about carrying out reform along similar lines.

The Japanese themselves appeared to share this belief. They presumed that financial deregulation and an accompanying shift to a market-based financial system would address the fundamental demographic and productivity problems facing an aging society and mature economy as follows: (1) a higher return on private financial assets would ameliorate the problem of increasing social welfare payments in a rapidly aging society, (2) capital markets would more efficiently allocate funds to emerging growth industries and lead to higher economic growth rates, and (3) Tokyo would compete successfully in global financial competition and become a leading financial center.[7]

The overall Japanese approach suggests acceptance of, or at least hope in, the power of deregulation and administrative reform to bring about far-reaching positive effects from the efficient functioning of free markets. It was anticipated that not only would a capital markets-based financial system lead to the creation of a strong financial services industry, but that it would also pressure both the banking system and nonfinancial corporations to restructure and become more efficient and competitive. The main thrust of deregulation would be aided by related reforms in a number of complementary areas such as the legal profession (more and better lawyers to support businesses in a regulatory system based on legal rules), corporate governance (greater shareholder orientation by corporate management to increase investor returns and stock market attractiveness), privatization of public corporations, labor flexibility, and pension system reform. The ultimate result would be a shift from a manufacturing-based, export-oriented economic model to a new service-oriented, postindustrial economic model for Japan.

Definitional uncertainties concerning basic issues related to the Big Bang program, such as its length and goals, complicate attempts at evaluating its results. For example, the announced length of the Big Bang was 1996–2001 (already a long period for a "bang"), but many important reform efforts began only under the Koizumi administration after 2001. The three broad societal goals of deregulation were cited by government planners but may have been exaggerated for political purposes. In addition, by the time the Japanese Government went beyond the 1996 announcement of the Big Bang into planning and implementing concrete measures in 1997–1998, it was necessarily reacting to a full-blown banking crisis[8] and focusing as much effort on stabilization of the financial system as on its reform.[9]

In seeking to re-evaluate the results of the Big Bang, this chapter adopts an expansive view of its length and its goals, that is, the Big Bang planners conceived a fundamental approach and long-term framework for ongoing financial and administrative reform that should include post-2001 reform efforts and the cited broad societal goals, even if these goals were not immediately or actively pursued. The thesis of this chapter is that despite the inability to achieve these ambitious societal goals, and contrary to conventional wisdom, Japan's reform efforts were "serious" and were not a failure. The Japanese Government did undertake significant reform and substantially, albeit not completely, transformed its administrative processes and financial regulatory system. The Japanese were largely successful in changing from a closed financial regulatory system based on an important role for government, administrative guidance and administrative discretion to a more open system based largely on markets, legal rules, and information disclosure/transparency. However, this change was insufficient to achieve large societal changes. Although financial deregulation could remove legal and administrative obstacles and thereby encourage growth and investment, other more important factors must operate successfully in order to achieve greater return on investment, gains in productivity, and a higher rate of economic growth.

It is necessary to evaluate Japan's efforts without resorting to crude, transformational standards arguably based on an idealized US model and a simplistic view of Japan's economic "failure" and bureaucratic dominance. To accomplish this, we must consider the process by which financial deregulation and administrative reform could achieve the three broad societal goals noted above, and evaluate the efforts and results for each step. This process was not clearly articulated at the time reform efforts were initiated. In retrospect, we can say that the first step would be government-led financial deregulation and administrative reform. The intermediate step would be financial institutions, corporate borrowers, and other market participants utilizing new competitive opportunities to gradually transform Japan's bank-oriented financial system to a market-centered system. The final step would be a more efficient financial system, combining with a number of other factors and broad societal participation, leading over time to achievement of the three broad societal goals and ultimately to a new postindustrial economic model (see Figure 10.1).

The ongoing re-examination of assumptions and changing perceptions following the 2008 financial crisis provide a good opportunity to reassess Japan's performance since the early 1990s. The specific issue addressed in this chapter concerns Japanese efforts to achieve market reforms and a sustained economic recovery. However, this inquiry also involves a broader fundamental issue related to the study of Japan: lingering notions of Japanese exceptionalism. Japan's supposed cultural characteristics (or even uniqueness) have been cited as a factor in both Japan's "success" through the 1980s and its "failure" since the early 1990s. Following the 2008 financial crisis, it has become clear that a number of industrialized countries have experienced their own "lost decade" in the 2000s with problems and causes similar to those described with respect to Japan at the beginning of this chapter.[10] Therefore, in a sense, Japan has heretofore been unfairly singled out as a "failure." This is likely due not only to the objective factor of Japan's extended period of low growth, but arguably also represents a reaction to its prior path-breaking "success" and perceived exceptionalism.

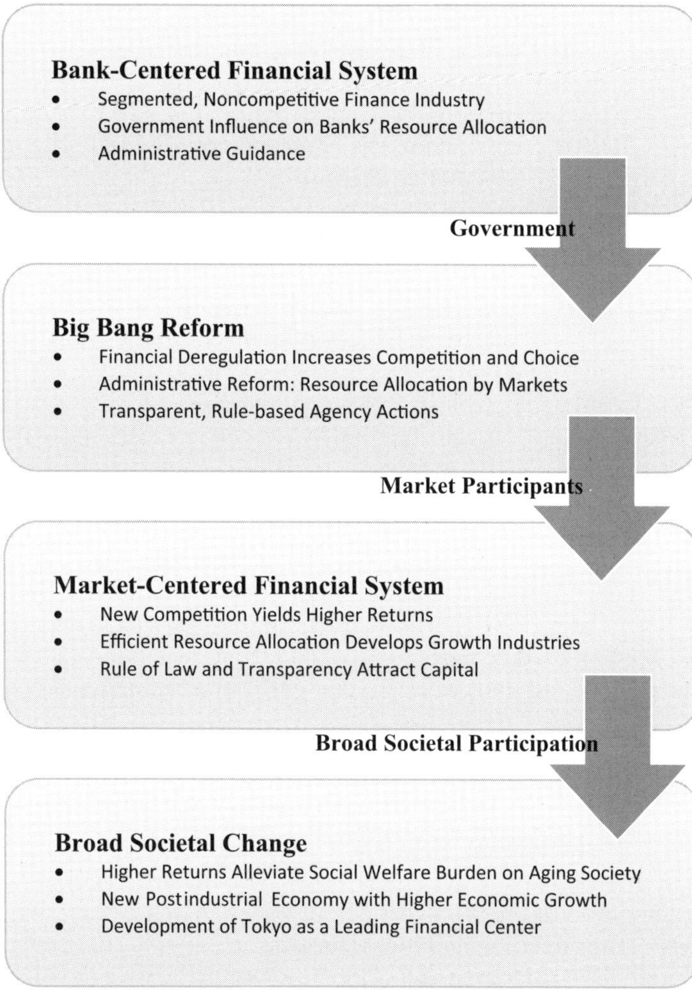

Bank-Centered Financial System
- Segmented, Noncompetitive Finance Industry
- Government Influence on Banks' Resource Allocation
- Administrative Guidance

Government

Big Bang Reform
- Financial Deregulation Increases Competition and Choice
- Administrative Reform: Resource Allocation by Markets
- Transparent, Rule-based Agency Actions

Market Participants

Market-Centered Financial System
- New Competition Yields Higher Returns
- Efficient Resource Allocation Develops Growth Industries
- Rule of Law and Transparency Attract Capital

Broad Societal Participation

Broad Societal Change
- Higher Returns Alleviate Social Welfare Burden on Aging Society
- New Postindustrial Economy with Higher Economic Growth
- Development of Tokyo as a Leading Financial Center

FIGURE 10.1 *Process of Big Bang leading to transformation to a Postindustrial Society.*

Of even greater significance than common problems is the relative ineffectiveness of common solutions. Japan's experience of extraordinary policy measures yielding very modest economic results is also no longer unique. In the wake of the 2008 crisis, the United States and other countries were forced to take extraordinary "Japan-like" measures in both fiscal and monetary policy, including large budget deficits and quantitative easing to increase the money supply. In the last few years, there has been both serious discussion in the United States concerning the possibility that America will repeat Japan's experience of slow growth within a lingering deflationary environment and sovereign debt crises in a number of developed countries in Europe.[11]

The 2008 financial crisis also challenged the assumptions of the wide-ranging positive effects of deregulation and the superiority of the US postindustrial model. It now appears that a portion of the gains of the financial services industry in the United States was due to a bubble or financial engineering unrelated to the real economy. The lack of regulation in areas such as over-the-counter derivatives is no longer solely praised as a key to financial innovation; the risks involved in such a course have also become readily apparent. This chapter is a broad survey that examines the appropriate standard for evaluation of financial system change in Japan, relevant data as available, and the results of reform for each step of the process outlined above: (1) financial deregulation and administrative reform, (2) transformation to a market-based finance system, and (3) achievement of the three broad social goals. It seeks to initiate a new discussion of Japan's reform efforts freed of the strong implicit assumptions and perceptions of the last two decades.

This chapter concludes that the Big Bang substantially achieved its immediate government-led goals of deregulation and administrative reform, but that the envisioned reform process was not generally successful beyond that initial stage. This illustrates the limits of what can be accomplished through deregulation of financial markets in the face of the persistence of past practices by market participants and strong headwinds such as low economic growth and poor stock market performance.

Financial deregulation and administrative reform under the Big Bang

The Big Bang reform program carried out wide-ranging substantive reform of financial laws covering banking, securities, and insurance. These reforms covered a much broader area and were more comprehensive than prior "Big Bangs" in New York and London that focused primarily on the deregulation of brokerage commissions.[12] There was substantial new legislation enacted beginning in 1997 that represented a dramatic acceleration of ongoing reform efforts. At the same time, the Japanese also recognized that financial system reform would require a fairly long-term and gradual process.

There is little disagreement that the Japanese carried out significant deregulatory reform of financial laws "on the books." However, the conventional wisdom holds that, judging partially by the lack of positive economic results, these reforms did not greatly affect regulatory practices. The suspicion remains that continuing governmental regulatory involvement may have hindered the development of competitive financial markets over the last two decades and achievement of the broad goals of reform. In addition, there are no statistical data available to demonstrate that Japan has substantially changed its regulatory style in the financial services area.

However, there is persuasive indirect evidence of significant change in regulatory style. Legislative changes broke up the powerful Ministry of Finance ("MOF") and replaced it in the financial services regulatory area with the new Financial Services Agency ("FSA") and a newly independent Bank of Japan ("BOJ"). An important practice in maintaining administrative guidance, the use of "informal" administrative directives not subject to legal challenge (*tsūtatsu*), was discontinued in 2000 and replaced by a system of guidelines (*kantoku shishin*) that are issued following a public consultation process. In addition, a new system of "American-style" no-action letters was introduced in 2001, although it is not widely utilized.[13]

Even prior to the formal breakup of the MOF, the position of "MOF-tan" at Japanese banks, which was a crucial role through the mid-1990s in maintaining close informal relations between banks and the MOF, was abolished. Today, much of the "give and take" between the banking industry and regulators occurs at the industry level through the chairman's office at the Japan Bankers' Association, while at the individual bank level, compliance officers have gained substantially in importance. Ultimately, deregulation and administrative reform greatly affected virtually every element of Japan's postwar banking system (e.g. industry segmentation and noncompetition, administrative guidance, the "convoy" system of bank bailouts, the role of main banks, etc.).

Apart from these structural and institutional changes, the movement from administrative discretion toward legal rules is reflected most clearly in a corresponding rise in the role of Japanese lawyers over the last decade. There has been significant new domestic demand in Japan for corporate legal services in areas including new financial products, compliance, and corporate governance. Japanese corporate law firms have grown very rapidly in the past decade to meet this demand and have essentially switched their primary role from one of advising on cross-border transactions to one of focusing on domestic work. This transformation of the role of the legal profession supports the view that there has been a real change in the Japanese style of administration, as businesses now consult with lawyers on legal rules and procedures rather than meet informally with government bureaucrats.[14]

Financial regulators have also significantly increased their involvement with lawyers. There was little, if any, consulting with lawyers by government agencies at the beginning of the Big Bang process in the mid-1990s. Today, not only do financial regulatory agencies consult regularly with outside attorneys, it has become very common for young lawyers at the leading corporate law firms to work temporarily inside regulatory agencies for a few years on "secondment." The FSA is the largest temporary employer of such lawyers, and other financial regulators also use them.[15] Although this trend is significant, its limits are indicated by a general lack of permanent lawyer positions at these agencies and by the lack of an enforcement division staffed by lawyers.

The prevailing viewpoint, argued most vigorously by foreign bankers in Japan and their attorneys, is that the Japanese regulatory system has not really changed. According to this view, the structure of regulatory agencies and the substance of regulations may look different, but the heavy hand of regulation is still present and it does not welcome foreign participants in Japan's financial markets. This is an important point since it directly relates to whether market participants were, in fact, free to compete fully in areas such as the provision of new financial products and services. However, this is a difficult argument to evaluate in a comparative context. It is often anecdotal and in every advanced economy, banks and financial services present significant risks and attract the highest level of regulatory interest of any industry.

The faults ascribed to Japanese regulatory agencies are also often vague, and can include phrases like "need to build trust" and "lack of communication." It is worth noting that such concerns would be consistent with a financial regulatory system that had moved substantially from an informal administrative model to a model based on legal rules. In such case, the old informal means of communication would necessarily need to be replaced with the enforcement of new rules. Such rules include FSA-published guidance and bank examination policies that could appear to be more one-sided and less interactive than the traditional approach, leading to new questions of trust and communication.

The standard for achieving significant reform should not require moving from a system of "heavy" rules-based regulation to a system of "light" principles-based regulation, as advocated by foreign financial institutions.[16] Rather, the key issue is one of regulatory style—that is, whether Japan has moved to a more open, rule-based system rather than relying on closed, informal interactions with government agencies. By this measure, Japan has arguably achieved substantial regulatory reform.

Transparency is related to clear rules, but it also depends on the public disclosure of information. Beginning with the Administrative Procedures Act of 1993, Japan has gradually moved to a system with public comments for proposed regulations, disclosure of discussions of deliberation councils that debate proposed legislation and regulations, and disclosure of enforcement actions. The website of any major government agency in Japan now contains a significant amount of information on relevant laws, policies, and activities disclosed in a timely manner. Ongoing corporate law reform has also resulted in the 2000s in increased information disclosure by public corporations (Financial Instruments Exchange Law or so-called J-SOX of 2006) that would help support stronger capital markets and a requirement for internal control systems that go beyond financial accounting and cover risk management policies (Companies Act of 2005).

Judging the extent of change in Japan's regulation and regulatory style in the financial services area is also complicated by governmental reaction to changed circumstances over time—it is not a unidirectional process. It is widely acknowledged that the initial Big Bang deregulation in 1998 increased competition in Japan's financial services industry, chiefly through the increased sales of mutual funds by banks. However, increased securities sales also revealed weaknesses in information disclosure and advice on suitability provided to customers, and that resulted in a degree of "reregulation" for investor protection under the Financial Instruments and Exchange Act of 2006.

Similarly, as noted previously, the initial 1998 reforms occurred at a time of an ongoing banking crisis that necessitated continuing close governmental supervision of the weak Japanese banking system. As this situation gradually improved over time, the FSA announced that it would move toward principles-based regulation, but has made only limited progress in that direction as compared to the United Kingdom. In sum, although issues remain and calls for more user-friendly regulation continue, the changes over time have been significant. Government-led deregulatory and administrative reform was, in fact, likely sufficient to remove legal and administrative obstacles and thereby permit the development of a market-centered financial system.

Transformation to a market-based financial system

This section considers whether government-led financial deregulation and administrative reform affected the behavior of market participants and led to a shift from a bank-dominated system of indirect finance to a capital market-dominated system of direct finance. As noted above (see Figure 10.1), such a shift would presumably be necessary to achieve greater financial market efficiency and achieve broad societal goals. This section concludes that progress to date has been slow and insufficient primarily because Japanese banks have continued with traditional inefficient banking practices rather than responding enthusiastically to government deregulation and new opportunities for competition. Japan remains a bank-dominated financial system, and banking practices have hindered the development of strong capital markets, particularly a corporate bond market commensurate with the size and maturity of Japan's economy.

Progress toward the goal of shifting to market-dominated finance can be measured generally through flow of funds data from the BOJ (excerpted in Table 10.1). Data show the total of all forms of corporate finance increasing in the 1980s, leveling in the 1990s, and gradually decreasing during the past decade. The substantial decrease between 1995 and 2005 was caused by a decline in loan volume, as stock issuance increased modestly during that time period. The ratio of loans to stocks ("shares and other equities") for nonfinancial corporations was roughly six times (6) in 1980, 5 in 1990, 3 in 2000, and 2 in 2009. In essence, the data indicate a very slow, but substantial movement in the direction of a greater role for equity finance.

TABLE 10.1 *Corporate finance* (Liabilities of nonfinancial corporations)

(Unit = trillion yen, percentage)

	1980	(%)	1985	(%)	1990	(%)	1995	(%)	2000	(%)	2005	(%)	2009	(%)
Loans	202	50.4	301	54.0	498	52.4	555	53.6	445	48.1	327	39.2	337	41.1
Securities other than shares	19	4.8	31	5.6	79	8.3	76	7.3	74	8.0	71	8.5	72	8.7
Shares and Other Equities	33	8.1	54	9.6	95	10.0	117	11.3	141	15.3	156	18.7	158	19.2
Deposit money	27	6.8	36	6.4	60	6.3	58	5.6	42	4.5	37	4.4	3	4.5
Inter-business credits	116	29.0	129	23.2	198	20.9	208	20.1	194	21.1	182	21.8	166	20.3
Others	3	0.9	6	1.2	20	2.1	21	2.0	28	3.0	62	7.4	50	6.1
Total	400	100.0	557	100.0	950	100.0	1,034	100.0	924	100.0	834	100.0	820	100.0

Source: Bank of Japan.

The question is whether this gradual shift to direct finance has made a real difference in the efficiency of Japan's financial system. The data are somewhat ambiguous. Stock issuance has increased relative to loan volume over the past decade primarily because of a decline in loan volume. The annual flow of funds data do not indicate that financial deregulation and other reform measures had any clear impact on the longstanding, gradual trend of moving from bank loans to equity financing. The gradual reduction in the volume of bank loans might also be substantially accounted for by tougher regulation in response to Japan's banking crisis and by an overall absence of corporate demand for funding in a weak economy.

Some academic commentators who closely follow the Japanese banking system have concluded that Japan has substantially transformed to a market-based financial system.[17] The reasons cited are the above data on the long-term trend of direct finance gradually replacing indirect finance, a loss of governmental protection of banks from capital markets, and the greater financing choices for large corporate borrowers. However, from the broader perspective of the financial system as a whole, most commentators still characterize Japan as having a bank-dominated finance system that is relatively inefficient.

This majority view focuses more on the comparison between bank loans and the weak corporate bond market. Commentators have long pointed to Japan's weak bond markets as the biggest difference between financial systems in Japan and the United States following the beginning of Japan's deregulation efforts in the 1980s.[18] Despite the substantial relative increase in direct equity finance, Japan's financial system continues to have an overreliance on bank lending and this is recognized by Japanese Government studies that call for greater diversification of financing sources.[19]

Generally speaking, a capital market system is presumably better than a bank-centered finance system for a large economy, as the higher costs of disclosure, regulation, and enforcement that accompany a market-based system are outweighed by the benefits of providing a large volume of cheap capital.[20] The same tradeoff is also generally true for individual corporations, as large businesses in the United States often favor bonds over bank loans due to lower cost and greater flexibility. Of even greater importance than providing low-cost funds is the potential for capital markets to allocate resources more efficiently to their greatest productive use. A robust Japanese corporate bond market may, therefore, be essential to provide a true alternative to bank lending and to obtain the full anticipated benefits of capital market efficiency.

From a comparative perspective, Japan's corporate bond market is now strikingly small compared to both the United States and the European Union, as measured, for example, by the size of the bond market to the economy.[21] Historically, legal and administrative obstacles hindered the development of a corporate bond market in Japan. Deregulation measures were undertaken (in particular, removal of issuer limitations in 1996) and resulted in the creation of a bond market infrastructure which is "reasonably well developed" to support market growth.[22] However, significant corporate bond market growth has not occurred. As of 2008, corporate bonds constituted only 5.8% of the Japanese bond market.[23]

This pattern—the removal of legal obstacles not leading to the development of a robust market—is by no means limited to corporate bonds. It also applies to a variety of new financial products such as exchange-traded funds (ETFs), securitizations, and real estate investment trusts (or REITS, although many consider the J-REIT market to be a relative or partial success) and the slow growth of liberalized markets such as over-the-counter foreign exchange and derivatives.[24] The failure of new financial products is often generally attributed to risk-averse Japanese investors and a corresponding lack of demand. However, there is persuasive anecdotal evidence of a healthy potential demand for relatively low-risk domestic corporate bonds from both institutional and individual investors in Japan.

We must, therefore, look to the supply side, that is, corporate issuers, for an explanation why a robust Japanese bond market has failed to develop. The most often-cited factor is corporations' easy access to bank loans due to the persistence of traditional relationship lending practices by Japanese banks, combined with the existing weak corporate bond market that fails to provide a fully viable alternative. Even weak corporate borrowers can readily obtain bank loans, and banks have continued to provide forbearance lending to "zombie" corporations.[25] On the other hand, there is nearly a complete lack of "junk" bond issuance by weaker corporations in Japan, although that particular market is also hampered by restrictions limiting many institutional investors to investment in highly rated bonds.

Big Bang reforms have significantly affected the banking industry. The roles of the main bank and keiretsu have weakened and the banking industry has undergone a dramatic consolidation across traditional group lines. However, the primary result of regulatory changes designed to increase competition has been banks reducing interest rates on loans to compete with one another. They have not been required to become more efficient profit-oriented lenders to compete with a corporate bond market. Japanese banks, like Japanese corporations generally, have traditionally emphasized market share over profitability and remain consistently less profitable than US banks.[26] Thus, the hope that increased competition from more efficient capital markets would also lead to a more efficient bank-led finance market has not been realized. Although the appeal of bonds for corporate issuers is generally thought to be their low cost compared to bank loans, the opposite is said to be true in Japan.[27]

There may be ingrained habits and existing images which discourage a corporate bond market. When Japanese think of corporate bonds, their image is of the small number of top-rated issuers rather than the "average" corporate issuers that are common in the United States. Ironically, until the Great Eastern Earthquake of 2011, the Tokyo Electric Power Company was considered the financially strongest corporation in Japan and was the largest bond issuer. Following the earthquake, it essentially became bankrupt and requires government support as would a failed large bank.

As a result, although there has been a substantial, if very gradual, increase in direct finance in Japan over time, there has probably not been a sufficient transformation of the financial system to obtain the benefits from market efficiency envisioned at the time of the Big Bang. The persistence of traditional bank lending and the failure of market participants to develop a corporate bond market despite deregulation is arguably the largest stumbling block in the process of governmental deregulation leading to achievement of broad societal goals. Ironically, one hope for the development of a corporate bond market may lie in strengthening bank regulation rather than in deregulation, that is, the possibility of tougher international capital adequacy requirements for banks following the 2008 financial crisis that would pressure all large Japanese banks to exit from low interest, unprofitable loans.

Failure to achieve broader societal goals

Despite substantial completion of the first step of government-led financial deregulation and administrative reform, the Big Bang failed to achieve the broader societal goals that were announced at the time of its inception. In this section, the chapter provides the available evidence on the lack of progress in achieving these goals. It also suggests some additional significant factors, beyond deregulation and market efficiency, that may be necessary to achieve such goals.

Higher return on private financial assets

One of the highly conspicuous arguments at the time of the Big Bang was the need and opportunity to invest some of the 1,200 trillion yen in private savings and obtain a higher market return than provided by bank savings accounts.[28] Achieving this goal would help provide ample assets for private retirement and for governmental social welfare payments, and would enable Japan to regain an important role in the international community. The Big Bang was expected to produce higher returns on private investment by increasing competition among financial service providers which, in turn, would produce a wider range of attractive financial products and investor-friendly services. However, the trend of household savings and investment has gone in the other direction—the percentage of bank savings ("cash and deposits") within all household financial assets has been increasing and now occupies nearly 55% (see Table 10.2). This contrasts with about 14% in the United States.[29] Conversely, Japanese households hold 6.4% of financial assets in shares and equities, while this percentage reaches 31.4% in the United States.[30]

TABLE 10.2 *Household financial assets*

(Unit = trillion yen, percentage)

	1980	(%)	1985	(%)	1990	(%)	1995	(%)	2000	(%)	2005	(%)	2009	(%)
Cash and Deposits	217	58.5	329	52.6	482	47.4	630	50.1	751	54.1	769	50.7	798	54.9
Bonds	27	7.4	48	7.7	64	6.3	74	5.9	48	3.5	40	2.7	42	2.9
Stocks and Other Equities	49	13.2	100	16.0	172	16.9	144	11.5	107	7.7	197	13.0	103	7.1
Investment Trusts	4	1.2	14	2.3	34	3.4	29	2.3	34	2.4	52	3.4	55	3.8
Insurance and Pension Reserves	50	13.4	102	16.3	212	20.8	319	25.4	378	27.2	391	25.8	393	27.0
Others	24	6.3	33	5.2	53	5.2	61	4.8	70	5.1	67	4.4	62	4.3
Total	372	100.0	627	100.0	1,017	100.0	1,256	100.0	1,389	100.0	1,517	100.0	1,453	100.0

Source: Bank of Japan.

The widely cited necessity of investing household savings and earning a higher return is as strong today as it was 15 years ago. In the interim, the total amount of private savings has increased from 1,200 trillion yen to over 1,500 trillion yen. Why has no progress been made?

There was, in fact, significant deregulation and encouragement of the asset management industry in Japan beginning in the mid-1990s. The number of financial services providers and products has increased, and today individuals can easily purchase stock investment trusts (the Japanese equivalent of stock mutual funds) and other investment securities at bank counters. However, other more important factors either were not present or had a negative impact.[31]

First is market performance. Individual investors (and the mutual funds which must attract such investors) tend to chase performance and invest during rising markets. The stock market in Japan, at least as measured by the Nikkei index, lost approximately 3/4 of its value when the bubble collapsed in the early 1990s and has been essentially flat for the past 20 years. Japanese investment in stocks has also been flat. In the United States as well, poor stock market returns following the tech stock market crash in 2000 reversed the trend of increased stock and bond ownership which had persisted from 1989 to 2001.[32] In both countries, stock ownership declined significantly following the 2008 financial crisis and stock market crash, and began to rise (end of 2010–early 2011) well after the stock market had staged a dramatic recovery from its 2009 low.

Second, employment instability, relatively high unemployment rates (for Japan), and low wage increases endured during much of the past two decades. Beginning around 1997, there has been a widespread trend for Japanese companies to rely extensively on part-time and temporary labor. New job openings and the percentage of graduating college seniors able to find full-time employment have plummeted over the past few years. This trend, together with the aging of society, has resulted in lower savings rates and has encouraged risk-averse behavior with financial assets.

Third is the lack of any necessity for many Japanese to invest in risk assets. In the United States, the trend of increasing household ownership of equities and bonds during the 1990s coincided with a decrease in traditional pensions in the form of defined benefit plans and an increase in 401(k) and other defined contribution plans.[33] This forced many individuals to be responsible for investing for their retirement. However, in Japan, most large employers still manage retirement funds for employees and provide a lump-sum benefit upon retirement despite the introduction of defined contribution retirement plans in 2001. There is accordingly little necessity for many individuals in Japan to accept market risk in order to achieve higher returns on assets for retirement.[34] One continuing area of proposed reform is to shift investment responsibility to individuals and provide tax incentives for individual investment accounts.[35]

Finally, government policies have worked at cross-purposes for fiscal and political reasons, and have encouraged low-return investments. One of the

most significant issues remaining on the deregulatory agenda is the fate of
Japan Post Bank, the former government post office which remains the largest
deposit-taker in Japan. In addition, large fiscal deficits and outstanding
amounts of government debt have led the Japanese Government to strongly
encourage investment in low-yielding government bonds. Both Japan Post
Bank deposits and government bonds had increased appeal to households
as a safe haven following the 2008 financial crisis, and both were heavily
advertised in media campaigns.

One potential bright spot in this otherwise bleak picture is the recent
asset increase by Japanese mutual funds and the continuing substantial share
of personal assets held by institutional investors (see Table 10.2). Pension
funds, in particular, are held out as the hope for professional management
of Japanese private assets, including the utilization of asset allocation strategies with significant exposure to equities and other risk assets. This trend
includes professional management of government funds, as under a significant 2001 reform, deposits from the postal bank are now professionally invested by the Government Pension Investment Fund (GPIF) rather
than being controlled and invested in pet programs by the MOF under the
Fiscal Investment Loan Program (FILP). However, Japanese institutional
investors remain more conservative in investments than their American
counterparts.[36]

Market allocation of capital to emerging growth industries

An oft-cited goal of both financial deregulation and government policies to
directly promote economic growth is investment in new growth industries.
There are no data available to measure progress toward this goal, as it is
difficult to identify or define "emerging growth companies." There are data
on the amount of bank loans going to small companies, and this number
has been declining during the past decade. However, the reality in Japan is
that the bulk of small businesses are likely companies that are in traditional,
low-growth industries rather than in emerging industries.

The best-known market for financing emerging companies, the venture
capital market, remains weak in Japan. In 2009, venture firms invested some
88 billion yen in Japan, compared with the equivalent amount of 532 billion
yen in Europe and 1,592 billion yen in the United States.[37] For evidence that
markets have been unable to efficiently allocate capital to growth industries,
one need only look to recent government initiatives by the Bank of Japan
to provide special low-interest loans to banks for lending to emerging
companies.[38] More generally, in 2010, the Japanese Government proposed a
national growth strategy of 10% across-the-board cuts in ministry budgets
in order to create a new government-led growth fund, again evidencing
frustration with the results of market activities.

Japan's failure to develop an active venture capital market contrasts with its early postwar history of entrepreneurs founding companies such as Sony and Honda. The contrast between Japan's early postwar success and more recent failure deserves further research, yet one general explanation would be that both Japanese lenders and businessmen have become accustomed to a mature, stable economy and have grown reluctant to take risks. More specifically, scholars in the United States have linked Japan's weak venture capital market to its bank-centered financial system and underdeveloped stock market, and especially to the inability of Japanese venture capitalists to "cash out" through a public stock offering.[39]

It is no longer a problem of regulation, as changes in Japanese corporate law, including liberalization of options and preferred shares, now provide Japanese entrepreneurs and venture capitalists the ability to make essentially the same deals as do Americans in Silicon Valley. The necessary legal infrastructure for a venture capital market now "looks to be in place."[40] In addition, during the last decade, competing emerging company stock markets have developed in Japan, including the "Mothers" market of the Tokyo Stock Exchange, the "Hercules" market of the Osaka Stock Exchange (formerly Nasdaq-Japan), and the Jasdaq Securities Exchange. And in fact, public stock offerings (IPOs) constitute the chief exit strategy for investors in the small Japanese venture capital market.[41]

As in the corporate bond market, the key factor appears to be the providers of capital and their persistence in traditional "bank-like" financing patterns. Loans play a large role in Japanese venture capital and venture funds often act like main banks rather than focusing on ownership and the potentially higher returns provided by future stock offerings. Indeed, most venture funds in Japan are not independent, but rather are sponsored by banks and other financial institutions. They are staffed by "salarymen," dispatched from the parent organization, who have no economic incentive to assume risk. Despite advances in the Japanese venture capital market over the past decade, the basic differences between suppliers of venture capital in Japan and the United States, as described by one commentator in 1997, continue to persist today.[42]

It should be noted that risk-averse attitudes of entrepreneurs in Japan may be rational since the consequences of failure may be greater in Japan than in the United States. In the United States, bankruptcy filings by failed young companies are common, and it is not unusual for an entrepreneur to experience several failures before ultimately achieving success. In Japan, bankruptcy is frowned upon, and an entrepreneur might be pressured to utilize personal assets in the case of a corporate failure or have a contractual obligation with the venture capitalist to do so; he would also be unlikely to receive a second chance.[43]

As evidence of risk aversion, we can look at an annual study that ranks venture capital environments on a comparative basis through annual surveys. The latest survey by Global Entrepreneurship Monitor (GEM) continues to show that Japan ranks lowest among 20 advanced countries surveyed in terms of entrepreneurial attitudes (see Table 10.3). However, Japan

TABLE 10.3 *Entrepreneurial attitudes and perceptions*

	Perceived opportunities	Perceived capabilities	Fear of failure*	Entrepreneurial intentions**	Entrepreneurship as a good career choice	High status to successful entrepreneurs	Media attention for entrepreneurship
Innovation-Driven Economies							
Belgium	15	37	28	5	46	49	33
Denmark	34	35	37	3	47	75	25
Finland	40	35	26	4	45	88	68
France	24	27	47	16	65	70	50
Germany	22	40	37	5	54	75	50
Greece	26	58	45	15	66	68	32
Hong Kong	14	19	37	7	45	55	66
Iceland	44	50	36	15	51	62	72
Israel	29	38	37	14	61	73	50
Italy	25	41	39	4	72	69	44
Japan	8	14	50	3	28	50	61

Republic of Korea	13	53	23	11	65	65	53
Netherlands	36	47	29	5	84	67	64
Norway	49	44	25	8	63	69	67
Slovenia	29	52	30	10	56	78	57
Spain	16	48	45	4	63	55	37
Switzerland	35	49	29	7	66	84	57
United Arab Emirates	45	68	26	36	70	75	69
United Kingdom	24	47	32	4	48	73	44
United States	28	56	27	7	66	75	67
average (unweighted)	28	43	34	9	58	69	53

*Denominator: 18–64 population perceiving good opportunities to start a business.
**Denominator: 18–64 population that is not involved in entrepreneurial activity.

Source: GEM Adult Population Survey (APS), 2009.

surprisingly has a relatively high score in the category of media attention for entrepreneurship. The authors of the study note the anomaly that despite the media attention, perceived opportunities for starting a business are low and fear of failure is high.[44] These findings were recently confirmed by a new survey employing a different methodology, the Global Entrepreneurship and Development Index, which also ranked Japan last among advanced countries.[45]

In this area, Japan is not only well behind the United States, but also substantially trails Europe, and entrepreneurial attitudes in Japan rank last among a large cross-section of advanced economies.[46] Despite legal reform and the rise of emerging company sections on stock exchanges, market participants have also failed to develop a robust venture capital market. The carryover of risk-averse banking practices to the nascent venture capital market appears to be an important factor hindering Japan's financial system from supporting emerging growth industries.

Tokyo as a leading financial center

Although Tokyo was widely regarded as a leading global financial center around 1990, the bursting of the bubble caused a dramatic decline from which the Tokyo financial market never truly recovered. The Nikkei 225 Average lost roughly 75% of its value and was unable to mount a sustained recovery during the following 20 years. The market capitalization of the Tokyo Stock Exchange was larger than the New York Stock Exchange in 1990, but by 2009, it constituted less than one-third of the value of the New York Stock Exchange (see Table 10.4). Tokyo had attracted stock listings from 127 foreign companies in 1990, but this number continually declined to a low of 17 companies by 2009.

Accordingly, one explicit goal of the Big Bang announced in 1996 was to restore the vigor of Tokyo's financial market so that it would "be on a par with New York and London by 2001."[47] It was anticipated that a robust capital market would provide substantial domestic benefits. Such a financial market would both create a newly important financial services industry with high-paying jobs and a significant role in a postindustrial society, and also provide efficient financial support for other sectors of the Japanese economy, including emerging growth industries. Authorities in Tokyo undertook significant deregulatory efforts as part of Big Bang reforms in an attempt to reinvigorate Tokyo's financial market.[48] Government study groups and plans over the past decade on the issue of Tokyo's competitiveness include a MOF study group in 2003, the Abe cabinet's economic plan in 2005 and a FSA study group in 2007.[49] If, however, substantial efforts at deregulation were ultimately not successful in revitalizing Tokyo's financial market, we must consider other possible factors.

TABLE 10.4 *10 Largest stock markets by domestic market capitalization*

(Unit = billion US dollars)					
1990		**1999**		**2009**	
1. Tokyo SE	2,929	1. NYSE Euronext (US)	11,438	1. NYSE Euronext (US)	11,838
2. NYSE Euronext (US)	2,692	2. Nasdaq OMX	5,205	2. Tokyo SE	3,306
3. London SE	850	3. Tokyo SE	4,463	3. Nasdaq OMX	3,239
4. Deutsch Börse	355	4. London SE	2,855	4. NYSE Euronext (Europe)	2,869
5. Nasdaq OMX	311	5. NYSE Euronext (Europe)	2,444	5. London SE	2,796
6. TSX Group	242	6. Deutsche Börse	1,432	6. Shanghai SE	2,705
7. SIX Swiss EX	158	7. TSX Group	789	7. Hong Kong EX	2,305
8. Borsa Italiana	149	8. Borsa Italiana	728	8. TSX Group	1,676
9. Johannesburg SE	137	9. SIX Swiss EX	693	9. BME Spanish EX	1,435
10. BME Spanish EX	111	10. Hong Kong EX	609	10. BM&Fbovespa	1,337

Source: World Federation of Exchanges, available at http://www.world-exchanges.org/statistics/time-series/market-capitalization.

Cross-listing decisions by individual corporations are not generally dictated by the level of regulation and the accompanying costs of compliance, but rather are subject to numerous practical factors. These would include the desire to raise capital, the cost of capital and valuation of a company's stock in that market, business connections in that market and increased visibility from a stock exchange listing, and geographic and cultural familiarity.

In addition to a lack of cross-listing by foreign issuers, an even more striking failure of Tokyo's capital market is its continued dominance by domestic Japanese securities firms. A lingering suspicion remains that this is due to an unwelcoming attitude by the Japanese Government. There has, in fact, long been some ambiguity in the general plans that the Japanese Government has put forward to make Tokyo a leading financial center. Is the primary goal to develop a strong and efficient Japanese financial services industry or, instead, to promote the creation of a strong international financial center at the possible cost of international firms dominating Japanese firms?[50]

Japanese Government reports to date treat these two goals as compatible. In fact, evidence from one market segment—foreign underwriters entering the samurai bond market following deregulation in 1995—suggests both that some Japanese issuers favored Japanese underwriters but that the entry of foreigners did increase competition and lower underwriting costs.[51] However, as neither goal of creating an efficient Japanese domestic industry or a strong international finance center has been achieved, it is difficult to say which would be given priority in the case of conflict. Foreigners note fears expressed in Japan about the theoretical possibility of rapid internationalization in Tokyo leading to domination by foreign firms in a "Wimbledon effect."[52] This phenomenon refers to the Wimbledon tennis tournament in London achieving world-class status at the cost of dominance by foreign players, and the same is said to apply to financial markets in London following its own Big Bang deregulation in 1986.

However, like cross-listing decisions for individual foreign issuers, there are a variety of practical factors that affect the attractiveness of a financial center. Various reasons are given for the steady decline of foreign firms in the Tokyo market over the past decade, including taxes and administrative infrastructure. Foreign firms often cite taxes, heavy regulation by the FSA, and insularity as reasons for this inability to attract widespread participation by foreign financial institutions.[53] A simpler and more persuasive explanation for the weak foreign presence in Tokyo is that foreign financial institutions have limited interest in Japan's stagnant market and are concentrating resources and expanding their presence in rapidly growing markets such as Shanghai and Hong Kong.

In retrospect, it seems likely that Tokyo's perceived role as a leading financial center in 1990, with a large number of foreign companies listed on the Tokyo Stock Exchange, was an anomaly or a bubble. At the time Japan had the greatest amount of capital available and was generally valuing company stock at a very high level. It was perhaps inevitable, or at least highly likely, that companies without a close business or other connection to Japan were attracted to a "hot" capital market, and that such companies would lose interest when the market cooled. The issue of the competitive position of Tokyo's financial market is sure to become prominent once again in light of recent international merger announcements among stock exchanges.

Conclusion

The evaluation of Japan's efforts in financial deregulation, administrative reform, and related areas remains an inexact business. Although data show that the three broad and ambitious societal goals of reform have not been achieved, there are no data that clearly indicate the causes. For example, it is not possible to measure directly whether actual regulatory practice in Japan has changed significantly. The conventional wisdom is that Japan's reform efforts have not been significant and, in any case, have failed. This view is based on a mixture of the substantive outcome of low economic growth, skepticism about any real change in bureaucratic processes, a crude transformational standard used to measure change based on a fascination (at least until 2008) with free markets and the US postindustrial model in an increasingly global economy, and perhaps a dash of Japanese exceptionalism in which Japan's "unique" features of bureaucratic-led development and cultural factors are now seen as ensuring failure rather than success.

This chapter argues that the opposite viewpoint that highlights the significance of reform efforts is equally, if not more, plausible. The available evidence, even if indirect, suggests that government-led Big Bang financial deregulation and administrative reform resulted in substantial deregulation of the banking, securities, and insurance industries, a regulatory style with greater information disclosure and transparency, and greater reliance on legal rules and market mechanisms than in the past. However, governmental reforms intended to develop strong capital markets had only limited impact on the behavior of financial institutions and corporate borrowers. A strong capital market system did not develop, and many of the anticipated benefits from capital market efficiency have not materialized.

What has been the major obstacle to the development of strong capital markets? The answer probably lies in solving the two great mysteries of Japanese finance—continuing low bank profitability and the failure to develop a bond market as an alternative to bank lending. The available evidence suggests in both cases that this result is not likely due to ongoing governmental interference, but rather to the persistence of traditional, inefficient banking practices. However, this remains an important area for further research. Even though Japan's program of financial deregulation was more extensive than that undertaken in New York or London, it was not nearly as successful in growing Japan's financial services industry or achieving other broad goals related to a service-oriented postindustrial society. This result clearly illustrates the limits of what can be accomplished through financial deregulation alone and the necessary contribution of other important factors. Japan faced very strong headwinds: a debilitating banking crisis, poor economic growth and stock market performance, deflationary pressure, mounting debts from government fiscal stimulus to keep the economy afloat, and unfortunate external shocks in 1997, 2008, and 2011.

In the environment following the 2008 financial crisis, deregulation is no longer held out as the panacea to solve all economic and social problems. The times arguably call for a greater governmental role throughout the developed world both to combat weak economies and financial systems and to help re-establish economic growth in a postindustrial world. Ironically, a more limited role for Japan's bureaucracy and its recent image as a cause of failure may now pose a barrier to the Japanese initiating the broad range of policy measures necessary to achieve the laudable goals associated with Big Bang reform efforts and to restructure the Japanese economy.

Such policy measures could include tax policy and administration, which heretofore have not been well integrated into overall government policy initiatives, reform of the social security system, and new free trade agreements (particularly participation in the Trans-Pacific Partnership). They could also address the issues discussed in this chapter, such as specifically encouraging the development of a corporate bond market and discouraging unprofitable banking practices as well as measures that focus on the development of household investment, venture capital, and Tokyo's financial market. The Big Bang achieved substantial, if by no means complete, success. Changes in regulatory style of the financial services industry should facilitate continuing reform in that sector. However, it is now time for other measures to make a greater contribution to the transition of Japan to a postindustrial society.

11

Endless Modernization: Fisheries Policy and Development in Postwar Japan

Satsuki Takahashi

The earthquake and tsunami of March 2011 destroyed nearly everything that the people of northeastern Japan (Tōhoku as well as Ibaraki and Chiba Prefectures) had built to develop their fisheries since the end of World War II.[1] All along the coast of northeastern Japan, concrete seawalls and port quays were demolished; fishing boats sunk or left aground; seaside restaurants and fish markets washed away; and hatcheries wrecked—millions of juvenile fish killed when their tanks were overwhelmed by the tsunami. The financial loss and emotional trauma to the region's fishing families is palpable, but the physical plant of the fisheries destroyed also serve in their absence as useful symbols of the modernization of Japan's fisheries accomplished during 60 years of fisheries development and management.

This chapter traces the historical trajectory of Japan's postwar fisheries policy and development as a means of demonstrating that policy makers have focused on the need for "modernization" (*kindaika*) even as the notion of what needed to be modernized, not to mention the meaning of the term "modernized," has changed significantly over the past six decades. Indeed, there have been three principal phases in terms of the primary direction of the "modernization" project for the fishing sector: mechanization, conservation, and neoliberalization. After a brief overview of the postwar history of fisheries modernization, the chapter discusses each of these three phases, showing the changes in the primary goals of what had to be modernized, and concludes with a brief discussion on how the postwar history of endless modernization is also embedded within the discussion of what might be next for post-disaster Japan.

Modernization after modernization

Japan's postwar coastal fisheries modernization began soon after the Potsdam Declaration and was flourishing by the time Japan entered the era of the high economic growth in the mid-1960s. In 1949, the Fisheries Law (*Gyogyō Hō*) set the legal foundations for modernizing the state's fishing sector. In 1963, the National Diet passed the Coastal Fisheries Promotion Act (*Engan Gyogyō tō Shinkō Hō*) as the primary law for guidance on coastal fisheries policies. Article I states:

> In responding to the nation's economic development and its improvement of social life, the purpose of this law is to promote the development of coastal fisheries. It also aims to improve the social status of those who are involved in the sector, allowing them to achieve lifestyles comparable to those in other industries by implementing necessary policies for improving the productivity of coastal fishing, enhancing welfare, and modernizing and rationalizing the sector.

These broad goals have been flexible and capacious, allowing for a wide variety of policy changes, all presumably designed to promote the sector and always encouraging further modernization. For the last 60 years, the Fisheries Agency (part of the Ministry of Agriculture, Forestry, and Fisheries, or MAFF) has pushed the fisheries industry to continue its capitalist industrialization by continually proclaiming the need to modernize fisheries, even as its depiction of what has to be modernized has been revised roughly every 30 years. There have been three general phases of the modernization policy project.

The first phase of "modernization" began soon after the end of World War II and aimed primarily at the mechanization of artisanal fishing in order to increase the seafood yield. The second phase took over the grand mission in the late 1970s. In responding both to local and global increasing concerns for environmental degradation, the government shifted its main goal to encourage scientific marine resource management. And the third, most recent phase calls for the rationalization of fishing family businesses in the early 2000s, responding in part to neoliberal initiatives to reduce budgetary deficits. These phases are distinguished primarily by the key policy goal set by the state, and labeled as the projected outcome of further "modernization" of the industry.

The consistent premise of Japan's postwar fisheries policy has been rooted in the discourses of "modernization," in many ways similar to the discourses of "development" in Nepal, as noted by Stacy Pigg, in Lesotho and Zambia by James Ferguson, in Colombia by Arturo Escobar, in various other nations by James Scott, and also in Indonesia by Tania Li.[2] Inspired by what Tania Li has called the "will to improve," I find it useful to consider the "will to modernize" in conceptualizing the core goals of Japanese fisheries policy. I use the "will to modernize" rather than the "will to improve" because modernization is a particular form of improvement, and one with distinctive consequences in Japan's postwar fisheries policy. By referring to improvement, Li talks about the fulfillment of an as-yet unrealized potential among a people or for a landscape. In the case of postwar Japan, modernization is a method of both improvement and survival, which closely relates to Japanese nationalism. Perhaps, with a mixture of the resentment and the pride of its lost empire, Japan has always been haunted by a desire to be acknowledged as an equal power to the West even as it enthusiastically presents itself as a unique nation. In his chapter on industrial policy, Lonny Carlile argues that neither the term "postindustrial state" nor "post-developmentalist" state adequately captures Japan's postwar economic trajectory. The last 60 years history of Japanese fisheries policy since the end of World War II, displaying a persistent desire for further modernization, may be useful for us to grasp how the postwar trajectory in one key primary industry has involved questions about the composition and future of Japan and its industries. As such, the pursuit of continuous improvement has involved the repetition of a mission that seeks to develop an as-yet unrealized potential among people, the land, and the seas. In order to help Japan survive as a "developed nation," the industries must keep improving to achieve their continuously revised potential, and this may yet be true in post-tsunami Japan as well.

Over the years, Japan's Fisheries Agency has announced one new direction after another in its quest for modernization of the nation's fisheries. Depending on the political and social context surrounding the industry, these have invariably produced images of what the industry and fishing people themselves should look like in order to be considered as elements and members of a modern state. These tasks of modernization are, therefore, closely related to negotiations of positionality. The discourses on Japan's status in international relations are, I claim, parallel to the discourses on the position of the fisheries industry within Japan.

Japan was the first non-Western industrialized nation and the country's discourses on modernization, especially in the first couple of decades after the end of World War II, resembled those in nations that are currently labeled as "developing countries." But over the years, with the emergence of "Japan's economic miracle," Japan had entered the club of advanced industrial nations; for example, Japan joined OECD (Organization for Economic Co-operation and Development) in 1965. As Japan became recognized more as a member of the developed countries, Japan's modernization discourses had increasingly involved reference to the goal of climbing the rungs occupied by the *original* Western members of the advanced industrial countries in order to become, not only statistically but also conceptually, a *truly* modern state. Even though the country has by any obvious measure accomplished this, to judge from the public rhetoric, it is still in the process of becoming modern; discourses on "modernization" continue to play a critical role in contemporary Japan. Over its 60-year postwar history, fisheries policy has always been focused on tasks connected to "modernization."

Phase 1: Mechanical modernization of fishing

Post-World War II fisheries law and policy structure

With the end of World War II in 1945, a new era began for Japan's fishing industry. Food scarcity inflated the price of fish, creating a temporary economic boom for the coastal fishing industry. The boom was an opportunity for existing fishing families to rebuild their business after the war and for newcomers to start their own fishing enterprises, aided by the relatively low cost of building a wooden boat or purchasing one second-hand.[3] Although this inflation lasted only three years, Japan's fishing industry continued growing due both to encouragement from the government and to the vast improvement of fishing technologies supported by new fisheries policies. The major postwar reform of the fishing industry was conducted under the US Occupation as part of the GHQ's (general headquarters) larger projects of capitalist industrialization and democratization of the economy. GHQ first worked on agriculture, seeking to end the quasifeudal nature of farming by changing land rights, or the so-called emancipation of farmland (*nōchi kaihō*). They then set their sights on fisheries.

In 1948, GHQ established the Fisheries Agency within the newly created MAFF (the Ministry of Agriculture, Forestry, and Fisheries). It also implemented the Fisheries Cooperative Act[4] (*Suisangyō Kyōdōkumiai Hō*), and the Fisheries Law (*Gyogyō Hō*) in 1949. Most Japanese industrial policies are guided by principles established, usually in quite general language, in basic sectoral laws, and the Fisheries Law is no exception; it establishes basic guidelines and also provides wide latitude to officials in the Fisheries Agency in pursuing them. Under this new Fisheries Law, fishermen's cooperatives became the primary stakeholders in fishing rights, which had previously been controlled by feudal lords and then aristocrats and landed elites since the Tokugawa Era (1603–1868). Since the original fisheries law had been established in 1741, Japanese coastal fishing has featured village-based fishing rights for near-shore species and by arrangement among different coastal villages for off-shore species. A later Fisheries Law was established by the Meiji government in 1902, but it was written primarily to give legal legitimacy to the customary arrangements from the Tokugawa period, and this law was used with only a few revisions until the new law was established in 1949.

Motorized fishing boats and modern fishing ports

Democratization and capitalist industrialization during the postwar era helped to fuel the growth of the fishing industry, making it easier for newcomers to join the trade. The relatively low cost of building a wooden, unmotorized fishing boat or purchasing a second-hand one also helped them to join in the coastal fishing business.[5] As a result, according to the National Census, the population involved in the fisheries industry—including coastal and offshore fishing—increased 32% from approximately 538,000 in 1940 to 710,000 in 1947.[6] Additionally, according to official MAFF statistics, the number of fishing boats increased 21% from 355,000 in 1939 to 430,000 in 1947.[7] Among those fishing boats, those weighing less than 5 metric tons—boats for coastal fishing—increased 28% from 53,000 in 1939 to 68,000 in 1947, and the numbers continued growing in the years thereafter. During the first decade after the end of World War II, the majority of coastal fishing boats were still small, wooden, and unmotorized, while off-shore fishing boats were increasingly motorized and more similar to the heavy industrialization then marking the Japanese economy.

Coastal fishing boats finally started to follow the motorized trend in the 1950s due both to the advancement of technology as well as to government support. Fishing engines used to be too large to be practical for small boats, but the improvement of technology produced smaller and more affordable engines for small coastal fishing boats.[8] In addition, generous government subsidies and the favorable loan deals also helped the technical modernization of the coastal fishing industry. The role of the Nōrinchūkin Bank—a quasigovernmental financial institution serving as the central bank for the agricultural, forestry, and fishery co-operatives—was especially important in encouraging coastal fishing families to purchase motorized boats and, subsequently, to continue updating their boats and equipment in order to improve landings and to make fishing operations more productive. According to MAFF's annual statistics (*Nōrin-suisan Tōkei*, or Agriculture, Forestry, and Fishery Statistics), from 1950 to 1957, more than 105,000 unmotorized boats disappeared, largely replaced by 35,511 motorized boats.

In the 1960s, the decade that is remembered as the era of high economic growth (*kōdo keizai seichō ki*), the government further promoted the technical modernization of coastal fishing with the 1963 implementation of the Coastal Fisheries Promotion Act (*Engan Gyogyō tō Shinkō Hō*). The main objective of the law was to improve the standard of living of coastal fishing families, which lagged behind that of workers in many of Japan's other rapidly developing industries. A number of government projects—for example, building of fishing ports, maintenance of fishing grounds, enhancement of marine resources, promotion of co-op businesses, improvement of seafood distribution and processing, adjustment/management of seafood imports, management of disasters, innovation of technology, etc.—flowed from the law, which aimed to transform the ostensibly backward industry in the name of modernization and rationality.[9] Consequently, the very appearance of the Japanese coasts changed significantly during the decades between the end of the war and the 1970s.

Among the different projects for improvement of coastal fishing during the 1950s–70s, the largest portion of the government budget was spent for building new fishing ports. The number of fishing ports in Japan sharply increased, especially after the passage of the Fishing Port Law (*Gyokō Hō*) in 1950. As an outcome of this law, the MAFF designated four phases for government support to aid in the construction of these new ports. From 1951 to 1955, 544 billion yen (roughly US $1.51 billion) was budgeted to build 450 fishing ports; in the second phase, 1956–1963, 551 billion yen ($1.53 billion) to build 604 fishing ports; 1 trillion yen ($2.78 billion) was allocated for 380 fishing ports from 1964 to 1968; and 2.3 trillion ($6.4 billion) yen for 370 fishing ports during the fourth phase, 1969–1973.

The concrete fishing port is the symbol of mechanically modernized fishing and the preferred base for Japan's motorized fishing fleets.[10] Before the development of these ports, many fishing villages kept their small, wooden boats on the beach in front of their houses, but the construction of concrete fishing ports transformed *gyoson* (fishing village) lives. The typical fishing village today includes a scenic panorama of concrete fishing port and high-tech motorized fishing boats moored one after another. The panorama was also aural as the contemporary fishing port is inundated with the sounds of boat engines at and near the docks. Although the scale varied depending on port, a coastal fishing port usually holds 100–200 fishing boats, a far cry from the days of small wooden boats dotting the coastline in front of the family home. Without a fishing port, daily interactions of fishing families were largely based on neighborhood groups consisting of a few families that kept their boats together on the beach. Each of the two coastal towns where I lived for a year has its own port that provides space and facilities for the fishing co-op members, including docking berths, fish markets, cargo transfer, and tackle storage. Although facility sizes differ from port to port, wherever you go along the Japanese coastline—including Japan's many small, remote islands—you will find the same scene.

Parallel with the motorization of the fishing fleets and the construction of fishing ports, the development and deployment of new fishing technology was also critical in Japan's postwar fisheries modernization. This included electronic fish finders, radios, and nylon fishing nets that replaced the earlier use of rope.[11] This equipment became standard among larger fleets first, but it was increasingly adopted by small-scale coastal fishing boats in the 1960s due to technological innovations that allowed these devices to be smaller and more affordable. Consequently, fishing technology development was primarily mechanical or electronic in nature, and subsequent fishing devices such as GPS and fishing track plotters became widely adopted among coastal fishing boats by the 1980s.[12]

From the end of World War II through the 1970s, the main agenda of Japanese fisheries policy was, thus, to improve landings by establishing a modern fishing system, constructing modern facilities, and adopting high-tech equipment; like much of Japan's economic modernization in the 1950s–1970s, it was a striking success. The average income of coastal fishing families also greatly improved. Times changed in the late 1970s, however, and coastal fisheries policy entered a new era of promoting resource conservation. Fishing families had been celebrated by the government as important contributors to the nation's project of technological modernization through the improvement of landings. But starting in the 1970s, the catch-all-you-can emphasis began to become a target of criticism, even seen as being backward.

Phase 2: Modernizing through scientific resource management

Emergence of new resource management policy

By the late 1970s, the new concept of *shigen kanri-gata gyogyō* (resource management-style fisheries, or officially translated as community-based fisheries resource management) emerged, becoming the major focus of Japan's fisheries policy for the next two decades. The concept was used by fisheries officials to call for greater efforts for recovering and maintaining marine resources, especially encouraging local fishing co-ops to take "voluntary" steps toward conservation. This emphasis on local voluntarism distinguished the new policy from the previous resource management system, which largely relied on the prefectural regulations and on the 1951 Fishery Resources Protection Law (*Suisan Shigen Hogo Hō*). These earlier government regulations had set basic restrictions—such as prohibited gear, protected areas, seasonal closure, and size limits—that applied to both commercial and recreational fishing activities within prefectural waters. The late 1970s witnessed the growth of new political and academic debates on the need for greater efforts for fisheries resource management, and terms such as *shigen kanri-gata gyogyō* and the like became commonly used vocabulary for fisheries officials and scholars alike.

Japanese fisheries resource management is often celebrated as a successful case in the discourses of environmental stewardship. Nonetheless, it is important to note that the related regimes have always been designed as an industrial policy rather than as environmental policy, unlike the cases in the United States, Canada, and European nations.[13] In Japan, ever since the first regime emerged in 1951 as the Fisheries Resources Protection Law was implemented, fisheries resource management has always been treated as a strategy to promote production efficiency for the development of the fishing industry. Article I of the Fisheries Resources Protection Law states that "the object of this law is to make contributions to the development of the fisheries industry through protecting and incubating marine resources." This stance clearly remained even when the state introduced the improvement of resource management by employing the Western scientific knowledge of marine conservation as the new policy agenda in the late 1970s. Japanese officials and scholars claimed that the main reason to adopt the new policy was to develop a survival strategy that allows the coastal fisheries to cope with a crisis in the sector, including sharp new constraints on deep sea fisheries, runaway oil prices, and slumping fish prices.[14] These dominant debates referred to overexploitation rarely as an environmental crisis, instead describing it more commonly as an economic crisis that causes high costs and low fish prices, ultimately weakening the industry. Thus, MAFF stepped in, as it conventionally did, to promote sustainable economic growth, not primarily because of environmental concerns.

In the 1970s, the Japanese fishing industry faced several potentially devastating crises within a few years. Prior to this period, Japanese deep-sea fisheries played a role in leading Japan's high economic growth, but they would fall into sharp decline for several reasons. The 1973 and 1979 oil shocks resulted in rapid increases in energy costs for deep-sea fisheries. In addition, the implementation of the 200-nautical-mile Exclusive Economic Zone (EEZ) by almost all coastal nations cost Japan access to fishing grounds around the world. In order to exclude foreign fleets and to pursue effective management of marine resources around its own territory, the United States first established its own EEZ under the Magnuson Fisheries Conservation and Management Act (Magnuson Act) in 1976; Japan and other countries followed suit in 1977.

The suddenness and enormity of the losses hitting Japanese deep-sea fisheries at this time forced a major shift in the structure of Japan's fisheries industry. In the wake of the post-EEZ losses for deep-sea fisheries already reeling from high energy costs, coastal fishing became the primary sector for the fisheries industry of Japan. The coastal fisheries at the time, however, were relatively small presences in the market and too unstable in terms of production in order to make up for the losses from the deep-sea fisheries in the Japanese fisheries industry as a whole. The improvement of the coastal fisheries, therefore, became a top priority in fisheries policy in the late 1970s. In many ways, the transformation was a success. MAFF reported that, in 2006, coastal fishing generated 1,287, 000 metric tons in total with a value of 524.8 billion yen (approximately, US$5.6 billion at US$1 = ¥93), which is 49% of the total landing value of marine fishing. But this transformation would also require new ways of thinking about how coastal fisheries could and should operate.

Western resource management logics and theories

Although the Japanese government hoped to improve the productivity and success of coastal fisheries, doing so simply by increasing landings through the adoption of bigger boats and more efficient equipment (which had been the consistent focus of previous fisheries policies) was made substantially more difficult by the prominence of resource management and conservation in the global fisheries agenda. Debates on overfishing, conservation, and resource management became particularly heated in the 1970s, significantly contributing to the American implementation of the Magnuson Act. But intellectually, the arguments were not new, as marine ecologists and resource economists had theorized about the mechanisms of overfishing since the early twentieth century. For decades, fish were considered an unlimited resource that could be utilized indefinitely, but the dramatic improvements in fishing efficiency through industrialization ultimately yielded declines in landings and the size of the fish that ended up in fishing nets. People wondered—where did the fish go? As they eventually learned that fish is not an eternal resource, the term "overfishing" entered mainstream debates. In 1918, a Russian fisheries scientist, Feodor I. Baranov, introduced a theoretical concept that later became the cornerstone of fisheries resource management: Maximum Sustainable Yield (MSY). If drawn graphically, the relationship between fishing efforts and yields (as limited by fish mortality) resembles a hump bridge; up to a certain point, increased fishing efforts mean an increased yield, but beyond that apex, further efforts start to lower yields because of depletion. The yield at the peak of the arch is the MSY for a given species; the area beyond the MSY describes overfishing. In other words, fish are renewable resources provided that fishing yields are lower than the rate of reproduction, but if extraction exceeds the ability of a species to reproduce, we end up with overfishing.

The United States and Canada have long employed this 1918 concept in their fisheries resource management schemes, and scientific models based on this concept have been the basis for many of their fisheries policies. These debates developed further after World War II. The Canadian economist H. Scott Gordon introduced the concept of Maximum Sustainable Economic Yield (MEY)[15] in one of the most widely noted theoretical contributions of the era, and this has been applied by the United States, Canada, and European nations in creating regimes for balancing the economic maximization of the fisheries industry and sustainable resource use. Although he did not mention fisheries management or related theories, Garrett Hardin made a crucial contribution in his well-known 1968 article "Tragedy of the Commons," published in *Science*, which explained the mechanisms behind the overexploitation of common natural resources.[16] This argument became highly influential in the broad field of natural resource management, including for fisheries.

Debates over fisheries resource management in the Western nations have, therefore, been around since at least 1918, and their fisheries policies have been constructed largely based on those scientific and economic theories. On the other hand, Japanese fisheries management had been mainly developed as conflict management between fleets rather than resource management. But as Japanese fisheries economists and scientists—such as Hasegawa Akira and Hirasawa Yutaka—began to study these theories and logics in the 1960s, they began to influence the country's fisheries policy debates. During my undergraduate years at a fisheries university in Tokyo in the late

1990s, I took a variety of courses on fisheries resource management, and I remember that MSY and MEY were the first theories that were taught in the required course for first-year students. Indeed, many of Japan's resource management narratives were constructed based on the language of Western-born natural sciences.

Resource management as a new modernization project

Fisheries scholars and officials, thus, considered scientific resource management as a new technology to develop the fisheries industry, and they treated the new resource management scheme as a modernization project. The previous agenda of fisheries policy, of course, had also focused on modernization, shifting from the backward and inefficient customs of premechanized fishing to more productive and technologically advanced practices, but this emphasis was replaced by a new project in which modernization meant management and restraint. As the academic literature and government documents suggest, the rationale behind this regime shift lay in the crises of the 1970s, not the debates of 1918. But through adopting Western scientific logics and methods, the new resource management system also played, I argue, two crucial roles that were important to the fisheries industry and those who were involved at the time: improving fishing's social status and connecting Japanese practices to those of other advanced or modern nations.

At the national level, the emphasis on a scientific resource management scheme helped improve the social status of the fisheries industry by demonstrating its modern capacities.[17] "Subordination" of the fishing sector to the other industries of Japan, however, remained in prevailing common discourses among fisheries officials, scholars, and fishing families. For them, it has been obvious that the high-tech and service industries as well as the agricultural industry are much more highly regarded in national politics. Also, the continuous policy discourses emphasizing modernization of the fishing sector constructed the haunting feelings of subordination and backwardness. It has been the task of prefectural fisheries officials, as "policy messengers," to convince fishing families of the necessity of modernization and to achieve the goal. The general line goes something like this: fisheries always face roughly a 10-year lag behind agriculture, a trope often repeated by those who study and supervise them with a sense of frustration and embarrassment. I occasionally heard such statements during my undergraduate lectures and my fieldtrips to government offices.

This narrative still exists in the 2000s, and it seems persistent enough to doubt that fisheries people will ever escape from the haunting feelings of backwardness. In the context of the late 1970s, the narrative had a great deal to do with discourses of Japan's "New Middle-Class." Farmers throughout the country—including those in northern Japan, far from the technological core in Tokyo—had achieved, statistically and consciously, membership in the "new middle-class" society of modern Japan by the mid-1970s,[18] but fisheries had yet to accomplish the goal, especially in the eyes of fisheries officials. Although more efficient, mechanized fishing had improved the average standard of living among fishing families by the late 1970s, as shown in government documents like the "Fisheries White Paper," fisheries officials continued to maintain that they had a responsibility to modernize fisheries and improve the social status of fishing families. In the pursuit of *further* modernization of Japan's fisheries, officials and scholars found a possibility in resource management. In the 1991 edition, the authors of the Fisheries White Paper wrote, "In order to provide a stable supply of seafood for our people and to achieve balanced development for the country, we include among our most important tasks the maintenance of the productivity of coastal fishing and the vitalization of fishing villages by promoting '*shigen kanri gata gyogyō*' (community-based fisheries management) and '*tsukuri sodateru gyogyō*' (marine ranching and stock enhancement)."[19] Therefore, the Fisheries Agency's goals were about encouraging economic development consistent with resource management and sustainability in the natural environment.

Resource management policy also aimed to demonstrate to international audiences Japan's membership in the group of advanced industrial nations by showing the country's ability to properly manage its marine resources. In Japan, environmental issues had long been largely associated with pollution and related public health issues, known as *kōgai* (public pollution)—such as the case of "Minamata disease," or mercury poisoning.[20] Resource management had been considerably less important. But from the late 1960s through the 1970s, Japanese environmental discourses started touching on resource management as the debates on natural resource crises were increasingly gaining public and political attention among other advanced industrial powers. Hardin's work on the "Tragedy of the Commons" sat alongside other studies concerning overexploitation of natural resources, and the Club of Rome's report "The Limits of Growth" had a major impact on public discourses on environmental resource crises. These arguments usually had a Malthusian flavor, pointing out that open access to common natural resources, with a growing resource-user population, would lead to the depletion of the resources. Correspondingly, they emphasized that the government should take responsibility for limiting access in order to conserve resources. Gordon's 1954 work had already introduced a similar argument about MEY in the context of fisheries about two decades earlier, but it was in the 1970s that most of the advanced industrial nations started to implement policies based on this general view.

In Japan, fishing activities had been limited and constrained by fishing rights and licenses since the Meiji Fisheries Law was implemented in 1902, long before the Malthusian arguments that shaped European and American policies. Although Japanese fisheries scholars and officials have long acknowledged that the Fisheries Law's roots lay in customary laws designed to maintain order (*chitsujo*) among fishermen rather than to conserve resources, many have also proudly claimed that a by-product was the Fisheries Law's capacity for resource management; in other words, Japanese coastal citizens had *traditionally* managed well their shared resources.[21] Even as they would argue that Japan had long had institutions, like the Fisheries Law, providing a capacity for resource management, or that such practices had long traditional roots, Japanese officials and scholars agreed— by recognizing the heated international debates on resource crisis—that the capacity of resource management should be enhanced so that Japan could demonstrate objectively and effectively its competence to international audiences. Thus, as noted by Tanaka Shōichi in his most widely read fisheries resource management textbooks, incorporating rational scientific resource management logics and methods—such as MEY and conservation methods attempting to maintain MEY—into the existing fisheries management system was recognized as a way to enhance resource management and also further modernize Japanese fisheries.[22]

In addition, the deployment of scientific resource management logics and methods has been important for the Fisheries Agency and Japanese fisheries scholars at international debate tables regarding marine resource management—most importantly, whales.[23] The improvement of Japan's "scientific and traditional" coastal resource management system was also used for proclaiming the country's capability of *rationally* and *wisely* managing overall marine resources. Developing the new resource management regime through combining modern scientific ideas with the "traditional" fisheries management scheme was also helpful for Japan to create its own image as a uniquely "modern-traditional" nation, similar to discourses of Japanese exceptionalism, known in Japanese as *nihonjinron*. This image consisting of two seemingly contradictory concepts was important for Japan's international political stance, as it represents Japan's attempt to become the first non-Western member of the leading advanced industrial nations.

Developing the new resource management regime

Political and academic debates on enhancing resource management continued growing after the late 1970s, leading to national efforts to develop a new resource management regime in the 1980s. In 1983, the Division of Agriculture and Fisheries declared its support for "*Shigen Kanri-gata Gyogyō no Suishin*" (Promotion of Fisheries Coupled with Resource Management). In 1984, the Fisheries Agency launched the "*Engan-iki Gyogyō Kanri Tekisei-ka Hōshiki Kaihatsu Jigyō*" (Development Project for the Enhancement of the Coastal-area Fisheries Management System) and the "*Engan-iki Gyogyō*

Moderu Jirei Chōsa Jigyō" (Coastal-area Fisheries Management Model-case Research Project), and then the "*Keikaku Eigyō Jissen Jigyō*" (Planned Fishing Management, nicknamed the "*eFISHency*" achievement project) in 1985. These national-level projects provided generous budgets to local governments and allowed a variety of projects dealing with coastal fisheries resource management to be launched at the prefectural level. In this way, developing coastal fisheries resource management schemes had become fisheries policy's main agenda during the 1980–90s.

In promoting this new resource management scheme, the Fisheries Agency emphasized two interrelated goals: fish stock enhancement and maintenance. One major technique in enhancing fish stocks was releasing hatchery-bred fish juveniles into the wild ocean. For this endeavor, generous budgets were devoted to the construction of fish hatcheries. For maintenance, however, financial resources and policy tools differed dramatically. The main method in maintaining "healthy" fish stocks was encouragement of local fishing co-ops to make voluntary efforts to control fishing activities. The budgets for this goal were spent mainly in educational activities designed to increase awareness among fishermen/ women regarding ideas of resource management and the importance of co-ops' voluntary efforts, though there were also subsidies for co-ops to carry out resource management activities. The projects had even entered the realm of the administrative slogan: the Fisheries Agency used the phrase "From 'fisheries that catch' to 'fisheries that generate and cultivate' ('*toru gyogyō*' *kara* '*tsukuri sodateru gyogyō*' *e*)."

Phase 3: Neoliberalism as modernization

Approximately three decades after the Japanese government shifted the primary directions in its fisheries modernization project in the late 1970s from mechanization to the promotion of scientific marine conservation, the state again turned its wheel around. In June 2001, the Diet passed the Basic Fisheries Law (*Suisan Kihon Hō*), which included familiar fundamental principles—like "securing the stable supply of seafood" and "healthy improvement of the fisheries industry"—but also encouraged the pursuit of significant cuts in government subsidies. This major shift in the fisheries policy was directed by the then-new Koizumi administration as part of its neoliberal agenda, which followed initiatives like the 1996 financial "Big Bang" and included the kinds of policies Bruce Aronson details in his chapter on Japan's regulatory reforms. Since this new law, the emphasis on resource management and related terminology have largely disappeared from official fisheries discourses. The text of the new law mentions resource degradation issues worldwide and calls for maintenance of resource management efforts. In practice, however, government support for the resource management-related projects has been cut drastically, and the fisheries advisors who had promoted them assiduously to the co-ops have shifted their interests in directions mandated by these subsidy cuts.

In place of resource conservation, but in line with its long-term goals and its recent neoliberal restrictions, the Fisheries Agency introduced a new policy that aimed to improve fishing families' "self-responsibility" in their finances and to encourage their independence from heavy government subsidies. Each year from 2001 to 2008, the Fisheries Agency's White Paper mentioned the creation of co-ops' sales businesses—such as a seafood restaurant run by women of fishing families—as an effective method for invigorating fishing villages and the continuing modernization of Japan's fishing industry. This is the modernization discourse under the new millennium's fisheries policy; it creates a new set of narratives specifying what is modern and what is outdated.

In the context of the new millennium, modernity is defined not only by collaboration in response to new challenges of environmental degradation, but also by attention to and competence in the logics and practices of market competition. The absence of such competence is seen—and criticized by fisheries officials—as an unacceptable feature that prevents the fishing industries from being modernized. The fisheries policy at the time that I spent in my field site consisted largely of prefectural fisheries advisors' suggestions to co-ops that they consider developing alternative ways to gain additional income hoping to make up for income loss from declining landings. These tended to focus on new business strategies for fishing families, like wholesale stands and other distribution nodes. Fisheries officials, however, see a long journey ahead. A fisheries advisor told me one day during my fieldwork with a sigh, "The fisheries industry still lags behind the agriculture industry. Farmers' markets have been expanding for the last ten years. Their rationalization (gōrika) though computerization (konpūtā-ka) has also been improved. We have to do a lot to catch up with them." In the past 60 years of postwar Japan's history, the notions of what it means to be "modern" in the narratives have shifted from one to another as fisheries policy has changed, but there are always endless tasks of "modernization" as long as the fishing industry exists.

Conclusion

The redevelopment debate that arose in the immediate aftermath of disaster in March 2011 revolved around the question of whether or not to restore the region's fisheries and port facilities to their predisaster state. The issue at the center of debate was whether post-disaster Japan had the means, the will, or even the desire to restore the region's fisheries to the way they had been before the 2011 tsunami. While at the time of publication of this book the question has yet to be resolved, it seems that the policies yet to emerge around the redevelopment of northeastern Japan, and the region's fisheries in particular, may serve as a useful demarcation between post-bubble and post-disaster Japan.

The discourse, thus, far suggests that similar notions of "modernization" may indeed be shaping post-disaster policy even as some of its architects argue that post-disaster Japan might yet depart from the constant drive for modernization that characterized Japan's postwar era.

During the six decades since the end of World War II, the Japanese government has consistently encouraged its fishing sector to modernize. This has taken dramatically different forms, as what it has meant to be modern has changed over time, but modernization has nevertheless been a consistent theme. The question remains, however, whether this will change in the aftermath of the 2011 disaster, which has been especially devastating for the fisheries industry and Japan's fishing families. Shortly after the 2011 earthquake and tsunami, Prime Minister Kan Naoto formed the Reconstruction Design Council (*Higashi Nihon Daishinsai Fukkō Kōsō Kaigi*) and its Working Group (*Kentō Bukai*) as an advisory body to generate policy suggestions for Japan's restoration and renovation from the unprecedented devastation. On 26 April 2011, in front of journalists at the Foreign Correspondents' Club of Tokyo, the Council's chairman, Iokibe Makoto, and the Working Group Leader, Iio Jun, explained that their task is to rebuild the devastated northeastern Japan region but also pointed out that "rebuilding does not simply mean to get things to the same state as before, but to create a new future for the people affected by the disaster."[24]

Although the council and its working group have given their own specific suggestions, they seem to agree upon the overall goal of their task. As one member of the Council's Working Group, Takemura Shinichi, emphasized at one meeting, "Instead of 'restoration of the old system,' what we utterly need is complete reformation or redesign of, so to speak, the 'New Japan.'"[25] This is not an isolated perspective. Specifically referring to the "old" and the "new" Japan, political scientist Mikuriya Takashi—who is the deputy chairman of the Reconstruction Design Council—wrote in the May 2011 issue of *Chūō Kōron*, "at last the long era of 'postwar' comes to an end, and we are entering the beginning of the new era, which we might call 'post-disaster."[26] For Mikuriya, "modernization" (*kindaika*) refers to "development of scientific technology, population growth, and high economic growth," and it symbolized Japan's postwar era.[27]

There is little doubt that the disasters of 2011 marked a turning point for Japan, but it is yet unclear whether the end of *kindaika* actually means the end of "modernization." Even if the term "*kindaika*" is to disappear from official policy narratives, modernization is conceptually alive in the continuing will to improve. The trajectory of postwar Japan's fisheries policy demonstrates that the history of fisheries management is built upon Japan's repeating efforts to construct a new, modern form of Japanese fisheries, even as the content of this idealized form has shifted over time. In this sense, the initial statements from the Reconstruction Design Council suggest that the era of modernization has not ended and perhaps never will, and further suggest that post-disaster Japan is likely to be another phase of the postwar era.

Part Four

Looking Out, Looking Back

The fears and uncertainties of the 1990s and beyond, compounded by the triple disasters of March 2011, had no real precedents in Japan's modern history. In the Meiji period (1868–1912), the national goals were clear, and neatly summed up in the slogan "rich nation, strong military" (*fukoku kyōhei*). Japan was engaged in a survival struggle to avoid colonization and to become strong enough not only to resist the great powers but also to become one of them. Its military and industrial might grew fast enough to enable it to defeat China and take Taiwan as its first colony in 1895, and to defeat Russia in 1905 and annex Korea in 1910—and then to launch an ultimately disastrous assault on China, Southeast Asia, and the United States in the 1930s and 1940s.

After the defeat, the goals had to change, but before long they became equally clear. Rebuilding and recovery were the initial goals, of course. But in 1960, Prime Minister Ikeda Hayato announced his plan to double real income by the end of the decade. In return for dedicating themselves to the new god of GNP growth and renouncing the divisive labor and political strife that had ended earlier that year with the passage of the revised US-Japan security treaty and quashing of the strike at Mitsui's Miike coal mine, Japanese would be rewarded with affluence that would enable enhanced consumerism.

Before long, Japan was held up as a model for the development of other countries, particularly in East and Southeast Asia, and Malaysia was among the first to adopt a "Look East" policy explicitly rejecting the western model in favor of that attributed to Japan. In 1979, Ezra Vogel published *Japan as Number One*, with the subtitle *Lessons for America*. Soon, executives from the United States were visiting their former pupil and junior partner to learn the secrets of its success, while Japanese hubris was reflected in the bits of gold foil one could order sprinkled on sushi at exclusive restaurants. Japan was seen, and saw itself, as the successful pioneer and model in solving the problems of late-industrial capitalism, from urban crowding to labor-management relations to industrial pollution.

The confidence, and the certainty about national goals, slipped away in the 1990s. The bubble burst, the Cold War ended, the population aged, rural areas hemorrhaged population and struggled to stay alive, and China continued its spectacularly rapid economic growth even longer than Japan had. Japan struggled to find its direction in what suddenly seemed to be a new and unfamiliar version of modernity, or postmodernity. There was much talk about the "Galapagos-ization" of Japan, a turning inward, a giving up of grand dreams, and an acceptance that Japan's global role and importance might shrink to the point where the nation would be ignored rather than copied by the rest of the world. It was no surprise that one response was to remember—or imagine—a time when things had been different.

Christine Yano takes us back to a time when the sky was the limit, when the world was about to become Japan's oyster. Showing the way in the joys of global travel, leisure, and cosmopolitanism were Japanese stewardesses for Pan Am, who traveled abroad even before the relaxation of currency restrictions in 1964 allowed other Japanese to follow. America became a different sort of model, offering employment and freedom for young women and lessons in the consumption of leisure travel and media for a generation who had not known the war, or who seemed to have forgotten it. Christopher Gerteis reminds us, however, that the past was not always so easily left behind. The NYK shipping line's redefinition of itself as Japan left the twentieth century and entered the twenty-first included new "corporate social responsibility" practices that involved the presenting of its past. Its attempt to focus on the supposed glitter, cosmopolitanism, and good relations with Asia up through the interwar years, and to paint itself as a passive victim of the Pacific War, only served to demonstrate the difficulty of escaping the shadow of the war and of reshaping the past to serve the present.

Hiraku Shimoda's description of the *Project X* television series argues that there may be dangers inherent in the nostalgia for the golden age of Japan's "greatest generation," the everymen (rarely are women foregrounded) who sacrificed and struggled to create the products on which growth and affluence were built. In the "good old days" of high growth, the series asserts, when "death from overwork" (*karōshi*) was not yet a legally recognized cause of death, inventiveness, nose-to-the-grindstone determination, production, and consumption gave Japan its purpose and identity. The message was appealing in the uncertain times of the early twenty-first century.

Unfortunately, imagined golden ages can never be recovered. The sages of old, be they the Duke of Zhou put forward as a model by Confucius, or the inventors of Cup Noodles or the Walkman, cannot show Japan how to solve the unprecedented problems of today. Even after the many crises that swept Japan in the wake of the Tōhoku earthquake and tsunami, some still seemed to think that it would be possible to turn back the clock or simply stay the course. These included the nuclear power industry, some elements of the Liberal Democratic Party, and more than a few in the Democratic Party of Japan. Others were pushing in new directions. Among them were the richest man in Japan, Son Masayoshi, the Korean-Japanese entrepreneur and CEO of SoftBank, who pushed for the building of a massive solar power network to replace Japan's dependence on nuclear power. Another was Mikitani Hiroshi, CEO of the internet company Rakuten, who advocated a thoroughgoing internationalization of Japanese corporate culture. Whether these or other ideas could bring back Japan's optimism, and again make it the sort of model it was for a time in the late twentieth century, remained to be seen.

12

Jet-Age Nationhood: Pan American World Airways in Postwar Japan

Christine Yano

In 1947, when Pan American Airways (in 1950 renamed Pan American World Airways, Inc.) began regular commercial service to Tokyo, it caused a tremendous stir in occupied Japan. Although Pan Am was not the first American carrier to fly to Japan (Northwest Orient Airlines began Tokyo service a few months earlier), the airline brought with it the kind of cachet that was unmatched by any other in the world. Japan Airlines, too, began flying internationally since 1954, but Pan Am possessed the prestige and routes that made it the favored airline for global travel.[1] Pan Am's commercial service to Tokyo in 1947 signaled the inauguration of the airline's famed round-the-world Flight 001 (traveling westward: San Francisco, Honolulu, Tokyo, Hong Kong, Bangkok, Delhi, Beirut, Istanbul, Frankfurt, London, and New York) and Flight 002 (traveling eastward, the same route in reverse).[2] The network of cities connected by Flights 001 and 002—including Tokyo—marked significant points of the globe within the context of the Cold War, delineating the borders of the global conflict through a dot-to-dot network. The imprimatur of the company's catchphrase—"world's most experienced airline"—thus indexed global power, prestige, and ultimately, politics.

   This chapter analyzes the central place of Pan Am in developing what I call Japan's "Jet-Age nationhood"—that is, citizenship defined and enacted within the context of high-speed mobility and incipient globalism. I examine the airline's activities in Japan from 1947 through 1986, when Pan Am, facing severe financial crises, sold its Pacific routes to United Airlines, and subsequently went bankrupt in 1991. Within that period, I focus particularly on the 1960s and 1970s—the heyday of the Jet Age—when the Japanese economy zoomed upward to a number three position in the world, and travel and international currency restrictions imposed during the Occupation were lifted, opening international travel broadly to Japanese citizens.[3] From 1964—the milestone year of the Tokyo Olympics—when Japanese could travel more freely internationally and increasingly possessed the capital and will to do so, it was Pan Am that provided the most reliable means. The exponential growth in overseas travel by Japanese may be seen by decades: 1960, 120,000 travelers; 1970, almost one million; 1980 nearly four million Japanese traveling abroad, many of whom were tourists.[4] The numbers of Japanese who traveled abroad rose from 1964 at a rate of over 25 percent yearly, and increasing numbers of these classified themselves as traveling not for business, but for pleasure.[5] This "turn to pleasure" came to define Jet Age nationhood in Japan as elsewhere. I base my analysis upon archival records (including those in the private collection of former Pan Am Japan employees), interviews, and participant observation at ongoing Pan Am events in Tokyo (annual Pan Am Alumni Association party,[6] World Wings International Tokyo Chapter events).

I trace the intertwining of Pan Am and Japan during the postwar years as a crossnational bond, American corporation to Japanese nation, taking the approach of what is called "critical corporate studies."[7] In a seminal work in this field, editors Purnima Bose and Laura Lyons note what has become a well-known adage tying corporations and nations together: popularly, what is good for corporation X is good for corporation X's home country:[8]

> Understanding how the collective, national, or even global good becomes articulated with particular corporate interests, how such equations become common sense, requires an examination of how corporations understand their role in the social contract as well as an understanding of how they endeavor to sell not only their products but also their way of doing business.[9]

The twist in the particular social contract I examine lies in the fact that the corporation (Pan American World Airways) extended its purview well beyond its home country, purportedly to underwrite the welfare of the globe. Pan Am's last Managing Director in Japan, Joe Hale, said of this global corporate purview: "Pan Am was a major force and recognized as everyone's airline in countries across the world."[10] This is confirmed by another Pan Am employee, who worked from 1964 to 1986, primarily in marketing: "When you look at the concept of Pan Am worldwide, . . . naturally it's a US carrier, but still we do not consider us as US We're international, we're a worldwide association. Once you have Pan Am, you have the whole world."[11] That is, chameleon-like, Pan Am became simultaneously national and global in its ports of call—thus Pan Am became a presence in postwar Japan that was both foreign *and* familiar.

Pan Am's version of corporate empire built upon the infrastructure and practices of political empire, but extended beyond to include something more difficult to regulate—global consumer desire. To desire Pan Am was to desire a palpable sense of oneself as a Pan Am passenger (or employee), which, during the 1960s and 1970s suggested a position of prestige and privilege based in modernity. To desire Pan Am meant also wanting the enticements of modern democratic access to global pleasures, such as tourism. This desire played upon elements of leisure, rather than work, as a fundamental component of being modern in postwar Japan.[12] As a Pan Am marketing director put it, successful overseas travel meant developing the "pleasure market" in Japan, as it grew from 15.1 percent of Japanese overseas travelers in 1964 to 49 percent in 1970.[13] The link between national position and individual desire, fostered in part through the audacity of the unspoken adage—"what is good for Pan Am is good for Japan"—permeated corporate practices in Japan during Pan Am's heyday.

As Flights 001 and 002 connected Tokyo to other global cities, circumscribing the boundaries of the Cold War, I ask the following questions of Japan's Jet-Age nationhood. What are the means by which Pan Am positioned itself as guardian of Japan's good? What kinds of symbolic measures secured such a relationship? And how did Pan Am help define and construct Japan and the Japanese citizenry's performance of their own modernity?

Japan's postwar relationship with mediatized *"Amerika"*

The historical conditions that made Pan Am's posturing possible lay partly in the image of America (*"Amerika"*) in postwar Japan, derived not only through the presence of the Occupation, but in large part through popular culture. As Sawa Kurotani points out, *"Amerika* is not just a Japanized pronunciation of the English word. It is a complex historical formation of the cultural and political other, a mirror against which Japan came to imagine its own totality as a modern nation-state."[14] Yet, in addition to *Amerika* as an oppositional mirror for postwar Japan, I argue that it was also a platform within which Japan came to imagine itself. It was a relationship that pulled both "against" and "within" to create the foreign-*and*-familiar contradiction within which Pan Am operated. Here, my discussion focuses on those elements mentioned by former Pan Am employees whom I interviewed in order to get a sense of what they thought influenced them in their view of *Amerika* and ultimately, Pan Am. They do not necessarily represent a cross-section of the Japanese population or opinion of the time, but rather occupied an elite position, here indexed by their education and English-language facility.

And yet they shared a widespread exposure to and infatuation with American popular culture as part of the prevailing mediascape. One Pan Am employee who worked from 1970 to 1986 recalls[15]:

I really loved American TV series. You know, "Lassie" and "Rebecca" and all this. And from that, I got [the image of a] very affluent country, where in Japan, we were still very poor. And a very large country and a lot of different atmosphere, I mean in terms of nature, and different races, all blended together. Country of opportunity, nothing is denied, everything goes as long as you work hard and opportunity's there, like American dream.[16]

Here are the familiar tropes of the American dream—affluence, expansiveness, opportunity, individual effort—as well as an element not much seen on television screens of this period, racial diversity. The programs she and others mentioned most, such as "Father Knows Best" and "My Three Sons," depicted white, middle-class, heteronormative, suburban life. This "American dream" should be situated more specifically as a hegemonic presence and globalized ideal, an impossible dream for Japanese that prompted *akogare* (longing, desire). As one Pan Am employee explained, "We were basically, [full of] *akogare*, [our] dream about the [American] culture that was different from us!"[17]

One American television show frequently mentioned by interviewees is the "Donna Reed Show" (ABC, aired in the United States from 1958 to 1966), a situation comedy featuring pretty, "all-American" girl-next-door actress Donna Reed portraying housewife Donna Stone, her handsome pediatrician husband Alex Stone (actor Carl Betz), and two children (actress-singer Shelley Fabares and Paul Peterson), living in an anonymous suburb in the United States. What seemed to strike the Japanese women I interviewed was the figure of Donna Reed as the quintessential modern American housewife, always tastefully attired in a shirtwaist dress, heels, and often pearls, while cheerfully doing her housework with modern appliances. Here is the recollection of Sachi Braden, a woman who flew for Pan Am from 1971 to 1981:

She [Donna Reed] showed up, she was doing a vacuum cleaner, with a skirt like this [she twirls], and then they were wearing high heels shoes and impeccable hair, and I go, "Oh my god!" And I thought, "My god, is that what they do?" I was curious! . . Oh, it's definitely *akogare*! But I didn't want to be Donna Reed; I wanted to see her.[18]

Indeed, it was this desire to see, rather than to be, Donna Reed that fueled *akogare* for *Amerika*. The Japanese I interviewed never envisioned themselves entering the lives of those they saw on the screen, but they speak of their intense desire to see the world of the mediatized image called *Amerika*.

Another stewardess who flew Pan Am from 1966 to 1986 described herself as a "vagabond with wanderlust," fascinated with foreign cultures since childhood. During the war, she and her brother found a small downed plane in a ditch in Kita-Kyushu where they lived, and would sit in it and dream of flying to far-off places. For her, dreams of *Amerika* (and other foreign countries) became intertwined with those of flying itself as the pathway by which she might fulfill her wanderlust through technologies of modernity. Flying represented freedom, knowledge, and a constant quest. She recounted: "I daydreamed all the time whenever I saw planes taking off. I was intent upon traveling the world. I always dreamed, what would it be like on the other side of the horizon?"[19] That horizon set one of its foci upon Hawai`i. While at Dōshisha University in the 1960s majoring in English literature, she experienced the "Hawai`i fever" that engulfed Japan at the time, with films such as Elvis Presley's *Blue Hawaii* (released in Japan in 1962), and popular Japanese actor Kayama Yūzō's *Hawai no Wakadaisho* [Hawaii's Young Guy] (1963), and older songs such as "Akogare no Hawaii Kōro" [Dreams of Hawaii] (1948). She herself learned ukulele and played Hawaiian songs such as "Blue Hawaii" and "Aloha `Oe." She said, "Everyone's dream was to go to Hawai`i!" For her, Pan Am represented an opportunity to fulfill her lifelong dream of seeing "the other side of the horizon"—fueled by literature, movies, and songs.

Several employees mentioned ways in which Pan Am symbolized the United States itself. One woman who flew in the 1970s reminisced: "I believe Pan Am was loved all over the world, because it was symbolic of the United States!"[20] Neither she nor other employees mentioned ongoing conflicts during this same period—the Vietnam War, violent student unrest, racial strife—that made the United States somewhat less than a global ideal. Instead, for these employees, America and Pan Am together stood for global prestige, achievement, and modernity. One stewardess recalled:

The day of the moon landing (21 July 1969, Japan time) after I finished my breakfast in the hotel, the Pan Am branch office called me on an urgent matter. I headed to Sogō Department store, . . . to the top floor where Nihon Terebi [Japan TV] studio was located. They wanted me along with others to be part of the television program to watch the news from the moon. The Pan Am crew appeared in uniform on the program. I thought I was really lucky to be there to witness the astronauts on this historical moment.. . . I was just a college student a few months prior. And now, living in America, visiting places all over the world which is a dream come true. And in addition to this, I got to watch the moon landing, live, while in my Pan Am uniform, simply made me cry with joy![21]

Her narrative highlights the mediatized image of *Amerika* and its global achievements, here symbolized by association with Pan Am, including its Japanese stewardesses in uniform. Thus, Pan Am became guardian of not only Japan's "good" (i.e. welfare, progress, modern achievements), but also that of the industrial world and its foremost technological innovations.

Pan Am and Japan's national sport

Japan's "good" within Pan Am's purview used media extensively, broadcasting at many levels, from spectacular events such as moon landings to regular programming. Just as television had vividly brought *Amerika* into Japanese homes, so, too, did Pan Am in Japan become part of domestic broadcasting. One such regular televised feature was that of Japan's national sport, sumo. In 1953, Pan Am and its marketing division accepted the suggestion by Japan's Sumo Association to present a trophy to tournament winners. The other trophy presentations at the time were the Emperor's trophy and those of the *Mainichi Shimbun* and Nihon Hōsō Kyōkai (NHK) broadcasting corporation. The Sumo Association felt that a new trophy presented by a major American corporation, and particularly one associated with a prestigious modern industry such as air travel, would help stimulate new interest in sumo. Here is how Isa Katsurō, then working for Pan Am's public relations office explained the prestige of the airline and the reason for the Sumo Association's request:

> Those days, really, Pan Am was *the* airline.. . . Pan Am was not only the airline, but the representative of American firms, like American banking business, financial or other related businesses, motor cars. So the name of Pan Am often appeared on the mass media, and Pan Am name was well-known by the [Japanese] public. I think this is one of the reasons the Sumo Association wanted Pan Am to give the Pan Am trophy to the winner [of the tournament].[22]

Pan Am had gained a reputation in Japan first as an airline, second as an airline to celebrities, and third, as an airline always in the news. Wanting to capitalize on this status, the Sumo Association sought Pan Am's cooperation.

The Pan Am sumo trophy claimed its own status as the outsized trophy with the most famous of presentations given at the very end of the tournament awards ceremony (and thereby special honor) by the company's marketing director in Japan (the first of whom was W.H.B. Ortwin). In May 1961—and for 30 years thereafter until 1991—that trophy and its presentation became one of the most familiar Pan Am media spectacles televised in Japan.[23] Pan Am's Public Relations Chief for the Far East, David Jones, took it upon himself to infuse the ceremony with both decorum and humor. A diminutive man (5'5", 134 pounds) always dressed for the occasion in the formal Japanese attire of *hakama* (Japanese wrapped pants) and *haori* (Japanese overcoat), Jones presented the huge trophy (1.15 meter/45 inches high, 40 kilos/88 pounds in weight) to the winning sumo wrestler, delivering the *hyōshōjō* (announcement of congratulations). Part of the humor was the relative size of the trophy and the man; part of the humor was in Jones' delivery of the *hyōshōjō*, often in regional dialect (of the area in which the tournament was being held) and exaggerated *gaijin* (foreigner) accent. Isa comments:

> [Jones was] just like small Japanese. That's why he's good. He was well-accepted. If he were tall and handsome, people would say, 'Oh, that's natural. Pan Am is Pan Am.' But he was like Japan: small, short. And that's one of the reasons, I think, [Japanese] accepted [him] easily. Of course, it's not all visual, but something about his personality [that was] very well accepted. I think he really liked things Japanese to begin with.. . . It's his *kokoro* [heart], heart is very much Japan-ized, really.[24]

Invoking *kokoro*—reputedly that innermost core of Japaneseness—demonstrates the degree of intimacy with which the public viewed Jones.[25] Ben Kinoshita, a Pan Am employee in charge of the Cargo Division, recalled, "He [Jones] was much more familiar [to us Japanese]. I guess the biggest thing he did was he had the Pan Am image filter into ordinary Japanese people."[26] A Japanese woman I interviewed explained, "That [Jones' presentation of sumo trophy] gave us a very, sort of, close feeling to Pan Am."[27] What Jones did was to humanize Pan Am for the Japanese public, in part through his small stature, in part through his humor. Much to the delight of the Japanese television audience, Jones' presentation became such a feature of the tournament that broadcaster NHK received angry calls from viewers if it ever cut the program short due to broadcasting time restraints or if an NHK announcer attempted to comment during Jones' presentation. The Japanese public wanted Jones, the American "with Japanese-style *kokoro*"—and Pan Am rode the coattails of his appealing persona. Jones became a celebrity in his own right, affectionately called "*hyōshōjō*-man," "*hyōshōjō*-san," or *hyōshō-Jones*."

From a marketing standpoint, Jones' presence was a stroke of genius.[28] As Hale, Pan Am Director of Western Japan, comments: "That was a marriage of two icons: the trophy itself, Pan Am, with sumo. I think so. I think for many people, when you go to see the sumo tournament on the last day, a lot of people only start to exit after Dave Jones' presentation is over. Only after that, people start to move [out of their seats]. It's visible. It's visible."[29] Consider what that marriage entailed: rather than an intimidating presence, Pan Am gained a very human, even self-deprecating face in the guise of Jones, who was smaller than the Japanese wrestlers to whom he presented the oversized trophy.[30]

Race played a subtle and often silent card, as well. According to his son Greg, David Jones was actually half Filipino, born in the Philippines to a Filipina mother (whom Greg describes as being of Spanish descent). As Greg explained, "If you look at him [father David] in his earlier years, he has a very dark complexion, he has very jet black hair. And so there's some of that Asian [blood]."[31] However, this racial factor was often overlooked in favor of his strong connection with the glamorous American company. Further, the trophy itself was huge, making Jones appear even smaller. Thus, part of the comedy for Japanese viewers—and one brought on with great relish by Jones himself—was to watch the diminutive American man maneuver the huge trophy into the arms of a towering Japanese champion. One of the most famous David Jones media moments came in January 1973 when Jones, who was about to present the trophy, staggered and fell on the sumo platform along with the trophy. A Japanese wrestler helped bring Jones to his feet, much to the Japanese public's mirth.

Besides offering the trophy with David Jones' famous *hyōshōjō*, Pan Am also occasionally offered prizes to sumo wrestlers. For example, in 1964, the very year that the government lifted international travel restrictions and welcomed foreign athletes at the Tokyo Olympics, Pan Am offered two tickets on their famous round-the-world flight to the winner of the tournament. In another instance, Pan Am offered tickets to Australia to the tournament winner. In each of these cases, sumo offered Pan Am great publicity, encouraging Japanese to travel to far off places via Pan Am, as much as Pan Am offered the sport its bit of modern glamor. Pan Am stood at the center of a swirl of Jet-Age mobility in, around, and through Japan.

Pan Am was also involved when Hawai`i-born Jesse Kuhaulua (sumo name Takamiyama) became the first foreign wrestler to earn a high title. Isa from public relations explained:

> When he [Jesse] made *jūryō* (ranked champion), I was with public relations. The *oyakata* [manager of the sumo stable] came to Pan Am, asked for apron, *keshō mawashi* [ceremonial skirt], and then the *oyakata* said this is the first American wrestler to become full-fledged *jūryō*, so we would like to ask you, Pan Am, to give him the first *keshō mawashi* apron. So we did that.[32]

Pan Am thus became synonymous with the United States and any of its representatives in Japan. As a corporation, the airline understood the public relations axiom of maximizing every opportunity to get one's name before the public, whether through humorous presentations, celebrity prizes, or wearable billboards (wrestler's *mawashi*).

Pan Am's glamor travelog

From 1959 to 1990, one of the Pan Am-linked media mainstays widely known to the Japanese public was "Kanetaka Kaoru Sekai no Tabi" [Kanetaka Kaoru's Travels of the World] (originally "Sekai Tobiaruki" [World-hopping]) hosted by Eurasian beauty Kanetaka Kaoru (a.k.a. "Rose"), and broadcast nationally on Tokyo Broadcasting Services (TBS) television on Sunday mornings from 9:00 to 9:30am.[33] With a nationwide network of 30 stations from Hokkaido to Okinawa, the estimated viewing audience in 1979 was over 13,000,000 per week. The program was developed by Kanetaka and her production company, Educational Aids Development, Inc., which contacted TBS and then Pan Am, seeking a tie-in relationship. In a letter dated 14 December 1979 from Kanetaka to the Managing Director of Pan Am, Kanetaka spells out the relationship: she and her team of four produce programs about places around the world; Pan Am receives a 50-second identification commercial at the beginning and a 15-second commercial at the end of each program.[34] This letter does not specify the kinds of transportation that Pan Am might provide, but airline officials indicate that was part of the tie-in.

As a 1979 letter from T. Katō of advertising agency Chūō Senkō to Richard Boynton, Pan Am's Director of Passenger Marketing in the Far East states: "This program has been one of Pan Am's core advertising activities in Japan for the last two decades and has greatly helped establish a solid image of Pan Am to the Japanese."[35] That image was one of cosmopolitanism and modernity built around Jet-Age nationhood. Beginning broadcasting in 1959 during a period when Japanese citizens themselves could not travel internationally freely, this program, its sponsor (Pan Am), and its host (Kanetaka), became the means for vicarious travel.

It was not the only one, as popular books such as Oda Makoto's 1961 *Nan de mo mite yarō* [I'll Give Anything a Look], Yamamoto Sukeyoshi's 1960 *Maachan Konnichiwa* [Hi, Mom], and others provided Japanese consumers with personal accounts of life abroad. Not unlike the Iwakura Mission comprised of elites who traveled abroad from 1871 to 1873 on official governmental fact-finding agenda to aid in the country's modernization, these postwar travelog narratives by private citizens purportedly brought eyewitness accounts of "the world" to Japan. However, whereas members of the Iwakura Mission traveled as part of work, postwar travelog writers traveled as part of play, even when their journeys afforded them less than pleasurable sights. Oda's in particular sparked the Japanese public's imagination as a decidedly unglamorous, dollar-a-day budget travelog with an intense focus on the margins of Euroamerican societies. Oda and Kanetaka—themselves elite—presented travel as a form of consumption, and even "consumerist multiculturalism."[36] Notably, there was a fundamental difference between the two: Oda's bestseller deliberately sought the gritty aspects of lives abroad; Kanetaka's, by contrast, was suffused through and through with Pan Am glamor.

Kanetaka's travelog rode the coattails of the powerful American corporation that served as its sponsor and carrier. As one Japanese woman born in 1948 recalled:

Pan Am represented *Amerika*. It brought us *Amerika*, and it brought us sort of culturally sophisticated image because this "Kanetaka Kaoru Sekai no Tabi" gave us a world . . . all those places, they gave us information,

different cultures, and so that brought us a window to the world. So this
was an airplane, and that was the carrier of culture, too. It was a window
for us. It was a carrier that was more bringing in [the world] than taking
us [out of Japan]. In those days it was difficult for us to go.[37]

This explanation demonstrates the relationship between Pan Am, Kanetaka's travelog, Japan, the United States, and "the world"—that is, Pan
Am provided Japan with an American "culturally sophisticated image"
of itself based in knowledge of "the world" as presented by the televised
travelog. Japanese viewers could share in Kanetaka's worldliness. The
world was less a threatening place than a series of enticingly exotic episodes
led by a beautiful Eurasian woman with linguistic and cultural fluency,
transported on "the world's most experienced airline." Kanetaka was the
ultimate tour guide: a cosmopolitan by birth, Japan's own jet setter, a dream
girl for postwar Japan whose own citizens could not travel abroad for
leisure until 1964. Gender played a role by which Kanetaka could function
as the beautiful feminine broker of knowledge and the world—not unlike
stewardesses in general, as well as tour bus guides in particular, in Japan.
In contrast with the male authors of travelog literature mentioned above
(e.g. Oda, Yamamoto) many of whom traveled at least initially as study-
abroad students, Kanetaka traveled as a female, alone, and seemed perfectly
at ease doing so. Consider the impossibilities broadcast weekly to living
rooms across Japan: a beautiful Eurasian woman with multilingual fluency,
who shows great confidence in traveling alone to places unknown, while
traversing the globe in a Pan Am jet. Given the scheduling of the show during
a time when many people were at home, such a glamorous Pan Am-fueled
travelog had a tremendous impact upon the Japanese postwar public.
    A Pan Am stewardess who flew from 1968 to1986 recalled watching Pan
Am and Kanetaka's show:

> Pan Am was *the* airline for anybody's dream at that time. Because we had
> on every week Kaoru Kanetaka. She's half Indian and half Japanese, I
> think. But she spoke fluent English and fluent Japanese, and many other
> languages. And she represented Pan Am, and she went around the world.
> Each week she introduced each city in the world. . . . Everybody watched
> it! She just introduced all different countries, and it always was with
> Pan Am. And of course in the show, the Pan Am logo comes up. . . . Pan
> Am made that program. I used to watch that [show]. So everybody [like
> me] just dreamed about Pan Am. That was the dream airlines. That's the
> number one airline everybody wanted to work or fly.[38]

The dream of Pan Am was the Japanese postwar dream of modernity,
mobility, and cosmopolitanism. Watching Kanetaka Kaoru live that dream
made for vicarious identification of themselves within it. This was not unlike
watching Donna Reed—but not necessarily becoming her, although here

there was somewhat closer proximity of the Japanese public to Kanetaka. I argue that this allure of viewing-without-becoming structures the *akogare* outlook of postwar Japan, surrounded by a rush of Americanisms (e.g. sights and sounds of media, food, clothing, images of Occupation personnel) while seeking oneself.[39]

Pan Am was not alone in using media tie-ins to enhance their image and presence. According to a survey conducted in 1979 by Video Research, other international airlines did the same, including Air France, Cathay Pacific, KLM, Singapore Airlines, and Japan Airlines.[40] The airlines understood well the power of the image and the allure of overseas travel, as well as the efficacy of television as the new, powerful medium that would convey that image instantaneously to the greatest numbers of people. As the memo by Chūō Senkō Advertising Co., Ltd. explained: "It goes without saying that TV in Japan is, as elsewhere, the strongest medium for advertising products or projecting corporate images. It is the core medium for all major advertisers in Japan. For airlines, it is equally important to utilize TV as a core medium as its consumer impact is stronger than print media."[41] The strength of television lay in its immediacy, bringing images into the home in what Andrew Painter calls "televisual quasi-intimacy."[42] With a program like "Kanetaka Kaoru Sekai no Tabi" that intimacy held sway as a means to visualizing the rest of the world—and thereby Japan itself—courtesy of Pan Am.

A wholly different kind of travelog linked Pan Am with media through the popular "Wakadaishō" [Young Guy] movie series produced by Tōhō studios with handsome heartthrob Kayama Yūzō.[43] In fact, Pan Am played a part in helping sponsor the "Wakadaishō" film series with Tōhō studios. Pan Am publicist Isa explained:

> Those days, making movies overseas location, producer had to think about moving the staff and the gears, and it cost you a lot. So those days, Japanese movie producers, major concern was transportation. Overseas location. So we were major sponsor with Tōhō Movie. We provide transportation to the Tōhō Production Movies.. . .There was a producer Fujimoto Sanezumi, later he became Executive Vice-President. He was very much in favor of Pan Am tie-up. And he accepted our request to use Pan Am in airplane scene in the movie.[44]

Pan Am planes appeared in at least five of the 17 "Wakadaishō" films, including ones in which lead actor Kayama Yūzō traveled to Hawai`i, the Swiss Alps, Hong Kong, Honolulu, Tahiti, and Rio de Janeiro. In addition, sumo presenter David Jones appeared in the Swiss Alps "Wakadaishō" film. This early product placement was crucial for helping create an image of Pan Am associated with a popular Japanese film star and his signature series.

In contrast to Kanetaka Kaoru as a beautiful mixed-race travel guide, Kayama Yūzō presented a different kind of Japanese presence in overseas locations—handsome, virile, with a kind of athleticism and energy that spoke well to postwar Japanese audiences. He was not a travel guide so much as a traveler himself, who demonstrated that one of the best ways to embrace a foreign locale was not by speaking its language, but by physically immersing himself in it. Kayama was an electric-guitar playing, often bare-chested, middle-class, collegiate leading man who could seemingly do everything, from water-skiing to sky-diving to judo to performing music, Ventures-style. In many ways, he represented the Japanese postwar generation's model of masculinity. Here was a new kind of Japan that was entirely modern *and* wholly Japanese with a face and body to match. And it was Pan Am that took him places that showed him (and Japan) off to best advantage. In 1967, Kayama appeared on the cover of the 16 March issue of popular magazine *Shūkan heibon* carrying a Pan Am flight bag and flanked by two Pan Am stewardesses. The message was clear: here was the epitome of postwar, globetrotting, airborne masculinity—hard at play with the bags, women, and airline to prove his place.

Pan Am as Japan: The power of image

Kanetaka and Kayama were not the only ones to be seen on the go by way of Pan Am. The Japanese public seemed to have an appetite for travel, or at least for reading and watching people doing it. The power of Pan Am in postwar Japan lay in part in the public's fascination with the airline industry itself as the forefront of modern life. Pan Am's Japan publicist in the 1960s, Isa, explained: "The public media, newspapers and the TV media, were much interested in airline operations, and they were keen to go after the world leading airlines, Pan Am."[45] For one, airplanes brought famous people to Japan, as well as transported Japan's own famous people abroad. Isa continued:

> The way Pan Am was treated back then [1960s, 1970s] was unimaginable today. For example, if someone [famous] came to Japan, the media would often report specifically that he or she came by Pan Am. All of the newspapers used to say Minister or State Head, very top, high people, came to Japan on Pan Am. Like [Joe] DiMaggio, Marilyn Monroe arrived on Pan Am for their honeymoon.... So the name Pan Am was ingrained in public's mind daily. So us PR guys didn't have to do much, for the name Pan Am was doing PR for itself, quite naturally.[46]

The classic publicity shot of the time showed a celebrity being greeted at Haneda International Airport in Tokyo with a Pan Am plane in the background. In short, the Japanese media placed a spotlight upon people's comings and goings at airports, including the vessels that took them places, chief among which were Pan Am planes.

Pan Am did not leave these things to chance. Instead, it courted the celebrity passenger, even as it occupied a prime position as a celebrity airline. Pan Am executive Joe Hale explained: "We had a very good. . .special service group for handling VIPs. I think that we did very well on that. We had a special unit around the world who were part of the airport office, but worked almost independently to be responsible to requests of Pan Am offices around the world.. . . Whatever it is [in requests], we will take care of that."[47] But Pan Am also garnered a fair share of ordinary Japanese passengers who opted for expertise over familiarity when they chose to fly internationally. One postwar Japanese passenger explained:

[Japanese travelers like myself would choose Pan Am] because the minute you walked in [the plane], it was America.. . . Once you get on the plane, it's their world [Pan Am's, America's] and I have to change there. It gives you a nice sort of preparation. And in those days, of course, Pan Am was *the* carrier. That was a real consideration—very safe, and big and reliable, good airline company.[48]

There may have been other reasons to choose to fly Pan Am when flying abroad. A Pan Am executive revealed:

We used to hear from [Japanese] passengers that one of the reasons that they preferred Pan Am is that in the early days, anyway, of JAL, they felt that JAL flight attendants looked down on the [Japanese] passengers, because in those days, international travel was a rarity that was reserved for the elite or the *gaijin* [foreigners]. And that the flight attendants were part of that elite group. And they [flight attendants] were looking down, saying, "A person like *that* is going to Hong Kong?" "Can you imagine this kind of person going to New York?" Like the Japanese passengers were *inakappe* [country bumpkins]. So some passengers felt they were better treated [on Pan Am].[49]

Whether it was for prestige or service, many Japanese passengers from high government officials to everyday travelers chose Pan Am for international flights during the mid-1960s and 1970s. The result was that when people in Japan thought of international travel during this period, they thought of Pan Am. In this way, Pan Am became part of a bundled set of associations: America, the world beyond Japan, and Japan itself configured as a modern, mobile nation.

Japanese employees of Pan Am learned this configuration firsthand as a source of pride. Pan Am was notable among American corporations for maintaining only a minimal number of American executives in their Japan offices. The rest of the staff, including managers, were Japanese. And in these positions of responsibility, Japanese employees were given what was considered an unheard of degree of autonomy. This was profound for many

Japanese employees, and many of them remarked on it. Ben Kinoshita, in charge of cargo, recalled:

> I was trying to think of what was significant about Pan Am was that people working there, the local [Japanese] people as well as the Americans who came over from the States, had no immediate feeling of nationality. We were all the same. We were all working for one company, and then the company recognized people as people and not because they are Japanese or American or what have you. So I never had even the feeling that I was Japanese. I was Pan Am.[50]

This blurring of identities into a singular entity—"Pan Am"—enabled Kinoshita and others I interviewed to take the company as their own. In becoming Pan Am, Kinoshita, like many others, found that their dreams and lives took on a sense of modernity's limitlessness. If Pan Am helped spell out Japan's Jet-Age nationhood, then the Japanese employees were among its first citizens.

Conclusion: Japan in Pan Am's own image

Pan Am performed Japan's modernity during the postwar era in several ways. First, it established Tokyo as a major hub of air travel, including Pan Am's renowned round-the-world service. Within the context of the Cold War, the high-speed mobility of air travel and the alliances that it could etch held tremendous symbolic value. Second, it became a household name through significant media placement in key films and regular television programs at a time when television itself was the newest broadcast medium. In short, Pan Am as an everyday media presence in Japan became less foreign and more familiar. Third, it employed hiring practices notable for their elevation of Japanese workers to positions of power and responsibility within the American corporation's bases in Tokyo and Osaka. These highly placed managers and directors put a significant Japanese face upon Pan Am. And fourth, Pan Am was a means by which Japan re-imagined itself as cosmopolitan, mobile, and airborne—that is, fully participating in the headiness of global connectedness. Part of the significance of Pan Am's presence is that the American airline helped the Japanese public envision itself as participating in what I dub "Jet-Age nationhood"—that is, citizenship characterized by global mobility, whether in media dreams or moving bodies. In this, Pan Am laid claim to both the aspirations and achievements of mobility in postwar Japan. Although the equation changed in the 1980s as Pan Am's fortunes fell while Japan Airlines' position rose, garnering a larger share of the Japanese market, during the 1960s and 1970s, Pan Am held a singular place as an icon of Japan's Jet-Age nationhood.

If mobility was a quintessential part of the modern experience, then this American corporation symbolized the acme of that possibility in Japan. Pan Am ushered in the Jet Age as a possibility of a modern Japan on the go at the highest levels. There were limits, however, to this cosmopolitanism. Note the particular configuration of postwar national desire—that is, the *akogare* that I have characterized as viewing-without-becoming. There was a wariness here that rested in part in the lingering residue of World War II and the Occupation that separated the victor from the vanquished, and reinscribed the degree to which Japan could not yet become a global citizen on the same level as other industrial nations. This residue often took on racialized undertones that overlapped with social class and global prestige. It arose from the tug of cultural nationalism with its sense of the separateness of Japan, amid foreign *and* familiar American corporations. Thus, the home for foreign corporations in Japan remained under constant surveillance during this time period, even for those who became as familiar as Pan Am.

This is a story that recognized *akogare* for *Amerika*, but asserted that this is only part of the picture. The relationship was made complex by recognizing Japan's agentive force. Indeed, Japanese organizations and individuals (e.g. Sumo Association, movie studios, television producers, Japanese travelers, Pan Am employees) took advantage of the airline's prestige for their own purposes, thereby finding gains in such an alliance. If Pan Am helped produce postwar Japan, then postwar Japan also took the reins in producing itself in the 1960s and 1970s through the glamor of that most modern of industries—international travel—under the auspices of the most prestigious company at the time, Pan American World Airways. These lessons of Jet-Age nationhood set Japan aloft in complex skies that both erased and reinscribed national boundaries. By the 1980s, when Pan Am's own fortunes had begun to wane, the American corporation's practices had been heavily borrowed and reframed in the image of other airlines more able to withstand the restructuring of the US airline deregulation of 1978. Regardless of Pan Am's declining fortunes in the 1980s, its effect upon postwar Japan of the 1960s and 1970s was indelible and complex. The airline that helped define Japan's Jet-Age presence may have looked like a glossy, even brash, carrier, but inevitably flying embodied all the seriousness of national play. Thus, when Pan Am flew out of Haneda for the last time in 1986, its wings carried a requiem for a particular mix of postwar nationhood wrought from Cold War strategies and Jet Age possibilities. The arc of excitement begun in 1947 came to a full stop under changed conditions that marked the end of not only an airline, but also an era.

13

Marketing History as Social Responsibility

Christopher Gerteis

In recent decades, it has become somewhat fashionable in Japan to recount one's own personal history of the war and postwar years through a variety of public and private media.[1] Several of the chapters in this volume examine how cultural and political elites have deployed narratives of tradition and modernity as a means of constructing modes of local and national identity. This chapter examines the role that historical narrative plays in the public relations agenda of corporate Japan by investigating the ramifications of the attention given to shaping public perception of the company's place in history. Most member companies of Japan's twentieth-century *keiretsu* (corporate conglomerates that included Mitsubishi, Mitsui, and Sumitomo) regularly published, before and after the war, official histories as a means of enhancing corporate prestige. As a result, company history narratives, like many tropes of national history, often obscure more than they illuminate about the corporate subject. This chapter unpacks the way in which corporate history narratives have in recent years become interwoven with philanthropic initiatives, so-called Corporate Social Responsibility (CSR) programs, in part developed to rehabilitate corporate reputation and enhance public perception of the private enterprise.

Although developed for different purposes, and a little later than in the United States and Europe, CSR programs in Japan were quickly integrated into pre-existing public relations practices with the common purpose of shaping public perception of corporations' social and fiduciary responsibilities for a variety of hot-button issues such as industrial pollution and racial and gender discrimination. An early adopter of recommendations from the Japan Business Federation (Keidanren), the Nippon Yūsen Kaisha (NYK) has, since the early 2000s, promoted CSR programming focused on company policies aimed to reduce the maritime transport company's

environmental impact while also underwriting education programs
in communities where NYK core businesses hold significant interests.
Importantly, NYK CSR initiatives also include significant employee-focused
human relations programming such as scholarships and vocational training
for employees across the globe.[2]

Since the beginning of the twenty-first century, it has become fashionable
for some Japanese companies to repackage their "history telling" enterprises
as social responsibility schemes advertising the organizations' commitment
to the social norms of the communities within which they operate. This
chapter argues that there has been a significant social cost, and potential
fiduciary risk, to the ways in which these organizations have shaped historical
memories of so-called golden eras of nineteenth and twentieth century
history. Most of the world's corporations deploy historical narrative—
whether to sell products, enhance brand value or establish corporate
prestige—as part of their overall marketing strategy. Corporations also
deploy historical narrative partly to ameliorate lingering memories of their
links to less pleasant aspects of the recent past. This line of inquiry broadens
our interrogation of the way history is shaped by examining the extent to
which social and fiduciary obligations come into conflict when it is in the
material interest of an organization to obscure past events even while under
the legal obligation to provide truthful information.[3]

While national jurisdictions define specific legal obligations, all corporations operating in the highly industrialized societies of Asia, Europe, and the
Americas share to some degree the fiduciary responsibility to provide truthful
information to their shareholders, employees, purveyors and customers.
The resultant interconnected milieu of social and fiduciary obligations
provides a fascinating opportunity for historical inquiry precisely because
many of these otherwise distinct types of corporations share in their use
of institutional history narratives to partly ameliorate lingering memories
of less pleasant aspects of the recent past. While it is understandable those
corporate executives would commission historical narratives that enhanced
corporate prestige or add brand value, this chapter argues that the resultant
commodification of history as public relations and marketing narrative is at
odds with corporate social and fiduciary responsibilities defined by custom
and law.

The Nippon Yūsen Kaisha

NYK executives have been intensely concerned about public perception
of the company's place in history since the early twentieth century.[4] NYK
regularly published, before and after the war, official histories. Multiple
agendas underpin NYK's official narratives, a fact which presents historians
with the means to further interrogate the idea that corporate history,
which first emerged at NYK as a genre of marketing and promotional

literature, can be presented as a manifestation of social responsibility and philanthropic activity. NYK's contemporary historical exhibitions and publications present a narrative of the past that promotes the company's role in the national maritime history of Japan in part by obscuring its central role in Japan's imperialist and militarist expansions of the nineteenth and twentieth centuries. From the company's official narratives, it is possible to learn the ways in which NYK's rise to global prominence parallels the trajectory of Japan's emergence as a global economic power. Importantly, the prewar and wartime incarnations of NYK did not conceal the company's intimate relationship with the emerging imperial state. Instead, NYK official histories and marketing propaganda clearly and proudly documented the company's exploits as an integral member of the imperial era military-industrial complex.

In the late 1980s, NYK managers responded to market competition and increasing labor costs by divesting the company of direct control of its sailing fleet and subcontracted ship operations to maritime management groups mostly based in Southeast Asia. The move transformed NYK into an *ersatz* holding company run by a relatively small workforce, based in Tokyo, who managed contractual relations with affiliated subsidiaries and subcontractors across the globe. The arrangement seemed satisfactory until the mid-1990s when the boom in trade between China and the consumer-focused economies of Europe and the Americas encouraged company officers to reclaim direct control of the NYK fleet and port facilities worldwide. The global megacarrier that emerged was more profitable and ethnically diverse. By 2008, NYK ranked among the top three marine transport companies in the world with more than ¥2.5 trillion (£19.2 billion) in total revenue and ¥160 billion (£1.23 billion) in net profit.[5] The globalization of NYK also resulted in a majority of the company's nearly 55,000 employees being nationals of countries whose populations still retained strong public memories of World War II.[6] This change in international status and employee demographics fostered a variety of challenges for NYK's Tokyo-based senior management, not the least of which was how to construct a global corporate identity that did not inflame memories of unpleasant aspects of the company's 120-year history.

NYK's earliest official histories, told in flowery marketing prose, tell us how fierce domestic competition compelled the fledgling company to shift the bulk of operations to overseas transport by linking the textile exporters of Yokohama and Shanghai with their overseas customers in Europe and the United States.[7] After several mergers with its remaining rivals, which also positioned the company to receive government favor, NYK was awarded a lucrative monopoly on troop and cargo transport during the First Sino-Japanese War (1894–95). As a core member of Japan's emerging military-industrial complex, NYK again benefited from government shipping transport contracts during the Russo-Japanese War (1904–05), in addition to gaining access to new ports and shipping routes made possible by Japan's expansion into China, which enabled the company to be a key player in the transport of cargo between Japan and its newly established colonies in Taiwan and Korea. By the start of World War I, NYK was Japan's primary intraempire and overseas deep water carrier and ranked among the seven largest shipping companies in the world.[8]

While bulk commodities cargo was NYK's primary business, human cargo was also an important source of revenue well into the twentieth century.[9] The majority of ships that comprised NYK's prewar fleet were mixed cargo and passenger vessels that, in addition to freight, also carried upper-class Japanese and Europeans in several dozen first- and second-class passenger berths. A surprising amount of NYK's early history can be gleaned from the marketing materials produced during the prewar and wartime era. In 1901, NYK published its first illustrated guide for upper-class travelers seeking passage throughout the Far East. As a paid supplement to the Meiji era periodical *Fūzoku gahō* (*Manners and Customs Illustrated*), the *Jōkyaku annai yūsen zue* (*Yūsen Passengers' Illustrated Guidebook*, or *Yūsen zue*) was more likely produced with a domestic agenda in keeping with the *Fūzoku gahō's* overall mission to educate the Meiji era upper-class in the ways of Western civilization. Offering short essays and captioned illustrations depicting the luxuries of shipboard life available to the elite transoceanic traveler, the guidebook joined a host of contemporary publications at the center of the Meiji discourse on "civilization and enlightenment."[10]

For the illustrated guide, NYK selected the 3,500 ton Scottish built *Kasuga Maru* to represent the ideal passenger ship of the era. Constructed by Napier and Sons in Glasgow and delivered to NYK in 1898, the *Kasuga Maru* was a moderately sized dual cargo-passenger ship that typified the vessels of the Yokohama-Shanghai-Seattle Line at the start of the twentieth century.[11] Importantly, *Fūzoku gahō* illustrators portrayed the *Kasuga Maru* as a cross-section of the emerging modern empire by dividing the ship into liminal spaces that also illustrate the many layered interconnections between capital and empire during the early twentieth century. Editor Noguchi Shōichi and illustrator Yamamoto Shōkoku portrayed the ship's first- and second-class passengers in the ship's social hall (main saloon), barber shop, smoking room, dining rooms, and stately cabins, as well as partaking in the modern amenities and culinary delights that the ship's crew provided for them. Noguchi described extravagant Western dining menus, while Yamamoto illustrated immaculately maintained first- and second-class accommodations. First-class passengers aboard the *Kasuga Maru* were expected to adhere to a formal standard of dress and conduct their activities with proper deportment.[12]

Like their European and American competitors, NYK ships of the era demarcated class lines as much by race and ethnicity as by wealth.[13] While Japanese and Chinese nationals able to pay the significantly more expensive first-class fare ate and socialized alongside their European and American contemporaries, more than half of the *Kasuga Maru's* passengers, and an unrecorded number of below-decks crew,[14] were Chinese and Korean nationals segregated from the Japanese lower-class passengers as well as the predominantly white European and American upper-class passengers. Japanese and Chinese third-class passengers were assigned separate communal sleeping and living spaces, and NYK even fashioned an "inter-class" steerage berth for lower-class Europeans and Americans whom the company thought would want to be segregated from what the NYK passenger guide referred to as the "Asiatic races."[15]

NYK's "Asiatic" third-class passengers were billeted according to national origin and were not granted access to organized deck side activities or upper-class below-deck communal spaces. Segregated by race and ethnicity, third-class passengers lived and slept in communal rooms of up to a hundred. Water was rationed and meals, prepared according to the company's determination of the passenger's ethnic cuisine, were cooked and served in ethnically designated communal quarters. The only specific comfort beyond food and a place to sleep offered to Chinese émigrés was the occasional "opium den" (ahenkutsu) where smokers could relieve their addiction in an environment that company propaganda claimed demonstrated the comfort of even the third-class NYK passenger experience.[16]

NYK continued to publish its annual illustrated travel guides until the mid-1920s when the company re-launched the serial as an English-language publication, Glimpses of the East, the purpose of which was to sell the exotic travel experience available to English-speaking travelers.[17] Published annually until 1944, a recurring feature of each year's edition was a recounting of the company's historic role in Japan's emergence as a modern imperial power, and each issue of Glimpses opened with a frank account of the company's collaboration with the imperial state. Successive decades of Glimpses tell us how NYK began dedicated passenger ship operations in the mid-1920s and further explain how in 1928 the company commissioned its first luxury passenger liners, which company managers marketed to what they perceived as an expanding number of wealthy world-travelers. These company mini-histories fondly recollect how NYK's interwar era passenger fleet marked the very best in a Golden Age of luxury passenger service.[18]

NYK marketing materials proudly present a narrative of shipping centered on the luxury passenger ships the company brought into service from the late 1920s. The first of NYK's luxury passenger ships were assigned to NYK's highest-profile trans-Pacific routes linking Hong Kong, Shanghai, Kobe, Yokohama, Honolulu, Seattle, San Francisco, and Los Angeles. NYK's European-styled luxury liners were a financial and public relations success, and in 1939, the company placed orders for two additional ships designed to carry some 900 passengers at speeds exceeding 25 knots, which promised to provide the fastest Pacific crossing in the industry. Had the twin 27,000 ton passenger liners been built as designed, they would have joined the ranks of the finest luxury passenger ships of the era. In late 1941, however, the Imperial Navy requisitioned both while still under construction at Mitsubishi's Nagasaki Shipyards. The navy re-fitted and launched them as aircraft carriers in 1942, along with three other smaller passenger ships that NYK had commissioned for the company's European passenger service. All NYK ships were put under direct government control in April 1942, and NYK histories tell us how only 36 cargo ships and one passenger liner, the *Hikawa Maru*, survived the war.

At the height of wartime patriotic fervor, *Glimpses* editors printed a message from company president Terai Hisanobu in which he wrote that NYK was bravely playing its part in

> the formation of the new World Order. Upon the conclusion of the present conflicts, the Company is prepared not only to resume its well-known world-wide services, but to devote its energy to the opening of services within the Co-Prosperity Sphere with special attention to inter-insular trade. It is hoped that the services hitherto monopolized by the British, American, and Dutch vessels between these districts, will thus be immensely improved, enhancing the enjoyment of freedom, happiness and prosperity of the vast number of native inhabitants at large, who were hitherto held down under the unjust oppressions, economic and otherwise, of their usurping overlords.[19]

The annual passenger guide included an unabashed narrative of co-expanding corporate and national empires up until the Pacific War. In fact, both the 1943 and 1944 issues of the annual guide similarly assert NYK's long-standing collaboration with the empire by laying out a historical narrative recounting NYK's service to the state during the annexations of Taiwan and Korea as well as the role NYK ships played in the subsidized transportation of Japanese subjects to Hawai'i and the Americas.[20]

The persuasiveness of these and NYK's other wartime propaganda publications is doubtful at best, but nonetheless demonstrative of the company's position at the nexus of wartime maritime transport. By 1944, the majority of the Japanese merchant fleet, long since under government control, lay at the bottom of the navigable waterways of East and Southeast Asia. While collaboration with the imperial state was compulsory, it is nevertheless significant that NYK's management, executives of what was essentially a shell corporation, produced patriotic public narrative that applauded the company's long-standing, intimate relationship with the modern empire.

Rescuing history from the past

After compulsory forfeiture of control of its remaining ships at the start of the Allied Occupation, NYK was allowed to resume normal operations in 1950, which enabled the company to begin rebuilding its cargo operations with the assistance of considerable government subsidies. In addition to resuming its cargo business, the company also refitted the *Hikawa Maru*, which had been used as a hospital ship during the war and to transport food and troops during the first half of the Allied Occupation, and returned it to service as a trans-Pacific passenger liner. The *Hikawa Maru* ferried dignitaries, students, and even Fulbright scholars between Japan and the United States until severe competition from the airline industry killed the passenger surface ship market in the early 1960s.

The end of NYK's trans-Pacific passenger service, however, also marked the beginning of the company's emergence as the dominant carrier of bulk materials and commercial cargo to and from Japan. Despite a profit-less decade between the mid-1950s and the mid-1960s, several waves of government-mandated industry consolidation positioned NYK to establish itself as a dominant player in the container cargo sector that grew alongside Japan's booming export trade. NYK was a major transporter of Japan's exported industrial production, and the rapid economic growth that characterized the postwar era was in part only possible because NYK was able to deliver the goods to marketplaces across the globe.

Despite a rich historical record of proud service to the empire, or perhaps because of it, NYK has, since 1945, taken great pains to downplay the extent to which earlier narratives celebrated the company's prewar and wartime accomplishments. The company was consumed with financial concerns well into the 1970s, but in the 1980s, NYK managers sought to re-establish the company's importance by commissioning an official history of NYK's first 100 years.[21] The economic challenges of the post-bubble years of the early and mid-1990s consumed the attention of company managers, but one small consequence of the company's shift in business plan and subsequent rapid growth in the early 2000s was an upgraded importance, and slightly different spin, put on the presentation of the company's historic role.

In 2002, NYK managers began a refurbishment of the company's maritime museum and repackaged its long-standing history-writing enterprise as part of the company's official social responsibility scheme. The majority of NYK's historical narrative has since been produced by personnel working from the NYK Maritime Museum located along the historic Yokohama waterfront. As cathedrals to the modern nation-state, history museums occupy the urban landscape as monumental acts of hubris disguised as philanthropy, and NYK's museum was similarly established in the early 1990s as a means to bolster corporate prestige by embodying the firm's historical importance. Reopened under the umbrella of NYK's social responsibility scheme in 2003, NYK executives charged the maritime museum staff with the tasks of preserving historical materials, communicating "marine philosophy" to the general public, and instilling "NYK Group Values—integrity, innovation and intensity—in the minds of employees around the world."[22] Managed by the company's corporate communications group, the museum is promoted by company officials as a forum for educating the general public, as well as employees of the NYK Group, about Japan's modern maritime history.[23]

To serve the museum's three-fold mission, the curatorial staff have organized temporary exhibits ranging from displays of marine art produced by local school children to educational exhibits explaining the danger consumer pollutants pose to the marine environment.[24] The museum even features monthly musical performances and occasional public lectures by marine scientists, NYK ships' officers, and company executives. Since re-opening in 2003, the museum has been visited by more than 100,000 members of the general public.[25] As a forum for public education, the museum does no worse, and no better, than the hundreds of maritime museums that bound the navigable waterways of Europe, Australia, and the Americas, and as such, the NYK Museum serves as the primary venue for staging the company's official historical narrative.[26] The museum, managed by the company's corporate communications group, is thus used as a forum for promoting the company's role in Japan's contemporary maritime industry as well as the nation's modern maritime history.[27]

From its historic building in Yokohama, the NYK Museum plays a central role in the formulation and embodiment of the company's institutional memory. As a phenomenon of the late twentieth century, company museums have helped to shape popular notions of history, nation, and culture in most of the world's highly industrialized societies.[28] Privately owned history museums often retell the history of a particular company within the meta-narrative provided by better known tropes of regional or national histories. NYK's museum, located on the ground floor of the company's fully restored 1920s' era Yokohama Office, offers visitors a spatial-temporal link to what the company refers to as its "Golden Era." The museum's nine permanent exhibits sequentially narrate the company's history through bilingual wall text (English and Japanese), period photographs, schematics, timelines, maps, and material relics— mostly nautical antiques recovered from NYK ships and offices from each of the historical eras portrayed.

Museum curators have filled the obvious narrative gaps left by the paucity of surviving relics with video segments from a commissioned documentary. The film is parsed into a dozen segments displayed on video screens embedded within the graphics and text of the permanent exhibit. "The NYK Story" (Nippon Yūsen Monogatari) recounts a heroic tragedy of the years leading up to, during, and just past World War II. Yet, the NYK documentary attends to the history of the company as a travel agent would précis their product. The resultant narrative fills important gaps in the museum's material narrative by providing visual evidence of shipboard life and exotic ports of call in an entertaining and somewhat informative format.

Much like a national history museum, the NYK museum's exhibit areas present the history of modern Japan as the product of world events spurred on by the advance of Western nations whose expansion into East Asia drove Japan to defend itself by pursuing the economic means to achieve world power status. Two exhibit areas, situated at the physical center of the museum's exhibit space, portray the historical narrative at the core of NYK's corporate identity. While NYK had been the lynchpin of Mitsubishi's cargo transport network since 1885, the NYK museum presents photos and artifacts of the company's 1930s' passenger service as material evidence of its finest era. The full-scale passenger ships of the 1920s and 1930s were the corporate prestige products of the interwar era, and the museum displays a variety of photographs and artifacts memorializing the sleek and stylish Art Deco interiors by designer Marc Simon from which visitors are able to discern some of the most appealing aspects of the first-class experience aboard NYK's interwar passenger liners.

The company's wartime exhibit sits directly beside its "Golden Era" display. Comparatively speaking, the Janus-faced exhibit is understated. It presents a wall-sized map depicting the last known locations of the 185 ships NYK lost during the war. Adjacent to the exhibit, museum curators have installed computer terminals offering patrons the opportunity to look up the names of deceased NYK sailors to determine which ship they died aboard and read brief accounts of their service to the company. While the war experience as recounted here is somber and rather modestly presented, the war exhibit nevertheless shares center stage with the exhibit celebrating what museum curators elected to portray as NYK's finest era.

Understatedness belies its purpose. The exhibit's accompanying wall text explains that NYK's participation in the war was involuntary, by asserting that the company and its officers had no choice but to join the war effort since all wartime shipping not already requisitioned by the Army or Navy was nationalized and put under the control of the government's *Senpaku Un'ei Kai* (Ship Management Association). There is some truth in the claim, but it is important to note that NYK's chief executive Ōtani Noboru was also appointed to head the Ship Management Association when it was formed in April 1942. While the head of the largest shipping corporation in Japan was the logical appointment, that Ōtani had been advanced to the position is indicative of NYK's multilayered complicity in the interests of the wartime state, a status not easily dispelled by claims that the company was simply compelled by imperial order.[29]

NYK's postwar war narrative de-emphasizes the company's role in the imperial expansionism that characterized the company's passage through the Meiji, Taishō, and early Shōwa eras. The exhibit does not mention the circumstances that led to the war, nor does it discuss the extent to which the company had been part of the military-industrial complex that prepared for and supplied the war. Through this exhibit, NYK pays tribute to the memory of the 5,000 merchant sailors and nearly 185 ships lost during the war. Yet, there is no mention of the cargo—military materiel for certain, but also human cargo—lost with these ships. An undetermined number of those lost at sea (passenger manifests were destroyed during the war) were colonial subjects and enemy prisoners in transit aboard ships that were in all but name still the responsibility of NYK personnel. In taking pains to explain how the NYK fleet had been requisitioned and put under direct control of the Army, Navy, or Ship Management Association, and thus not NYK's responsibility, the exhibit also illustrates the extent to which NYK's postwar managers and history writers still understood the sunken wartime ships to be NYK's "lost fleet."

On the surface, it seems that the loss or forfeiture of the majority of the NYK merchant fleet, followed by a brief interregnum of operation under Allied control, allowed company officials to assert a break from their wartime past and rebuild their company free of the specific histories of the company's earlier complicities. Indeed, it is perhaps the near total loss of the wartime fleet—only 37 of more than 200 ships remained afloat in 1945— which enabled the company to assert a physical break from the past. The few merchant cargo ships that survived the war were retired by the mid-1950s, and it seems likely that the purpose of the exhibit commemorating NYK's sunken heroes is to further diminish public memory of wartime complicity without losing the brand value of the company's past.

Selling nostalgia as history

While cargo transport remained NYK's dominant business throughout the postwar era, NYK moved in the 1990s to exploit public memories of the interwar era passenger liners by re-entering the luxury passenger service. Its first foray into the postairline passenger service business, however, came in the form of the Los Angeles-based cruise ship line Crystal Cruises. NYK marketers used the moment of *Crystal Harmony's* first call on New York as an opportunity to mark NYK's re-emergence as a company of global importance. One company advertising leaflet asserts: "almost a half-century after NYK's wartime losses, the gleaming, all-white *Crystal Harmony* arrived in New York . . . [and] amidst the festivities and formalities of the occasion there was also a historic notation to her visit: she was the very first Japanese luxury liner to visit New York in forty years."[30]

Catering to the lucrative American market, Crystal Cruises began as a one-ship operation. Despite a stagnant economy in Japan, economic growth in the United States bolstered NYK's California-based cruise business. NYK cruise ships regularly won industry-wide customer satisfaction awards, and industry analysts lauded NYK's return to the passenger market. The success of Crystal Cruises' first ship, *Crystal Harmony*, encouraged the company to launch two additional luxury cruise ships for the American market: the *Crystal Symphony* in 1995 and the *Crystal Serenity* in 2003.[31] Hoping to experience similar success in home waters, NYK re-launched its Japan-based passenger business in 1991 with the 600-passenger ship *Asuka*. After a slow start in the post-bubble recessionary economy of the mid-1990s, NYK's *Asuka* business grew into a successful enterprise by offering to its middle-class Japanese clientele long and short-distance luxury cruises with an annual global circumnavigation cruise for its elite passenger base. In 2005, in order to relieve the aging *Asuka*, NYK refitted and relaunched the Los Angeles-based *Crystal Harmony* as the 800-passenger *Asuka II* to serve the Japanese market with intercoastal and regional cruises punctuated by a biannual circumnavigation.[32]

Considering that the bulk of NYK's profitability comes from the cargo transport business, NYK's cruise ship lines receive a considerable amount of attention within corporate communications and marketing propaganda. While profitable, NYK's cruise business accounted for less than one percent of net operating profit in 2009, and cruise operations only became profitable in 2005. Recent refitting and refurbishment of its cruise ships operating out of Yokohama and Los Angeles indicates that the company intends to remain in the cruise business.[33] However, NYK's investment in its cruise line is only partly explained by the company's optimistic outlook on its potential to gain additional market share in an uncertain financial climate. The cruise business holds a disproportionate position of importance within the company's public profile because it functions as a prestige product line aimed at enhancing the corporation's brand image.[34]

While the company does make money at it, NYK's contemporary cruise business is an attempt to leverage the company's historical prominence in the luxury passenger carriage business. NYK marketing materials and corporate communications often use the public image of the company's cruise line to enhance public recognition of its historical connection to the interwar passenger ship business. Like many other corporate institutions, NYK deploys historical narrative as a means of influencing public perception of the company's long-term commitment to qualities desired by the targeted clientele.[35]

NYK offers its Japanese cruise ship clientele a taste of the "good life" in the form of well-ordered shipboard activities with prescribed activities and a minimum standard of deportment that includes a sense of culture and class, in the form of fine dining and exotic ports of call that draw upon the customer's nostalgic link to public memories of NYK's interwar era passenger ships. NYK's American product line offers the same well-ordered sense of class and culture, but also offers its majority non-Japanese clientele several opportunities to become familiar with the history and prestige at the core of their host's corporate identity. Reading materials, shipboard activities, and even memorabilia offer the cruising customer an historicized experience designed to enhance their perception of the cruising experience within an historical framework. The shipboard enterprise in Japan and the United States also includes a gift shop that sells a range of reproductions of advertising materials and artifacts from what NYK has branded as the "Golden Age" of passenger shipping.

The NYK museum is tightly integrated with the company's prestige cruise business. The museum archives provide historical materials for all aspects of the company's marketing strategy, but also produce narratives for company publications that feature the company's historic passenger business. Indeed, the relationship between passenger operations and the museum is also quite contemporary. The museum's first two directors each finished their seafaring careers in command of one of NYK's three cruise ships—a plum assignment among the company's 800 captains. Even further evidence is found on the third floor of the museum building, which houses NYK's cruise sales center. The museum and cruise center, under the command of a former cruise ship captain, foster an integrated platform for NYK's maritime history enterprise.

Writing history for internal audiences

While marketing products is a primary purpose of the company's history writing enterprise, NYK has also deployed historical narrative as an integral part of its employee relations programs, and in this, the NYK museum serves as a primary venue for internal as well as external audiences. While by the mid-2000s, Japanese remained the language of NYK's Tokyo-based management, English was the language of daily operations for all 45,000 employees working outside Japan.[36] Importantly, the employee demographics of NYK in the early twenty-first century were in some ways similar to those of the late nineteenth century. NYK's Meiji era ship crews were by necessity multiethnic: NYK purchased its ships from Europe and recruited its ships' officers and senior engineering crew from Europe and the United States. The foreign senior crew served as mentors to a small number of handpicked Japanese whom the company aspired to put in their stead, but a great many below decks crew, especially fire crew who fed coal to the great boilers in the bowels of the ship, were Korean and Chinese colonials whose unrecorded, underpaid labor meant much to the company's profitability. By the mid-1920s, the majority of NYK ships were captained and officered by Japanese nationals, but NYK continued to employ a multiethnic crew below deck.

NYK managers aspired to a monoethnic above deck workforce, which many Japanese of the era perceived as evidence of having achieved technical parity with Western shippers. The preference for all-Japanese crews, above and below deck, became much easier to manage when NYK transitioned from coal- to oil-fired ships, which required far fewer below-deck crew with higher levels of technical specialization, and Japan's merchant maritime fleet of the 1930s and 1940s was crewed by only Japanese nationals. The employment structure persisted throughout the first three decades of the postwar era, but the company's inability to attract new recruits from Japan's high school graduates, who by the 1980s, were more interested in white-collar than blue-collar maritime careers, resulted in a rapid ageing of NYK's ship crews.

NYK managers responded to their "ageing problem" by re-registering NYK ships under flags of convenience and subcontracting sailing operations to primarily Southeast Asian maritime logistics partners. It has not been possible to determine the exact reason why company managers took the decision to reflag their fleet, but while it was indeed common industry practice during the 1980s, it seems likely that company managers also did not perceive an advantage in directly managing the multiethnic organization that would result from the declining numbers of young Japanese men entering into the maritime trades. The decision of the early 1980s was made all the more significant when in the late 1990s the company reversed its early policy and began to again re-flag a Filipino crewed fleet under Japanese officers.

Internal communications within a large corporation can provide a fascinating perspective on operational dynamics, especially the ways in which a company's management teams seek to communicate with their employees. In the late 1990s, NYK's Japanese language employee magazine *YŪSEN*, and English language *SEASCOPE*, began to feature stories narrating the company's central role in the migration of peoples across the globe. Although reader-impact data is not available, these two magazines do provide a unique window on the institutional uses of historical narrative deployed as part of NYK's employee management scheme.

In July 2000, the English-language *SEASCOPE*, distributed to all of NYK's ships, dock facilities, and offices worldwide, featured a story highlighting the important role NYK played in the transportation of Japanese overseas migrants. "The history of emigration from Japan to South America started with the voyage of the *Sakura Maru* when she left the port of Yokohama on 27 February 1899." The writer tells us that all of the *Sakura Maru*'s "790 emigrants were male and went there to work at a sugar cane farm through contracts they had with the trading company, Morioka-shōkai." While the story fails to explain how most such contracts were signed without benefit of literacy or full disclosure, and were tantamount to contracts of indenture, the story does go on to explain how "as a result of differences in diet, the harsh climate and the rugged natural features of this new country, a large number of the new arrivals succumbed to illness and sadly died."[37]

Despite this grisly turn, the NYK emigration narrative did serve a purpose. The article further explains that "although emigration to Peru through contracts with a trading company was abolished in 1923, many people continued to cross the Pacific Ocean to Peru with the aim of advancing into commercial fields." By way of personalizing the narrative, the story further narrates how "in the mid-summer of 1934 newly-married Mr. Naoichi Fujimori accompanied by his wife Mutsue, emigrated to Peru on NYK's *Bokuyo Maru* sailing from Yokohama to Callao. This couple's son Mr. Alberto Fujimori is the first Peruvian President of Japanese descent."[38]

While it seems bizarre that an internal magazine would fix on such a distant connection between NYK and the then head-of-state, Fujimori—who in 2012 sat in a Peruvian jail cell—Fujimori was at the time of publication in 2000 still lauded across Japan for having boldly directed the retaking of the Japanese Ambassadorial Residence in Lima from Túpac Amaru (MRTA) guerrillas in 1997.[39] A few months after publication of the *SEASCOPE* story, though there is no likely connection between the story and subsequent events, Fujimori was able to leverage his fame and claim patrilineal right of citizenship when he fled to Japan to escape prosecution for his role in orchestrating the extra-judicial killings and kidnappings conducted by the anti-Communist death squad Grupo Colina.[40]

The public relations benefit of NYK's historical connection to Fujimori is somewhat doubtful, given the crimes for which he was ultimately convicted. Nevertheless, the rhetorical effort appears to have been part of an overall attempt by NYK's internal communications team to shape institutional memory of the company's involvement in the human cargo business. Indeed, *SEASCOPE* and *YŪSEN* ran several stories from the late 1990s to the mid-2000s highlighting the famous people, sports teams, and social groups—from a Nobel physicist to Japan's first Fulbright scholars—who had taken passage on NYK ships.[41] Many of the stories focus on the honor bestowed upon the company by the patronage of the NYK Line's many VIP passengers, but a telling few attempt to impart a different air to the role played by the company in the human migrations of the twentieth century.

By an odd circumstance of history, it was the NYK Line that carried Rabbi Zorach Warhaftig and a few dozen other Polish Jews when they fled from Lithuania in 1941. Warhaftig is credited with having engineered the escape of as many as 5,000 Jews to the Americas and Dutch Caribbean. When visas from the Dutch consulate were cut off, Warhaftig turned to Japanese consul Sugihara Chiune, who issued some 6,000 visas to Jewish refugees before his consulate was also closed.[42] Explains the *SEASCOPE* story on the affair: "after working extremely hard to help the Jewish refugees, Mr. Warhaftig and his family boarded *Hikawa Maru* (an NYK vessel) in Yokohama on 5 June, 1941, destined for Vancouver, Canada." In his book, Warhaftig writes:

> The sea was calm and the voyage was peaceful. It was as if we were having a summer holiday onboard and we spent the time sunbathing on deck. The shadow of the war and the storm faded away, and the troubles and the tense nature caused by them disappeared. However, I didn't have a peaceful mind because of the strong responsibility I had to help the Jewish refugees with the troubles they faced.[43]

Hundreds of Jews paid passage out of Europe on NYK ships, and while the story does carry some value as a human interest piece, the narrative ends with a selection from Warhaftig's own travel journal that resembles contemporary touristic narratives of the NYK experience, albeit in the heavy shadow of the destruction of European Jewry.

While there seems little doubt that the communication group does not employ skilled history writers, it might yet stand to question why the NYK communications group chose to draw such tenuous historical connections for its English-speaking audience. The historical narrative appeared as the company was experiencing significant demographic change and, ineffective as it appears, the internal historical narrative that emerged during the 1990s seems indicative of an uneasy awareness of the company's increased global exposure to public criticism for its role as a purveyor of maritime services to the imperial state.[44]

NYK's postwar war narrative de-emphasizes the company's role in imperial expansionism and coerced transportations that characterized NYK's passage through the Meiji, Taishō, and early Shōwa eras. The exhibit does not mention the circumstances that led to the war, nor does it discuss the extent to which the company had been part of the military-industrial complex that prepared for and supplied the war. Through this exhibit, NYK pays tribute to the memory of the 5,000 merchant sailors and hundreds of ships lost during the war. It seems that the near total loss of the NYK merchant fleet in 1945 provided NYK's postwar managers with the opportunity to claim a physical break from their wartime past and thus rebuild their company free of the specific histories of the company's earlier complicities embodied by its lost fleet. Indeed, the few ships that survived the war were retired by the early mid-1950s—all except for the interwar passenger liner *Hikawa Maru*.

Institutional mnemonics

Most maritime heritage organizations are shaped by a contemporary fascination with the history of technology, and no maritime museum seems complete without the physicality of a ship for its visitors to wander. Since 1945, the corporeal body of the *Hikawa Maru*, the last survivor of NYK's historical fleet, has provided a useful spatial-temporal link to the interwar era. Permanently berthed near Yokohama's Yamashita Park since the early 1960s, the *Hikawa Maru* exhibit is the last surviving relic of the company's "Golden Era." and serves as a crucial aspect of the company's effort to evoke nostalgia for a set of products and services rendered to the upper classes of the early twentieth century as a means of marketing a vaguely similar set of products and services to the urban middle classes of contemporary Japan. In 2007, NYK completed an extensive refurbishment of the ship, which had lain in neglect at its permanent mooring in Yokohama since 1960, and reopened it as an extension of the NYK Museum. Yet the ship, which also saw service during the war as a medical support vessel in Southeast Asia, also embodied unpleasant memories of the company's wartime complicity. Perhaps symbolic of their uneasy relationship with its history, company officials have several times remade the ship and its story in ways that seem to further diminish public memory of the less laudable moments of its past.

When launched in 1929, the *Hikawa Maru* was designed as a cargo-carrying passenger vessel. It completed more than 70 trans-Pacific voyages on the Seattle line between 1930 and 1941, at which point the company responded to increased political tensions between the United States and Japan by reassigning the ship to service on the European line. After several voyages carrying Japanese and other evacuees from Europe, the ship was requisitioned by the government in 1942, refitted as a hospital ship, and put into service tending wounded soldiers in Southeast Asia. Seized by the Allied Occupation in 1945, the ship was used to carry personnel between the United States and Japan until 1947 when it was reassigned to alternately carry coal and food until released to NYK control in 1950.[45]

NYK continued to use the *Hikawa Maru* as a cargo vessel until 1953, when it was refurbished as a passenger carrier and reassigned as the company's first postwar trans-Pacific passenger liner. The ship traveled between Yokohama and Seattle until August 1960, when it was retired and permanently moored on the Yokohama waterfront where it served as a floating youth hostel and wedding venue. In the early 1970s, the youth hostel was closed and the ship was converted into a joint operation with the City of Yokohama that featured a maritime museum, restaurant, banquet facility, and summertime beer garden. The restaurant, banquet hall, and beer garden closed in 2002, and the ship's future remained uncertain until 2007 when NYK agreed to completely refurbish and reopen the ship as a historical exhibit of the NYK Museum in April 2008.[46]

Since 2008, the company has exhibited the refurbished *Hikawa Maru* as a memorial to designer Marc Simon's sleek Art Deco interiors, the faded ghost of which can be experienced by walking through the refurbished exhibits of first-class cabins and social spaces, the smoking salon, and the dining room. The designated walking tour, illustrated with graphics and bilingual wall text, guides visitors from the upper-deck first-class accommodations to the third-class berths and service areas of the ship's lower decks. The exhibit is designed and maintained by museum staff, and many of the wall-sized displays deployed to explain the exhibit feature visual materials and text drawn directly from the pages of *SEASCOPE* and *YŪSEN*, most of which can also be found on display at the museum nearby in Minato Mirai.

A recent reacquisition, the contemporary ship exhibit was meant to supplement the museum, but has drawn far more visitors than the primary facility, which is situated about two kilometers from the ship's mooring at Yamashita Park. The *Hikawa Maru* has long been a popular waterfront attraction, drawing more than 26,000,000 visitors in its first 45 years moored on the Yokohama waterfront, and attracting more than 100,000 visitors in the first year after its refurbishment and reopening in April 2008.[47] Although the ship attracts a small number of merchant mariners while they are in port, the primary audiences are school children and families out for a day on the waterfront, and the numbers of visitors are evidence that the ship is a popular venue from which NYK seeks to promote the company's role in Japan's modern maritime heritage. Yet, the ship is only one of many corporate venues and publications that obfuscate NYK's role in the history of imperial Japan.

Conclusion

Corporations in part flourish by evading critical discussion of their social function, and CSR schemes deploy an array of devices as a means of achieving this end.[48] Surprisingly, many companies, large and small, host their own museums, and the case of NYK is an excellent example of how corporate museums manufacture historical memory as a means of enhancing brand recognition, selling products, and obscuring less pleasant aspects of institutional histories. As an arm of the company's social responsibility program, the NYK historical enterprise is part of a philanthropic scheme that promotes a carefully crafted narrative of the company's role in the history of modern Japan. Indeed, NYK's history-telling enterprise is so well integrated within the other parts of the company's internal and external communications apparatus that it is remarkably easy to forget that the museum and ship exhibit are managed by the public relations organ of a for-profit corporation.

The integrated history enterprise nevertheless exemplifies an institutional uneasiness with the historical narratives it attempts to create. NYK's museum exhibits and employee magazines offer little more than a facsimile of the national history narrative presented by museums such as the Yūshūkan at Yasukuni Shrine and the National Shōwa Memorial Museum, both in Tokyo. On consequence is that NYK's external narrative is under-informative and offers little more than the opportunity for the visitor to spend a pleasant day on the Yokohama waterfront. NYK's internal narrative selectively, and uncritically, draws from historical materials originally crafted to emphasize the company's enthusiastic participation in imperial and militarist narratives, which further underscores what I think to be an embedded institutional fear of employee relations problems between NYK's Japan-based managers and its majority non-Japanese workforce. Human relations programming comprises part of many public relations schemes, but the reason for this particular shape to NYK's public relations agenda may be the fact that the significant shift in employee demographics since 2000 may have left NYK managers feeling anxious about what their Asian employees might do after learning about the company's twentieth-century history.

NYK merchant ships did not shoot, bomb, or gas anyone and the official narrative is that the company was compelled by imperial order to collaborate with the war effort, and lost nearly all of its merchant fleet as a result. Significantly, in the company's version of history, the human story is also lost at sea. Hundreds of thousands of civilians and soldiers in Asia and the

Pacific lost their lives because of the war materiel and soldiers transported aboard NYK ships, for which NYK received ample compensation—up until the end, when the corporation was all but lost at sea.

It is important to note, however, that the wartime government and its marine transport contractors were closely entwined elements of the same military force, and total loss, whether sunk at sea or lost through forced divestiture of capital inventory at the conclusion of the war, does not appear to have fully resolved the historical concerns of NYK officials. While it is convenient for postwar company executives to deploy historical narratives that underpin the assertion that the wartime company was merely following orders, it seems that the NYK Group, which today transports goods across the globe and employs more than 33,000 Asians, might indeed benefit from a vision of historical responsibility that seeks to reconcile rather than obfuscate its multiple collusions with the imperial and wartime state.

The stories presented by NYK bring to bear the question as to what constitutes legitimate historical narrative. Recent scholarship on historical memory in Japan and Germany demonstrates that all public memory is at some level constructed within contested discourses.[49] NYK's history-telling enterprise opens the question as to whether it is "socially responsible" for a corporation to present itself as absolved of its past without seeking reconciliation for the very worst deeds undertaken by its employees, corporate officers, and majority shareholders. Many postwar German citizens chastised their postwar corporate leaders for not admitting the extent to which their institutional collaborations with the Nazi regime did grave harm to tens of millions of individuals. Few in Japan have questioned the same.

Corporations have in law the fiduciary responsibility to provide truthful information. Nevertheless, the obfuscation of an unpleasant past may be one way that corporate executives protect shareholder value since publicizing past indiscretions could invite civil action. Indeed, several civil cases brought against the American subsidiaries of major German and Japanese corporations have precipitated settlements despite legal roadblocks claiming the issue of war liability was resolved by the treaties that ended World War II.[50]

Yet, there are historic sites, such as the slave auction at Colonial Williamsburg in the United States and the "Killing Fields" at Choeung Ek in Cambodia, that function as profitable tourist enterprises by specifically recalling past horrors on a scale that seems well beyond any indiscretion or collaboration perpetrated by NYK. The crucial point of difference, however, is that the historical narratives deployed by NYK are also likely intended to ameliorate an institutional fear of conflict between Japanese management and a predominantly Asian workforce—a situation that perversely resembles social and political tensions within the imagined Greater East Asian Co-Prosperity Sphere of the wartime era. The institutional structures constructed by NYK to promote corporate social responsibility since the start of the twenty-first century seem to emphasize the lingering ambiguities of postwar Japan's relationship with its prewar and wartime past. Ironically, it also seems likely that NYK's history telling enterprise exposes the company to fiduciary risk by using the company's social responsibility scheme as a forum for presenting marketing narrative as history.

14

Memorializing the Spirit of Wit and Grit in Postindustrial Japan

Hiraku Shimoda

In one of his nonfiction moments, the novelist Murakami Haruki worried about Japan's future legacy. Reflecting upon Japan's rapid, export-fueled economic success in the second half of the twentieth century, he pondered what ultimately came of it. "The Toyota Corolla, the Sony Walkman, electric bread makers and *karaoke*, too . . . um, what else? There might be more but I can't think of any," he wrote in 1997. "If Japan in the twenty-first century were to fall from the height of its prosperity"—if that sundry of gadgets and frivolities were all that modern Japan would leave behind for posterity—"Wouldn't that be a rather meager and empty legacy? We couldn't really complain if future historians were to poke fun at us for this." He asked, "Could it be that we live in a country where the best we can do is a Walkman?"[1]

The turn of the twenty-first century presented many good reasons for not only baby boomers like Murakami but also countless others to feel uneasy about the postwar generation and what their seemingly spectacular industrial success had brought to bear upon contemporary society. All the handwringing about the so-called Lost Decade, *kakusa shakai* (social inequity), and *rōjin taikoku* (aging society) made some look askance at the true meaning of postwar affluence and those who had delivered it. Now that the seven million baby boomers were riding off into the sunset, could it really be that the mere Walkman was their only worthwhile keepsake? If that were true, postindustrial Japan would be a poor place indeed; back in 1997, Murakami did not yet know that even the Walkman would soon be consigned to the technological dustbin.

In contrast, a far more sanguine and buoyant interpretation of the Walkman and other postwar artifacts has been put forth elsewhere. According to this viewpoint, these products are more than just so many ephemeral contrivances. They are proud and enduring symbols of a distinctly remarkable age, crystallization of an undying spirit of innovation and industry. This storyline insists that we pay thankful tribute to the postwar generation that gave the world these worthy icons, for it was their ingenuity and hard work that bestowed redemption and prosperity upon a lost country, and laid an unshakable foundation on which an even brighter future might be built.

This simultaneously rousing and comforting vision of Japan's postwar experience is broadcast by the documentary series *Project X: Challengers*, which aired weekly between March 2000 and December 2005 on NHK. Every Tuesday night, *Project X* presented a dramatized remembrance of some remarkable feat that was achieved during the postwar. At the heart of the show are the trials and triumphs of technical innovators who brought us the VHS, the bullet train, the LCD television, and other testaments to Japan's industrial success. We have, among 177 episodes, the story of Japanese salesmen who worked desperately in the 1960s to sell the then-unknown Sony transistor radios in America. There is, too, the tale of food engineers who gained 30 pounds while testing the now-ubiquitous Cup Noodle in the 1970s. Viewers learn of lab technicians who literally risked their behinds trying to perfect the experimental "washlet." Even seemingly modest achievements like the photocopier, sonar fish finders, and running shoes are presented with no less pomp and zeal. All such tales, drawn mainly from the "high speed growth era" (1955–1973), are told in an ultimately triumphant and heart-warming narrative that asks the audience to map their own lives over the same field of dreams. Sepia-toned reenactments, grainy black-and-white snapshots, teary interviews with the participants themselves, now visibly aged but not so in spirit—they all reach but one conclusion: "We did good."

Of course, *Project X* is hardly the only famous celebration of the postwar experience. But it is an especially useful and telling medium for historians who seek to understand the struggles over the legacy of Japan's industrial success, and how that past might come to be remembered by an anxious postindustrial society. *Project X* is also a good opportunity to observe the convergence of history and media that took place around the turn of the twenty-first century, for *Project X* in fact ran alongside a broader movement, often carried forth in popular media, to resuscitate the Shōwa era—and its supposed ethos of industry—in the annals of Japanese history.

The descriptor "social phenomenon" gets tossed about a little too easily, but *Project X* probably qualifies as one. It certainly pulled in the numbers as a hit television show. At the height of its popularity, in 2002, the show boasted a 20% rating, reaching some 12–15 million viewers each week.[2] *Project X* quickly became a flagship program for NHK, and the center of considerable public attention. A typical airing provoked as many as 10,000 viewers to share their reactions with NHK.[3] Books based on the show, written by its creator and producer Imai Akira, regularly topped best-seller lists for nonfiction.[4] The word "Project X" came to be synonymous with syrupy success stories, an adjective to describe any painfully sincere and overwrought act of dramatization.[5] The show even earned enough attention to warrant a brief *New York Times* piece in 2003, which called it "an improbable television hit and a cultural phenomenon."[6]

In its heyday, *Project X* received extensive—though certainly not always positive—media coverage, as well as some critical acclaim and industry awards.[7] There was a sense that *Project X* was admirably edifying and beneficial in a way that television rarely is, a view that emerges best in a 2003 PTA survey. Parents identified *Project X* as the television program they would most like their children to watch, and they did so in a landslide.[8] Such a glowing assessment of *Project X* might be outliving the show itself. In 2010, or 5 years after it went off the air, a Mitsubishi Electric Engineering Corporation survey asked 327 employees which television show they would like to leave behind for posterity. *Project X* came in top among male respondents, and second among all respondents.[9] Its perceived didactic value is also conveyed by reports that the show has been used in schools and corporate training regimens.[10] If nothing else, *Project X* pushed the singer-songwriter Nakajima Miyuki's career to new heights. Her opening theme song spent an unprecedented 174 consecutive weeks on the Oricon Top 100 chart.[11] "Chijō no hoshi" will always be associated with *Project X*, as its emotionally soaring and poignant, anthemic pitch matched the show note for note.

NHK's official description of *Project X* captures both the program's appeal and, ultimately, the problem with its means and message:

> *Project X* tells the untold story of organizations and groups featuring anonymous Japanese who, with burning passion and fiery sense of mission in their hearts, carried out innovative initiatives in the postwar era.
>
> That social phenomenon still fresh in our memories; the development of new products that dramatically changed our lives; enormous projects that demonstrated the true inner strength of the Japanese: [these are the subjects of *Project X*.] In the postwar, the Japanese people have wielded their wisdom, and let individual ability flower as teamwork. What kinds of people were behind the scenes in the age-defining events of postwar Japan? What drama lay in the shadows of success, and how were the many obstacles overcome through ingenuity?
>
> The Japanese of the twenty-first century now face yet another challenge. By depicting our predecessors' tales of challenge and innovation, this show seeks to endow the Japanese people with the courage to confront new challenges.[12]

As the blurb breathlessly advertises, one of the documentary's main attractions is its purported populist sensibility. It is true that the people who are prominently featured are not famous public figures. The heroes of *Project X* tend to be ordinary engineers, designers, technicians, and other corporate cogs who would have been unfamiliar to their viewing audience. CEOs, tycoons, and captains of industry are beside the point here. This "everyman" positionality is in sharp contrast against, say, the long-running series "Watashi no rirekisho" in *Nikkei shinbun*, which is another brand of personalized postwar corporate history popularized in mass media, but one that is always narrated from the top-down by the iconic leader himself. As the show's opening theme song entreats, "Why do we look only up at the sky?" while "no one remembers the stars right here on earth."[13]

Likewise, there is, at least ostensibly, a focus here on individuals as opposed to large groups. Blue-chip corporations such as Matsushita, Toyota, and Canon do make their appearances, but the emphasis is not on the company as such. Rather, the protagonist is usually a small team of just a few visionary employees. Indeed, one recurring narrative setup is that this small team gets shunned by the corporate brass who are skeptical of their bold initiative. Or perhaps they had already been marginalized as the so-called *madogiwazoku*, middle-aged office outcasts who have stumbled off the corporate ladder. These underdog mavericks must then fight the corporate current to prove their dream's worth (this, we are told, is how the Victor VHS, the Casio digital camera, and Honda's CVCC engine technology came to be). It is not big capital *per se* that receives credit for postwar innovation, but the derring-do of its single members, often overlooked and underestimated.

The final complement to this bottom-up, grassroots vision of postwar success is the absence of the state. Powerful ministries such as the former Ministry of International Trade and Industry and the bureaucratic elite seldom enter the picture. In that sense, *Project X* refutes the institutional explanation of the so-called Japanese Miracle, which credits adroit state leadership for postwar economic success.[14] Instead, the spotlight—quite literally, when these folks enter the studio—is on ordinary people whose extraordinary moment is now finally being made known to the public.

Such claims and practices make *Project X* look like the small-screen's crack at *minshūshi*, or populist history. The focus on the quotidian "rank-and-file" workers reflects the producers' self-conceit as the champion of the people. Their subjects are often placed in tension against the prevailing context, in this case, the hierarchical corporate structure and naysayers who surround them. These small-time heroes struggle in a hostile world in which truly creative and transformative aspiration must bubble from below, not from the top. Their narratives de-center the state and other traditional sources of power that typically dominate elitist history. The documentary proclaims, quite loudly and self-consciously, its intent to uncover that which had earlier been ignored or forgotten, and to restore the historical agency of the common folk. These also happen to be hallmarks of academic *minshūshi* as penned by professional historians in the early postwar years.[15] The likes of Irokawa Daikichi, Yasumaru Yoshio, and Kano Masanao viewed history from the bottom-up, and excavated the historical significance of everyday thought and practices that lay beneath prevailing authority structures and institutions—"to pump up the groundwater of history," as Irokawa put it in his seminal *Meiji seishinshi* back in 1964.[16]

Aside from its apparent aspiration to *minshūshi* ideals, *Project X* tickles the historian in other ways, too. First of all, *Project X* could well be regarded as bona fide oral history. Through taped interviews and studio appearances, we see and hear the participants speak about their past experiences for themselves (even if their voices are mediated, framed, and edited, like most oral histories). There are also some remarkable behind-the-scenes nuggets that might make a historian tip her cap to the show. On several occasions, the show debunked some aspect of "official history," like the time the producer Imai Akira discovered that the person who developed the first fully domestically produced gastro fiberscope was not someone credited by Olympus' official corporate history.[17] Similarly, the production staff found out that Toshiba's internal records regarding its electric rice cooker celebrated "their own technical engineers and extraordinary sales staff" instead of acknowledging the appliance's true origin—a tiny family-run subcontractor on the verge of bankruptcy. The staff, naturally, turned its cameras onto the latter.[18] All these points also testify to the show's high production value. Each team, led by one of 13 directors supported by a crew of writers, editors, and researchers, spent about four months researching and producing each 45-minute episode—a luxury by industry standards.[19]

What we might well have here, then, is a legitimate and widely received form of public history. As a historical documentary, *Project X* seems akin to museums, commemorative monuments, and heritage sites. Like many such sources of historical knowledge, *Project X* has transmitted an accessible, visualized, and humanized narrative about the past to a vast audience, who have often been moved to identify with that rosy vision of the past. Certainly, this would be in keeping with the way many enchanted viewers and avid supporters have often praised the program.

But that understanding, however common it may be, misses the mark. A deeper historiographical inquiry, once it cuts past the sweet, thick sentimentality, reveals a message with dangerous implications. What *Project X* in fact propagates is a dubious ideology of wit and grit, one that is complicit with a strain of neoconservative ethnic nationalism that emerged, not coincidentally, just around the same time. More than anything else, we have here a making of a popular and seductive mythology. No historian can afford to discount such a powerful yet problematic means to unduly dramatize and reify the past.

For all its gestures to a populist impulse, *Project X* actually features a rather stilted cast. The heroes of this postwar narrative are mostly engineers, industrial designers, and other corporate white-collar employees with a technical bent. They may not be famous, and they may not be the traditional elite, but they are, for the most part, duly trained and educated workers with the commensurate social status and job security. These technical experts are a far cry from the riotous peasants, persecuted radicals, and desperate outcasts that inhabit academic *minshūshi*. Some relatively blue-collar types—rescue personnel, construction managers, master craftsmen, and the like—also make their appearances but, even when taken together, these subjects hardly constitute the full ensemble of social history. *Project X* is a battle hymn of the technocracy, not of "the people" at large. Democratic inclusivity here only goes so far, and anonymity is relative.

Accordingly, women clearly get shortchanged in this technology-laden remembrance of the postwar. Of the 177 total episodes, just three feature women centrally: the Equal Employment Opportunity Law of 1985, the female climbers of Mount Everest in 1975, and the women's softball team at the 2000 Sydney Olympics. Sometimes, a woman plays the muse, sparking inspiration in the male protagonist; the rice cooker, the modular "dining kitchen," and the Tokyo Tower among others are melodramatically presented as a dedication to love. Other times, she extends a helping hand to her husband along the way, as happened with the making of the Toto washlet and the Nisshin Cup Noodle. For the most part, however, women are relegated to twiddling their thumbs as lonesome housewives and patient mothers, silently waiting for their busy absentee husbands to come home. At best, women are supporting cast; mostly, though, they are altogether absent, as the producer himself has conceded.[20] This point was not lost upon some viewers. A 54-year-old housewife from Kobe, who otherwise enjoys the show, complained to *Mainichi shinbun* about precisely this. "I'm no hard-core feminist," she wrote, "Still, I can't help feeling that the program presents women as a figure in the shadows, depicting them as 'the woman behind the man' and 'the wife who always sticks by her husband.'"[21] The University of Tokyo professor Shiomi Toshiyuki raised a similar point. He, too, was a fan of the show but wondered what it might have looked like had it been produced by a woman.[22]

From this rather bare subject base, *Project X* constantly—and recklessly—extrapolates something grand about "the Japanese" at large. Consider, for example, how frequently the program's official description refers to "the Japanese people." The show presumes a nationalist frame of mind. Its creator Imai Akira unapologetically narrated *Project X* as a national parable, and a most glorious one at that. Among his many comments to that effect: "The more I do *Project X*, the more I come to love the Japanese;" "Our boldness upon facing a crisis; then, having done great work, the dignity to return to the quiet of everyday life without fanfare. The Japanese people are really amazing;" and "The Japanese are said to lack individuality, but I think the complete opposite. There is no other ethnicity that is so imbued with individuality, daring, and originality."[23] The promotional sleeve to one of his *Project X* books exclaims, "Once upon a time in this country, there were anonymous men who made possible the impossible. Dreams come true.

This is the true inner strength of the Japanese."[24] Even after discounting for marketing hyperbole, such naked chauvinism is still enough to make any *minshūshi* historian blush. In fact, the flagrant ethno-nationalist assumption and reaffirmation expose *Project X* as a "reverse *minshūshi*."[25] Practitioners of *minshūshi* were openly hostile to nationalist historiography, and they used their subaltern subjects to counteract the totalizing effects of such historical thought. They worked from history's margins to chip away at the fictive totality of ethnic nationalism.[26] *Project X*, by contrast, seeks to nationalize and totalize the postwar as a singular, formulaic experience for all and, moreover, one that was unimpeachably good. Within this exuberantly nationalist framework, a few technical innovators all too easily become shorthand for the exalted Japanese whole.

What supposedly makes these innovators so admirable is their single-minded dedication to their duty. *Project X* insists that these men toiled tirelessly not for the sake of self-advancement, their company, or profit. Rather, they burned the midnight oil and sacrificed themselves—sometimes even paying with their lives—because they simply wanted to do their jobs. Kunii Masahiko, a long-time NHK announcer, a host of the show, and a baby boomer himself, once described the *Project X* generation like this: "Things were really simple. Unless they pulled it off, they couldn't feed their families. Or maybe it would be good for society. It's all clear-cut. So they just did it. They would just get started. If they got stuck, that's when they first used their head. That's what made them strong."[27] Celebrated as an ideal here are the aesthetics of a desperate struggle, the alacrity to unthinkingly throw themselves headlong into the task before them. Such praising of selfless devotion and self-erosion is ironic given the show's claims to honoring the individual. And yet that is precisely what the protagonists of *Project X* always do; they work the grind, skip meals, neglect their families, and put themselves in harm's way with no regard for their own well-being. All this sounds suspiciously like an ode to self-sacrifice and self-denial, which is an all too familiar trope from an old cultural repertoire that was last heard in wartime. "Until we win, we shall not want," promised the steadfast subjects of imperial Japan at war.[28] "Extinguish the self in service to the state," intoned another slogan from the 1930s.[29] The postwar heroes of *Project X* may not be giving themselves to the state, but they are still lauded for willingly obliterating the self for a higher cause. No wonder some chided the show as "promotional programming for 'overworking oneself to death' (*karōshi*)."[30]

It does not even take a historian to make this connection between *Project X* and romanticized collectivism from Japan's militarized past. The nonfiction writer Yoshida Tsukasa, in reviewing Imai Akira's overtly inspirational *Project X* book in 2001, was reminded of the wartime catchphrase "Make known the true inner strength of our hundred million people!"[31] A 2003 *Mainichi shinbun* article, which reported that even popular TV dramas were increasingly set in idealized, inspired, and cooperative *Project X*-like workplaces, invoked another mobilization slogan and tabbed it "The *Project X*-for-Our-One-Hundred-Million Phenomenon."[32] Not coincidentally, the women of *Project X* reprise their wartime role as defenders of the home front, stoically supporting their husbands, now clad in suits instead of fatigues, as they fight their distant battles. Such well-worn devices, all of which help to slyly naturalize wartime practices, make a heroic return in *Project X*, and weave a subtle and seamless continuity from wartime into the postwar present. An appealing focus on technical mastery might distinguish *Project X*, but lurking below that shiny modern gloss is something much darker from Japan's imperial past. (It only seems apt that some spiteful colleagues at NHK reportedly nicknamed the show's brash producer "Emperor Imai.")[33]

Indeed, the Pacific War looms large here as a constant background presence. This is natural given that *Project X* is an anthology of the postwar, with many episodes drawn from the immediate postwar years, but the war is no ordinary background material here. *Project X* praises the war's positive, if unintended, yield, thus redeeming the wartime experience and making it more palatable. Viewers are reminded that the bullet train is "a fighter plane reincarnate," and that it became possible because talented former Imperial Army and Navy engineers decided to apply their military expertise to civilian railroad needs. The raging engine in the Prince Skyline R380, which defeated the Porsche 906 in the 1967 Japan Grand Prix, is descended from the engine that propelled the vaunted Zero fighter. Even the precise, reliable mechanism found in the "washlet" encapsulates the know-how honed by hydraulics specialists in the Imperial Navy who had worked on fuel delivery systems in Mitsubishi bombers. The war, *Project X* insists, was not without its technical merit, which the transwar and postwar generations worked hard to recast into tools of peace and prosperity. *Project X* is a tale of victory that could not be theirs in wartime. The shadow of war is magically made light, and the notion of "the useful war" is carried to a new height.[34]

If any of this sounds familiar—redeeming the war, glorifying past struggles, honoring selfless devotion, and reaffirming the Japanese ethnicity—it might be because these yearnings have been given new life by the popular neonationalist movement that gained relevance in the early Heisei era (1989–present). This development earned its greatest notoriety for promoting a so-called revisionist history textbook in the late 1990s, and its agenda has been publicized through other controversies such as the "comfort women," the Nanjing Massacre, and Yasukuni Shrine. The likes of Nishio Kanji the German literary scholar, Fujioka Nobukatsu the education scholar, and the comic artist Kobayashi Yoshinori, raised the banner of self-proclaimed "historical liberalism" in a highly public, visible way. They did so to oppose what they regarded as a "masochistic view of Japanese history" that pervaded postwar education and the intellectual environment, in which they felt their country was forced to endure excessive guilt for its imperial past. Agitating in the name of ethnic pride, national sovereignty, and spiritual revitalization, they managed to attract considerable admiration as well as scorn. Though far from a coherent movement—their personal and ideological feuds have led to much internal splintering—they did give ethnic nationalism renewed public visibility and momentum around the turn of the twenty-first century.[35]

Project X is best considered alongside that concurrent intellectual development because they share many similarities in both their means and end. Both can be understood as a search for historical redemption and Japan's equivalent of "the Greatest Generation."[36] Of course, the direct generational counterpart in Japan could never boast of having saved the world from fascism, militarism, and racism. As the postwar generation saw it, the flag of their fathers was an ignominious white. Nonetheless, it was still possible to turn instead, as *Project X* did, to the baby boom generation and claim that they, along with the transwar generation, had delivered salvation through their commitment to peaceful industry. By rebuilding from the ashes and carrying their country to affluence, they atoned for whatever ways in which their fathers might have strayed. Besides, the wartime past was not without its fruits, for it had gifted us precious seeds of technical knowledge, and those who sacrificed in war deserve our pity, for we have sacrificed alike in peace. Such is the emotional logic that connects the overachieving postwar generation with the prior, less fortunate, one, many of whom did not survive to see a brighter Japan. Neoconservative thought has worked to validate the wartime generation through a similar emotional connection. We are constantly reminded that it was their dutiful, well-intended suffering that made possible the bountiful present that we now take for granted.[37] If we are to feel any shame, they argue, it is not for our past as such, but for failing to honor that past properly. The writer Obata Kazuyuki saw *Project X* as also arguing that Japan's past deserves to be rehabilitated. "Now that the postwar and its busy bee mentality can only be spoken of in the negative," he wrote, "it is valid to reflect upon this past and cry out, 'Don't be so masochistic!'" as *Project X* so often does.[38]

Tension, or sometimes outright hostility, with the outside world is another common denominator between *Project X* and the nationalist "historical liberals." The latter are more vitriolic and unapologetic on this point— they live to provoke other countries, especially the neighbors in Asia—but *Project X* carries its own set of complexes toward foreign countries, too. One persistent narrative frame is that of "us versus the world." Japan must produce its own passenger plane instead of buying from Douglas. Canon must build a fully domestic copier and not rely on foreign patents. The Mazda rotary engine must conquer the world at Le Mans. Komatsu bulldozers must beat Caterpillar on its home turf. This is more than a healthy rivalry; a competitive mercantilist streak in *Project X* puts Japan in a tense, precarious confrontation against the world beyond. At the same time, the opposite extreme is true as well. When a "project X" goes overseas, it also does so to extend a generous humanitarian hand. Our doctors save a three year-old burn victim in Russia. Our master craftsman helps restore Angkor Wat.

Our cartographers map Guinea. Our expertise removes landmines from Cambodia. The end result is that either Japan is busy beating the world, or Japan is busy saving it; one is no less gratifying than the other. Taken together, though, they also betray an odd blend of insecurity and arrogance toward the rest of the world.

Just as *Project X* reached a wide public audience through television, neonationalists have also worked the mass media to advance their agenda. For example, Kobayashi Yoshinori, a firebrand ideologue of a motley ideology, gave the war a rousing, sentimental makeover through his highly accessible *manga*, such as the *Gōmanizumu sengen* series.[39] Of course, *manga* had been used earlier to spread far less flattering images of the war, as Nakazawa Keiji's *Hadashi no Gen* and Mizuki Shigeru's *Sōin gyokusai seyo!* did back in the 1970s, but now their hawkish counterparts were firing back on the same field in the 1990s. The "historical liberalism" movement has secured useful allies in media, most notably, the Fuji Sankei Group (which includes *Sankei shinbun* and Fusōsha, the publisher of the revisionist textbook and the weekly *SPA!* where Kobayashi's *Gōmanizumu sengen* was first serialized), but also Bungei Shunjū (which publishes the *Project X* book series), Gentōsha, and the PHP Institute. Whether their motive is ideological or commercial, powerful industry partners have allowed nationalist messages to reach their public audience and provide easy access to their worldview, much as NHK beamed its *Project X* vision of the postwar into millions of living rooms across Japan. Most academic historians can only dream of such a tall pulpit.

Perhaps the most important and compelling similarity between *Project X* and popular neonationalism is their shared emphasis on the visceral. Both seek to create pathos-laden histories that evoke strong emotional responses and profound sympathy in their audience. Their arguments openly speak to the heart as much as the mind. According to Nagahara Keiji, a critic of the so-called liberal historians, they obligate national history to instill a feeling of "pride and romanticism" in its consumers.[40] *Project X* also does just that. Those taken by the *Project X* narrative repeatedly use the word *kandō*— "emotionally moving"—to describe the show's psychological impact upon them.[41] Although this word is trite, it does testify to the show's ability to reach deep into the audience's gut and move them to tears. The high school rugby coach Yamaguchi Yoshiharu, a protagonist in one of the most highly rated episodes, fervently insisted, "The history of the world clearly demonstrates that an ethnicity without *kandō* will perish. This means that the Japanese people, who have now lost that *kandō*, are in real danger."[42] To deliver that much-needed rapture, however, history must be made bright. This is exactly the province of the revisionist "liberals." By insisting that history is not a social science but a narrative, they have propagated what Nagahara dismisses as not history but "rekishi monogatari"—a historical tale, "an illusion cast as a product of the nation-state ideology, which is formed by hiding and forgetting inconvenient historical truths as too 'dark' and 'masochistic,' while emphasizing and committing to memory only that which is convenient."[43] It is when history is reduced to an emotionally affective and predetermined narrative that it finds a welcome partner in mass media, which traffics in just such facile consumables. Given that television especially induces synchronic unity by propagating "national time" and "national narratives," the synergy between television and nationalist history grows stronger still.[44]

As the fiery rugby coach Yamaguchi indicated, both *Project X* and neonationalism sought to fill a supposed sense of emptiness in Japanese society as it limped into a second decade of economic malaise. Fans of *Project X* credit it as having "energized"—the word *genki* comes up no less than *kandō*—a people who had supposedly lost their will and self-esteem.[45] The producer Imai Akira prescribed *Project X* as an antidote to what he perceived as a decline in the nation's confidence that has only grown steeper since the bubble burst.[46] And many supporters happily swallowed this idea, accepting the premise that a Japan beset with postindustrial angst needed something as maudlin and uplifting as *Project X*. The literary critic Kawamura Jirō was impressed by the show's "burning sense of purpose" and how it shined a ray of hope upon "a now-demoralized Japan."[47] The essayist Nakano Midori, despite her objections against the show's dramatic tendencies, echoed a similar sentiment. *Project X*, she explained, seems "even more beautiful, nostalgic, and holy" to its viewers because "today's Japanese are disillusioned by themselves. They have fallen into the doldrums of self-hatred."[48] Such a view held that an anemic, flaccid postindustrial Japan needs a shot of blood, sweat, and tears from its hard-working industrial past, when, it is said, labor of love was the norm. All this sounds much like the kind of public service the neonationalists have called upon themselves to perform. They, too, have sought to rally a supposedly self-loathing people—the alleged victims of "historical masochism"—around the illusion of a glorious collective past that may or may not have existed.

This is not to say that *Project X* was part of a systemic revisionist conspiracy as such. Nothing suggests that Imai Akira was in cahoots with the likes of Kobayashi Yoshinori. The similarities between *Project X* and "historical liberalism" may be unintentional, but they are not entirely coincidental, either. They occupied—and expanded—the same "rekishi mondai" ("The History Problem") milieu around the turn of the twenty-first century, in which competing historical sensibilities clashed quite publicly in mass media.[49] Revisionist efforts of the mid- to late-1990s may well have primed many viewers to receive the *Project X* mythology by the time it hit the air in 2000. To sing the praises of the postwar may well have seemed like a logical next step in the historical rehabilitation of Shōwa Japan. In short, *Project X* corroborated, but not necessarily collaborated with, concurrent neonationalism.

Not much about this particular wrangling over the past is fundamentally new. It is simply the latest chapter in a long postwar struggle over how to historicize the Shōwa era, in which, as Carol Gluck described it, various "custodians of the past" shaped "public memory."[50] Throughout the postwar, historical accounting of the past has been a way to hash out contemporary ideological tensions, a battlefield in a proxy war between conflicting assessments of modernity. No matter the time or the place, the present has always seemed worrisome and the future uncertain. And because they always will, some will inevitably look to the past for guidance and comfort; that is a universal condition. If anything is new here, perhaps it is the medium. The technology of television and other forms of popular media has made dramatic, visualized representations of the past easily accessible for a broader audience than ever before, threatening to overwhelm competing interpretations that do not enjoy the same access. The conservative ethnographer Ōtsuki Takahiro likened Kobayashi Yoshinori's *manga* to "bringing nukes to a bamboo-spear fight in the village of intellectuals" for being highly accessible.[51] If that is true, then a primetime NHK show like *Project X* surely qualifies as a weapon of mass destruction, too. The writer Sekikawa Natsuo went so far as to blame an outright absence of alternative interpretations for allowing *Project X* to thrive. He surmised that *Project X* deftly filled a lacuna carved by historical ignorance. "We are captured by these success stories because we do not know the high speed growth era in any empirical way," he wrote in a book review of Imai Akira's collection of glib inspirational quotes by the heroes of *Project X* ("Real salesmen can sell ice to the Eskimos!"). As Sekikawa proposed, "Perhaps the reason why all these old words seem fresh to us is simply because we have neglected to historicize [the postwar]."[52] He suggests that the likes of *Project X* have stepped in where academic historians have fallen short, gaining the attention of a vast, torpid audience that others have failed to rouse.

The result is what is best described as a popular mythology—part history, part fiction, and all heart—that fulfills multiple common desires, some that are specific to Heisei Japan and some more general. One is a nostalgic yearning for the solace that Japan once basked in a golden sun not so long ago. Even if that golden age was, in truth, more gilded than *Project X* would have it, this warm soothing rendering of the past allows those who fret about the present to receive *Project X* as proof of what we once were, and what we could once again become. In this sense, to call *Project X* a requiem for Japan's postwar past, as some have done, seems inadequate.[53] It also looks forward as a hopeful augury for old-school industrial capitalism in a postindustrial world, projecting a future in which "Made in Japan" will continue to not only command a price premium, but articulate some deeper meaning about the country that produced it. Every episode of *Project X* ends on this note as it looks wistfully both backward and forward in time. Nakajima Miyuki's "Headlight/Taillight," which brings each episode to a close, metaphorically illuminates the path that lies both before and behind, and promises that "the journey is not yet over."[54]

Reinforcing this faith in an enduring identity of wit and grit is the mythical spirit of craftsmanship, or *monozukuri*. *Project X* is a paean to the salad days when Japan could make things, and do so seemingly better than anyone else in the world. The idealized *shokunin*—the relentless, uncompromising master craftsman—is the heart and soul of numerous episodes. Some protagonists are literally such expert craftsmen, but many more who are not still embody the same spirit of obsessive devotion to technical perfection. A necessary partner to this *monozukuri* ideal is the "neighborhood workshop" (*machi kōba*) romanticism. When viewers learn that the electric rice cooker was birthed in one such nameless mom-and-pop outfit, and that the quartz wristwatch was invented in the valleys of Shinano, it feeds the hope that innovative manufacturing is a deeply embedded, everyday part of modern Japanese life, and that breakthrough ingenuity might spring suddenly from any quarter of society; that the word *monozukuri* is often rendered in *kana* (the Japanese syllabary, as opposed to *kanji*, or Chinese characters) suggests that it is native to Japan. This heady notion could provide comfort at a time when Japan was said to be losing its vaunted manufacturing edge to other parts of Asia. Everything seems to be made in China nowadays, and Samsung just might eclipse Sony, but so long as we stoke our *monozukuri* fire, *Project X* assures us, Japan will always have a fighting chance. Some even regarded the *Project X* spirit of *monozukuri* as a beacon that would guide Japan away from the siren calls of monetary abstractions and formless speculation—so very postmodern in their empty seductiveness—that had led to the 80s' bubble, and back toward the safe harbor of hard stuff.[55]

Thinking beyond its Japan-specific setting, the *Project X* mythology just might be the perfect fable of modernity at large. The two cornerstones of *Project X* are innovation and perseverance, or wit and grit, as it were. The former—that is, mastery of ever-accelerating science and technology—is the engine that drives material progress. However, that technical knowledge is nothing without good old elbow grease, as *Project X* likes to remind us. Innovators are not necessarily geniuses, we are told; rather, they are optimistic, determined people who, by the dint of sheer desire and diligence, managed to impose their will upon their times. Thus, *Project X* reaffirms faith in the transformative power of human agency and industry. The teleological idea that scientific mastery, when combined with individual subjectivity, leads to a progressively better tomorrow is a foundational conceit within modernity.[56] Of course, how this perfectly modern ideology of wit and grit plays out in so-called postmodern times remains to be seen.

Grayed men in tired suits who remind us of our fathers and grandfathers; a moving soundtrack shamelessly tugging at the heartstrings; the firm, declarative narration that ends in the conclusive "-*datta*." They leave little room for alternatives, all but daring viewers to not fall for the folksy heroics on display. Such is the dramatic determinism in television that the scriptwriter Yamada Taichi once critiqued as "story fascism," and one that *Project X* proudly put before an eager audience in the early twenty-first century.[57] The intentional scriptedness of *Project X* makes it one form of "historical liberalism" that liberates the viewers from having to think too much. The dazzling, extravagant production will ably carry viewers to a happy destiny; they will prevail, and you will cry. Exit stage right, roll credits.

But people do think, and they do not always cry. And there lies the best hope for the definitive end to *sengo* (the postwar) that would lead Japan into what Gluck called its "post-postwar future," which can only begin with a morally autonomous and intellectually responsible reckoning of its past.[58] Far from letting historical time flow on past the bubble and pushing Japan off toward a "post postwar," *Project X* helped instead to "stall time," as Miyazaki Tetsuya the public commentator has observed. Unlike another NHK hit show *Oshin*, which helped Japan in the 1980s bid farewell to prewar Meiji-style developmentalism, Miyazaki argues that *Project X* in the early 2000s failed to serve as a necessary rite of parting—"a funeral"—from Shōwa.[59] If anything, it has strengthened a cloying romantic attachment to a bygone era. Fortunately, however, not everyone is seduced by the lovely but empty packaging of history as an anthology of feel-good episodes that are conveniently divorced from context and critique. Plenty of people have seen *Project X* for what it is. As the writer Yoshida Tsukasa put it, "This ballad to the baby boomers' youth is also a tale of conquest that celebrates the war of economic aggression that Japan waged upon the world. In that sense, it is like erecting a war memorial to those corporate warriors."[60] Taking a lighter note, more than a few viewers were able to laugh at the *Project X* mythology by parodying it and otherwise receiving it as unintentional comedy. As the University of Tokyo media scholar Kitada Akihiro argued, many viewers possessed enough media literacy and cynicism to make a laughing stock out of *Project X* and all its predictable piety. "For viewers who appreciate irony," Kitada points out, programs like *Project X*, which "narrate a false front (*tatemae*) with a straight face, while feigning neutrality and fairness and concealing their edited artifice, strike them as being phony."[61] Despite the undeniable allure of the *Project X* mythology, it has hardly obviated the plurality of remembrances and judgments on the postwar. *Project X*, like the neonationalists, may have staked one claim upon Japan's recent past, but that past is still very much up for grabs.

It only seems fitting that the show, for all its popularity and publicity, died an ignominious death partly because of its overcommitment to manipulating the audience's emotions. In May 2005, the program came under fire for gross exaggerations and factual errors in an episode that aired that month. In explaining this editorial finagling, one NHK official later admitted, "Viewers all across the country were watching us. We had to provide *kandō*."[62] NHK publicly apologized at the end of May; five months later, it announced that *Project X* would end its six-year run in December.[63] Having tied itself to an exceedingly emotional rendering of history, perhaps it was comeuppance that *Project X* choked on that very thing.

Obituaries were mixed. Shiga Nobuo, the chairman of the Japan Council for Better Radio and Television, thought *Project X* had run its course. "Its duty is done," he concluded.[64] "Even salarymen do not need a cheerleader forever," wrote one columnist.[65] Others waved a fond farewell to the show that had done the same for the baby boom generation, like the 65-year-old part-time worker from Gifu Prefecture who thanked the show for giving her "hope and courage."[66] *Project X* may no longer be on air, but it spawned an enduring genre of reality television that might be called "work entertainment."[67] These progenies are less historically inclined, but they have inherited the same faith that the Japanese are as ingenious, hard-working, and enterprising as ever. The Nikkei Index will always be fickle, Japan's international competitiveness ranking might continue its freefall, and prime ministers still come and go, but the spirit of innovation and industry supposedly does not.

Still, as an ode to twentieth-century industrial manufacturing, *Project X* might already feel as quaint and analog as the original Walkman. Even the venerable ideal of *monozukuri* has sometimes been discounted as passé, a dangerous illusion in a postindustrial world where "First World" manufacturing gets crushed by cheap global labor and commoditization, and value-added is increasingly found instead in abstract information services.[68] The economics commentator Ikeda Nobuo flipped a dismissive hand at *Project X* re-runs in 2008 by announcing, "Those happy days, when unquestioning, selfless, and earnest pursuit of assigned goals was rewarded, are unfortunately over."[69] That may or may not be true; not yet over, though, is the struggle to memorialize those seemingly "happy days" by those who are told, time and again, that they live in less happy days and could really use a happier tomorrow.

15

Bookending Postwar Japan: Seeing a Whole Greater than the Sum of its Parts

Stephen Vlastos

If my contribution to this volume is to reflect on what the chapters tell us about Japan today, I begin by drawing attention to the rhetorically smart but defensive posture struck by the editors, Christopher Gerteis and Timothy S. George, in the first sentence of the introduction, "Of course Japan matters." Lest the reader be tempted to take up the rhetorical gambit and challenge the premise, the editors follow with examples of how Japan does matter today, citing familiar markers of national importance such as Japan having the world's third highest GDP just behind China's, and its historic role as the first non-Western country to industrialize and command world power status. But why the need to reassure readers that Japan warrants their attention? Why begin a book titled *Japan Since 1945* by launching a preemptive strike on the specter of "Japan passing?"[1]

The contemporary context and proximate causes, no doubt, are the strikingly different trajectories of China and Japan today. China was the first large economy to resume high growth after the 2008 global recession and, at this writing, is still going gangbusters; Japan's modest post-2008 recovery had already weakened before the cascading catastrophes triggered by the 11 March 2011 tsunami knocked the economy and national psyche back into negative growth. The metaphor of "Japan passing" darkly projects a future of increasing marginality. Japan's inability to sustain strong economic growth since 1990, four decades of declining fertility which has yet to bottom out, historically high rates (for the postwar period) of unemployment and underemployment among school leavers and displaced middle-aged white and blue collar workers, and a foreign policy that can't seem to decide between placating and provoking China, Russia, North and sometimes South Korea: these are all real and troubling symptoms of a country whose spectacular postwar ascent is off the fast track.

Being on the slow track, however, should not be mistaken for permanent decline. Being historians and historically informed social scientists, the contributors to this volume know well just how often "expert" opinion has gotten Japan all wrong. As Walter LaFeber notes in *The Clash: U.S. Japan Relations throughout History*, in 1950, five years into the Allied Occupation, John Foster Dulles "was pessimistic about Japan's economic prospects" unless the China market opened up, because "the low quality" of Japanese goods would preclude them from selling to the West.[2] Only two decades later, Herman Kahn, guru of the Hudson Institute, published *The Emerging Japanese Superstate* (1970), which confidently predicted that Japan would surpass the United States in GDP by the end of the century, making the twenty-first century the "Japanese century."[3] At the time, both Dulles' and Kahn's pronouncements were generally accepted as valid.

The particular challenge facing Japan scholars endeavoring to write about a country that invites extremes of over- and underestimation is to strike the mean: to see through the trends of the day to ways in which Japan is really quite ordinary. Here, history has a useful role to play, and the chapters in this volume, according to Gerteis and George, do just this in "examin[ing] the historical context to the social, cultural, and political underpinnings of Japan's postwar and postindustrial trajectories."[4]

Notably successful in finding the mean is Bruce Aronson's chapter, "Reassessing Japan's 'Big Bang': Twenty Years of Financial Regulatory Reform." His level-headed assessment of the real and partial successes of the Liberal Democratic Party's (LDP) leap into financial regulatory reform revises—and one would hope disposes of—the facile declaration of failure intoned by academic and finance experts, many of whom first gained prominence on the talking head circuit by bemoaning Japan Inc's inexorable assault on world markets. Now, Aronson observes, expert opinion is hostage to "myths of [Japan's] bureaucratic incompetence and rigid cultural traits."[5]

The uniformly negative assessment of Japan's "Big Bang" is one example of the new consensus on Japan to find failure everywhere. Japan's recent condition of low economic growth, aging population, ineffectual political leadership, and vulnerability to natural disasters is hardly unique among rich and economically developed countries around the world—yet the feverish pitch of neoliberal scolding and their dire forecasts (echoed by Japan's neoliberal true believers) are out of all proportion to actual changes in Japanese society or Japan's place in the world economy today. Yes, Japan has not done well in the twenty-first century; but if China is the new norm of success, not only Japan but most OECD countries are on the fast track to scoliotic irrelevance.[6]

The pessimistic outlook on Japan, which appears immune to facts and figures, is blowback from euphoria engendered by Japan's postwar successes.

If Japan had not sustained such a spectacularly long run of high economic growth, at one point nearly overtaking the United States in nominal per capita GDP, the Japan of today would appear much more ordinary. This is one of the editors' important observations: the effect of Japan's rise from ashes to riches in less than a half century, Gerteis and George tell us in the introduction, was to naturalize high economic growth, and "the Japanese themselves came to see Japan's 'economic miracle' as part-and-parcel with what it meant to be Japanese."[7] Japanese were egged on in this regard by Anglo-American modernization theorists, for whom Japan offered proof positive of capitalism's unlimited capacity to create consumers without borders. These experts, moreover, bought into some version of *Nihonjin ron*, the theory of Japanese forming a unique ethnic nation, and propagated the notion that Japanese values of harmony and communitarianism would produce endless growth while avoiding the ills of America's crime-ridden, low achieving, and contentious society. This was the thesis of *Japan as Number One*, authored by Ezra Vogel, Harvard's renowned East Asian sociologist.[8] The book quickly became, and has remained, the best-settling book on Japan. Vogel, meanwhile, now writes books about China.

Without the prior reification of Japan's long run of high economic growth as in the DNA of postwar Japanese, both Japan's "economic miracle" and the ensuing "lost decade" can be seen as phases of global post-World War II capitalism. Japan benefited greatly from the political economy of Cold War capitalism. Japan emerged from the Allied Occupation with high levels of human capital, plentiful rural reserves of industrial labor, favorable global terms of trade between value-added manufacture and primary commodity prices, more or less unrestricted access to the US market during its most dynamic stage of expansion, membership in the Bretton Woods system of international economic institutions without reciprocal obligations, and so forth. Viewed this way, the miracle was less miraculous. At the same time, Japan's relatively low economic growth since 1990 is less daunting when viewed alongside that of other rich, developed countries. Japan was the first G7 country to be knocked back on its heels by the excesses of finance capitalism—but as readers hardly need to be reminded, not the last. Japan has been losing jobs in manufacturing, but manufacturing has held up comparatively well in a global economy where intellectual property flows rapidly from advanced to emerging economies, whether by direct investment, outright sale, or theft, and corporations are free to invest wherever wages, working conditions, and environmental safeguards are lowest. Can it be that Japan, for so long a follower of Anglo-American capitalism, is now walking point?

Hiraku Shimoda's engaging riff on the phenomenally popular NHK television program *Project X*, "Memorializing the Spirit of Wit and Grit in Postindustrial Japan," takes the producers to task for promoting "a cloying romantic attachment to a bygone era." The program, which aired weekly for five years on Japan's public television stations beginning in March 2000, celebrated the boot-strap entrepreneurialism of "idealized *shokunin*—the relentless, uncompromising master craftsman" who produced such iconic products of the postwar economic miracle as the electric rice cooker and quartz watch.[9] Shimoda sardonically and critically remarks on the program's ideological resonances with contemporary Japanese strains of ethnic nationalism and neoliberal proscriptions for economic revitalization. I wish, however, he had extended his analysis and considered *Project X* as a Japanese-inflected lament for the particular social formation of post-World War II capitalism, which in First World countries produced upward mobility, middle-class incomes even in families with a single wage earner, and considerable job security and pensions for male, white collar, and unionized blue collar workers. The nostalgia for postwar capitalism Shimoda skewers in *Project X* is not limited to Japan; isn't it part of the appeal of contemporary US hit television dramas like AMC's *Mad Men*? Of course, the cultural articulations of capitalist values diverge sharply across the Pacific. Given Shimoda's own considerable wit, I would have loved a comparison of the ideological work of *Project X* and *The Apprentice* as, respectively, Japanese and American-inflected mystifications of entrepreneurialism.

Gerteis and George assert toward the end of the introduction that Japan "might yet serve as an indicator for the economic and social trajectories" of similarly rich, postindustrial societies.[10] Though there is some waffling on whether the reader is to understand Japan's role as the canary in the coal mine or a beacon pointing to a better future, let's accept the premise and ask what guidance the volume's chapters offer.

Three chapters provide quite fascinating and informative case studies of industries and communities in decline well before the bubble burst: Satsuki Takahashi examines three waves of modernization of the fishing industry in Tōhoku villages; Martin Dusinberre reveals the tensions that arose in a small port city on the Inland Sea between protecting its natural resources and cultural heritage and inviting in an industry, nuclear power, to anchor employment and retain young adults; and Timothy George compares and contrasts four communities' efforts to stabilize economically and demographically by mobilizing elements of the past. As case studies with few common threads, they do not provide a valid basis for generalization. How well they fit together as a unit is also questionable, in that in Takahashi's study, central government fishery policies drive the process of adaptation, while in Dusinberre's and George's communities, citizens, not always united in purpose, set the agenda. Nevertheless, each case study provides evidence of modest levels of success; the overall picture the authors paint is far from bleak. Most of all one sees the resiliency of Japan's small towns and a refusal to accept their own obsolescence. This augers well.

A leitmotif that links a number of the chapters is contemporary uncertainty over the place of Japan's half century of empire and war. As Christopher Gerteis' interesting case study of Nippon Yūsen Kaisha's (NYK) floating museums and glossy publications shows, the authorized NYK narrative of the corporation's rise to world class standing in maritime transport "obscure[s] its central role in Japan's imperialist and militarist expansions of the nintieth and twentieth century."[11] Martin Dusinberre identifies the same phenomenon in Kaminoseki's determined effort to celebrate its distant past as port of call in the Edo period, when it hosted Korean embassies and Dutch officials, while totally occluding the port's more consequential role after the 1894–5 Sino-Japanese War as a gateway to colonized Korea. Some of the chapters, on the other hand, reveal how even the Asia-Pacific War is positively figured into larger narratives of postwar progress. The producers of *Project X*, for example, were not embarrassed to point out the role of wartime technology in peaceful postwar industrial achievements, as in the case of Japan's famed bullet trains of the mid-1960s.

The intellectual contribution of this volume to the historiography of modern Japan, at least in my judgment, is not what the title appears to promise, that is, chapters that individually and collectively tell the story of Japan's passage from surrender and occupation through 35 years of high economic growth to the present "lost decade." In fact, with few exceptions, the chapters cluster either at the beginning or at the end of "postwar" without traversing the territory of high economic growth.[12] In other words, the more familiar "postwar," the subject of Andrew Gordon, ed., *Postwar Japan as History*—the Japan of bullet trains, surging exports, soaring land and stock prices, ever higher favorable trade balances, rock-bottom unemployment, nearly iron-clad job security for the majority of male household heads, white or blue collar—functions like the "Ghost of Christmas Present" in this collection, luminous with lessons learned from the "dark valley" of wartime Japan and cautionary as to what will follow. The volume's intervention, rather, is to juxtapose the early postwar (a devastated, defeated country occupied by a foreign power) with post-bubble Japan, still prosperous but angst-filled and without clear direction. This is visually conveyed in the brilliantly designed dust jacket, which splices together into single-frame photographs of a downtown Tokyo street soon after 1945 and 60 years later. We have considered the varied messages of the latter group of chapters. What about the former?

The editors group together four chapters to form the section "Legacies of War and Occupation." David Tobaru Obermiller shows how in the early years of the US Occupation of Okinawa, US military officials inadvertently planted the seeds of native Okinawan ethnic nationalism, which progressives subsequently mobilized to obstruct or limit US use of military bases. Katarzyna Cwiertka revises the historiography of the Occupation period in demonstrating that the black market both preceded and outlasted both the extreme period of food scarcity in the mid- to-late 1940s, and the Occupation itself. Sally A. Hastings adds to the historiography of Japanese women's history by showing how Japanese nurses achieved political representation and furthered their collective interests under the 1947 Constitution. Tetsuya Fujiwara reveals the struggles and eventual success of Japanese disabled veterans, who, like nurses, skillfully utilized freedoms guaranteed in the new constitution to push through their demands for a more secure livelihood and respect. Laura Hein narrates the very political, and progressive, origins of the Kanagawa Prefectural Modern Art Museum, the first museum in Japan dedicated to modern art, in the founders' commitment to the incubation of a counterfascist popular culture.

Each of the Occupation-period chapters is quite fascinating in detail, and each connects the particular case studied to larger forces at work in Japan after 1945. Whether entirely by design or not, the editors' pairing of Occupation period and post-bubble chapters makes an important point. The reader encounters the devastation and privation of the early Occupation years but equally a period of intellectual ferment and organizational dynamism across numerous sectors of postwar Japanese society. Taken together, these chapters do not form a mosaic; they are, rather, missing pieces, or to extend the metaphor, brightly painted tiles that fill in spaces in John W. Dower's monumental work, *Embracing Defeat: Japan in the Wake of World War II*.

The juxtaposition of the immediate postwar and post-bubble should remind readers that history is a process of relentless change beyond the capacity of any observer to predict. No one standing amidst the ruins of fire-bombed Tokyo in 1945 could imagine the Tokyo of the 1964 Olympics. In the late 1960s, when the GDP was rising at double-digit rates in successive years, who even considered the possibility that 20 years later the Nikkei would lose a third of its value and some of Japan's biggest banks would go bust, let alone the tent city in Yoyogi Park sheltering 500 unemployed and homeless Japanese over New Year's 2011? Above all, this volume is a telling reminder that nobody has the foggiest idea of what Japan will become another two decades hence.

Notes

Chapter 1

1   Gordon, Andrew, ed. *Postwar Japan As History* (Berkeley: University of California Press, 1993).

Part I

1   The subject of the total numbers of people killed during the Asia-Pacific War (1931–45) is still very controversial. While estimates range between 15 and 20 million, the total number of war dead, civilian and military, will never be known. For a sobering discussion of this issue, see John Dower's epilogue "From War to Peace" in John W. Dower, *War Without Mercy: Race and Power in the Pacific War* (New York: Pantheon Books, 1986), 293–317.

Chapter 2

1   See, especially, Garon and Mochizuki, Gordon, and Hein in *Postwar Japan as History*. ed. Andrew Gordon (Berkeley: University of California Press, 1993).

2   For example, Hiromi Mizuno, *Science for the Empire: Scientific Nationalism in Modern Japan* (Stanford: Stanford University Press, 2009). Sven Saaler and J. Victor Koschmann, eds, *Pan-Asianism in Modern Japanese History: Colonialism, Regionalism and Borders* (London: Routledge, 2007). E. Taylor Atkins, *Primitive Selves: Koreana in the Japanese Colonial Gaze, 1910–1945* (Berkeley, University of California Press, 2010). Kenneth J. Ruoff, *Imperial Japan at its Zenith: The Wartime Celebration of the Empire's 2,600th Anniversary* (Ithaca, Cornell University Press, 2010).

3   Dower, Cumings, Gluck in *Postwar Japan as History*.

4   Laura Hein, "Revisiting the Occupation of Japan," *Cold War History*, 11:4 (August 2011):1–21, 2011.

5   Tessa Morris-Suzuki, *Exodus to North Korea: Shadows from Japan's Cold War* (Plymouth UK: Rowman & Littlefield, 2007). Chalmers Johnson, *The Sorrows of Empire: Militarism, Secrecy, and the End of the Republic* (New York: Metropolitan Books, 2004).

6   Sarah C. Maza, *The Myth of the French Bourgeoisie: An Essay on the Social Imaginary, 1750–1850* (Cambridge MA: Harvard University Press, 2003). Quotes 10 and 14.

7 Franziska Seraphim, *War Memory and Social Politics in Japan* (Cambridge: Harvard University Asia Center, 2006).

8 Slaymaker and Winther-Tamaki, panel on Reputation of Paris in Japan, at Association of Asian Studies meeting, Philadelphia 2010. See also Tansman, Alan, ed. *The Culture of Japanese Fascism* (Durham, NC, and London: Duke University Press, 2009).

9 J. Victor Koschmann and Carol Gluck in *Postwar Japan as History*, 64–95, 395–423, quotes 395–396 and 73–74.

10 This was the original official translation of the museum's name, which is now known in English as the Museum of Modern Art, Kamakura and Hayama.

11 Osaragi Jirō, "Jo", Uchiyama Iwatarō, *Hankotsu 77 nen* (Yokohama: Kanagawa Shinbunsha, 1968), 3–5, quotes 4. Uchiyama was appointed governor on 25 January 1946 and won his first election on 5 April 1947.

12 Sasaki Seiichi, "Kamakura Kinbi Bijutsukan no Shuppatsu." In *Kanagawa Kenritsu Kindai Bijutsukan 30-nen no Ayumi: Shiryō-Tenrankai Sōmokuroku, 1951–1981* (Kamakura: Kanagawa Kenritsu Kindai Bijutsukan, 1982), 12–16, esp. 12.

13 Uchiyama Iwatarō, *Hankotsu 77 nen* (Yokohama: Kanagawa Shinbunsha, 1968), 222.

14 Takemae Eiji, *Inside GHQ: The Allied Occupation of Japan and its Legacy*, trans. and adapted by Robert Ricketts and Sebastian Swann (London: Continuum, 2002).

15 Uchiyama, 165–67. Osaragi in Uchiyama, 4–5. Uchiyama pointed out that in the late 1940s, the Occupation employed about 100,000 local people, at a time when almost no one else in the prefecture was hiring. 158.

16 Satō Kaori, "GHQ no Bijutsu Gyōsei: CIE Bijutsu Kinen Bukka ni yoru 'Bijutsu no Minshūka' to Yashiro Yukio," *Kindai Gasetsu*, 12 (2003): 80–95. Yashiro focused on improving Japan's international image by sending art abroad, while Uchiyama was more concerned about giving Japanese opportunities to view art.

17 "Report on Field Trip to Fukuoka, Saga, etc." in folder "Reports of Staff Visits" by J. M. Plumer 6 May 1949, 6, RG 331 UD 1647 5074 and "Report on Arts and Monuments: Recommendations of Outgoing Adviser in Fine Art." In folder "Correspondence and Memoranda" by J. M. Plumer, 20 June 1949 NARA RG 331 UD 1698–5848, both SCAP, CI&E, Religion and Cultural Resources Division. Arts & Monuments Branch in US National Archives.

18 Plumer, "Reports on Staff Visits." 6.

19 Sasaki Seiichi, "Kamakura Kinbi Bijutsukan no Shuppatsu," 12–16, esp. 13; Interview with Hijikata Yukue, Kamakura, 27 February 2009.

20 Interview with Mizusawa Tsutomu. Kamakura, 16 April 2005.

21 Sarah Maza, *The Myth of the French Bourgeoisie*, 10.

22 "Modern Art Patronage and Democratic Citizenship in Japan," *The Journal of Asian Studies*, 69.3 (August 2010): 821–41.

23 Hobsbawm, Eric, and Terence Ranger, eds, *The Invention of Tradition* (Cambridge: Cambridge University Press, 1983). In an aside that showed

that neither wartime behavior nor the constructedness of history escaped his thoughts, Wakimura commented to interviewers that Hasegawa Jin, a personal friend, had been very close to Ishiwara Kanji but that Hasegawa failed to include that fact in his otherwise encyclopedic *History of Japanese Oil Painting* (Nihon Yōga Shi), Yonekura Mamoru, "Tokujiku Nohahikae—Wakimura Yoshitarō," part 19 "Hasegawa Jin: Garō, Gaka, Shūshūka," *E*, 16–19, esp. 18–19.

24 Charles Merewether. "Disjunctive Modernity: The Practice of Artistic Experimentation in Postwar Japan," 1–33, in *Art, Anti-art, Non-art: Experimentations in the Public Sphere in Postwar Japan, 1950–70*, ed. Charles Merewether with Rika Iezumi Hiro (Los Angeles: Getty Research Institute, 2007).

25 Sakai Tadayasu, "Kishida Ryūsei dōjozu kifun no keii ni suite." In his *Sono toshi mo mata –Kamakura Kindai Bijutsukan o Meguru Hitobito* (Kamakura: Kamakura Shunjūsha, 2004), 39–41.

26 Jiro Osaragi, *The Journey*, Ivan Morris trans. (Rutland VT & Tokyo, 1960), 7–8. Osaragi Jirō. 1951. "Saisho no chihō Bijutsukan", *Mainichi News*, 21 November. Reprinted in Kanagawa Kenritsu Kindai Bijutsukan, ed. *Chisa na Hako: Kamakura Kindai Bijutsukan no 50 nen, 1951–2000* (Tokyo: Kyūryūdō, 2001), 75. Osaragi lent art objects for a 1968 ceramics show called "Watakushi no Atsumeta Yakimono." See Asahi Akira "Sōchō no denwa no aruji—futari no sensei," *Tosetsu*, 581 (December 1956): 37–40.

27 Pierre Bourdieu, *Distinction: A Social Critique of the Judgment of Taste*. Trans. Richard Nice (Cambridge, MA: Harvard University Press, 1984). Wakimura Yoshitarō, *Shumi no Kachi* (Tokyo: Iwanami, 1950, Revised ed. 1967), 127.

28 Watanabe Kazutami, "Kaisetsu." *Osaragi Jirō Nonfikushon Zenshū* Vol. 1 (Tokyo: Asahi Shinbunsha, 1971), 323–43.

29 Osaragi also wrote the script for the 1928 film version of the earliest episodes. See *Talking Silents 5: Kurama Tengu and The Frightful Era of Kurama Tengu* (Kurama Tengu Kyōfu jidai), Directed by Yamaguchi Teppei, 1928. Distributed by Digital Meme, 2008. Tsuyoshi Ishiharu, *Mark Twain in Japan: The Cultural Representation of a Cultural Icon* (Columbia: University of Missouri Press, 2005) shows that Osaragi muted the egalitarian message of *The Prince and the Pauper* (51–4) during World War II.

30 Kanagawa ken Bijutsu—Bakumatsu Meiji Shoki hen, *Kanagawa ken Bijutsu—Bakumatsu Meiji Shoki* (Kamakura: Kanagawa Kenritsu Kindai Bijutsukan, 1970), 1.

31 Sakai Tadayasu, "Kaisō no Bijutsukan Funtōki," *Chisa na Hako: Kamakura Kindai Bijutsukan no 50 nen, 1951–2000*, The Museum of Modern Art, Kamakura (Tokyo: Kyūryūdō, 2001), 29.

32 Ellen P. Conant, ed., "Introduction: A Historiographical Overview," *Challenging Past and Present: The Metamorphosis of Nineteenth-century Japanese Art* (Honolulu: University of Hawai'i Press, 2006), 1–30, quote 3. See also Sawatari Kiyoko, "Innovational Adaptations: Contacts between Japanese and Western Artists in Yokohama, 1859–99," 83–113.

33 Hijikata Teiichi, "Maegaki," *Kanagawa ken Bijutsu Fūdōki*, in Kanagawa ken Bijutsu—Bakumatsu Meiji Shoki, ed. (Kamakura: Kanagawa Kenritsu Kindai Bijutsukan, 1970), ix–xiv, esp. ix.

34 Joel Mokyr, *The Gifts of Athena: Historical Origins of the Knowledge Economy* (Princeton: Princeton University Press, 2002).

35 Nagasu Kazuji, "Chōji," in Hijikata Teiichi Tsuitō Kankōkai, *Hijikata Teiichi Tsuisō*, 3–4, quote 4.

36 Eiko Ikegami, *Bonds of Civility: Aesthetic Networks and Political Origins of Japanese Culture* (Cambridge: Cambridge University Press, 2005).

37 Wakimura, *Nijūisseiki o Nozonde*, 305–11, 323–24.

38 Detroit in Wakimura, *Shumi no Kachi*. 1967, 133; Sumitomo in Wakimura Yoshitarō, Suzuki Haruo, and Yui Tsunehiko, "Bunka no Shiensha to shite no Kigyōka," *Keiei to Rekishi*, 12 (1991): 2–19. Yamamoto in Wakimura Yoshitarō, "Saeki Yūzō no Gagyō to Shūshūka." Originally published in *Saeki Yūzō Zengashū* by Saeki Yūzō Zengashū Kankō Iinkai Kōdansha, 1968, republished in Wakimura Yoshitarō, *Wakimura Yoshitarō Chosakushū*, (Tokyo: Nihon Keieishi Kenkyūjo, 1976) 4, 343–55, esp. 347–8.

39 Tetsuo Najita, *Ordinary Economies in Japan: A Historical Perspective, 1750–1950* (Berkeley: University of California Press, 2009). Najita's work develops the theme of diverse Tokugawa modernities.

40 Irokawa Daikichi, *The Culture of the Meiji Period* (Princeton: Princeton University Press, 1988).

41 Hijikata Teiichi "Kindai Bijutsukan Sōseiki," *Geijutsu Shinchō* July 1951, reprinted in *Chisa na Hako*, 42–7. esp. 43.

42 Plumer, "Report on Arts and Monuments: Recommendations of Outgoing Adviser in Fine Art," 20 June 1949, NARA RG 331 UD 1697 5780. See also "Three Exhibitions in Occupied Japan" by Sherman E. Lee, 4 Dec 1947, NARA RG 331 UD 1699 5862, SCAP, CI&E, Religion and Cultural Resources Division. Arts & Monuments Branch.

43 Hijikata, "Kindai Bijutsukan Sōseiki," 43.

44 Hijikata Teiichi, "Atogaki" in *Hijikata Teiichi Chosakushū* Vol. 7 *Kindai Nihon no Gakaron 2* (Tokyo: Heibonsha, 1976), 429–36, quotes 435. Kendall H. Brown, "Out of the Dark Valley: Japanese Woodblock Prints and War, 1937–1945," *Impressions: Official Publication of the Ukiyo-e Society of America*, 23 (2001): 65–85.

45 Hijikata 17 January 1951 *Mainichi* article "Gendai Bijutsukan e no Chūmon" quoted in Sasaki, "Kamakura Kinbi Bijutsukan no Shuppatsu," 14.

46 Hijikata Teiichi 1951. "Kindai Bijutsukan Sōseiki", *Geijutsu Shinchō* July 1951, 43–4.

47 Hijikata, "Kindai Bijutsukan Sōseiki," republished in Wakimura Yoshitarō, *Wakimura Yoshitarō Chosakushū*, (Tokyo: Nihon Keieishi Kenkyūjo, 1976) 4, 343–55, esp. 347–8. 56–69, quote 57–8.

48 Hijikata Teiichi, "Kanagawa Kenritsu Bijutsukan," *Atorie*, 303, February 1952. Reprinted in *Chisa na hako*, 38–9.

49 This is discussed briefly in Bert Winther-Tamaki, *Art in the Encounter of Nations: Japanese and American Artists in the Early Postwar Years*

(Honolulu: University of Hawai'i, 2001) 16 and at greater length in Mitsuda Yuri, "'Bijutsu Hihyō' (1952–1957), shi to sono jidai—'gendai bijutsu' to 'gendai bijutsu hihyō' no seiritsu," *Fuji Xerox Art Bulletin*, 2: 1–52.

50 Mitsuda, 27. As late as 2008 the national museum described its central task as showing the "maturity of Japanese-style and Western-style paintings," while in 2012 the museum proclaimed that "it can be said that modern Japanese painting reached its maturity around this [1912–26] period." These characterizations presuppose exactly the kind of unified path to national modernity that the Kamakura museum questioned. Website of the National Museum of Modern Art, Tokyo. http://www.momat.go.jp/english/artmuseum/index.html. (Accessed 17 September, 2008 and 21 May, 2012).

51 Masaaki Morishita, *The Empty Museum: Western Cultures and the Artistic Field in Modern Japan* (Surrey: Ashgate, 2010).

52 Tange Kenzō, "Kokuritsu Kindai Bijutsu ni tō" *Geijutsu Shinchō*, 4.1 (January 1953): 32–5, quotes 32 and 34–35. Sasaki Seiichi summarized Tange's stance as taking "the opportunity created by the national art museum to address what had been unstated and so breathe out the great pain of self-condemnation regarding Japanese modernity that had been lodged in his heart up until then." Sasaki, "Kamakura Kinbi Bijutsukan no Shuppatsu," 15.

53 Hijikata, "Maegaki," ix. Also see Tsuruta Heihachirō, "Kanagawa Kenritsu Kindai Bijutsukan" in *Nihon Yōga to Kanagawa Kenritsu Kindai Bijutsukan* (Tokyo: Asahi Shinbunsha ed., 1983), 125–35.

54 "Ryūsei no Kai—Hito to geijutsu," discussion with Wakimura Yoshitarō, Hijikata Teiichi, Maekawa Seirō, and Tomiyama Hideo, *Toshi*, 356 (April 1979): 2–19, quote 5–6.

55 Sakai Tadayasu Interview, Tokyo, 24 February 2009. Hijikata Yukue Interview, Kamakura, 27 February 2009.

56 As Alicia Volk puts it, "Saeki is considered to have accomplished, before his mental collapse and death at the age of thirty in a suburb of Paris, an uncontrived and intuitive marriage of Japanese and Western aesthetics." Christine M. E. Guth, Alicia Volk, and Emiko Yamanashi. *Japan & Paris: Impressionism, Postimpressionism, and the Modern Era*, (Honolulu: Honolulu Academy of Arts, 2004): 114.

57 Wakimura Yoshitarō, "Hijikata Teiichi shi to watashi — Kishida Ryūsei to Saeki Yūzō," In Hijikata Teiichi Tsuitō Kankōkai, ed. *Hijikata Teiichi Tsuisō*, 109–14.

58 Mark Sandler, "The Living Artist: Matsumoto Shunsuke's Reply to the State," *Art Journal*, 55.3 (Fall 1996): 49–74.

59 Bert Winther-Tamaki, "'The Mexico Boom' in the Japanese art world, 1955," paper given at conference Japanese art since 1945: The First PONJA GenKon Symposium, Yale April 2005. Summary at http://www.yale.edu/macmillan/ceas/japanartabstracts.pdf . (Accessed 13 October, 2010). Hijikata Teiichi, *Mekishiko kaiga*, (Mexican painting), (Tokyo: Misuzu, 1955).

60 Wakimura "Perusha Jūtan no bi" in *Shumi no Kachi*, 147–66.

61 Sasaki Kōzō, "Hijikata Ikka" (The House of Hijikata), in Hijikata Teiichi Tsuitō Kankōkai, *Hijikata Teiichi Tsuisō*, 48–9.

62 Yagyū Fujio, "Wasurenagusa," in *Chisa na Hako*, 68–70, quote 68. Yagyū Fujio, "1950 nendai no Omoide," in *Kanagawa Kenritsu Kindai Bijutsukan*

30-nen no Ayumi: Shiryō-Tenrankai Sōmokuroku, 1951–81, (Kamakura: Kanagawa Kenritsu Kindai Bijutsukan, 1982), 17–20, esp. p 17.

63   Tanikawa Tetsuzō, "Bijutsu Kōkishika to shite no Wakimura-san" in *Wakimura Yoshitarō Chosakushū Geppō*, Vol. 2 (Tokyo: Nihon Keieishi Kenkyūjo, 1975), 2.

Chapter 3

For Minamata, I wish to thank: Herbert Bix, Albert Craig, John Dower, Endō Kunio, Carol Gluck, Andrew Gordon, Gotō Takanori, Hamamoto Tsuginori, the late Harada Masazumi, Ōya (formerly Hirakida) Rimiko, Hirotsu Toshio, Hiyoshi Fumiko, Horikawa Saburō, Irokawa Daikichi, Ishimure Michiko, Jitsukawa Yūta, the late Kawamoto Teruo, Maruyama Sadami, Margaret McKean, Mochizuki Toshikazu, Nakanishi Junko, Ogata Masato, the late Onitsuka Iwao, Ori Arisa, Michael Reich, Aileen Smith, the late Sugimoto Eiko, Takakura Shirō, Togashi Sadao, the late Ui Jun, Frank Upham, Yahagi Tadashi, Yamanaka Toshiharu, Yanagida Kōichi, Yoshii Masazumi, Yoshimoto Tetsurō, Yoshinaga Toshio. For Tsumago: Horikawa Saburō, Kobayashi Toshihiko. For Otaru: Horikawa Saburō, Ogawara Tadashi, Yamaguchi Tamotsu. For Uwa: Gail Bernstein, Ninomiya Takashi, Ninomiya Yōko, Taniguchi Kayo, Utsunomiya Haruko, Utsunomiya Shōichi. Research was supported by the Northeast Asia Council of the Association for Asian Studies, the University of Rhode Island Center for the Humanities, the University of Rhode Island Council for Research, and the University of Rhode Island Foundation. All photographs in this chapter are ©Timothy S. George.

1   André Sorenson and Carolin Funck, eds, *Living Cities in Japan: Citizens' Movements, Machizukuri, and Local Environments* (London and New York: Routledge, 2007) is a collection of studies on this phenomenon focusing almost exclusively on areas in and near major cities.

2   Timothy S. George, *Minamata: Pollution and the Struggle for Democracy in Postwar Japan* (Cambridge, MA: Harvard University Asia Center, 2001) focuses mainly on the story up to 1973, using the responses to Minamata disease as a lens through which to examine the ongoing redefinition by citizens of postwar democracy. Frank K. Upham discusses Minamata in "Unplaced Persons and Movements for Place," in *Postwar Japan as History*, ed. Andrew Gordon (Berkeley: University of California Press, 1993), 325–46.

3   George, *Minamata*, 35–6.

4   Minamata-shi, "Tōkei jōhō: jinkō, setai," www.minamatacity.jp/jpn/so-go/to-kei/to-kei_top.htm. (accessed 24 October 2010).

5   A total of 24,881 had applied for certification, with most rejected but over 7,000 still awaiting decisions. Minamata Shiritsu Minamatabyō Shiryōkan, "Minamatabyō nintei shinsei shori jōkyō," www.minamata195651.jp/list.html#3. (accessed 24 October 2010).

6   Carol Gluck, "The Past in the Present," in *Postwar Japan as History*, ed. Andrew Gordon (Berkeley: University of California Press, 1993), 89.

7   Jennifer Robertson, "It Takes a Village: Internationalization and Nostalgia in Postwar Japan," in *Mirror of Modernity: Invented Traditions in Modern Japan*, ed. Stephen Vlastos (Berkeley: University of California Press, 1998), 110–29.

8   In English, see the helpful survey by Watanabe Shun'ichi, "*Toshi keikaku* vs. Machizukuri: Emerging Paradigm of Civil Society in Japan, 1950–80," in Sorenson and Funck, 39–55.

9   Three essays in the Sorenson and Funck collection deal with Kōbe since the quake: Carolin Funck, "Machizukuri, Civil Society, and the Transformation of Japanese City Planning: Cases from Kōbe" (pp. 137–56); Itō Atsuko, "Earthquake Reconstruction Machizukuri and Citizen Participation" (pp. 157–71); and Nunokawa Hiroshi, "Machizukuri and Historical Awareness in the Old Town of Kōbe," 172–86.

10 Tsumago is part of the town of Nagiso, which has a total population of just under 5,000 and is in the Kiso district (*gun*) in Nagano Prefecture. Much of my understanding of Tsumago comes from a wide-ranging personal interview on 5 June 2008 with Kobayashi Toshihiko, a founding member and current head of the Tsumago o Aisuru Kai, who gave a detailed overview of events in Tsumago since he arrived there in 1951 as a town agricultural officer. Kobayashi and his work in Tsumago are the subject of a special issue of the journal *Fushin kenkyū*: "Tsumago-juku: Kobayashi Toshihiko no sekai," *Fushin kenkyū* 21 (June 1987). This issue includes transcripts of interviews with Kobayashi by Miyazawa Tomoko ("Kobayashi Toshihiko no sekai: Kobayashi Toshihiko, (kikite) Miyazawa Tomoko," pp. 11–78), an autobiographical essay by Miyazawa ("Tsumago-juku: dentōteki na machinami kankyō hozen to watashi," pp. 78–94), and a list of articles Kobayashi has published on the preservation movement in Tsumago (p. 95).

11 "Tsumago o Aisuru Kai kessei no yobikake," in the Rekishi Shiryōkan, Tsumago.

12 "Tsumago-juku o mamoru jūmin kenshō," in the Rekishi Shiryōkan, Tsumago.

13 Horikawa Saburō, "Rekishiteki kankyō hozon to chiiki saisei," in *Kōza shakaigaku 12: Kankyō*, ed. Funabashi Harutoshi and Iijima Nobuko (Tokyo: Tokyo Daigaku Shuppankai, 1998), 125.

14 For part of a visit to Otaru in 2008, I was guided by Horikawa Saburō, an environmental sociologist at Hōsei University who has studied Otaru since 1984. The discussion of Otaru here is based largely on his work and on interviews with two long-time local activists, Ogawara Tadashi (interviewed on 13 and 15 June 2008) and Yamaguchi Tamotsu (14 June 2008). Among the works by Horikawa I have found useful are "Rekishiteki kankyō hozon to chiiki saisei," in *Kōza shakaigaku 12: Kankyō*, ed. Funabashi Harutoshi and Iijima Nobuko (Tokyo: Tokyo Daigaku Shuppankai, 1998), p. 103–32; Otaru-shi ni okeru rekishiteki kankyō hozon to kankō kaihatsu (3): 1999-nendo Hōsei Daigaku shakai gakubu shakai chōsa jisshū hōkokusho (Tokyo: Hōsei Daigaku Shakai Gakubu Shakai Chōsa Jisshūshitsu, 2000, a collection edited by Horikawa); *Otaru unga hozon mondai kanren nenpyō: 1959–2006* (Tokyo: Hōsei Daigaku shakai gakubu kenkyūhi purojekuto "kōkyōen to kihan riron," 2008, edited by Horikawa and Morihisa Satoshi); and *Toshi gabanansu no*

shakaigakuteki jisshō kenkyū, (Tokyo: Hōsei Daigaku Shakai Gakubu Shakai Chōsa Jisshūshitsu, 2008, edited by Horikawa and Morihisa Satoshi).

15 Otaru's population declined from a peak of just under 200,000 in 1960 to 133,000 in 2010, about what it was in 1925. Otaru-shi, "Otaru-shi no purofiru," www.city.otaru.hokkaido.jp/sisei_tokei/otaru/profile/pro.html. (accessed 24 October 2010).

16 "Shuisho" (prospectus) issued by festival organizers, quoted in Horikawa, "Rekishiteki kankyō hozon to chiiki saisei," 119.

17 See the explanation on the city's website at www.city.otaru.hokkaido.jp/simin/ sumai/machidukuri/kifujyourei/. (accessed 24 October 2010).

18 Horikawa, "Rekishiteki kankyō hozon to chiiki saisei," 125–8.

19 Quoted in Horikawa, "Rekishiteki kankyō hozon to chiiki saisei," 130, note 11.

20 Gail Bernstein, *Haruko's World: A Japanese Farm Woman and Her Community* (Stanford: Stanford University Press, 1983). The l996 printing includes a new "Epilogue," and covers Bernstein's later visits to Uwa up to 1993 and news from the Utsunomiya family through November 1995. With an introduction from her, I visited Uwa and met the Utsunomiyas in 2008. As readers of *Haruko's World* might expect, they insisted that I stay with them, and they took charge of my schedule to be sure I saw as much of Uwa and met as many people as possible.

21 Uwa-machi shi Hensan Iinkai, ed. *Uwa-machi shi II* (Uwa-machi: Uwa-machi, 2001), 329, 330. Uwa was combined with neighboring towns to create Seiyo City in 2004.

22 The Nakanomachi o Mamoru Kai (Association to Protect Nakanomachi) was established in 1983, and describes its purpose as to "preserve the Bakumatsu historical views and buildings centering on Nakanomachi, pass them on to later generations, and to raise the historical standing of Seiyo City and the cultural awareness of the citizens." See "Nakanomachi o Mamoru Kai kaisoku," passed 31 March 1983.

23 Text of speech distributed by Minamata City.

24 Hirakida Rimiko, Global People's Forum, United Nations World Summit on Sustainable Development, Johannesburg, August 2002.

25 Oiwa Keibō, narrated by Ogata Masato, *Rowing the Eternal Sea: The Story of a Minamata Fisherman* (trans. Karen Colligan-Taylor) (Lanham, MD: Rowman & Littlefield, 2001), 93; idem, *Tokoyo no fune o kogite* (Yokohama: Seori Shobō, 1996), 96–8.

26 Oiwa, narrated by Ogata Masato, *Rowing the Eternal Sea,* 123; idem, *Tokoyo no Fune o Kogite,* 159.

27 Kurihara Akira, "Minamata kara kangaeru 11—inori" (lecture, Minamata Tokyo Ten, 12 Oct. 1996).

28 Yoshimoto Tetsurō, *Watashi no jimotogaku: Minamata kara no Hasshin* (Tokyo: NEC Kurieitibu, 1995).

29 The plans are available on Minamata's website, www.minamatacity.jp/. (accessed 24 October 2010).

30 Irokawa Daikichi, *Minamata: sono sabetsu no fūdo to rekishi* (Minamata: Han Kōgai Minamata Kyōtō Kaigi Jimukyoku, 1980), 75 ff.

31 Carol Gluck, *Japan's Modern Myths: Ideology in the Late Meiji Period* (Princeton: Princeton University Press, 1985), 49–60.

32 Asahi Shinbun, *Japan Almanac 1995* (Tokyo: Asahi Shinbun, 1994), 52.

33 Asahi Shinbun, *Japan Almanac 1999* (Tokyo: Asahi Shinbun, 1998), 134.

Chapter 4

1 Dedicated to the memory of Ueda Kichisuke and Nishiyama Hiroshi.

2 Narita Ryūichi, *"Kokyō" to iu monogatari* (Tokyo: Yoshikawakō Bunkan, 1998), 2–3; David W. Hughes, *Traditional Folk Song in Modern Japan: sources, sentiment and society* (Folkestone: Global Oriental, 2008), 1–2, 243.

3 Stephen Dodd, *Writing Home: Representations of the Native Place in Modern Japanese Literature* (Cambridge, MA; London: Harvard University Press, 2004), 81, 52–61.

4 See Marilyn Ivy, *Discourses of the Vanishing: Modernity, Phantasm, Japan* (Chicago; London: University of Chicago Press, 1995), 29–65.

5 Fujioka Wakao, *Disukabaa Japan: Karei naru shuppatsu* (Tokyo: Mainichi Shinbun, 1972), 40, 42–56. Emphasis in the original.

6 Millie Creighton, "Consuming Rural Japan: The Marketing of Tradition and Nostalgia in the Japanese Travel Industry," *Ethnology* 36. 3 (1997), 239.

7 Tanaka Sen'ichi, "Furusato oyobi furusato-kan no hen'yō," *Nihon Minzokugaku* 206, Special Feature: "Furusato o tou" (1996), 9.

8 Creighton, "Consuming Rural Japan," 243; Yasui Manami, " 'Furusato' kenkyū no bunseki shikaku," *Nihon Minzokugaku* 209 (1997), 78; Christine R. Yano, *Tears of Longing: Nostalgia and the Nation in Japanese Popular Song* (Cambridge, MA.; London: Harvard University Press, 2002), 174–76.

9 Quoted in Yano, *Tears of Longing*, 170.

10 Jennifer Robertson, "Furusato Japan: The Culture and Politics of Nostalgia," *Politics, Culture and Society* 1, 4 (1988), 495, 513–14; Yano, *Tears of Longing*, 178.

11 Ian Reader, "Back to the Future: Images of Nostalgia and Renewal in a Japanese Religious Context," *Japanese Journal of Religious Studies* 14, 4 (1987), 290; William W. Kelly, "Rationalization and Nostalgia: Cultural Dynamics of New Middle-Class Japan," *American Ethnologist* 13, 4 (1986), 613.

12 Yagi Tōru, "Ie, josei, haka: joseitachi ni totte no furusato," *Nihon Minzokugaku* 206, Special Feature: "Furusato wo tou" (1996), 48.

13 Yasui Manami, "Machi-zukuri, mura-okoshi to furusato monogatari," in *Matsuri to ibento*, ed. Komatsu Kazuhiko (Tokyo: Shōgakukan, 1997), 208, 218; Iwamoto Michiya, ed. *Furusato shigenka to minzokugaku* (Tokyo: Yoshikawakō Bunkan, 2007).

14 *Kaminoseki Kōhō* (hereafter abbreviated as KK), 5 January 1979.

15 KK, 5 June 1981; 5 July 1981; 20 November 1971.

16 Martin Dusinberre, *Hard Times in the Hometown: A History of Community Survival in Modern Japan* (Honolulu: University of Hawai'i Press, 2012), chapters 10–11.

17 This paragraph is influenced by Kuraishi Tadahiko, "Toshi seikatsusha no furusato-kan," *Nihon Minzokugaku* 206, Special Feature: "Furusato o tou" (1996), 17–18.

18 Ivy, *Discourses of the Vanishing*, 48.

19 Ronald P. Toby, *State and Diplomacy in Early Modern Japan: Asia in the development of the Tokugawa bakufu* (Princeton: Princeton University Press, 1984).

20 The painting, the *Tsūshinshi bune Kaminoseki zaikō-zu*, is housed in Chōsenji Temple, Kaminoseki.

21 Kaminoseki-chō kaidoku no kai, *Hōreki-do Chōsen tsūshinshi: shinshi raichō(ge) kihan(chū) Kaminoseki kiroku* (Kaminoseki: Kaminoseki-chō kyōikuiinkai, 2003), passim.

22 Nishiyama talked me through the iconography of the sign in May 2004, just a few months before it was blown down.

23 Thomas C. Smith, "Family Farm By-Employments in Preindustrial Japan," *The Journal of Economic History* 29, 4 (1969), 687–715; Dusinberre, *Hard Times in the Hometown*, chapter 2.

24 Kawamura Toshiyuki, *Furusato tanbō Kaminoseki* (Kaminoseki: Kaminoseki-chō no hatten o kangaeru kai: 2 volumes, 1984, 1986), Vol. 2, 67.

25 *Chūgoku Shinbun*, 15 December 1982.

26 Kimura Kenji, *Zaichō Nihonjin no shakaishi* (Tokyo: Miraisha, 1989), 11, 14.

27 Jonathan Dresner, "International Labour Migrants' Return to Meiji-era Yamaguchi and Hiroshima: Economic and Social Effects," *International Migration* 46, 3 (2008), 71–8.

28 Ibid., 71.

29 See Mariko Asano Tamanoi, *Memory Maps: The State and Manchuria in Postwar Japan* (Honolulu: University of Hawai'i Press, 2009).

30 The video is no longer to be found in the town history museum, and I could not trace it during a visit to Kaminoseki in 2011.

31 Chūgoku Denryoku Kabushiki Gaisha, *Fūdoki: Furusato no Rekishi Wo Tazunete* (Kaminoseki: Chūgoku Denryoku Kaminoseki Ritchi Chōsa Jimusho, 1994), 8–9.

32 Interview with the late Ueda Kichisuke, 15 March 2005.

33 Interview with the late Nishiyama Hiroshi, 8 January 2005.

34 Kaminoseki Kyōdoshi Gakushū Ninjatai, *Komikku Chōsen Tsūshinshi Monogatari: Umi to Toki o koete* (Kaminoseki: Kaminoseki Kyōdoshi Gakushū Ninjatai, 1997), 13.

35 See, for example, Kaminoseki-chō kaidoku no kai, *Hōreki-do Chōsen tsūshinshi*.

36 Ironically, the Yoshida household is now part of a historical museum complex in Shimo-Kamakari that celebrates that town's links to the Korean Embassies.

37 Interview with Nishiyama Hiroshi, 5 December 2003.

38 *Chūgoku Shinbun,* 19 July 2006.

39 Sven Saaler, *Politics, Memory and Public Opinion: The History Textbook Controversy and Japanese Society* (Munich: Iudicium, 2005), 91.

40 Eiichiro Azuma, "'Pioneers of Overseas Japanese Development': Japanese American History and the Making of Expansionist Orthodoxy in Imperial Japan," *The Journal of Asian Studies* 67. 4 (2008), 1187–1226.

41 Kaminoseki-chō Kyōiku Iinkai Kyōiku Bunkaka, *Yamaguchi-ken Shitei Bunkazai: Shikairō Hozon Shūri Kōji HōKokusho* (Kaminoseki: Kaminoseki Kyōiku Iinkai, 2002).

42 Daikichi Irokawa, *The Culture of the Meiji Period*, trans. Marius B. Jansen (ed.) (Princeton: Princeton University Press, 1985 [1970]).

43 Ogata owned at least 24 properties in Murotsu, and he also donated the land on which the elementary school was built to the village: Dusinberre, *Hard Times in the Hometown*, chapter 4.

44 I am influenced here by Harry Harootunian, "Shadowing History: National narratives and the persistence of the everyday," *Cultural Studies* 18, 2. 3 (March/May 2004), 181–200.

45 Anonymous interview, 2008.

46 Prasenjit Duara, *Rescuing History from the Nation: Questioning Narratives of Modern China* (Chicago: University of Chicago Press, 1995).

Chapter 5

1 Quoted in Norma Field, *In the Realm of a Dying Emperor: Japan at Century's End* (Random House, 1993), 77.

2 Moreover, using "Uchinā" and "Ryūkyū" reflected a conscious decision to use the more ancient terms for the island(s), as Uchinā is the name of the island in the indigenous language, Uchināguchi, and Ryūkyū derives from the fourteenth-century characters used by the Ming Dynasty to denote the archipelago. "Okinawa," as signifier, is hardly an innocuous term. When Meiji Japan invaded and conquered the Ryūkyū Kingdom in the 1870s, it was decided that continuing to call the islands "Ryūkyū" would allow China (the Qing Dynasty) to claim suzerainty. Hence, the Meiji oligarchy designated the islands as Okinawa Prefecture and named the largest island Okinawa. The etymology of "Okinawa" is thoroughly modern, as the *kanji* (Chinese characters) used to write "Okinawa" have no historical or cultural connection to the islands.

3 Arasaki Moriteru and Nakano Yoshio, *Okinawa Sengo Shi*, (Tokyo: Iwanami, 1976), 51.

4 Okinawa People's Party, "Declaration Concerning Reversion of the Ryūkyū Islands to Japan," 21 March 1951. Emphasis added. Freimuth Papers.

5 Although many historians have often treated the Ryūkyūs as a natural part of Japan, the intensive efforts by Tokyo to assimilate the Ryūkyūan people as proper Japanese subjects belie this uncritical view of Ryūkyūan-

Japanese relations. In fact, the term "Ryūkyūs" became a contested term, as it represented a time when the Ryūkyūs, both politically and culturally, identified more with Chinese civilization, and the term "Ryūkyūs" was invented by China. In order to create a clean break with the Ryūkyūan past, Tokyo renamed the islands Okinawa Prefecture in 1879. Over the next 70 years of successful assimilation policies, "Okinawa" became synonymous with the period of control by Japan, and "Ryūkyū" became an anachronism. Throughout this chapter, the terms "Okinawa" and "Ryūkyū" will be used interchangeably and inconsistently to reflect the ambiguous identity of the people of the Ryūkyūs.

6 M. D. Morris, *Okinawa: A Tiger by the Tail* (New York: Hawthorn Books, Inc., 1968), 26.

7 Morris, *Okinawa*, 26.

8 *The Okinawas of the Loo Choo Islands*, 108. Emphasis added.

9 Ibid., 103. It was also claimed that one could distinguish the two groups based on the manner of walking. Japanese supposedly walked with their toes pointed in, whereas Okinawans walked with their toes pointed outward.

10 "Psychological Warfare Plan," Headquarters Tenth Army, Office of the A.C. of S., G -2, 18 November 1944, 173–5. Reprinted in *Okinawakenshi Shiryōhen 2 The Okinawas of the Loo Choo Islands, etc* (Okinawa Haebaru: Okinawaken kyoikuiinka, 1996).

11 Ibid., 216 and 258. Ironically, during the Vietnam War, North Vietnam used similar questions to great effect in getting American black soldiers to ask, "whose war am I fighting?"

12 Ibid., 220, 221, 262.

13 Ibid., 176.

14 Hanna never made a critical distinction in the nomenclature in naming the islands, as he used the term "Okinawa" to describe both Japan's 70-year control of the islands and the era of the Ryūkyū Kingdom. For someone who was keen in preserving the Ryūkyūan past, it is ironic that he did not use the term he was trying to preserve.

15 Higaonna Museum also went by the name Okinawa Chinretsukan.

16 Willard Hanna, "Okinawa Exhibit Pamphlet," Watkins Collection, 29, 139 (emphasis added).

17 Ruth Ann Keyso, *Women of Okinawa: Nine Voices from a Garrison Island* (Cornell University, 2000), 60.

18 Entertainment Circuit, Memorandum Number 55, US Naval Military Government, 7 November 1945. Watkin Papers, 29, 148.

19 Hanna, "Okinawa: Ten Years Later," Watkins Collection, 46, 173.

20 Keyso, *Women of Okinawa*, 60.

21 Ibid.

22 Hanna, "Okinawa: Ten Years Later," Watkins Collection, 46, 173.

23 Keyso, *Women of Okinawa*, 57.

24 Aoyama Yōji, *Beikoku kisha ga mita Okinawa Shōwa Nijūnen* (Okinawa-shi: Aragusuku Insatsu, 1985), 78–9.

25 Keyso, *Women of Okinawa*, 57.

26 Memorandum to DCMG on Government Physical Set-up, Civilians Affairs Dept, 9 Jan. 1946, Watkins Collection, 36, 56.

27 Watkins War Diary, "Government-Capital," 31 December 1945, Watkins Collection, 36, 56.

28 Nakasone Gen'wa, *Okinawa kara Ryūkyū e: Beigunsei Konranki no Seiji Jikenshi* (Naha-shi: Gekkan Okinawasha, 1973), 192–4.

29 Watkins War Diary, "Caldwell-Watkins Policies," 16 February 1946. Hiyane Teruo, et al., ed., *Papers of James T. Watkins IV: Historical Records of Postwar Okinawa and the Beginning of US Occupancy*, Vol. 36 (Ginowan, Okinawa: Ryokurindō Shoten, date unknown), 66.

30 Watkins War Diary, "Art Treasures," 31 December 1945. Hiyane Teruo, et al., ed., *Papers of James T. Watkins IV: Historical Records of Postwar Okinawa and the Beginning of US Occupancy*, Vol. 89 (Ginowan, Okinawa: Ryokurindō Shoten, date unknown), 92–3.

31 During the 70 years of prewar Japanese domination, Tokyo had always appointed a mainland Japanese to be governor of Okinawa Prefecture.

32 Nicholas Evan Sarantakes, *Keystone: The American Occupation of Okinawa and US-Japanese Relations* (College Station: Texas A & M University Press, 2000), 34 (emphasis added).

33 "Report of Organization of the Okinawa People's Party," 27 July 1947. Freimuth Papers.

34 Higa, "The Okinawan Reversion Movement," 2.

35 "Report of Organization of the Okinawa People's Party," 27 July 1947. Freimuth Papers.

36 When he wrote his 1953 analysis of American policies toward Okinawa, Tull wrote that "since so little is known about the Ryūkyūs, inclusion of considerable background information is deemed critical" because not having such information would make it impossible for a "critical appraisal of American policies and how they have been implemented." If Tull encountered such little information in 1953, the situation for Sheetz in 1949 likely was far worse.

37 Tull, who left RYCOM shortly after Sheetz's departure in mid-1950, entered graduate school at the University of Chicago in 1951. While pursuing his MA in sociology, Tull wrote his MA thesis based upon his personal experience in Okinawa. Thus, due to his direct experience, I am treating his MA thesis as a primary document. His MA thesis remains the single most important primary document during this pivotal time.

38 Tull, "The Ryūkyū Islands, Japan's Oldest Colony—America's Newest; An Analysis of Policy and Propaganda," 17.

39 George Kerr, "Memorandum to Harold Coolidge, Executive Secretary Pacific Science Board," 28 June 1952. Folder "Proposed 'Tension' Project (An Investigation of the beginning of the Reversionist Movement of the 1950s)" located in the University of the Ryūkyūs Library, Kerr Collection (accessed 3 February 2000).

40 George Kerr, "Memorandum for the Civil Administrator, USCAR," on the subject of "Cultural Rehabilitation: Three Recommended Reconstruction Projects." 3 October 1952. Folder "SIRI & USCAR Correspondence" located in the University of the Ryūkyūs Library, Kerr Collection (accessed 3 February 2000).

41 Headquarters, Military Government of the Ryūkyū Islands, Programs and Statistics Section, *Ryūkyū Statistical Bulletin*, No. 3, March, 1950.

42 JCS 1231/14, "Directive for United States Civil Administration of the Ryūkyū Islands, 4 October 1950, Foreign Relations of the United States (FRUS), 1950, 6, 1313–19. USCAR also was a euphemism in that "Civil Administration" was an attempt to hide the reality the islands were still firmly under military command.

43 Personal Memo from James Tull to Colonel Schaeffer, Subject: "Central Government Structure," 14 December 1950. Taira Tetsuo's victory for Okinawa Gunto governor and subsequent call for reversion reinforced Tull's analysis of the problem. USCAR attempted to address Tull's criticism by abolishing the Gunto system and replacing it with a centralized government, the GRI, in 1952.

44 *Okinawa Sengo Shashin shi Amerika yû—no 10 nen* (Naha: Gekkan Okinawashi, 1979), 2. *Okinawa Encyclopedia*, "Okinawa daikyaka jiten jyōkan," (Naha-shi: Okinawa taimusu sha, 1983), 440. Also see Nakasone Gen'wa, *Okinawa kara Ryūkyū e*, and Phil Nelson, "Independent State of Okinawa," http://www.crwflags.com/fotw/flags/jp-47_50.html (accessed 16 November 2001).

45 *Ryūkyū Daigaku Yonjū Nen* (Okinawa: Ryūkyū Daigaku, 1990), 4.

46 USCAR, Okinawa: Keystone of the Pacific. Publication date unknown, though the most probable date would be the late 1950s. One US military officer, testifying in front of a Senate Appropriations Committee, asserted that American financial support would "be tangible evidence that the United States is interested in the cultural welfare of the Ryūkyū Islands." Senate Appropriations Committee, Supplemental Appropriation Bill for 1955, 620.

47 Headquarters, Military Government of the Ryūkyū Islands, Programs and Statistics Section, *Ryūkyū Statistical Bulletin*, No. 3, March, 1950.

48 As quoted in George Kerr, *Okinawa: The History of an Island People* Revised Edition with an afterword by Mitsugu Sakihara (Boston: Tuttle Publishing, 2000), 381–2.

49 Ibid.

50 According to William Hanna, it was Yamashiro who first suggested building a future university on the ruins of Shuri Castle. William Hanna, "Okinawa: Ten Years Later," 23 December 1945 (Bangkok: American Universities Field Staff, 1955). Watkins Collection, 46, 178.

51 Discussion with Edward Freimuth.

52 *Ryūkyū Daigaku Yonjū Nen* (Okinawa: Ryūkyū Daigaku, 1990), 7.

53 Author's photo.

54 http://www.okinawakai.org/past&present/shuri%20gate/Shuri%20no%20 Mon.htm (accessed 12 November 2005).

55 Colonel Walter Murray, Deputy Civil Administrator to Gen. David Ogden, Civil Administrator, Subject: "National Standard for GRI," 22 July 1954. RG 260 HCRI-LN, 1603–06, Box 29, Folder: Designs (Flag, others).

56 Edward Freimuth, USCAR Liaison Officer, to Colonel Walter Murray, Deputy Civil Administrator to General David Ogden, Civil Administrator, Subject: "Re: National Standard for GRI," 26 July 1954. RG 260 HCRI-LN, 1603-06, Box 29, Folder: Designs (Flags, others).

57 Ibid., Freimuth also questioned the current design, called the "Tomoebata," based on the Shō royal family's house colors. Even though "discussions with people in the University at Shuri, the seat of the old kingdom," had suggested that the people would accept it, Freimuth wondered if the rest of the people would even know that the Tomoebata flag was based upon that of the Shō household, and even more fundamentally, he was "uncertain whether the same reaction would be received from other than Shuri people."

58 Edward Freimuth, "Flags for Okinawa," undated ten-page report. Freimuth collection.

59 Ibid.

60 Item #4, Questionnaire by CO, 29th Army Band, of Meeting called by Mr. Houston, USCAR PIO, 21 January 1959. US National Archives II, RG 260 HCRI-PA, CAD 1957–71, Box 107, Folder "29th Army Band-Education Program."

61 Carl Bartzt, Director of Office of Public Information USCAR, to Lt. Col. Hood, Coordinator USARYIS PIO, Subject: 29th Army Band Concert Schedule, 14 November 1957.

62 Yamazato Eikichi, "Nippon wa sokoku ja nai," *China Post*, June 18–22, 1969.

63 Mitsugu Sakihara, "Preface" in *A Brief History of Early Okinawa Based on the Omoro Sōshi* (Tokyo: Honpo Shoseki Press, 1987), v.

64 Ibid., "Preface" vi. Emphasis added.

65 "Ōta Masahide's Appeal in Front of the Supreme Court of Japan," trans., *The Ryūkyūanist*, 35 (Winter 1996–97).

66 Numata Chieko, "Checking the Center: Popular Referenda in Japan," *Social Science Japan Journal*, 9, 1 (April 2006), 19–31.

67 "U.S.-Japan Defense Contradictions and the Nago Plebiscite." JPRI Critique 5:1, January 1998. http://www.jpri.org/publications/critiques/critique_V_1.html (accessed 29 August 2010).

68 Chalmers Johnson, "The U.S. General Accounting Office's Report on the Proposed Marine Corps Floating Heliport off Okinawa," *Japan Policy Research Institute*, no. 14, June, 1998.

69 Chalmers Johnson, "Okinawa between the United States and Japan," *Japan Policy Research Institute*, no. 24, January 2002. Johnson indicates that Obuchi's office redirected funds from the Foreign Ministry, meant to entertain LDP members when traveling abroad, to Okinawa in the form of a "Special Compensation Fund," run through a front organization.

70   "Obuchi pledges 10 bil. yen for Okinawa development," *Kyodo News Service*, 11 Dec. 1998. http://www.thefreelibrary.com/ Obuchi+pledges+10+bil.+yen+for+Okinawa+development-a053484435.

71   "Samitto Okinawa kaisai zōshō gaishō kaikō wa Fukuoka, Miyazaki de/ saishū kyokumen de taigyaku," *Ryūkyū shinpō*, 29 April 1999. http:// Ryūkyūshimpo.jp/news/storyid-96406-storytopic-86.html (accessed 30 August 2010).

72   "2000 en satsu, kennai 190 man maihakkō," *Ryūkyū shinpō*, 19 August 2000. http://Ryūkyūshimpo.jp/news/storyid-115449-storytopic-86.html (accessed 30 August 2010).

73   Johnson, "Okinawa between the United States and Japan," *Japan Policy Research Institute*, no. 24 January 2002.

74   In 1960, President Eisenhower was supposed to visit Japan to sign the renewed US-Japan Security Pact with Prime Minister Kishi Nobusuke, but the ANPO (anti-Security Treaty) demonstrations forced the cancelation of their meeting. In order to save face, the President abruptly decided to visit Okinawa on 19 June. His handlers had been assured that the Okinawans would welcome the president warmly, but instead he witnessed angry demonstrations that forced Eisenhower to retreat to the US air base at Kadena and hold meetings with the Okinawan governor ensconced safely on the base. Forty years and one month later, President Clinton went to Okinawa, though he made no reference to Eisenhower's visit.

75   "Clinton's Speech at the War Monument," *The Japan Times*, 22 July 2000. http://search.japantimes.co.jp/print/nn20000722d5.html (accessed 2 October 2010).

76   "Photo of G8 Summit Leaders in front of Shurijo," http://www.life.com/ image/1305516 (accessed 10 September 2010).

77   "Ryukyu ōkoku no Gusukugun, sekaiisan ni tōroku," *Ryūkyū shinpō*, 30 November 2000. http://Ryūkyūshimpo.jp/news/storyid-114803-storytopic-86.html (accessed 3 September 2010). Five castle (*gusuku* or *jō*) sites include Nakijingusuku, Zakimigusuku, Katsurengusuku, Nakagusuku, and Shurigusuku. The four other sites are Sonohyan Utaki Ishi-mon, the stone gate of Shuri Castle; Tama Uden, the Shō family's tomb; the royal garden at Shikina-en; and the Seifa Utaki.

78   "'Kettei' no shirase ni kansei/sekai isan tōroku," *Ryūkyū shinpō*, 30 November 2000. http://ryukyushimpo.jp/news/storyid-114803-storytopic-86.html (accessed 3 September 2010).

Chapter 6

1   John W. Masland, "Neighborhood Associations in Japan," *Far Eastern Survey* 23 (1946): 355.

2   For a superb account of food shortages in the immediate postwar period, see John Dower, *War Without Mercy: Race and Power in the Pacific War* (New York: Pantheon, 1986), 89–97.

3   For example, Thomas R. H. Havens, *Valley of Darkness: The Japanese People and World War Two* (New York: Norton, 1978); H. T. Cook and T. F. Cook, *Japan at War: An Oral History* (New York: The New Press, 1992); Akimoto Ritsuo, *Sensō to minshū: Taiheiyō sensōka no toshi seikatsu* (Tokyo: Gakuyō Shobō, 1974); Yamanaka Hisashi, *Kurashi no naka no taiheiyō sensō* (Tokyo: Iwanami shoten, 1989).

4   For example Takemae Eiji, *The Allied Occupation of Japan* (New York/ London: Continuum, 2002), 409.

5   Chris Aldous, "Contesting Famine: Hunger and Nutrition in Occupied Japan, 1945–52," *Journal of American-East Asian Relations* 17 (2010): 230–56.

6   Ibid., 255.

7   Nōrinshō sōmukyoku chōsaka, *Chōsa shiryō dai 25 gō: Nihon ni okeru shokuyō nōgyō jijō ni kan suru FAO ate 1948 nendoji hōkokusho* (Internal document of the Ministry of Agriculture and Forestry, 20 October 1948). Nutritional surveys were also conducted by the ministry before 1945. See, for example, Shimizu Katsuyoshi, ed., *Senjika kokumin eiyō no genjō hōkokusho*, Vol. 21 in the series *Jūgonen sensō kyokuhi shiryōshū* (Tokyo: Fuji shuppan, 1990).

8   Bruce F. Johnston, *Japanese Food Management in World War II* (Stanford: Stanford University Press, 1953); Bernd Martin, "Agriculture and food supply in Japan during the Second World War," in *Agriculture and Food Supply in the Second World War*, ed. Bernd Martin and Alan S. Milward (St. Katharinen: Scripta Mercaturae Verlag, 1985), 181–205; Anke Scherer, "Drawbacks to Controls on Food Distribution: Food Shortages, the Black Market and Economic Crime," in *Japan's Wartime Economy*, ed. Erich Pauer (London and New York: Routledge, 1999), 106–23; Steven J. Fuchs, "Feeding the Japanese: Food Policy, Land Reform, and Japan's Economic Recovery," in *Democracy in Occupied Japan: The US Occupation and Japanese Politics and Society*, ed. Mark Caprio and Yoneyuki Sugita (London and New York: Routledge, 2007), 26–47; Aldous, "Contesting Famine."

9   Owen Griffiths, "Need, Greed, and Protest in Japan's Black Market 1938–49," *Journal of Social History* 4 (2002): 825.

10 Ibid.

11 See, for example, Andrew Gordon, *A Modern History of Japan: From Tokugawa Times to the Present* (Oxford and New York: Oxford University Press, 2002) and Ishikawa Hiroko and Ehara Ayako, ed., *Kingendai no shokubunka* (Tokyo: Kōgaku shuppan, 2002).

12 Carol Gluck, "The Past in the Present," in *Postwar Japan as History*, ed. Andrew Gordon (Berkley: California University Press, 1993), 64.

13 Kōdansha, ed., *Shōwa: Niman nichi no zenkiroku*, Vol. 7 (Tokyo: Kōdansha, 1989), 106.

14 Economic and Scientific Section, Natural Resources Section, Public Health and Welfare Section, *Food Situation during the Second Year of Occupation* (Tokyo: Supreme Commander for the Allied Powers, 1948), 56. National Archives, College Park, Maryland. RG 331, Folder 35, Box 8395.

15 Shimokawa Akifumi and Katei Sōgō Kenkyūkai, eds, *Shōwa, Heisei kateishi nenpyō, 1926–95* (Tokyo: Kawade shobō, 1997), 114–16.

16 Jerome B. Cohen, *Japan's Economy in War and Reconstruction* (Minneapolis: University of Minnesota Press, 1949), 378–9, 385.

17 Cohen, *Japan's Economy in War and Reconstruction*, 373; Howard F. Smith, "Food Controls in Occupied Japan," *Agricultural History* 3 (1949): 221. See also Johnston, *Japanese Food Management*, 187–204.

18 Some authors differentiate the term *rinpo* from that of *tonarigumi*, as a smaller unit of up to 5 households. However, due to local differences in size, differentiating the two does not make much sense. In the occupation-period documents, as well as English-language literature on the topic, the term "neighborhood associations" refers to both *tonarigumi* and *rinpo*.

19 Kurt Steiner, *Local Government in Japan* (Stanford: Stanford University Press, 1965), 59.

20 Akimoto, *Sensō to minshū*, 48.

21 Ralph J. D. Braibanti, "Neighborhood Associations in Japan and their Democratic Potentialities," *The Far Eastern Quarterly* 2 (1948): 140.

22 Simon Partner, "Daily Life of Civilians in Wartime Japan, 1937–1945," in *Daily Life of Civilians in Wartime Asia*, ed. S. Lone (Westport, CT: Greenwood Press, 2007), 135.

23 Steiner, *Local Government in Japan*, 57.

24 Neighborhood associations functioned in the rural areas as well, but since food rationing was primarily an urban phenomenon, this chapter will focus on the urban situation.

25 Braibanti, "Neighborhood Associations in Japan," 151; See also Erich Pauer, "A New Order for Japanese Society: Planned Economy, Neighbourhood Associations and Food Distribution in Japanese Cities in the Second World War," in *Japan's War Economy*, ed. E. Pauer (London: Routledge, 1999), 95.

26 Partner, "Daily Life of Civilians in Wartime Japan," 137.

27 Most probably head of the "Block Association."

28 Kodera Yukio, ed., *Senji no nichijō: Aru saibankan fujin no nikki* (Tokyo: Hakubunkan, 2005), 118, 123.

29 Hazama Michiko, "Dainiji sekai taisenka no Amagasaki no kurashi VI," *Michishirube: Amagasaki kyōdoshi kenkyūkai kaishi* 36 (2008): 36–9.

30 Tomoko Aoyama, *Reading Food in Modern Japanese Literature* (Honolulu: Hawai'i University Press, 2008), 35.

31 Braibanti, "Neighborhood Associations in Japan," 155–6.

32 Ebato Akira, *Senji seikatsu to tonarigumi kairanban* (Tokyo: Chūō kōron 2001), 114–9.

33 Ibid.

34 Ibid., 123–7.

35 Braibanti, "Neighborhood Associations in Japan," 152.

36 Ibid., Masland, "Neighborhood Associations in Japan," 355.

37 Scherer, " Drawbacks to Controls on Food Distribution," 112, 115; "Shokuryō eidan kanbu o kiso," *Mainichi Shinbun*, 11 June 1947, 2.

38 Tokyo-fu Metropolitan Police, "Special Explanation of Rice Ration Books in Tokyo-fu," in *Handbook for Village and Neighborhood Ration Boards*, 7–10. Archival material. US Strategic Bombing Survey RG243, M1652 roll 61. National Archives, College Park, Maryland.

39 Ibid., 6.

40 Takemae Eiji, *The Allied Occupation of Japan* (New York and London: Continuum, 2002), 296.

41 Steiner, *Local Government in Japan*, 72.

42 Economic and Scientific Section, Price Control and Rationing Division. *Food Situation during the First Year of Occupation* (Tokyo: Supreme Commander for the Allied Powers, 1947), 3. National Archives, College Park, Maryland. RG 331, Folder 35, Box 8395.

43 H. F. Alber, "Draft Memorandum on Timing of the Establishment of the Staple Food Kodan," dated 18 June 1947, 3. National Archives, College Park, Maryland. RG 331, Box 8395.2, Folder 36 "Tonagirumi Dissolution."

44 Takemae, *The Allied Occupation of Japan*, 301, 304.

45 The Food Management Board, Ministry of Agriculture and Forestry, "A Report Relative to the Abolition of Tonarigumi System and Staple Food Ration Distribution," 31 March 1947, Folder 36 "Tonagirumi Dissolution," Box 8395, RG 331.

46 Takemae, *The Allied Occupation of Japan*, 304. See also Steiner, *Local Government in Japan*, 73.

47 "Chōnaikai haishi wa shigatsu tsuitachi," *Mainichi Shinbun* (Osaka edition) 25 January 1947, 2. Research on food-related articles in the Osaka edition of Mainichi Shinbun was carried out by my research-collaborator, Yasuhara Miho, as part of our forthcoming monograph *Shinbō to zeitaku: Gaishoku ga miseru senchū, sengo no seikatsu.*

48 "A Statement by the President of Food Management Board on the Subject of the Abolition of Tonari-Gumi and Staple Food Ration Distribution." National Archives, Maryland. RG 331, Box 8395, Folder 36 "Tonagirumi Dissolution."

49 The Food Management Board, 31 March 1947, Enclosure 1 and 3; The Food Management Board, "A Report Relative to the Measures the Food Management Board, Ministry of Agriculture and Forestry has taken with regard to standard Staple Food Rations since the Total and Complete Abolition of *Tonarigumi* System or its Similar Organization." National Archives, Maryland. RG 331, Box 8395, Folder 36 "Tonarigumi Dissolution."

50 Ibid.

51 Food Management Bureau No. 828, 24 March 1947. RG 331, Box 8397, Folder 27 "Ministry Instructions to Prefectures."

52 The Food Management Board, 31 March 1947, Enclosure 4. The Food Management Board, "A Report Relative to the Measures the Food Management Board, Ministry of Agriculture and Forestry has taken with regard to standard Staple Food Rations since the Total and Complete

Abolition of *Tonarigumi* System or its Similar Organization." National Archives, Maryland. RG 331, Box 8395, Folder 36 "Tonarigumi Dissolution."

53 Food Management Board, "A Report Relative to the Abolition of Tonarigumi System," 2.

54 Steiner, *Local Government in Japan*, 74.

55 B. F. Johnston, "Memorandum on the elimination of Tonari Gumi (Neighbourhood Associations) from Food Rationing," 17 June 1947, 1–2. National Archives, College Park, Maryland. RG 331, Box 8395, Folder 36 "Tonarigumi Dissolution."

56 "Kyū chōnaikaichō nado tsuihō: Daigae soshiki wa kongetsuchū ni kaisan," *Mainichi Shinbun* (Osaka edition), 3 May 1947, 1. See also Steiner, *Local Government in Japan*, 74.

57 "Michibata ni hottoku mochikomi haiyū. Tonarigumi haishigo no shimin seikatsu no jitsujō," *Mainichi Shinbun* (Osaka edition), 22 June 1947, 2.

58 Johnston, "Memorandum on the elimination of Tonari Gumi," 2–3.

59 24-Shokuryo no. 426. 26 January 1949. NARA, Maryland. RG 331, Folder 36 "Tonarigumi Dissolution," Box 8395.

60 *Mainichi Shinbun* (Osaka edition), 5 February 1946, 1.

61 Alber, "Draft Memorandum on Timing of the Establishment of the Staple Food Kodan," 3.

62 Ibid., 2.

63 Ibid., 4.

64 Smith, p. 222; "Shushoku ryūtsū chitsujo kaikakuan ima kokkai e," *Mainichi Shinbun* (Osaka edition), 29 November 1947, p. 1. See also http://www.shugiin.go.jp/itdb_housei.nsf/html/houritsu/00119471230247.htm (accessed 1 March 2010).

65 Steven J. Fuchs, "Feeding the Japanese: Food Policy, Land Reform, and Japan's Economic Recovery," 27.

66 Steven J. Fuchs, "Feeding the Japanese: MacArthur, Washington and the Rebuilding of Japan through Food Policy" (Ph.D. diss., State University of New York, 2002), 303–4.

67 Steiner, *Local Government in Japan*, 75.

68 Ibid., 75, 228.

69 Gregory J. Kasza, *The Conscription Society: Administered Mass Organizations* (New Haven and London: Yale University Press, 1995), 72–102.

70 Steiner, *Local Government in Japan*, 228–9.

Chapter 7

1 Shoichi Itoh, "After the Election: Will Japan be Different," *Brookings Northeast Asia Commentary* 31 (September 2009) http://www.brookings.edu/opinions/2009/09_japan_election_itoh.aspx. (accessed 19 January 2011).

2   On the vulnerability of Koizumi's assassins, see Sally Ann Hastings, "Assassins, Madonnas, and Career Women: Reflections on Six Decades of Women's Suffrage in Japan," *Asian Cultural Studies* 35 (2009):237.

3   http://www.nurse.or.jp/toukei/pdf/toukei01.pdf. (accessed 1 May 2009).

4   Ezra F. Vogel, *Japan's New Middle Class: The Salary Man and His Family in a Tokyo Suburb* (Berkeley: University of California Press, 1963).

5   Mariko Asano Tamanoi, "Women's Voices: Their Critique of the Anthropology of Japan," *Annual Review of Anthropology* 19 (1990):19–20, provides a review of some of this literature. Two outstanding examples are Gail Lee Bernstein, *Haruko's World: A Japanese Farm Woman and her Community* (Stanford: Stanford University Press, 1983) and Anne E. Imamura, *Urban Housewives: At Home and in the Community* (Honolulu: University of Hawaii Press, 1987).

6   Kathleen S. Uno, "Death of 'Good Wife, Wise Mother'?" in *Postwar Japan as History*, ed. Andrew Gordon (Berkeley: University of California Press, 1993), 305, and Frank K. Upham, "Unplaced Persons and Movements for Place," in *Postwar Japan as History*, ed. Andrew Gordon (Berkeley: University of California Press, 1993), 332.

7   Upham, "Unplaced Persons," 333–7 and Sandra Buckley, "Altered States: The Body Politics of 'Being Woman,'" in *Postwar Japan as History*, ed. Andrew Gordon (Berkeley: University of California Press, 1993), 353–5.

8   Olive Checkland, *Humanitarianism and the Emperor's Japan, 1877–1977* (New York: St. Martin's Press, 1994), 37.

9   Sarah Soh makes this point with respect to the neglect of prostitutes, arguing that prostitution is stigmatized care work. C. Sarah Soh, *The Comfort Women: Sexual Violence and Postcolonial Memory in Korea and Japan* (Chicago: University of Chicago Press, 2008), 202.

10 Takie Sugiyama Lebra, *Japanese Women: Constraint and Fulfillment* (Honolulu: University of Hawaii Press, 1984), 55.

11 Lebra, *Japanese Women*, 178.

12 Dorothy Robins-Mowry, *The Hidden Sun: Women of Modern Japan* (Boulder, CO: Westview Press, 1983), 249.

13 Ruth Campbell, "Nursing Homes and Long-term Care in Japan," *Pacific Affairs* 57. 1 (Spring 1984):81.

14 Blenda Larson, "Report from Japan and Korea," *American Journal of Nursing* 48. 10 (October 1948):630–2.

15 Yuka Yasui Fujikura, "Public Health Nursing in Japan: In the Country, in the City," *American Journal of Nursing* 56. 11 (November 1956):1416.

16 See the photograph of striking nurses at the Keiō University Hospital in April 1971 in Robins-Mowry, *The Hidden Sun*, 185.

17 See the chronology on the JNA website, http://www.nurse.or.jp/jna/english/nursing/system.html#history, (accessed 4 May 2009). See also *JNA News*, 38 (March 2007), 2.

18 Ochiai Emiko, "Modern Japan through the Eyes of an Old Midwife: From an Oral Life History to Social History," in *Gender and Japanese History*, ed.

Wakita Haruko, Anne Bouchy, and Ueno Chizuko (2 Volumes; Osaka: Osaka University Press, 1999), 1:240–2.

19   Checkland, *Humanitarianism and the Emperor's Japan, 1877–1977*, 33. See also Aya Takahashi, *Development of the Japanese Nursing Profession: Adopting and Adapting Western Influences* (London: RoutledgeCurzon, 2004).

20   See, for instance, Fujime Yuki, "One Midwife's Life: Shibahara Urako, Birth Control, and Early Shôwa Reproductive Activism," in *Gender and Japanese History*, ed. Wakita et al., 1:299.

21   See, Sally Ann Hastings, "Women Legislators in the Postwar Diet," in *Reimaging Japanese Women*, ed. Anne Imamura (Berkeley: University of California Press, 1996), 273; Ogai Tokuko, "The Stars of Democracy: The First Thirty-nine Female Members of the Japanese Diet," *US-Japan Women's Journal*, English 11 Supplement (1996): 91 shows that two-thirds of those elected identified themselves as having occupations.

22   On Shibahara, see Fujime, "One Midwife's Life."

23   Crawford F. Sams, *"Medic," The Mission of an American Military Doctor in Occupied Japan and Wartorn Korea*, ed. Zabelle Zakarian (Armonk, New York: M. E. Sharpe, 1998), 140.

24   Shina Kan, "Japanese Women Move Forward," *Far Eastern Survey* 19. 12 (1950):124.

25   *Nihon Josei Jinmei Jiten* (Tokyo: Nihon tosho senta, 1998).

26   Sams, *"Medic,"* mentions their status. Inoue's close relationships with Alt and Ohlsen are clear from the fact that when Inoue visited the United States in 1951 as part of a Diet delegation, she met with Alt's parents and siblings in Baltimore and with Ohlsen's family in Chicago. Inoue Natsue, *Amerika Kango Jigyō no Ittan* (Tokyo: Bunkōdo, 1951), 54–5.

27   Herbert Passin, "The House of Councillors: Promise and Achievement," in *Japan at the Polls: The House of Councillors Election of 1974*, ed. Michael K. Blaker (Washington, DC: American Enterprise Institute for Public Policy Research, 1976), 8.

28   Kan, "Japanese Women Move Forward," 124. Kan says the legislation was passed in 1947, but Sams *"Medic,"* 142, makes clear that the final passage was in 1948.

29   Tiana Norgren, *Abortion Before Birth Control: The Politics of Reproduction in Postwar Japan* (Princeton: Princeton University Press, 2001), 175 n. 44.

30   Norgren, *Abortion Before Birth Control*, 42, 176 n. 48.

31   Sams, *"Medic,"* 143.

32   *Hoken to josan* 7. 6 (June 1953):4.

33   There are short biographical sketches of her in *Jinji Kōshinroku* (18th edition, Tokyo: 1955) and *Seijika Jinmei Jiten* (Tokyo: Nichigai asoshietsu, 1990). Yokoyama's self-identity as an Edokko is in *Hoken to Josan* 7. 12 (December 1953).

34   *Hoken to Josan* 6. 2 (February 1952):26–7. Ichikawa Ishi died at age 72 on 17 January 1952, in Setagaya.

35 *Hoken to Josan* 3. 4 (April 1949):24; Nihon kango kyōkai, *Nihon Kango Kyōkaishi* (Tokyo: Nihon kango kyōkai shuppanbu, 1967), 1:213–4.

36 *Kango* 3, 1 (January 1951):58 and 3. 3 (March 1951):62.

37 *Hoken to Josan* 6, 1 (June 1952):35–6; photograph, 38.

38 Yokoyama Fuku, "Sōkai o mae ni," *Hoken to Josan* 6. 4 (April 1952):3.

39 Yokoyama Fuku, "Ugoki," *Hoken to Josan* 6. 12 (December 1952):33.

40 Yokoyama Fuku, "Sōkai o mae ni," *Hoken to Josan* 6. 4 (April 1952):3.

41 Tokyo-to, Itabashi-ku, *Itabashi-ku Shi* (Tokyo: Tokyo-to, Itabashi-ku, 1954), 573.

42 *Asahi Shinbun*, 3 and 6 June 1950.

43 *Hoken to Josan* 6. 2 (February 1952):27.

44 *Hoken to Josan* 6. 10 (October 1952):35.

45 *Asahi Shinbun*, 27 April 1953.

46 See, for instance, the list of candidates provided in *Asahi Shinbun*, 23 April 1953.

47 Mentioned in *Jinji Kōshinroku* (1955).

48 *Fujinkai Tenbo*, May 1957, 14.

49 *Hoken to Josan* 8. 1 (January 1954):38–40.

50 Tomioka Jirō, *Nihon Iryō Rōdō Undō Shi* (Tokyo: Keisō shobō, 1972), 111.

51 The text of the statement, dated 19 November 1956, is given in Tomioka, *Nihon Iryō Rōdō*, 111.

52 William E. Steslicke, *Doctors in Politics: The Political Life of the Japan Medical Association* (New York: Praeger Publishers, 1973), 75.

53 Tomioka, *Nihon Iryō Rōdō*, 111.

54 The date is from Ishihara Akira, *Kango Nijūnen Shi* (Tokyo: Mejikaru furendo sha, 1967), 176.

55 Nihon kango kyōkai, ed., *Nihon Kango Kyōkai Shi*, Vol. 3 (1968–1977) (Tokyo: Nihon kango kyōkai shuppanbu, 1978), 11. Hereafter, NKKS.

56 Details of Hayashi's life are from Yukinaga Masae, *Kango Jinmei Jiten* (Tokyo: Igaku shoin, 1968), 206–7.

57 Her statement can be found in Tokyo-to senkyo kanri iinkai, *Senkyo Kiroku*, 1950–1959 Tokyo: Tokyo-to, 1959, 534.

58 NKKS 3:11.

59 Yumaki Masu, "Rijikai hōkoku," *Kango* 12, 7 (June 1960):6.

60 The proceedings of the Nihon kango renmei kessei taikai appear in *Kango* 12. 7 (June 1960):76–80.

61 Steslicke, *Doctors in Politics*, 59.

62 *Kango* 13. 7 (July 1961). For the resolution, see 50–51; for the election results, see 100–101. Inoue Natsue ran against Hayashi, receiving only 26 votes to Hayashi's 508.

63 Steslicke, *Doctors in Politics*, 109.

64 Her statement appeared in *Asahi Shinbun*, 17 June 1962.

65 A picture of the JNA Building decked out for the election appears in the opening pages of *Kango* 14, 6 (June 1962). A picture of Hayashi with the campaign car is in the opening pages of *Kango* 14. 8 (August 1962).

66 *Asahi Shinbun*, 29 and 30 June 1962.

67 Opening pages, *Kango* 14. 8 (August 1962).

68 *Kango* 14. 10 (October 1962):1. A photograph shows her at her desk in the Independents Club.

69 *Kango* 16. 6 (June 1964):47–8.

70 Details of Ishimoto's life are from Yukinaga, *Kango jinmei jiten*, 21.

71 Kaneko Mitsu, "Rijikai hōkoku," *Kango* 20, 6 (June 1968):12.

72 Miyagawa Takayoshi, *Rekidai Kokkai Giin Keireki Yōran* (Tokyo: Seiji Kōhō Sentā, 1990), 1187.

73 *Fujin tenbo*, 157 (November–December 1967): 4.

74 *Fujin tenbo*, 174 (June 1969):2.

75 Shūgiin Sangiin, *Gikai seido Hyakunenshi: Kizokuin Sangiin Giin Meikan* (Tokyo: Ōkura-sho, 1990), 248.

76 http://www.nurse.or.jp/jna/english/statistics/index.html (accessed 3 November 2010).

77 http://www.shimizukayoko.gr.jp/profile/index.html (accessed 3 May 2009).

78 *JNA News*, 31 (October 2001):3.

79 On nurses as "housewives," see Susan Orpett Long, "The Sociological Context of Nursing in Japan," *Culture, Medicine and Psychiatry* 8 (1984):141–63.

Chapter 8

1 Special thanks to Ruselle Meade and Edmont Katz for translating sections of this chapter.

2 *Asahi Shimbun*, 21 February 2010.

3 Wakamatsu Kōji, *Caterpillar* (Tokyo: Yūgakusha, 2010), 8.

4 Yamada Akira, "Shintai shōgaisha undō no rekishi to taisaku rinen no hatten," in *Shōgaisha to Shakaihoshō*, eds, Kojima Mitsuko, Sanada Naoshi, and Hata Yasuo (Kyoto: Hōritsu Bunkasha, 1979), 200–43; "Nihon ni okeru shōgaisha fukushi no rekishi," in *Shōgaisha no Fukushi to Jinken (Kōza Shōgaisha no Fukushi I)*, eds, Ichibangase Yasuko and Satō Susumu (Tokyo: Kōseikan, 1987), 43–128.

5 Murakami Kimiko, *Senryōki no Fukushi Seisaku* (Tokyo: Keisō Shobō, 1987).

6 Ueno Masumi, "Hakui bokinsha issō-undō nimiru shōigunjin no sengo" *Nihongakuhō* 23 (2003), 95–116; — "Hakui bokinsha to wa dare ka: Kōseishō zenkoku jittai chōsa ni miru shōigunjin no sengo," *Machikaneyama Ronsō* 29 (2005), 31–59; — "Sengo Nihon no shōigunjin mondai: senryōki no shōigunjin engo," *Minshūshi Kenkyu* 71 (2006), 3–12.

7 Imamura Yuzuru, "Shōisha wa sukuwareruka?" *Kōsei Jihō* 4. 8 (1 August 1949), 7.

8 On 15 September 1945, the Japanese government reported that 2567 hospitals and sanitariums had 101,509 patients with a total bed capacity of 155,654. According to reports received from the Imperial Japanese Army, approximately 78,000 wounded veterans were treated in 268 hospitals in Japan and 9 hospitals in Korea on 15 August 1945. General Headquarters/ Supreme Commander for the Allied Powers Records: Public Health & Welfare Section-BOX 9447-01991, Memorandum for Record, Subject Brief Summary Japanese Hospital Status.

9 Murakami, *Senryōki no Fukushi Seisaku*, 165–6.

10 The Japanese military disability pension system set three prime categories *kōshō*, *kanshō*, and *mokushō*. Special *kōshō* is the severest disability due to military service, while second-degree *mokushō* is the slightest one. *Kōshō* is divided into eight subcategories (special, one through seven). *Kanshō* is divided into four subcategories (one through four). *Mokushō* is divided into two subcategories. A special provision of the Pension Law was introduced for injured ex-soldiers; those who had received the sixth-degree *kōshō* under the Pension Law kept the same payment, those who had from less than the seventh-degree *kōshō* received a temporary stipend, and the government stopped the pension for those who were only slightly injured. Takashima Masurō, "Gunjin onkyū wa dono yōni fukkatsu suru ka," *Toki no Hōrei* 108 (1953), 5–11; Sōri-fu, Onkyū-kyoku. *Onkyū-kyoku 100 nen* (Tokyo: Ōkura-shō, Insatsu-kyoku, 1975), 299; Sano Risaburō, "Shōigunjin shogū no kaizen ha," *Shakaijigyō* 35, 1 (1952), 26.

11 Kōseishō 50 Nenshi Henshū Iin, *Kōseishō 50 Nenshi, Kijutsu-hen* (Tokyo: Chuōhōki Shuppan, 1988), 583–4.

12 Before GHQ announced SCAPIN 775, GHQ advanced poor relief efforts through negotiation with the Japanese authorities by the end of 1945. GHQ released "Affair on Stockpile of Rationed Goods for Relief" on 22 November 1945. Then, GHQ announced SCAPIN 404, "Affair on Outreach Program and Welfare Relief," on 8 December. On the other hand, the Japanese government issued its "Memorandum on Outline of Urgent Life Support for Needy People" on 22 November, and "Affair on Relief Welfare" on 31 December (answer to SCAPIN 404). Thus, SCAPIN 775 was consequently deemed an official response to "Memorandum on Outline of Urgent Life Support for Needy People." Murakami Kimiko, "Senryōki ni okeru shōisha taisaku no dōkō: shintai shōgaisha fukushi-hō seiritsu made," *Shakai Fukushigaku* 6 (1982), 52.

13 Shakai Hoshō Kenkyūjo, *Nihon Shakai Hoshō I* (Tokyo: Shiseido, 1975), 7; Murakami, *Senryōki no Shakai Fukushi*, 166.

14 Tanaka Sumie, "Sagamihara no shōigunjin tachi," *Chuō Kōron*, 768 (Fall 1952), 150.

15 At its peak, the National Hospital Patients' League enrolled about 53,000 patient members from 130 national hospitals. Yamada Akira, "Shintai shōgaisha undō no rekishi to taisaku rinen no hatten," in *Shōgaisha to Shakai*

hoshō, Kodama Mitsuko, Sanada Yoshi, Hata Yasuo, eds, (Kyoto: Hōritsu Bunkasha, 1979), 200.

16 Aochi Shin, "Shōigunjin: sensō giseisha no jittai," *Fujin Kōron* 36, 10 (October 1951), 107–8.

17 Tanaka, "Sagamihara no shōigunjin tachi," 147–8; *Asahi Shimbun*, 14 October 1951.

18 Kimura Takuji, "Senshōbyōsha senbotsusha izokutō engo-hō no seitei to gunjin onkyū no fukkatsu: kyū gunjin dantai e no eikyō o chūshin ni," *Jinmin no Rekishigaku* 134 (1997), 5–6.

19 Nippon Shōigunjin Kai, *Nippon Shōigunjin Kai 15 Nenshi* (Tokyo: Chiyoda Shōji, 1967), 10–11; *Nisshō Gekkan (Monthly Paper of the JDVA)*, Vol. 1, 20 May 1953, 2.

20 Nomura Kichisaburō was a navy admiral with a five-degree *kōshō*.

21 *Nisshō Gekkan*, Vol. 1, 20 May 1953, 1.

22 Kaba Atsushi was an army lieutenant general with a five-degree *kōshō*.

23 *Nisshō Gekkan*, Vol. 1, 20 May 1953, 1.

24 Nippon Shōigunjin Kai, *Nippon Shōigunjin Kai 15 Nenshi*, 13–14.

25 Ibid., 15.

26 *Nisshō Gekkan*, Vol. 1, 20 May 1953, 2.

27 *Nisshō Gekkan*, Vol. 1, 20 May 1953, 1.

28 Kimura, "Senshōbyōsha senbotsusha izokutō engo-hō no seitei to gunjin onkyū no fukkatsu," 4.

29 Of the 15 council members, five members were former military personnel or civilian personnel, who represented the expected beneficiary groups of military pensioners. Nippon Shōigunjin Kai, *Nippon Shōigunjin Kai 15 Nenshi*, 9–10.

30 The extended suspension of the military pension also meant that the prewar military pension system was not reintroduced. Kimura, "Senshōbyōsha senbotsusha izokutō engo-hō no seitei to gunjin onkyū no fukkatsu," 4.

31 To be entitled to military pensions, commissioned officers (*shōkō*) and noncommissioned officers (*kashikan*) needed 13 years and 12 years of service, respectively. In addition, salaries for commissioned officers reflected a military rank-based pay scale. Yamamura Nobuo, "Gunji onkyū wa dō naru ka," *Jinjigyōsei* 3. 7 (July 1952), 22.

32 Military officials regardless of military rank received additional benefits such as military service benefit (*senmu kasan*), Ibid., 21; Kimura, "Senshōbyōsha senbotsusha izokutō engo-hō no seitei to gunjin onkyū no fukkatsu," 4.

33 Yoshihara Kazumasa, "Gunjin onkyū fukkatsu no kōsō: onkyū hō tokurei shingikai kengi no gaiyō," *Toki no Hōrei* 82 (1952), 31.

34 Although the prewar pension system covered soldiers other than commissioned and noncommissioned officers, the new system would cover draftees who served more than seven years in the military regardless of military rank. The Council calculated that the estimated budget of

¥65 million for the expected 1.83 million recipients would divide into survivor's benefits payable to families (*kōmu fujoryo*) (85.4%), increased military pensions (*zoka onkyū*) for injured or sick veterans (4.7%), conventional military pensions (*futsū onkyū*) for elderly veterans (7.2%), and benefits payable to families of those who died after discharge (2.7%). Ibid., 32–4.

35 According to a survey conducted by the *Nippon Hōsō Kyōkai* (Japan Broadcast Corporation) on 25 November 1952, many Japanese citizens opposed the reintroduction of military pensions because of a sense of caution and aversion to commissioned soldiers' privileges. Ibid., 32.

36 Hirose Shunji, "Gunji onkyū no fukkatsu: 28 nendo yosan no shōten," *Meisō* 4, 5 (August 1953), 121.

37 For the campaign during the Fifteenth Diet, about 300 members from 31 prefectures were involved. *Nisshō Gekkan*, Vol. 1, 20 May 1953, 2–3.

38 Ibid.

39 *Nisshō Gekkan*, Vol. 3, 30 July 1953, 3.

40 Hirose, "Gunji onkyū no fukkatsu: 28 nendo yosan no shōten," 120–1.

41 Ibid., Vol. 7, 20 November 1953, 1.

42 Ibid., Vol. 10, 20 February 1954, 2.

43 Ibid., Vol. 8, 20 December 1953.

44 Ibid., Vol. 10, 20 February 1954, 3.

45 Ibid.

46 Ibid.

47 Ibid., Vol. 11, 1 April 1954, 3.

48 Ibid.

49 The JDVA acceded to the WVF on 27 May 1956.

50 *Nisshō Gekkan*, Vol. 7, 20 November 1953, 3.

51 Ibid., Vol. 9, 20 January 1954, 2.

52 Ibid., Vol. 8, 20 December 1954, 1.

53 Ibid., Vol. 8, 20 December 1953, 1; Vol. 9, 20 January 1954, 1.

54 Ibid., Vol. 9, 20 January 1954, 1.

55 The first and second convention of the JDVA reached unanimous decisions on release of war criminals. The JDVA, thereafter, repeatedly demanded their release. Ibid., Vol. 17, 1 November 1954, 3; Vol. 23, 1 June 1965, 3.

56 Ibid., Vol. 15, 1 September 1954, 1.

57 Ibid., Vol. 24, 1 August 1954, 4.

58 Ibid., Vol. 26, 1 October 1954, 3.

59 Ibid., Vol. 27, 1 December 1954, 3.

60 Ibid., Vol. 26, 1 September 1954, 3.

61 Ibid., Vol. 17, 1 November 1954, 3.

62 Ibid.

Chapter 9

1   Daniel Bell, *The Coming of Post-Industrial Society* (New York: Basic Books, 1973).

2   Peter F. Drucker, *The Age of Discontinuity* (New York: Harper & Row, 1969); Fritz Machlup, *The Production and Distribution of Knowledge in the United States* (Princeton, NJ: Princeton University Press, 1962).

3   John Zysman and Abraham Newman, eds *How Revolutionary Was the Digital Revolution?* (Stanford, CA: Stanford University Press, 2006).

4   Jean-François Lyotard, *The Postmodern Condition* (Minneapolis, MN: University of Minnesota Press, 1984).

5   Michael J. Piore and Charles F. Sabel, *The Second Industrial Divide* (New York: Basic Books, 1984).

6   Emiko Ochiai, "Reconstruction of the Intimate and Public Spheres in Asian Modernity," *Journal of Intimate and Public Spheres* (2010).

7   Manuel Castells, *The Rise of the Network Society* (Malden, MA: Blackwell Publishers, 1996).

8   Linda Weiss, *The Myth of the Powerless State* (Ithaca, NY: Cornell University Press, 1998). Jonah D. Levy, "The State Also Rises" in Jonah D. Levy, ed., *The State After Statism* (Cambridge, MA: Harvard University Press, 2006).

9   Ardath W. Burks, *Japan* (Boulder, CO: Westview Press, 1984).

10 For useful discussion see Carolyn S. Stevens, "You Are What You Buy: Postmodern Consumption And Fandom Of Japanese Popular Culture," *Japanese Studies* (2010).

11 Glenn D. Hook and Michael Weiner, eds, *The Internationalization of Japan* (London; New York: Routledge, 1992).

12 Ikuo Kume, *Disparaged Success* (Ithaca, NY; London: Cornell University Press, 1998).

13 Florian Coulmas, Harald Conrad, Arnette Schad-Seifert, and Gabriele Vogt, eds, *The Demographic Challenge* (Leiden and Boston: Brill, 2008); John Creighton Campbell, *How Policies Change* (Princeton, NJ: Princeton University Press, 1992).

14 For example, Chalmers A. Johnson, *The Industrial Policy Debate* (San Francisco, CA: ICS Press, 1984).

15 For example, Arthur J. Alexander, *In the Shadow of the Miracle: The Japanese Economy Since the End of High-Speed Growth* (Lanham, MD: Lexington Books, 2002); Marie Anchordoguy, "Japan's Developmental State in the 1990s and Beyond" in Davide Arase, ed., *The Challenge of Change: East Asia in the New Millennium* (Berkeley, CA: Institute of East Asian Studies, University of California, 2003); Richard Katz, *Japan, the System That Soured : The Rise and Fall of the Japanese Economic Miracle* (Armonk, NY: M. E. Sharpe, 1998); Edward J. Lincoln, *Arthritic Japan* (Washington, DC: Brookings Institution Press, 2001).

16 Chalmers A. Johnson, *MITI and the Japanese Miracle* (Stanford, CA: Stanford University Press, 1982), 19.

17 Chalmers A. Johnson, "The Developmental State: Odyssey of a Concept" in Meredith Woo-Cumings, ed., *The Developmental State*, ed. (Ithaca, NY; London: Cornell University Press, 1999), 38–9; Johnson, *MITI and the Japanese Miracle*, 314–20.

18 Jonah D. Levy, Mari Miura, and Gene Park, "Exiting *Etatisme?*" in Levy, ed., *The State after Statism*. As a theoretical possibility one could also envision a post-developmental state that transforms itself into a plan ideological state.

19 See Junnosuke Masumi, *Contemporary Politics in Japan* (Berkeley, CA: University of California Press, 1995), for detailed treatment.

20 Alice H. Amsden, *Asia's Next Giant: South Korea and Late Industrialization* (New York: Oxford University Press, 1989).

21 Laura Elizabeth Hein, *Fueling Growth* (Cambridge, MA: Council on East Asian Studies Distributed by Harvard University Press, 1990).

22 Inoguchi Takashi and Iwai Tomoaki, *Zoku Giin no Kenkyū* (Tokyo: Nihon keizai shinbun sha, 1985); Ellis Krauss and Michio Muramatsu, "The Conservative Policy Line and the Development of Patterned Pluralism," in Yasusuke Murakami and Hugh T. Patrick, eds, *The Political Economy of Japan, Volume 1* (Stanford, CA: Stanford University Press, 1987); Satō Seizaburō and Matsuzaki Tetsuhisa, *Jimintō Seiken* (Tokyo: Chūō Kōronsha, 1986).

23 Kent E. Calder, *Crisis and Compensation* (Princeton, NJ: Princeton University Press, 1988).

24 Gavan McCormack, *The Emptiness of Japanese Affluence* (Armonk, NY: M.E. Sharpe, 1996); Brian Woodall, *Japan under Construction* (Berkeley, CA: University of California Press, 1996).

25 Masumi, *Contemporary Politics in Japan*.

26 Johnson, *MITI and the Japanese Miracle*, 291.

27 Scott Callon, *Divided Sun* (Stanford, CA: Stanford University Press, 1995).

28 For example, Anchordoguy, "Japan's Developmental Sate in the 1990s and Beyond."

29 Mark Tilton, *Restrained Trade* (Ithaca, NY: Cornell University Press, 1996).

30 For example, Eisuke Sakakibara, *Structural Reform in Japan* (Washington, DC: Brookings Institution Press, 2003).

31 Lonny E. Carlile, "The Evolution of the Administrative Reform Movement," in Lonny E. Carlile and Mark Tilton, eds, *Is Japan Really Changing Its Ways?* (Washington, DC: Brookings Institution Press, 1998), 76–110.

32 Rinchō Gyōkakushin OB Kai, *Rinchō gyōkakushin* (Tokyo: Zaidan Hōjin Gyōsei Kanri Kenkyū Sentā, 1987), 162–239.

33 Ibid, 169.

34 Ibid, 174–5.

35 Ibid, 191.

36 Ibid, 195–200.

37 Carlile, "The Evolution of the Administrative Reform Movement."

38 Anchordoguy, "Japan's Developmental State in the 1990s and Beyond."

39   Carlile, "The Evolution of the Administrative Reform Movement." The administrative reform program was one part of a six-part "structural reform" package that in addition consisted of fiscal reform, social security reform, economic reform, financial system reform, and education reform.

40   Sangyō Kōzō Shingikai, "21 seiki keizai sangyō kōzō no kadai to tenbō," (Tokyo: Sangyō Kōzō Shingikai, 2000).

41   Industrial Struture Council, "Challenges and Prospects for Economic and Industrial Policy in the 21st Century" (Tokyo: Industrial Struture Council, 2000).

42   Ibid, 5

43   Shingikai, "21 seiki keizai sangyō kōzō no kadai to tenbō," 29.

44   Steven Kent Vogel, *Freer Markets, More Rules* (Ithaca, NY: Cornell University Press, 1996).

45   Yasu Taniwaki, "Emerging Broadband Market and the Relevant Policy Agenda in Japan," *Journal of Interactive Advertising* 4, 1 (2003).

46   Kenji Kushida, "Japan's Telecommunications Regime Shift," in John Zysman and Abraham Newman, eds, *How Revolutionary Was The Digital Revolution?* (Stanford, CA: Stanford University Press, 2006), 126.

47   Vogel, *Freer Markets, More Rules*.

48   This is the ministry's name as of 2012. At the time of its creation in 2001, it had the rather unwieldy English name of Ministry of Public Management, Home Affairs, Posts and Telecommunications.

49   Quoted in Yagi Takashi, " e-Japan senryaku no sōkatsu to kongo no IT seisaku," *FUJITSU* 58, 6 (2007).

50   Lonny E. Carlile, "From Outbound to Inbound," in Hiroshi Itoh, ed., *The Impact of Globalization on Japan's Public Policy* (Lewiston, NY: Edwin Mellen Press, 2008).

51   Fukuyama Junzō, "Kankō rikkoku jitsugen e no torikumi," *Chōsa to Jōhō*, 554 (2006).

52   JTA website.

53   Sherry L. Martin and Gill Steel, *Democratic Reform in Japan* (Boulder, CO: Lynne Rienner Publishers, 2008).

Chapter 10

Much of the research for this chapter was conducted while I was a Visiting Scholar at the Institute for Monetary and Economic Studies, Bank of Japan. I would like to thank Wataru Takahashi, Michio Ayuse, Keiko Harimoto, and other participants in a Bank of Japan seminar held on 26 August 2010, Janet Hunter, Christopher Gerteis, and other contributors to this book, and Hideki Kanda, Tetsuo Morishita, and Akihiro Wani for their helpful comments on earlier drafts. Views expressed in this chapter are those of the author and do not necessarily reflect the official views of the Bank of Japan.

1   Richard Katz, "Comment, The Japan Fallacy: Today's U.S. Crisis Is Not Like Tokyo's Lost Decade." *Foreign Affairs,* March/April (2009); Takatoshi Ito, *The Japanese Economy* (Cambridge: MIT Press, 1992), 408.

2   The term "Big Bang" refers to banking policy changes undertaken in London in 1986. A number of deregulatory, market opening measures, such as the deregulation of fixed brokerage commissions for stock trading, were implemented simultaneously ("Big Bang Day") and are often credited with improving Britain's financial sector and its international competitiveness as a financial center. An earlier deregulation of brokerage commissions in New York in 1975 is also generally seen as producing positive results. Japan hoped to achieve similar success with a "Japanese version of the Big Bang" (*Nihonban Biggu Bangu*).

3   For a discussion of Japan's efforts to adjust its economic model to a postindustrial society, see Lonny Carlile, "Toward a Post-Industrial Policy or a Post-Developmental State?" in this volume.

4   Laura Hein, "Growth Versus Success: Japan's Economic Policy in Historical Perspective," in *Postwar Japan as History*, ed. Andrew Gordon (Berkeley and Los Angeles: University of California Press, 1993).

5   Henry Hansmann and Reiner Kraakman, "The End of History for Corporate Law," *Georgetown Law Journal* 89 (2001): 439–68. Based partly on this assumption of convergence, law specialists looked for a transformation in Japanese corporate governance from a stakeholder-based system to a shareholder-based system. See Curtis J. Milhaupt, "A Lost Decade for Japanese Corporate Governance Reform?: What's Changed, What Hasn't, and Why." in *Institutional Change in Japan,* ed. Magnus Blomstrom and Sumner La Croix (London and New York: Routledge, 2006), 97–119. Business school faculty speculated in the "varieties of capitalism" literature whether a Japanese "government-coordinated economy" could transform into a "liberal market economy." See Richard Deeg and Gregory Jackson, "Toward a More Dynamic Theory of Capitalist Variety," *Socio-Economic Review* 5. 1 (2007): 149–79.

6   For example, John O. Haley, "Heisei Renewal or Heisei Transformation: Are Legal Reforms Really Changing Japan?" *Journal of Japanese Law* 19 (2005): 5–18.

7   Ministry of Finance, "Financial System Reform—Toward the Early Achievement of Reform," 13 June 1997. http://www.fsa.go.jp/p_mof/english/ big-bang/ebb32.htm and http://www.fsa.go.jp/p_mof/english/big-bang/ebb25. htm. (accessed 9 March 2011); Tetsuro Toya, *The Political Economy of the Japanese Big Bang* (Oxford: Oxford University Press, 2006).

8   Thomas Cargill, Michael Hutchinson, and Takatoshi Ito, *Financial Policy and Central Banking in Japan* (Cambridge, MA: MIT Press, 2000).

9   Ministry of Finance, Discussion Group on New Finance Trends, "Organization of Discussion Points," (in Japanese) [joint study group with members from 13 Japanese Government agencies and industry observers]. 17 June 1998. http:// www.fsa.go.jp/p_mof/singikai/nagare/tosin/1a031aa2.htm. (accessed 9 March 2011); Takeo Hoshi and Hugh Patrick, *Crisis and Change in the Japanese Financial System* (Boston, MA: Kluwer Academic Publishers, 2000), 16.

10 Italy's economic growth rate in the 2000s was a miniscule 0.27%, lower than that of Japan (0.73%). Global investors have lost confidence in Italy, which faced a sovereign debt crisis in 2011, as investors were leery of buying Italian government bonds. These same investors continue to think of Japan as a safe

haven and flock there to purchase Japanese Government bonds at the first sign of instability in global financial markets, despite even larger government debts in Japan and its supposed economic "failure."

11   James Bullard, "Seven Faces of 'The Peril.'" *Federal Reserve Bank of St. Louis Review* September–October (2010): 1–40.

12   Yasuyuki Fuchita, "Revisiting the Debate Over Competitiveness of Japan's Markets and the Global Financial Center Concept," *Nomura Capital Market Review* 10 (2007): 1. http://ssrn.com/abstract=988855. (accessed 30 September 2010).

13   Financial Services Agency, "Details of the Financial Services Agency No Action Letter System," 2011. http://www.fsa.go.jp/en/refer/noact/index_menu.html. (accessed 1 March 2011).

14   Bruce E. Aronson, "The Brave New World of Lawyers in Japan: Proceedings of a Panel Discussion on the Growth of Corporate Law Firms and the Role of Lawyers in Japan," *Columbia Journal of Asian Law* 21 (2007): 45–86.

15   Bruce E. Aronson, "Changes in the Role of Lawyers and Corporate Governance in Japan—How Do We Measure Whether Legal Reform Leads to Real Change?" *Washington University Global Studies Law Review* 8 (2009): 223–40, 231.

16   International Bankers' Association, "Recommendations to Promote Tokyo as a Global financial Center," 16 March 2007. http://www.ibajapan.org/StoreImages/Editor/IBA_paper_on_Tokyo_as_a_Global_Financial_Center_E. pdf, 12 (accessed 9 March 2011).

17   Takeo Hoshi and Hugh Patrick, *Crisis and Change in the Japanese Financial System*, 2000.

18   Takatoshi Ito, *The Japanese Economy* 1992, 105.

19   Council on Economic and Fiscal Policy, "The Report of the Special Board of Inquiry for Examining 'Japan's 21st Century Vision'," The Special Board of Inquiry for Examining Japan's 21st Century Vision. April 2005. http://www5. cao.go.jp/keizai-shimon/english/publication/pdf/050419visionsummary_fulltext.pdf, 30–1 (accessed 9 March 2011).

20   Hideki Kanda, "Regulatory Differences in Bank And Capital Markets Regulation." *University of Tokyo Journal of Law and Politics* 2 (2005): 29–40.

21   Japan Securities Dealers' Association, Study Group to Vitalize the Corporate Bond Market (Japan Securities Dealers' Association), "Toward Vitalization of the Corporate Bond Market," 22 June 2010. http://www.jsda.or.jp/html/en/newsroom/researches-studies/pdf/100930_finalreport_e.pdf, 1 (accessed 9 March 2011).

22   Hibiki Ichiue, "Development of Japan's Credit Markets, in Bank for International Settlements, Developing Corporate Bond Markets in Asia." *BIS papers No. 26*, 1 February 2006: 88–95, 92.

23   Japan Securities Dealers' Association, "Toward Vitalization of the Corporate Bond Market." 22 June 2010.

24   Sayuri Shirai, "Promoting Tokyo as an International Financial Centre," In *Competition among Financial Centres in Asia-Pacific: Prospects, Benefits,*

Risks and Policy Challenges, ed. Soogil Young, Dosoung Choi, Jesus Seade and Sayuri Shirai (Institute of Southeast Asian Studies, 2009).

25 Ricardo J. Caballero, Takeo Hoshi, and Anil K. Kashyap. "Zombie Lending and Depressed Restructuring in Japan," *MIT Economics Working Paper No. 06-06*. http://ssrn.com/abstract=889727. (accessed 30 September 2010).

26 Over the last decade, Japanese banks had lower profitability in terms of both net interest rate spread (1% lower) and return on assets (1.2% lower). Masahiko Igata, Toshio Taki, and Hiroshi Yoshikawa, "Examining the US Corporate Bond Market and the Changing Environment for Japan's Corporate Bond Market" *Normura Journal of Capital Markets* 5 (Winter 2009): 1. 22.

27 Japan Securities Dealers' Association, "Toward Vitalization of the Corporate Bond Market." 22 June 2010, 4.

28 Ministry of Finance, "Financial System Reform" 13 June 1997.

29 Japan Securities Dealers' Association, "Toward Vitalization of the Corporate Bond Market." 22 June 2010, Appendix 8, 3.

30 Bank of Japan, "Flow of Funds (3rd Quarter of 2010)—Japan and US Overview," 17 December 2010(a). http://www.boj.or.jp/en/statistics/sj/sjhiq.pdf. (accessed 9 March 2011).

31 Ministry of Finance, Study Group on Structural Changes in Flows of Funds in 21st Century, English outline of report on *Changes in Household Savings Rate and Financial Asset Selection Behavior and their Impacts on the Flow of Funds in Japan,* 2001: April. http://www.mof.go.jp/english/tosin/henkaku/hk004.htm. (accessed 9 March 2011).

32 Investment Company Institute and Securities Industry and Financial Markets Association 2008, "Equity and Bond Ownership in America," http://www.ici.org/pdf/rpt_08_equity_owners.pdf, 7 (accessed 9 March 2011).

33 Ibid., 1.

34 Ministry of Finance, Changes in Household Savings Rate and Financial Asset Selection Behavior and their Impacts on the Flow of Funds in Japan 2001.

35 Investment Company Institute and Securities Industry and Financial Markets Association 2008, "Equity and Bond Ownership in America."

36 Bank of Japan, "Flow of Funds (3rd Quarter of 2010)—Japan and US Overview," 17 December 2010(a). http://www.boj.or.jp/en/statistics/sj/sjhiq.pdf. (accessed 9 March 2011).

37 Venture Enterprise Center. 15 December 2010. "Recovery and Prospects for Venture Business in 2010," (annual venture white paper, summary report) (January 2011) (in Japanese), available at http://www.vec.or.jp/2011/02/01/001-33/ (shortened summary entitled "2010 Survey Results on Trends in Venture Capital Investment," 15 December 2010, is also available in English at http://www.vec.or.jp/2010/12/15/brief/). (accessed 9 March 2011), English Figure 6.

38 Bank of Japan, Establishment of "Principal Terms and Conditions for the Fund-Provisioning Measure to Support Strengthening the Foundations

for Economic Growth," 15 June 2010 (b). http://www.boj.or.jp/en/mopo/
measures/mkt_ope/len_b/index.htm/. (accessed 9 March 2011).

39 Bernard S. Black and Ronald Gilson, "Venture Capital and the Structure
    of Capital Markets: Banks Versus Stock Markets." *Journal of Financial
    Economics* 47 (1998): 243–77; Curtis J. Mihaupt, "The Market for Innovation
    in the United States and Japan: Venture Capital and the Comparative
    Corporate Governance Debate." *Northwestern University Law Review* 91
    (1997): 865–98.

40 Zenichi Shishido, "Why Japanese Entrepreneurs Don't Give up Control to
    Venture Capitalists," Working Paper. http://ssrn.com/abstract_id=1370519
    5 April 2009, 2 (accessed 1 March 2011).

41 Venture Enterprise Center. 15 December 2010. "Recovery and Prospects for
    Venture Business in 2010," Japanese 1.

42 Mihaupt, "The Market for Innovation in the United States and Japan:
    Venture Capital and the Comparative Corporate Governance Debate."1997:
    865–98.

43 Shishido, "Why Japanese Entrepreneurs Don't Give up Control to Venture
    Capitalists." 5 April 2009, 20.

44 Niles Bosma and Jonathan Levie, "Global Enterprise Monitor, 2009 Global
    Report," 2009. http://www.gemconsortium.org/download/1285854461939/
    GEM%202009%20Global%20Report%20Rev%20140410.pdf, 18 (accessed
    30 September 2010).

45 Zoltán J. Acs, and László Szerb, "The Global Entrepreneurship and
    Development Index (GEDI)," paper presented at Summer Conference 2010
    on "Opening Up Innovation: Strategy, Organization and Technology,"
    Imperial College London Business School. April 2010, http://www2.druid.dk/
    conferences/viewpaper.php?id=502261&cf=43 (accessed 9 March 2011).

46 Venture Enterprise Center. 15 December 2010. "Recovery and Prospects for
    Venture Business in 2010," English Figure 6.

47 Ministry of Finance, "Financial System Reform," 13 June 1997.

48 Fuchita , "Revisiting the Debate Over Competitiveness of Japan's Markets and
    the Global Financial Center Concept,"2007

49 See Shirai, "Promoting Tokyo as an International Center," 2009.

50 Toya, *The Political Economy of the Japanese Big Bang*, 2006, 106–7.

51 Mark M. Spiegel, and Jose A. Lopez, "Foreign entry into Underwriting
    Services: Evidence from Japan's 'Big Bang' Deregulation," *Federal Reserve
    Bank of San Francisco*, Working Paper Series, Working Paper 2009–14. June
    2009. http://www.frbsf.org/publications/economics/papers/2009/wp09-14bk.
    pdf. (accessed 9 March 2011).

52 Nicole Pohl, "Foreign Penetration of Japan's Investment-Banking Market: Will
    Japan Experience the Wimbledon Effect?" July 2002, http://iis-db.stanford.
    edu/pubs/20028/Pohl.pdf. (accessed 9 March 2011).

53 Catherine Makino, "Asia Seeks Business Hub: Frantic Battle to be Financial
    Capital," *ACCJ Journal* 2007: August. http://www.accj.or.jp/doclib/journal/
    Aug07.pdf, 28 (accessed 9 March 2011).

Chapter 11

This research on which this chapter is based was funded by the National Science Foundation under a Doctoral Dissertation Research Improvement Grant (DDRIG, Award # 0612838) and a Rapid Response Research Grant (RAPID, Award # 1137856). An earlier version of this essay is included as a chapter in my dissertation, *Surviving Modernization: State, Community, and the Environment in Two Japanese Fishing Towns* (Rutgers University, 2010). I would like to thank Bonnie J. McCay, David Leheny, and the other contributors to this book for their comments and suggestions.

1   The discussions on the postwar transitions in Japanese fisheries policies in this chapter mainly focus on so-called coastal fisheries (*engan gyogyō*). There is no rigid definition of what coastal fisheries are, but the term is often used to refer to the fishing activities that are operated by fishing boats weighing less than five metric tons and targeting species within the boundary of one's own prefecture with prefectural licenses and/or with the fishing rights of one's own co-op.

2   Arturo Escobar, *Encountering Development: The Making and Unmaking of the Third World* (Princeton, NJ: Princeton University Press, 1995); James Ferguson, *The Anti-Politics Machine: "Development," Depoliticization, and Bureaucratic Power in Lesotho* (Minneapolis, MS: University of Minnesota Press, 1994); James Ferguson, *Expectation of Modernity: Myths and Meanings of Urban Life on the Zambian Copperbelt* (Berkeley, CA: University of California Press, 1999); Tania Murray Li, *The Will to Improve: Governmentality, Development, and the Practice of Politics* (Durham, NC: Duke University Press, 2007); Stacy Leigh Pigg, "Inventing Social Categories through Place: Social Representations and Development in Nepal," *Comparative Studies in Society and History* 34. 3 (1992); James C. Scott, *Seeing Like a State: How Certain Schemes to Improve the Human Condition Have Failed* (New Haven, CT: Yale University Press, 1998).

3   Yutaka Hirasawa, *GyogyōSeisan No Hatten Kouzou* (Tokyo: Miraisha, 1961).

4   I use the official English translations for the names of Japanese laws based on Japanese Law Translation, http://www.japaneselawtranslation.go.jp (accessed in February 2010).

5   Yutaka Hirasawa, *Nihon Suisan Dokuhon* (Tokyo: Tōyō Keizai Shinpōsha, 1973).

6   Hirasawa, *GyogyōSeisan No Hatten Kouzou*, 351.

7   Hisao Iwasaki, *Nihon Gyogyō No TenKaikatei: Sengo 50 Nen Gaishi* (Tokyo: Kajisha, 1997), 33.

8   Kazuo Yamaguchi, *Nihon No Gyogyō* (Tokyo: Kōbunkan, 1959); Yutaka Hirasawa, *Shigenkanri Gata Gyogyō E No Ikō (the Shift to Collaborative Resource Management)* (Tokyo: Hokuto Shobo, 1986).

9   Iwasaki, *Nihon Gyogyō No Tenkaikatei: Sengo 50 Nen Gaishi*, 102.

10 Shōichirō Ōtsu and Shunji Sakai, *Gendai Gyosonmin No Henhyou Katei* (Tokyo: Ochanomizu shobō, 1981).

11 Hirasawa, *Gyogyōseisan No Hatten Kouzou.*

12 Iwasaki, Nihon Gyogyō No Tenkaikatei: Sengo 50 Nen Gaishi.

13 Hirasawa, *Nihon Suisan Dokuhon*, 21.

14 Hirasawa, *ShigenKanri Gata Gyogyō E No Ikō*; Shigen Kyōkai, *Tsukuru Gyogyō* (Tokyo: Shigen Kyōkai 1983); Iwasaki, *Nihon Gyogyō No TenkaiKatei: Sengo 50 Nen Gaishi.*

15 H. Scott Gordon, "The Economic Theory of a Common Property Resource: The Fishery" *Journal of Political Economy* 62 (1954).

16 Garrett Hardin, "The Tragedy of the Commons" *Science* 162 (1969).

17 Iwasaki, Nihon Gyogyō No Tenkaikatei: Sengo 50 Nen Gaishi (the Development Process of Japanese Fisheries: An Overview of Postwar History of Fifty Years).

18 William W. Kelly, "Rationalization and Nostalgia: Cultural Dynamics of New Middle-Class Japan" *American Ethnologist* 13. 4 (1986).

19 The English translations are employed from the fisheries vocabulary chart, listing terminologies in both Japanese and English, provided by MAFF, http://www.aafs.or.jp/info/Yougo/JE82.htm (accessed February 2010).

20 For English audiences, Timothy George provides an in-depth history of Minamata Disease and related struggles among the people of Minamata. Timothy George, *Minamata: Pollution and the Struggle for Democracy in Postwar Japan* (Cambridge, MA: Harvard University Asia Center, 2001).

21 Tadashi Yamamoto, "Collective Fishery Management Developed in Japan" (paper presented at the Microbehavior and Macroresults: Proceedings of the Tenth Biennial Conference of the International Institute of Fisheries Economics and Trade, Corvallis, OR, 10–14 July 2000).

22 Shōichi Tanaka, *Suisan Shigen-Gaku Sōron*, Vol. Revised volume (Tokyo: Kōseisha Kōseikaku, 1985).

23 Kazumi Sakuramoto, Hidehiro Katō, and Shōichi Tanaka, *Geirui Shigen No Kenkyū to Kanri* (Tokyo: Kōseisha Kōseikaku, 1991).

24 http://www.fccj.or.jp/node/6560 (accessed in May 2011).

25 http://www.cas.go.jp/jp/fukkou/pdf/kentou1/takemura.pdf (accessed in May 2011).

26 Takahashi Mikuriya, "'Postwar' Ends, 'Post-disaster' Begins," *Chūō Kōron* 2011, 27.

27 Ibid., 28.

Chapter 12

1 The inauguration of Japan Airlines' international flights provided the impetus for Pan Am—ever attentive to the possibilities of competition—to begin a program of hiring stewardesses who could speak Japanese. Because of US immigration laws, Pan Am hired Japanese Americans for this purpose until 1966, when laws changed and the airline began hiring Japanese women. See

Christine R. Yano, *Airborne Dreams: "Nisei" Stewardesses and Pan American World Airways* (Durham, NC: Duke University Press, 2011).

2   The connection between San Francisco and New York was left open, since Pan Am was supposed to be an exclusively international carrier.

3   Lonny Carlile lists the following disincentives to overseas travel by Japanese: "Most passports issued were valid for one trip only. Any international travel had to be approved by a Ministry of Finance committee. There was a $500 limit on the amount of foreign exchange that could be taken out of Japan and travel for the purpose of tourism was not considered a valid reason for authorization" (Lonny Carlile, "Economic Development and the Evolution of Japanese Overseas Tourism, 1964–94," *Tourism Recreation Research* 21 (1996), 11). These restrictions changed in 1964, when Japan liberalized these policies as one of the conditions for entry into the Organisation for Economic Cooperation and Development (OECD). However, note that in 1964, overseas travel for most Japanese was prohibitively costly.

4   Andrew Gordon, *A Modern History of Japan*, 2nd ed. (Oxford: Oxford University Press, 2009), 252.

5   Carlile, "Economic Development," 12. See further on the same page, Table 1, Key Statistics Relating to Japanese Overseas Tourism. Bruce Suttmeier, "Ethnography as Consumption: Travel and National Identity in Oda Makoto's *Nan de mo mite yarō" Journal of Japanese Studies* 35 (2009), 63.

6   In 2009, 120 people attended the Pan Am Retired Employees' Association party, held at the Foreign Press Club in Tokyo, not far from the former Pan Am offices in Marunouchi.

7   Although my emphasis here is on the crossing primarily from West (i.e. America) to East (i.e. Japan), it is important to acknowledge crossings in the opposite direction that were important during the era. East-to-West (Japan to Euroamerica) crossings of the period include Japanese war brides (an estimated 50,000 emigrated from Japan to the United States 1946 to 1965) and Zen Buddhism (D.T. Suzuki's move to New York City in 1951; influence upon avant-garde Beat movement in 1950s; first Zen monastery in the United States established 1967).

8   Although this is a popular adage in the form of a quotation attributed to then General Motors CEO Charles Wilson upon his nomination as Secretary of Defense in 1953 ("What is good for General Motors is good for the United States"), the adage is a misquotation of "For years I thought what was good for the country was good for General Motors and vice versa" ("Armed Forces: Engine Charlie," *Time*, 6 October 1961, (accessed 22 April 2011), http://www.time.com/time/magazine/article/0,9171,827790-1,00.html). Although the infamous, misquoted passage implies far greater American corporate arrogance, both versions demonstrate the close ties between nations and business institutions.

9   Purnima Bose and Laura Lyons, "Introduction: Toward a Critical Corporate Studies," in *Cultural Critique and the Global Corporation,* ed. Purnima Bose and Laura Lyons, (Bloomington, IN: Indiana University Press, 2010), 3–4.

10   Joseph Hale, "A Snapshot from the Heart," in *Pan Am kaisōroku* [Pan Am
     Memoirs], (Tokyo: Pan American Alumni Association, 2004), 113.

11   Naura, pers. comm., 15 June 2009.

12   David Leheny, *The Rules of Play: National Identity and the Shaping of
     Japanese Leisure* (Ithaca, NY: Cornell University Press, 2003), 1.

13   Naura, pers. comm., 15 June 2009; Carlile, "Economic Development," 12.

14   Sawa Kurotani, *Home Away from Home: Japanese Corporate Wives in the
     United States* (Durham, NC: Duke University Press, 2005).

15   Many of the former Pan Am employees I interviewed stayed with the company
     until the end in 1986. At that point, most, but not all transferred over to
     United Airlines with great sadness and reluctance.

16   Stiller, pers. comm., 3 May 2009.

17   Braden, pers. comm., 13 February 2008.

18   Braden, pers. comm., 13 February 2008.

19   Grantham, pers. comm., 31 July 2006.

20   Arima Neriko, [Untitled], in *Pan Am Kaisōroku*, (Tokyo: Pan American
     Alumni Association, 2004), 17.

21   Kawauchi Kazuko, [Untitled], in *Pan Am Kaisōroku*, 74.

22   Isa, pers. comm., 17 October 2009.

23   Jones officially left Pan Am in 1974; however, his popularity exceeded his
     post, so he continued presenting the Pan Am trophy until the trophy itself
     was retired in 1991. In 1991, Japan Airlines wanted to take over the trophy;
     however, the sumo governing body refused, saying that the trophy was too
     long and strongly associated with Pan American World Airways. As such, the
     trophy remains in the possession of the sumo association and is occasionally
     put on display in their small museum in Tokyo.

24   Isa, pers. comm., 17 October 2009.

25   Brian Moeran, "Individual, Group, and *Seishin*: Japan's Internal
     Cultural Debate," in *Japanese Culture and Behavior: Selected Readings*, ed.
     Takie Lebra and William S. Lebra (Honolulu, HI: University of Hawaii Press,
     1986), 74.

26   Kinoshita, pers. comm., 17 October 2009.

27   Ohta, pers. comm., 6 June 2009.

28   At least as early as 1973, Jones headed up his own public relations company,
     Public Relations Services International. In the private collection of former
     employees of Pan Am Japan is a letter dated 31 December 1973 from Malcolm
     McDonald, Managing Director of Pan Am to David Jones of Public Relations
     Services International, confirming a "working relationship" between the public
     relations firm and Pan Am. The letter states that the services rendered to Pan
     Am will include: "Pan Am tie-ins with each Sumo Tournament, the Sekai No
     Tabi TV program and the National Football League TV promotion within
     Japan"—effective 1 January, 1974 for one year.

29   Hale, pers. comm., 24 August 2009.

30 One might easily draw a contrast between the sight of diminutive Jones alongside huge Japanese sumo wrestlers, compared with the iconic photograph of General Douglas MacArthur towering over Emperor Hirohito at their first meeting in September 1945.

31 Jones, pers. comm., 31 May 2010.

32 Isa, pers. comm., 17 October 2009.

33 The original title of the show in 1959 was "Kanetaka Kaoru Sekai Tobi-aruki" (Kanetaka Kaoru World Hopping). In 1960, the title was changed to the more sedate "Kanetaka Kaoru Sekai no Tabi."

34 Kanetaka Kaoru, (Educational Aids Development Inc.), 14 December 1979, private collection.

35 Kato, T., 27 July 1979, private collection.

36 Suttmeier, "Ethnography as Consumption," 62–3.

37 Ohta, pers. comm., 6 June 2009.

38 Munroe, pers. comm., 22 February 2008.

39 This mode of consuming through seeing—what Suttmeier calls his "ubiquitous discourse of 'looking,'" "his focus on 'seeing' as the central mode of his encounters abroad"—parallels that of Oda's travelog (Oda Makoto, *Nan de mo Mite Yarō* (Tokyo: Kawade Shobou Shinsha, 1961). Suttmeier, "Ethnography as Consumption," 75.

40 Quoted in a private memo from T. Katō of the Chūō Senkō Advertising Co., Ltd. To Richard Boynton, Director of Passenger Marketing for the Far East division of Pan Am. The memo lists the international airline, name of program, television station, day of week, and on-air time. The shows themselves do not necessarily deal directly with travel. For example, there were Edo period detective serials ("Denshichi Torimono-chō" with Cathay Pacific), comedy shows ("Deko-Boko College" with Singapore Airlines), quiz shows ("Panel Quiz, Attack 25" with Air France), and sports shows ("Big Event Golf" with Japan Airlines).

41 Katō, [unpublished letter], 1979.

42 Andrew Painter. "Japanese Daytime Television, Popular Culture, and Ideology," in *Contemporary Japan and Popular Culture*, ed. John Whittier Treat (Honolulu, HI: University of Hawaii Press, 1996), p. 198.

43 The "Wakadaishō" movies comprised a series of 19 films produced by Tōhō Studios between 1961 and 1981, directed by seven different directors. Kayama Yūzō became the iconic actor whose name and image were synonymous with the series (although Kusakiri Masao appeared instead in two of the less popular films).

44 Isa, pers. comm., 17 October 2009.

45 Isa, pers. comm., 17 October 2009.

46 Isa, pers. comm., 17 October 2009.

47 Hale, pers. comm., 24 August 2009.

48 Ohta, pers. comm., 6 June 2009.

49 Hale, pers. comm., 24 August 2009.

50 Kinoshita, pers. comm., 17 October 2009.

Chapter 13

1   Hiraku Shimoda examines a particularly fascinating form of this
    phenomenon in his contribution to this volume, but several other scholars
    have also examined the ways in which private and public individuals have
    deployed historical narrative to shape public memory of their relationship
    to the prewar and wartime eras. Gerald Figal, "How to Jibunshi: Making
    and Marketing Self-Histories of Shōwa Among the Masses in Postwar
    Japan," *Journal of Asian Studies* 55. 4 (1996): 902–33; Jordan Sand,
    "Monumentalizing the Everyday: The Edo-Tokyo Museum," *Critical Asian
    Studies* 33, 3 (2001): 351–78; Carol Gluck, *Rekishi de kangaeru* (Tokyo:
    Iwanami Shoten, 2007); Aaron Moore, *The Peril of Self-Discipline: Soldiers
    Record the Rise and Fall of the Japanese Empire* (Cambridge, MA: Harvard
    University Press, 2012); and Aaron Moore, "To Defile a Sacred Memory:
    Japanese Peace and War Museums in a Comparative Context," in Nicholas
    Martin, ed. *Aftermath: Legacies and Memories of War in Europe* (London:
    Ashgate, 2013).

2   The ideas behind CSR programs today first developed out of the fiduciary
    concerns of US-based multinational corporations during the social and
    environmental scandals that defined the early 1970s. The private sector
    interest in CSR schemes among Japan's multinationals arose from a
    combination of international pressure to conform to international standards
    of corporate governance as well as from domestic pressure from the
    manufacturers' association Keidanren, which asserted that the adoption of
    philanthropic schemes like those found in CSR programs worldwide would
    help to persuade the state bureaucracy to loosen regulatory controls over
    the private sector. See Keidanren, "Charter for Good Corporate Behavior,
    1991." www.keidanren.or.jp/english/speech/spe001/s01001/s01a.html
    (accessed 22 January 2009); "Market Evolution and CSR Management,
    2003," www.doyukai.or.jp/en/policyproposals/articles/pdf/030326_1.
    pdf. (accessed 22 May 2011); "Keidanren Charter of Corporate Behavior,
    2004," www.keidanren.or.jp/english/policy/cgcb.html (accessed 22 January
    2009); and *The Earth is Our Home: Social and Environmental Report*,
    NYK Group, 2002. www.nyk.com/english/csr/report/past/pdf/2009.pdf.
    (accessed 22 May 2011).

3   Bruce Aronson has elsewhere argued, though not specifically regarding
    CSR or history telling enterprises, that the board members of Japanese
    corporations have a "duty of oversight, i.e., a duty to establish and
    monitor an information and reporting system designed to prevent and
    detect wrongdoing by the corporation's employees." This chapter proposes
    that the redeployment of historical narratives reconstructed by company
    employees as part of a broader scheme to represent corporate social policy
    could constitute an activity falling under the directors' duty of oversight.
    See Bruce E. Aronson, "Learning from Toyota's Troubles: The Debate on
    Board Oversight, Board Structure, and Director Independence in Japan,"
    Zeitschrift Für Japanisches Recht : Zugleich DJJV-Mitteilungen 15. 30
    (2010): 67–87. See also *Kaisha-hō* (Companies Act), Law No. 86 of 2005.
    www.japaneselawtranslation.go.jp. (accessed 2 March 2012).

4   William Wray's account of the financial relationships that underpinned the first 40 years of NYK history is the only English language scholarly study to date. All extant Japanese language studies of the company have been published directly by, or underwritten by, the company itself. William D, Wray, *Mitsubishi and the N.Y.K., 1870–1914: Business Strategy in the Japanese Shipping Industry* (Cambridge, MA: Council on East Asian Studies, Harvard University, 1984).

5   Nippon Yūsen Kaisha, "Annual Report 2008: New Horizon 2010," (Nippon Yūsen Kaisha: Tokyo, 2008), 6–8; and "NYK Corporate Profile, Social Contribution Activities," www.nykline.co.jp/english/profile/csr/social/local_museum.htm (accessed 22 January 2009).

6   "Human Resources Data," *CSR Report 2009*, NYK Group, 2009: 50–1. www.nyk.com/english/csr/report/past/pdf/2009.pdf. (accessed 22 May 2011).

7   Nihon Yūsen Kabushiki Kaisha, *Nippon Yūsen Kabushiki Kaisha Gojūjenshi* (Tokyo: Nihon Yūsen Kabushiki Kaisha, 1935); Nippon Yūsen Kabushikigaisha, *Wagasha Kakukōro no Enkaku* (Tokyo: Nihon Yūsen Kabushiki Kaisha, 1935); and *The Travel Bulletin* (Tokyo: N. Y. K. Line, 1900–21); *Handbook of information/N.Y.K. Line (Nippon Yusen Kaisha)* (Tokyo: N. Y. K. Line, 1921–26); *Glimpses of the East: Nippon Yusen Kaisha's Official Guide [Glimpses of the East: Official Shipper's Guide and Commercial Year-book of the World]* (Tokyo: Nihon Yusen Kaisha, 1926–44).

8   Wray, *Mitsubishi and N.Y.K.*, 1984, 213–25, 227–87, 289–307.

9   By the 1890s, railroads, which could reach more domestic destinations faster, had replaced the maritime carriers as the primary means of domestic postal carriage.

10   Yoshida Etsushi, "Fuzoku Gahō o sansaku suru," *Meiji Daigaku Toshokan Kyō*, (3) 1999, 114–29. On the cultural missions of the Meiji era, see Carol Gluck, *Japan's Modern Myths: Ideology in the Late Meiji Period* (Princeton, NJ: Princeton University Press, 1985); Irokawa Daikichi, *The Culture of the Meiji Period* (Princeton, NJ: Princeton University Press, 1985); Sharon Minichiello, ed., *Japan's Competing Modernities Issues in Culture and Democracy, 1900–1930* (Honolulu, HI: University of Hawaiì Press, 1998); and Jordan Sand, *House and Home in Modern Japan: Reforming Everyday Life 1880–1930* (Cambridge, MA: Harvard University Press, 2003).

11   The *Kasuga Maru* was retired and sold for scrap in 1935. *Handbook of information/N.Y.K. Line (Nippon Yūsen Kaisha)* (Tokyo: N. Y. K. Line, 1921), 4–6.

12   Noguchi Katsuichi (editor) and Yamamoto Shōkoku (illustrator), *Jōkyaku Annai Yūsen Zue* (Tokyo: Tokyōdō, 1901.10).

13   Robert Eric Barde, *Immigration at the Golden Gate: Passenger Ships, Exclusion, and Angel Island* (Westport, CT: Praeger, 2008).

14   Below decks, Chinese and Korean laborers were also often employed to shovel coal, while a handful of Japanese and European deck officers managed the ship's overall operation.

15   The *Yūsen zue* also depicts the occasional non-Japanese domestic service worker—waiters, maids, and saloon attendants, but neglects the bulk of the ships' crew. Noguchi and Yamamoto, *Yūsen zue*, 1901. 10.

16 Yamada Michio, *Fune ni Miru Nihonjin Iminshi: Kasuga Maru kara Kurūzu Kyakusen e* (Tokyo: Chūō Kōron Sha, 1998), 33–44.

17 *The Travel Bulletin* (Tokyo, N. Y. K. Line, 1900–21); *Handbook of information/N.Y.K. Line (Nippon Yusen Kaisha)* (Tokyo: N. Y. K. Line, 1921–26); *Glimpses of the East: Nippon Yusen Kaisha's Official Guide [Glimpses of the East: Official Shipper's Guide and Commercial Year-book of the World]* (Tokyo: Nihon Yusen Kaisha, 1926–44).

18 Yamada Michio, *Fune ni Miru Nihonjin Iminshi*, 1998; and Hayashi Yoshinori, *Futatsuhiki no Hata no Moto ni: Nihon Yūsen Hyakunen no Ayumi* (Tōkyō: Nihon Yūsen Kabushiki Kaisha, 1986).

19 *Glimpses of the East: Nippon Yūsen Kaisha's Official Guide* Tokyo: Nihon Yūsen Kaisha, 1942, 4.

20 Ibid., 7–14.

21 Kizu Shigetoshi, *Nihon Yūsen Senpaku 100-nenshi* (Tokyō: Kaijinsha, 1984).

22 Nippon Yūsen Kaisha, "Annual Report 2008: New Horizon 2010" (Tokyō: Nippon Yūsen Kaisha, 2008), 15.

23 "Hakubutsukan e yōkoso rekishi hakubutsukan no shakai kōken katsudō," *YŪSEN*, 2006. 2, Tokubetsu hen.

24 A calendar of temporary exhibits and special events is maintained on the NYK website at www.nyk.com/rekishi/exhibitions/event/index.htm (accessed 4 March 2012).

25 Personal communication with NYK Communications Group staff, 28 January 2009.

26 See "Smith's Master Index to Maritime Museum Websites at www. maritimemuseums.net/ (accessed 23 January 2009).

27 "Hakubutsukan e yōkoso rekishi hakubutsukan no shakai kōken katsudō," *YŪSEN*, 2006. 2, Tokubetsu hen.

28 For more information on the Wells Fargo, Boeing, Mercedes Benz, Sony, and Toyota museums, see their websites at www.wellsfargohistory.com/museums/museums.htm, www.museumofflight.org/, www.museum-mercedes-benz.com/, www.sony.co.jp/SonyInfo/CorporateInfo/History/Museum/, and www.toyota.co.jp/Museum/ (accessed 23 February 2009).

29 Hayashi Jōji, "Zōtai shita kansen ni tai suru jinsai kyōkyū no jittai" in *Teikoku Rikukaigun Hojo Kantei: Sōryokusen ni Hitsuyō to Sareta Shien Kanteigun no Zenbō* (Tokyō: Gakken, 2002); Bōeichō Bōei Kenshūjo Senshishitsu, *Kaigun Gunsenbi. 2* (Asagumo Shimbunsha, 1975), 280–5.

30 NYK Crystal Cruises, "Crystal and its Noble Parents: Nippon Yūsen Kaisha (NYK Line)," www.crystalcruises.com/files/NYK_History.pdf (accessed 4 March 2012).

31 "Cruise Service," www.nyk.com/engliSH/service/cruise/index.htm. (accessed 4 March 2012).

32 Ibid.

33 In 2009, NYK's cruise line generated a £9 million operating profit on £310 million total revenue, a three percent margin of return that accounted for less than one percent of the company's total operating profit. "NYK Annual

Report 2010," Nippon Yūsen Kabushiki Kaisha, 2010. www.nyk.com/english/ir/library/annual/pdf/2010.pdf. (accessed 27 September 2010).

34 NYK Crystal Cruises, "Crystal and its Noble Parents: Nippon Yūsen Kaisha (NYK Line)." Available online at: http://www.crystalcruises.com/files/NYK_History.pdf. (accessed 26 January 2009).

35 NYK Corporate Communications Group, "Profile," www.nyk.com/english/profile/profile/. (accessed 21 September 2010); NYK Corporate Communications Group, "Publications," Available at: http://www.nyk.com/english/profile/publications/. Accessed 21 September 2010; NYK Crystal Cruises, "Crystal and its Noble Parents: Nippon Yūsen Kaisha (NYK Line)." www.crystalcruises.com/files/NYK_History.pdf. (accessed 26 January 2009).

36 NYK CSR Group Report 2010, "Human Resources Data (as of 31 March, 2009)," 11, IV. www.nyk.com (accessed 29 October 2010).

37 NYK Communications Group, "First Emigration Ship to Peru," SEASCOPE, 157, July 2000.

38 Ibid.

39 Diana Jean Schemo, "How Peruvian Hostage Crisis Became Trip Into the Sureal," The New York Times, 26 April 1997. www.nytimes.com (accessed 29 October 2010).

40 Simon Romero, "Peru's Ex-President Convicted of Human Rights Abuses," The New York Times, 7 April 2009. www.nytimes.com (accessed 29 October 2010).

41 "Hiyōfune ni notta Nōberu butsurigakusha," YŪSEN, 2002.8, p. 15; "Gakudō sōkai fune 'Tsushima maru'," YŪSEN, 2004.9, p. 33; "Nichibei yakyū kōryōshi," YŪSEN, 2005.12, p 44; "Rekishi no iki shōnin Hikawa Maru—sono mitsu" YŪSEN, 2007. 6. 59.

42 Paul Lewis, "Rabbi Zorach Warhaftig Dies; Rescuer of Polish Jews Was 96," New York Times, 7 October 2002. www.nytimes.com (accessed 27 October 2010).

43 NYK Communications Group, "Memories on the Hikawa Maru by a Survivor of the Holocaust," NYK Group Newsletter SEASCOPE, June 2003, No. 192.

44 Janklowicz-Mann, Dana, Amir Mann, Martin Landau, and Sujin Nam, Shanghai Ghetto (New York: Docurama, 2004).

45 Yūsen OB Hikawamaru Kenkyūkai, Hikawamaru to sono jidai (Tokyo: Kaibundō Shuppan, 2008); and "The Reborn Hikawa Maru Makes its Debut," SEASCOPE, June 2008, No 252; "Witness to History: Hikawa Maru Part II," SEASCOPE, December 2007, No. 246.

46 Yūsen OB Hikawa Maru Kenkyūkai Hikawa Maru to Sono Jidai (Tokyo: Kaibundō Shuppan, 2008).

47 Personal communication with NYK Communications Group staff, 28 January 2009; and "Witness to History: Hikawa Maru Part II," SEASCOPE, December 2007, No. 246.

48 Nick Nissley and Andrea Casey, "The Politics of the Exhibition: Viewing Corporate Museums Through the Paradigmatic Lens of Organizational Memory," British Journal of Management 13, (2002): 35–45.

49 Franziska Seraphim, *War Memory and Social Politics in Japan, 1945–2005*. Harvard East Asian monographs, 278 (Cambridge, MA: Harvard University Asia Center, 2006); and Philip A Seaton, *Japan's Contested War Memories The "Memory Rifts" in Historical Consciousness of World War II* (London: Routledge, 2007).

50 Laura Hein, "War Compensation: Claims Against the Japanese Government and Japanese Corporations for War Crimes" in John Torpey. *Politics and the Past: On Repairing Historical Injustices* (Lanham, Md: Rowman & Littlefield Publishers, 2003), 127–47; William Underwood. "Redress Crossroads in Japan: Decisive Phase in Campaigns to Compensate Korean and Chinese Wartime Forced Laborers." *The Asia-Pacific Journal: Japan Focus*. 3387. Available at http://www.japanfocus.org/-William-Underwood/3387.

Chapter 14

The author gratefully acknowledges the generous support of the Elinor Nims Brink Fund at Vassar College, and a Grant-in-Aid for Scientific Research from the Japan Society for the Promotion of Science for underwriting this project. He also thanks Professors Hayashi Kaori and Kitada Akihiro of the University of Tokyo Interfaculty Initiative on Informational Studies for their kind assistance.

1 Murakami Haruki, "Wōkuman o waruku iu wake ja nai desu ga," *Murakami Asahidō Wa ika ni Shite Kitaerareta ka* (Tokyo: Asahi, 1997), 310, 312.

2 Japan Computer System Sellers Association, *JCSSA News* 43 (summer, 2007), 4; "NHK Purojekuto X daijigyō no butaiura tsutae sannenme," *Yomiuri Shinbun*, evening ed., 15 May 2002, 12.

3 Ibid., p. 5; "NHK ninki dokumentarī Purojekuto X no butaiura," *Mainichi Shinbun*, evening ed., 9 July 2001, 2; "NHK 'Purojekuto X chōsenshatachi' nebarizuyoku tettei shuzai," *Sankei Shinbun*, 21 April 2001, 16.

4 "Purojekuto X kandō shutsuen no kannen," *Yomiuri Shinbun*, 23 September 2001, 11.

5 *Shūkan Asashi* 44, 1 (2002): 82–92.

6 Norimitsu Onishi, "Tokyo Journal: At Long Last, the Salarymen are Given Their Due," *The New York Times*, 21 August 2003.

7 It won four awards in 2001: the 49th Kikuchi Kan Award from Bungei Shunjū; the 9th Hashida Award from the Hashida Cultural Foundation; the Television Journalists Award from the Association of All Japan TV Program Production Companies; and the 27th Hōsō Bunka Foundation Award for Cultural Broadcasting. "Kenkyūsha no omoi monogatari ni," *Yomiuiri Shinbun*, 24 October 2001, 31; "Nebarizuyoku," *Sankei Shinbun*, 21 April 2001, 16; "Ei BBC suijun ijō 'Purojekuto X,'" *Sports Nippon*, 13 August 2001, 23.

8 Nihon PTA, "Katei kyōiku ni okeru terebi media chōsa chōsa kekka hōkokusho" (March, 2004), 18. 27.4% of respondents named *Project X*, while the second-place shows received just 9.7%.

9 "Gose ni nokoshitai terebi bangumi," *Business Media Makoto*, bizmakoto.jp (accessed 27 April 2010). The venerable *Sazae-san* came in first.

10 "NHK 'Purojekuto X' mumei no ijin ni supotto," *Nikkan Sports*, 29 October 2000, 24; "NHK 'Purojekuto X' Kunii Masahiko-shi ni miryoku kiku," *Nikkan Sports*, 11 August 2001, 22.

11 "Kodomo ni yume o ataetai NHK 'Purojekuto X' ten," *Yomiuri Shinbun*, evening ed., 6 August 2004, 7.

12 http://www.nhk.or.jp/projectx/index.htm (accessed 1 June 2006; this site has since been removed).

13 Nakajima Miyuki, "Chijō no hoshi" (Tokyo: Yamaha Music Communication, 2000).

14 Chalmers Johnson, *MITI and the Japanese Miracle* (Stanford: Stanford University Press, 1982); Richard J. Samuels, *The Business of the Japanese State* (Ithaca: Cornell University Press, 1987).

15 Haga Noboru, *Minshūshi no Teigen to Kadai* (Tokyo: Yūzankaku, 1999), 78–87; Sasaki Junnosuke, *Minshūshi o Manabu to iu Koto* (Tokyo: Yoshikawa kōbunkan, 2006), 166–91.

16 Irokawa Daikichi, *Meiji Seishinshi* (Tokyo: Kōga, 1964), "maegaki."

17 "Otoko no fukken," evening ed., *Sankei Shinbun*, 10 October 2001, 5; "'Purojekuto X' no purodūsā Imai Akira-san Nihonjin no daitansa ni odoroku," *Mainichi Shinbun*, 6 November 2000, 15.

18 "Ichioku sōPurojekuto X genshō?" *Sankei Shinbun*, 21 April 2001, 16.

19 "Purojekuto X chōsenshatachi: shūnen no gyakuten geki," *Yomiuri Shinbun*, evening ed., 6 August 2004, 7.

20 "Otoko no fukken," *Sankei Shinbun*, evening ed., 10 October 2001, 5.

21 "Okashiizo! Purojekuto X," *Mainichi Shinbun*, 12 March 2002, 4.

22 "'Purojekuto X' eiyū sasaeta onnatachi wa?" *Mainichi Shinbun*, 28 February 2003, 14.

23 "Purojekuto X o yareba yaru hodo Nihonjin o suku ni narimashita," *Zaikai* 50, 19 (2002): 96; "NHK ninki dokumentarī 'Purojekuto X' no butaiura," *Mainichi Shinbun*, evening ed., 9 July 2001, 2; "Yakushiji kondō to Purojekuto X," *Sankei Shinbun*, evening ed., 16 November 2000, 4.

24 Imai Akira, *Purojekuto X Rīdatachi no Kotoba* (Tokyo: Bungei Shunjū, 2001).

25 Thanks to Timothy S. George for pointing this out.

26 Haga Noboru, *Minshūshi no Teigen to Kadai* (Tokyo: Yūzankaku, 1999), 78–86; Kodowaki Teiji and Amakusa Ken, eds, *Minshūshi no Kiten* (Tokyo: Sanshōdō, 1974), 1–4; Minshūshi kenkyūkai, ed. *Minshūshi Kenkyū no Shiten* (Tokyo: San'ichi shobō, 1997), 1–2.

27 "NHK Purojekuto X," *Nikkan Sports*, 11 August 2001, 22.

28 *Asahi Shinbun*, 27 November 1942, 3.

29 Gavan McCormack and Yoshio Sugimoto, *Democracy in Contemporary Japan* (New York: M.E. Sharpe, 1986), 10.

30 "'Kōdo seichō jidai no banka' ka? NHK 'Purojekuto X' ni igi ari!" *Shūkan Asahi* 108, 57 (2003): 25. As a fatal form of work-induced stress, *karōshi* is often considered a phenomenon that is distinct to postwar Japan.

31 "Purojekuto X rīdātachi no kotoba," *Asahi Shinbun*, 2 September 2001, 11.

32 "NHK Purojekuto X," *Mainichi Shinbun*, 21 April 2003, 15.

33 "Jijitsu gonin no mama hōsō, kajō na enshutsu, gōin na sutōrī zukuri 'Purojekuto X' hōsō shitaku nai kako," *Shūkan Asahi* 110, 25 (2005): 28.

34 John Dower, "The Useful War," *Daedalus* 119. 3 (summer, 1990): 49–70.

35 One useful, though critical, summary of this movement is Nagahara Keiji, *Jiyūshugi Shikan Hihan* (Tokyo: Iwanami, 2000).

36 Tom Brokaw, *The Greatest Generation* (New York: Random House, 1998).

37 For example, Kobayashi Yoshinori, *Gōmanizumu Sengen* Vol. 4 (Tokyo: Fusōsha, 1994), 67.

38 "NHK ninki dokumentarī," *Mainichi Shinbun*, evening ed., 9 July 2001, 2.

39 See, especially, Kobayashi Yoshinori, *Shin Gōmanizumu Sengen Special Sensōron* 3 vols, (Tokyo: Gentōsha, 1998–2003); *Shin Gōmanizumu Sengen Special Yasukuniron* (Tokyo: Gentōsha, 2005).

40 Nagahara Keiji, *Rekishi Kyōkasho o Dō Tsukuruka* (Tokyo: Iwanami, 2001), 125.

41 "'Purojekuto X Chōsenshatachi' shichōritsu daikentō," *Mainichi Shinbun*, Osaka ed., 11 November 2000, 1; "Yakushiji kondō to Purojekuto X," *Sankei Shinbun*, evening ed., 16 November 2000, 4; "Purojekuto X rīdātachi no kotoba," *Mainichi Shinbun*, 8 August 2001, 15.

42 Imai Akira, *Purojekuto X za Man* (Tokyo: NHK, 2002), 161. The telling subtitle of this book is *subete wa kandō kara hajimaru.*

43 Nagahara, *Rekishi Kyōkasho*, 128.

44 Yoshimi Shun'ya, "Terebi o dakishimeru sengo" in Yoshimi and Tsuchiya Reiko, eds, *Taishū Bunka to Media* (Kyoto: Minerva, 2010), 188–92.

45 For example, "Kenkyūsha no omoi," *Yomiuri Shinbun*, 24 October 2001, 31; *Sankei Shinbun*, 21 April 2001, 16; *Mainichi Shinbun*, Osaka ed., 11 November 2000, 1; "NHK Purojekuto X Chōsenshatachi," *Sankei Shinbun*, evening ed., 16 November 2001, 4.

46 "Yakushiji kondō to Purojekuto X," *Sankei Shinbun*, evening ed., 16 November 2000, 4.

47 "'Purojekuto X' no atsui kokorozashi," *Asahi Shinbun*, evening ed., 13 April 2001, 16.

48 "Otoko no fukken," *Sankei Shinbun*, evening ed., 10 October 2001, 6.

49 Thanks to Jordan Sand for suggesting this idea of a shared milieu.

50 Carol Gluck, "The Past in the Present," in Andrew Gordon, ed., *Postwar Japan as History* (Berkeley: University of California Press, 1993), 64–95.

51 *Gōmanizumu Sengen* Vol. 6, 14.

52 "Nonfikushon 'Purojekuto X' ga ichii," *Yomiuri Shinbun*, 23 September 2001, 12.

53 "Purojekuto X," *Asahi Shinbun*, 2 September 2001, 11; *Voice* 287 (2001): 267.

54 Nakajima Miyuki, "Heddoraito-tēruraito" (Tokyo: Yamaha Music Communications, 2000).

55 "'Purojekuto X Chōsenshatachi' tēma kyoku ni makenu hakuryoku eizō," *Yomiuri Shinbun*, 20 July 2004, 20.

56 Here again, *Project X* counters a basic goal in *minshūshi* to critique triumphant developmentalist views of history such as the so-called modernization school. Haga Noboru, *Minshūshi no Sōzō* (Tokyo: NHK Books, 1974), 72–104.

57 "NHK ninki dokumentarī," *Mainichi Shinbun*, evening ed., 9 July 2001, 2. Hayden White might call this narrative practice the "emplotment" of history as a romance. Hayden White, *Metahistory* (Baltimore: The Johns Hopkins University Press, 1973).

58 Gluck, 95.

59 "Sararīman Purojekuto X to iu mayaku," *AERA* 15, 36 (2002): 16. *Oshin* (1983–4) follows the life of the eponymous character from her provincial childhood in the late Meiji era to the Shōwa present. It remains the most watched TV drama ever in Japan.

60 "Purojekuto X," *Mainichi Shinbun*, 2 September 2001, 11.

61 "'Purojekuto X' o warau kanjusei seijiteki romanshugi," *Asahi Shinbun*, evening ed., 17 February 2003, 14.

62 "NHK mondai tsuzuku 'Purojekuto X,'" *Mainichi Shinbun*, 28 June 2005, 29.

63 "NHK Sōkyokuchō ga shazai," *Asahi Shinbun*, 26 May 2005, 39. In fact, this was not the first time *Project X* came under fire for hyperbole, factual errors, and other mishaps. In its second season, episodes dealing with the H-II rocket and environmentalists at Shirakami Mountain Range were critiqued for misinformation. NHK publicly admitted to the latter. "Shitsubō shita 'Purojekuto X' no misurīdo," *Sankei Shinbun*, 13 July 2001, 17; "Shirakami sanchi atsukatta Purojekuto X 'bangumi ni ninshiki no ayamari," *Yomiuri Shinbun*, 2 August 2001, 28. In 2004, NHK was criticized for its *Project X* exhibition in Tokyo Dome City held in August. *Asahi Shinbun* reported that companies that had been featured in past episodes were strong-armed by NHK brass into providing as much as ¥3,150,000 in "cooperation money" to finance the exhibit. This led to a Diet hearing, and became the latest in a series of scandals and bad publicity that plagued NHK and its strident chairman Ebisawa Katsuji around 2004. "NHK 'Purojekuto X' ten hōsō kigyō kara kyōenkin," *Asahi Shinbun*, September 10, 2004, 3, 37. A summary of *Project X* controversies, both small and large, is in "Jijitsu gonin no mama," *Shūkan Asahi* 110, 25 (2005): 27–9.

64 "'Purojekuto X' raishun endingu," *Sankei Shinbun*, 23 September 2005, 30.

65 "NHK 'Purojekuto X' sutaffu kaitai shite denaose," *Sports Hōchi*, 3 June 2005, 17.

66 "'Purojekuto X' shūryō ni kangai," *Mainichi Shinbun*, 21 January 2006, 6; "Purojekuto X kara ōku no kandō," *Mainichi Shinbun*, 28 October 2005, 4.

67 *Kanburia Kyūden* (TV Tokyo), *Gaia no Yoake* (TV Tokyo), *Kigyō Damashii* (Tokyo MX), *Wafū Sōhonke* (TV Osaka), *Purofesshonaru Shigoto no Ryūgi* (NHK), and *Shigotogaku no Susume* (NHK) are some examples of this genre.

68 For example, Noguchi Yukio, *Monozukuri Gensō ga Nihon Keizai o Dame ni Suru* (Tokyo: Diamond, 2007).

69 Ikeda Nobuo, "'Purojekuto X' to iu sakkaku," blog.goo.ne.jp/ikedanobuo (2 December 2008).

Chapter 15

1   The term "Japan passing" references Japan's decline in world GDP rankings to third behind China, and US diplomacy, which, especially during the Clinton Administration, appeared to take Japan for granted, as in President Clinton's visit to China in 1998 without even a meet-and-greet in Tokyo.

2   Walter LaFeber, *The Clash: U.S.-Japanese Relations throughout History* (New York: W.W. Norton, 1997), 302.

3   Herman Kahn, *The Emerging Japanese Superstate: Challenge and response* (Englewood Cliffs, NJ: Prentice-Hall, 1970).

4   Gerteis and George, 4.

5   See Aronson, 166. Perhaps, a moniker for regulatory reform so closely identified with Thatcher's 1986 deregulation of UK financial institutions egged the skeptics on in promising more than could possibly be delivered.

6   Japan's per capita GDP in the first decade of the twenty-first century, before the 2011 disaster, was slightly below, at, or somewhat above those of other OECD countries.

7   Gerteis and George, 4.

8   Ezra F. Vogel, *Japan as Number One: Lessons for America* (Cambridge, MA: Harvard University Press, 1979).

9   Shimoda, 254.

10 Gerteis and George, 4.

11 Gerteis, 225.

12 Christine Yano's contribution to the volume is the single exception. Nevertheless, her entertaining analysis of the unique place Pan American Airlines occupied in the postwar popular imagination focuses on the *akogare* for world travel that took root during the occupation period.

Index